THE OPÉRA
MAGAZINE
VOLUME XIII

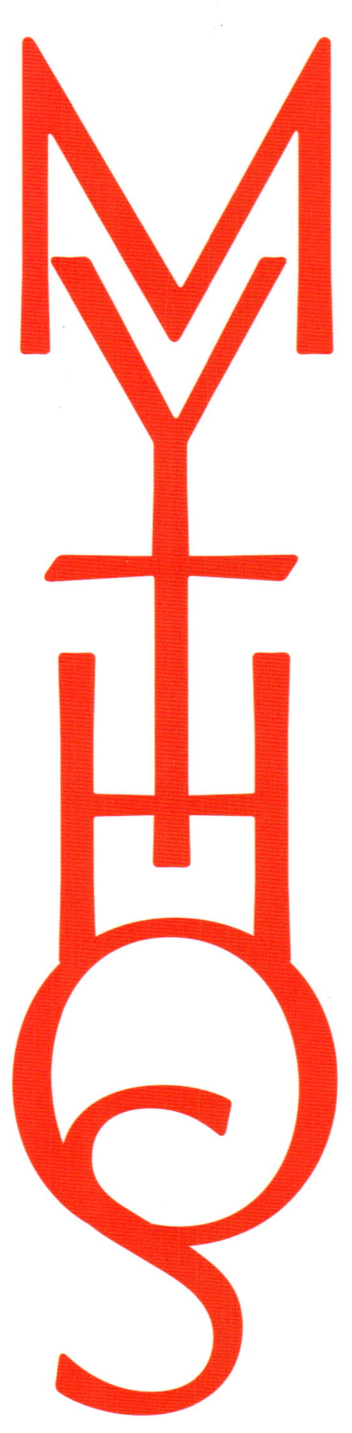

MAGAZINE FOR
CLASSIC & CONTEMPORARY
NUDE PHOTOGRAPHY

PRELUDIO

I. KOSMOS

II. HEROS

PRELUDIO

IN THE ANCIENT TELLING OF TALES, WHERE GODS WALKED AMONG MEN AND MORTALS DARED THE HEAVENS, THE NOTION OF MYTHOS DID NOT MERELY SERVE AS ENTERTAINMENT – IT WAS THE MIRROR OF THE SOUL AND THE FLESH. THE HUMAN BODY, UNCLOTHED AND UNASHAMED, STOOD AS A SYMBOL OF TRUTH, VULNERABILITY, AND DIVINE PROPORTION. IN GREEK MYTHOLOGY, THE NUDE FORM WAS NOT BASE BUT EXALTED:

CONSIDER APHRODITE, BORN OF SEA FOAM, RISING IN THE RADIANT NAKEDNESS, HER BEAUTY A FORCE OF NATURE ITSELF. HERCULES, SCULPTED IN HEROIC NUDITY, BORE THE MARKS OF LABOR AND VIRTUE UPON HIS SINEWED LIMBS. THE ROMANS, INHERITORS OF HELLENIC GRANDEUR, PRESERVED THIS REVERENCE. THEIR STATUES OF MARS AND VENUS, UNCLAD YET DIGNIFIED, SPOKE OF POWER AND PASSION UNBOUND BY GARMENT.

NUDITY, IN THESE MYTHIC FRAMES, WAS NOT INDECENCY, BUT REVELATION – OF CHARACTER, OF FATE, OF DIVINE ESSENCE. THUS, MYTHOS, THAT SACRED TAPESTRY OF LORE, HAS EVER EMBRACED THE HUMAN FORM AS BOTH CANVAS AND CIPHER. NUDITY THEREIN IS NOT SCANDALOUS, BUT SACRED; NOT PROFANE, BUT PROFOUND. IT IS THE BODY AS TRUTH, THE SKIN AS STORY, THE MORTAL AS MYTH — IN THIS LIGHT, WE SEE NOT SHAME, BUT SPLENDOR.

WELCOME TO
THE OPÉRA VOLUME XIII

MATTHIAS STRAUB,
EDITOR

I.
KOSMOS

THE ARRANGEMENT OR ADORNMENT OF SOMETHING, LIKE THE STARS IN THE SKY. IN ESSENCE, IT ENCOMPASSES BOTH THE PHYSICAL UNIVERSE AND THE CONCEPT OF ORDER AND BEAUTY WITHIN IT.

9

MARIA KNOFE

WHITE SANDS

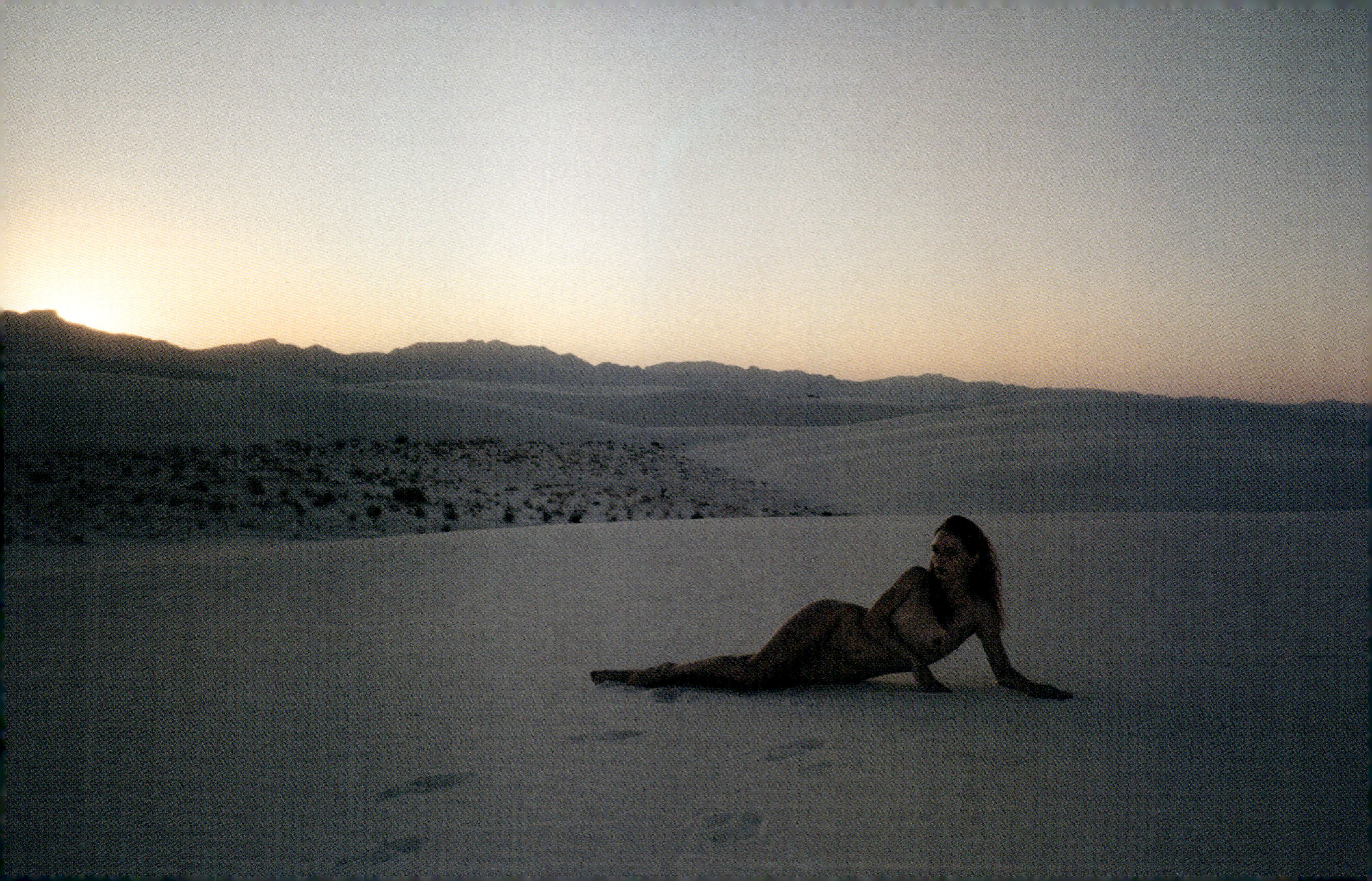

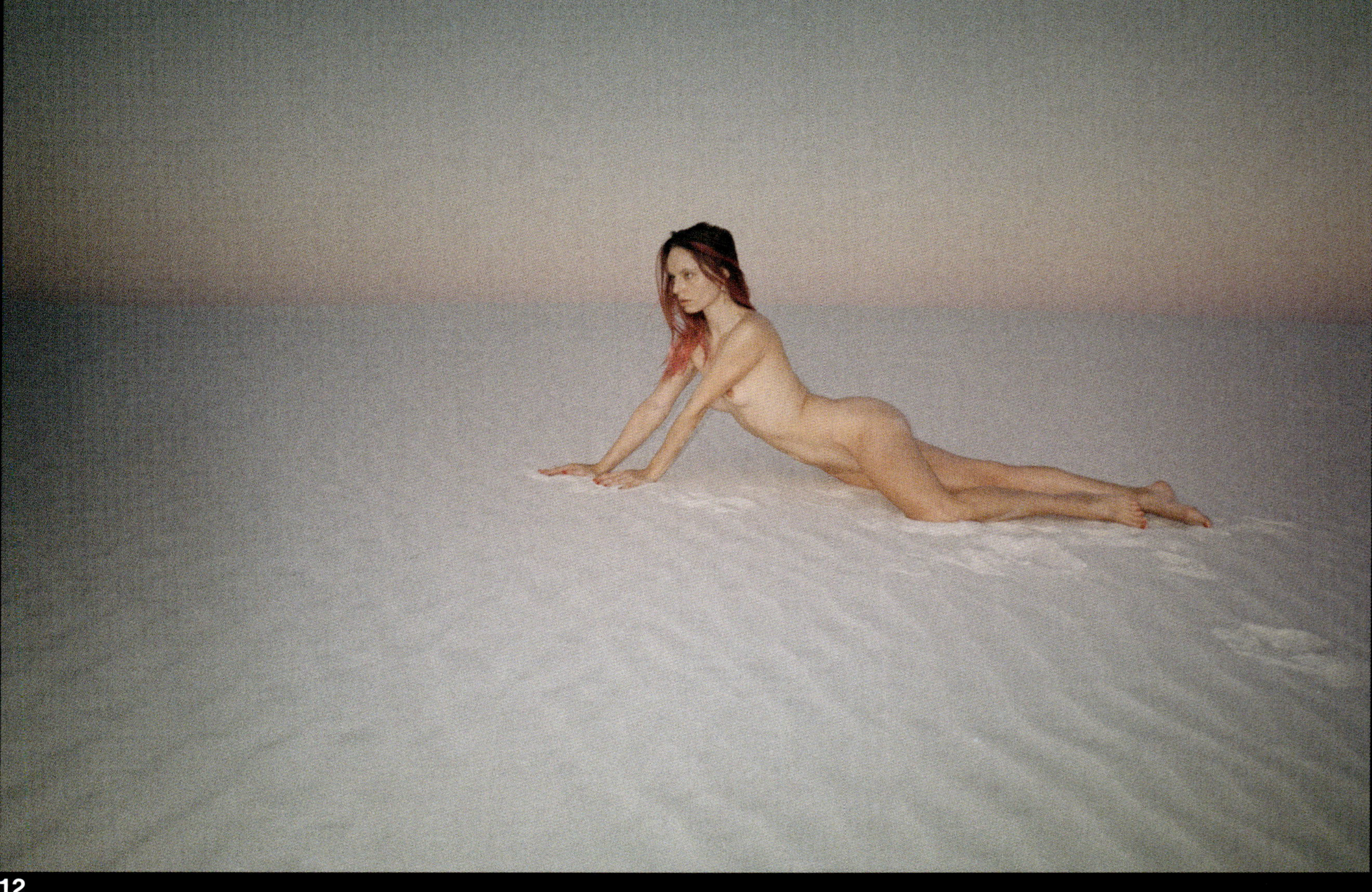

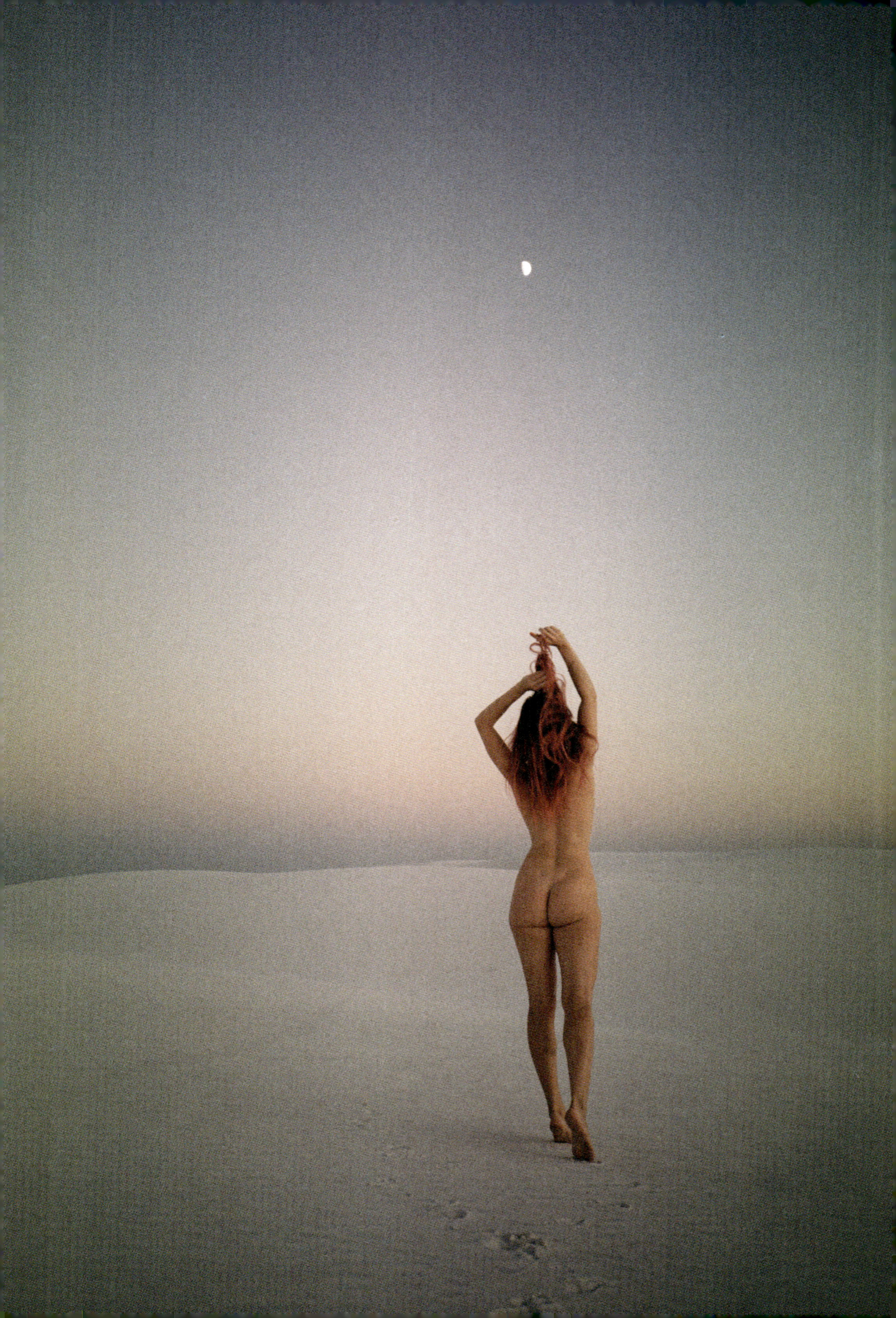

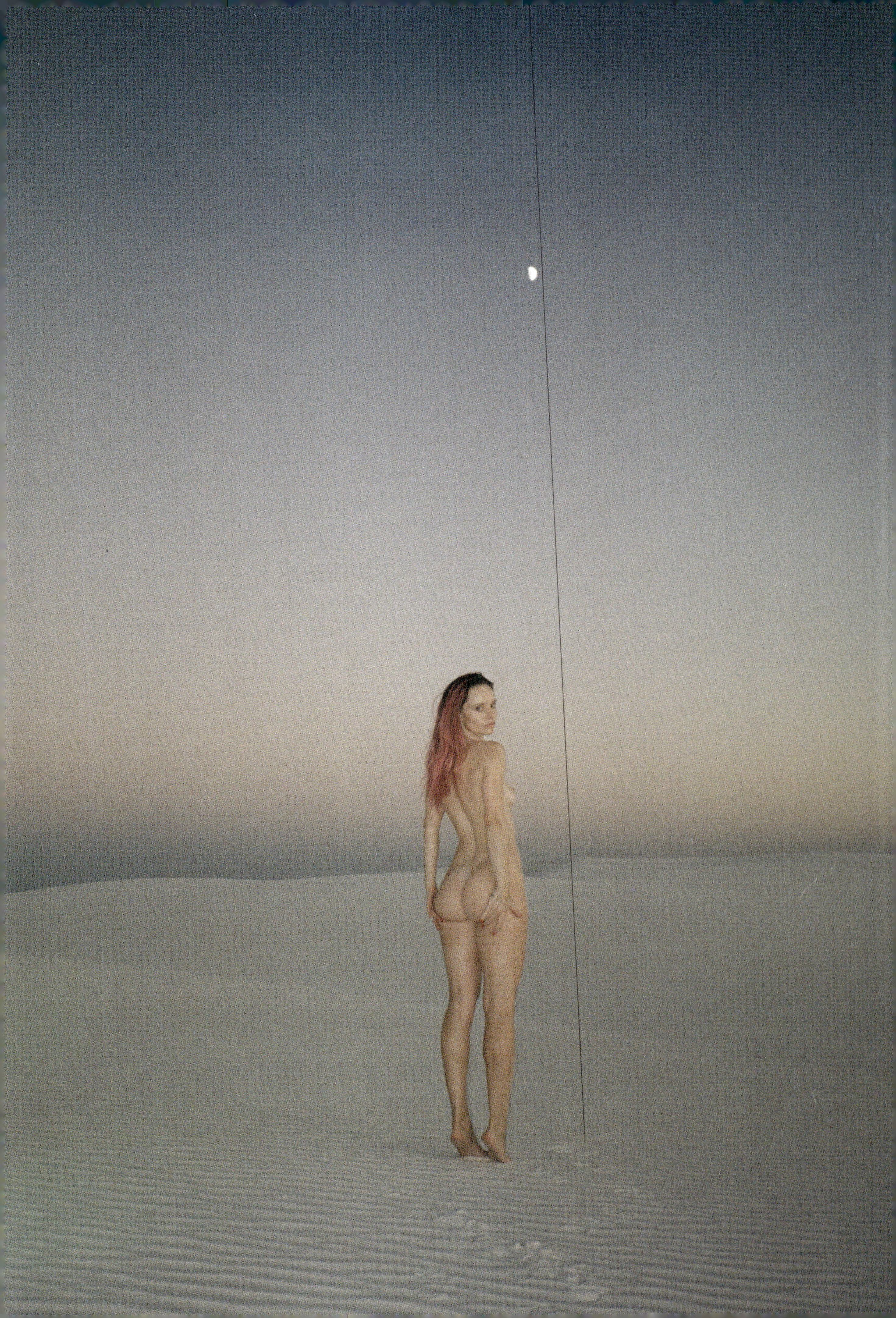

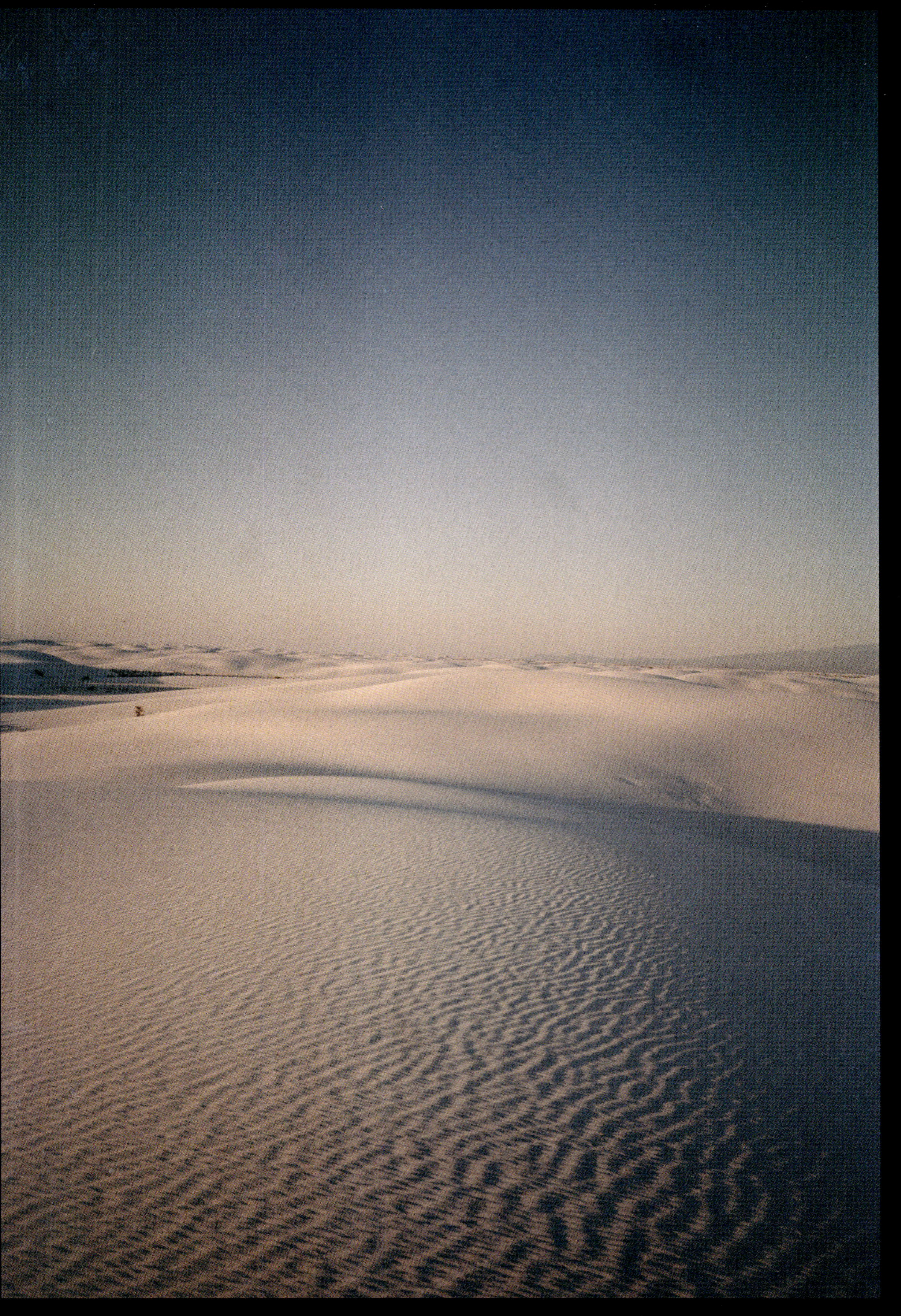

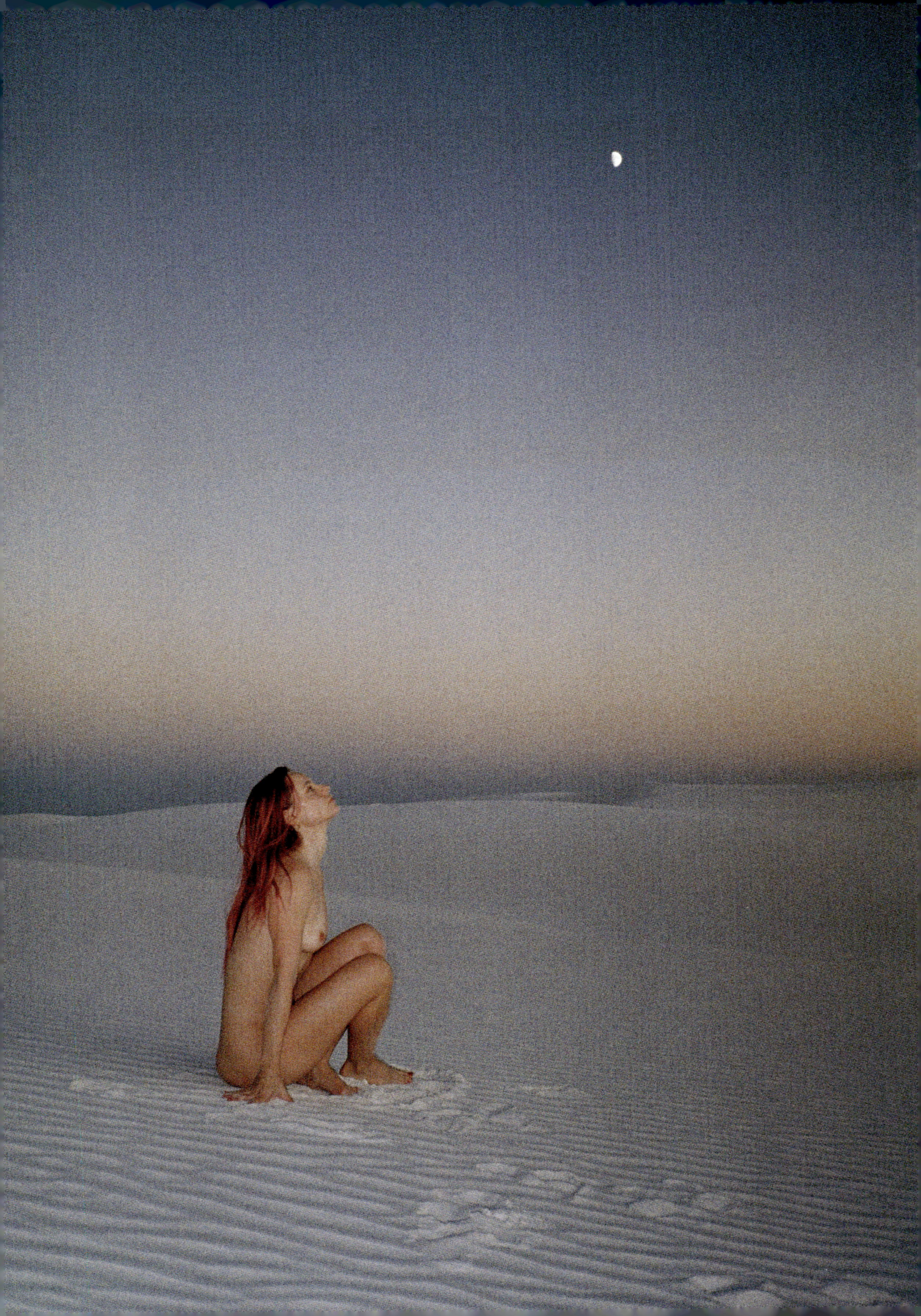

JAMES HENSBY

18

RHODES & CRETE

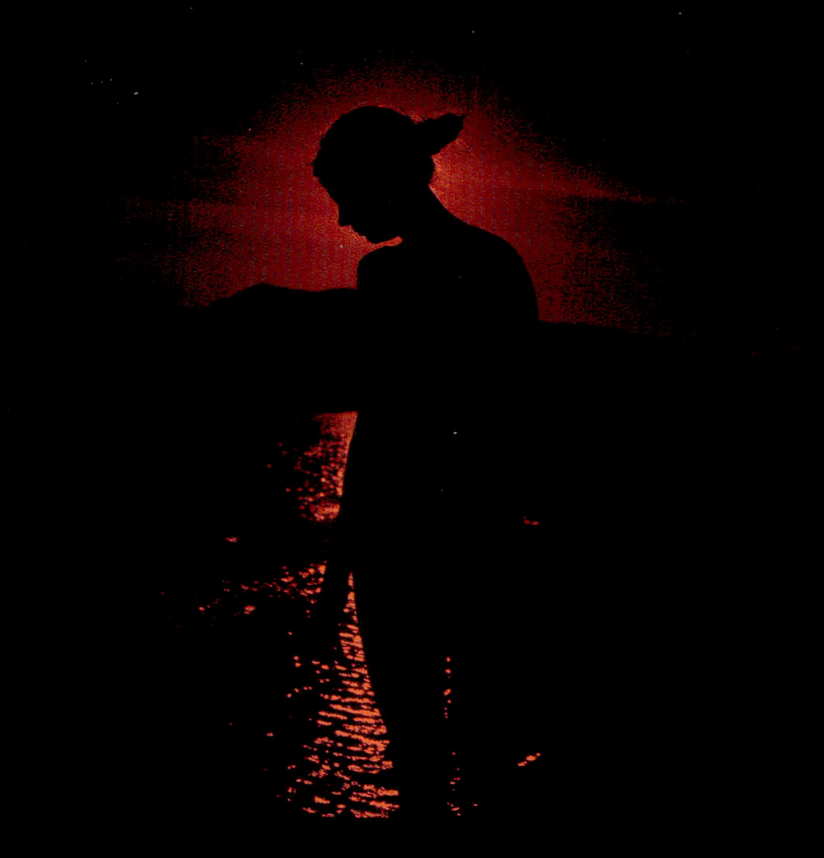

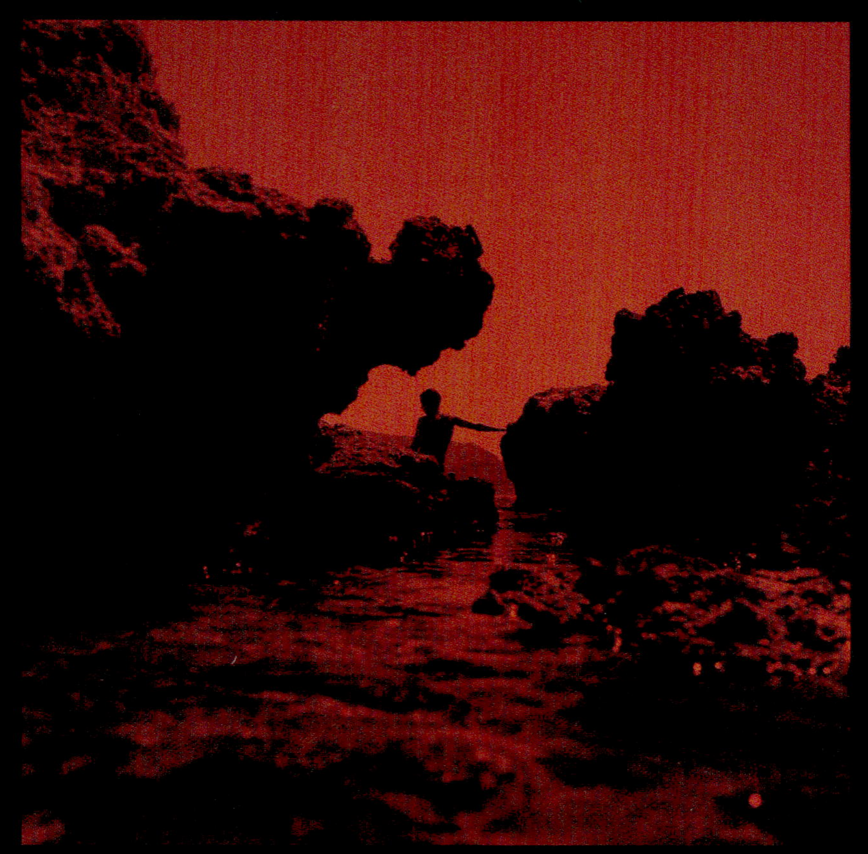

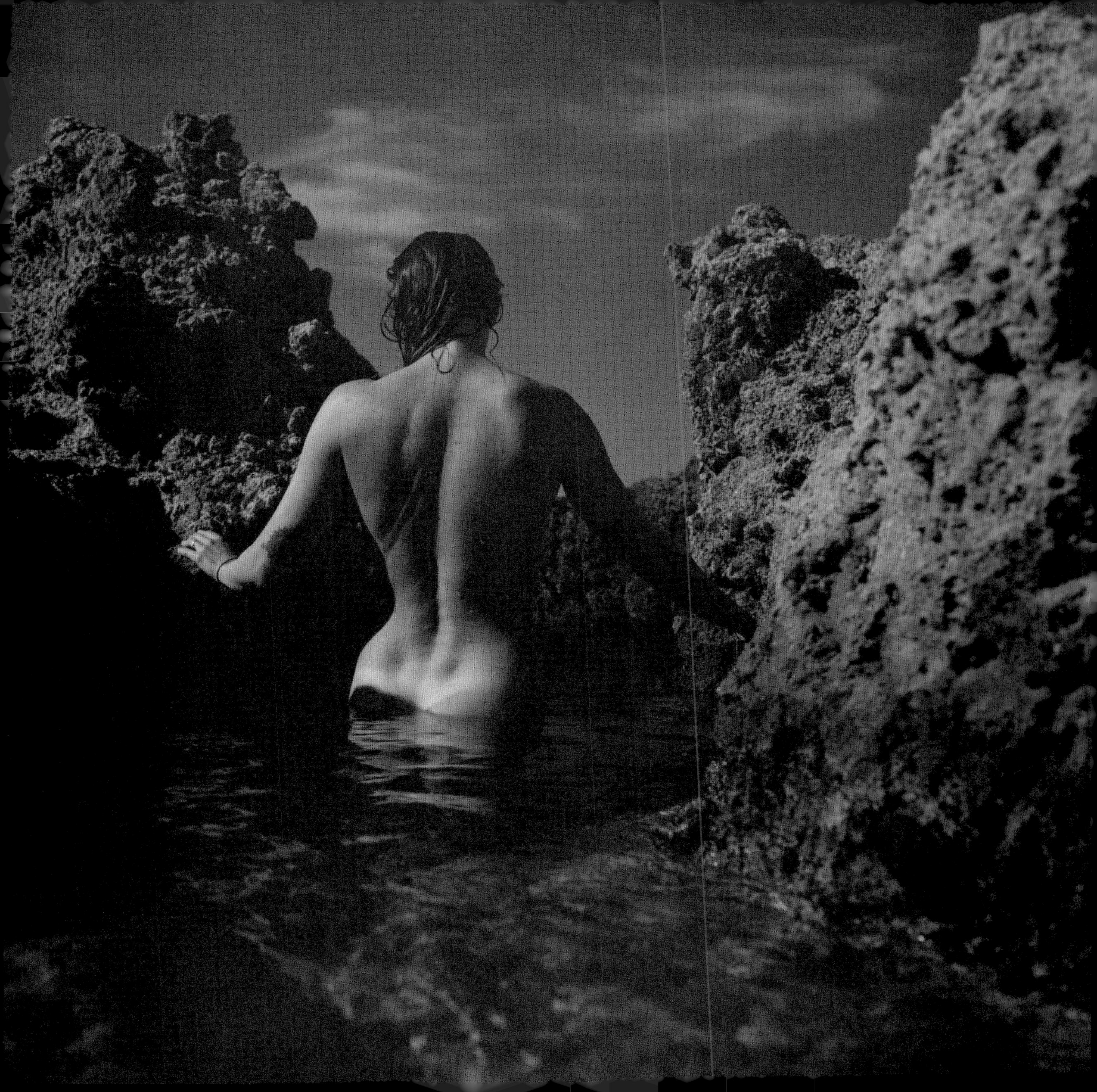

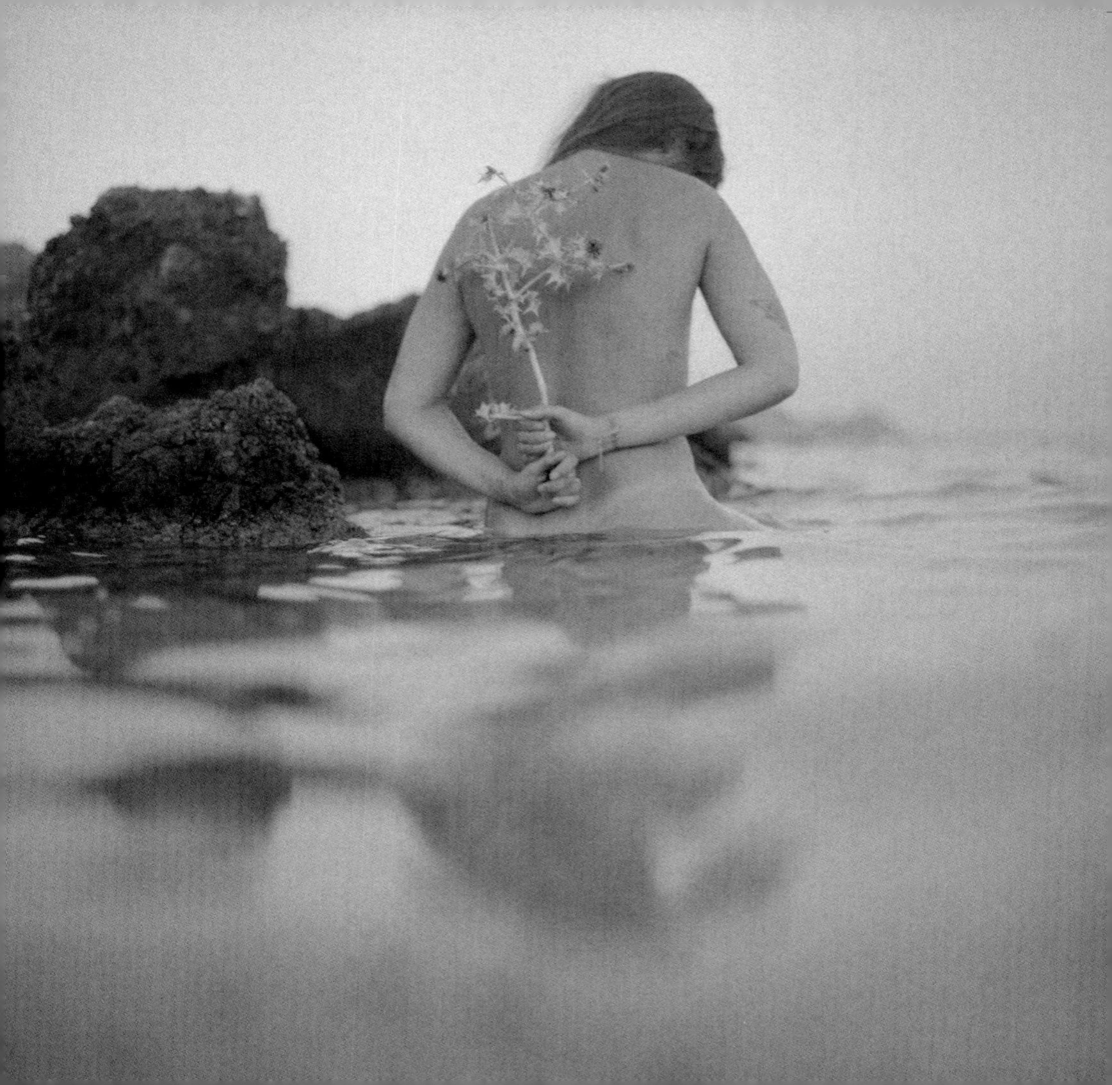

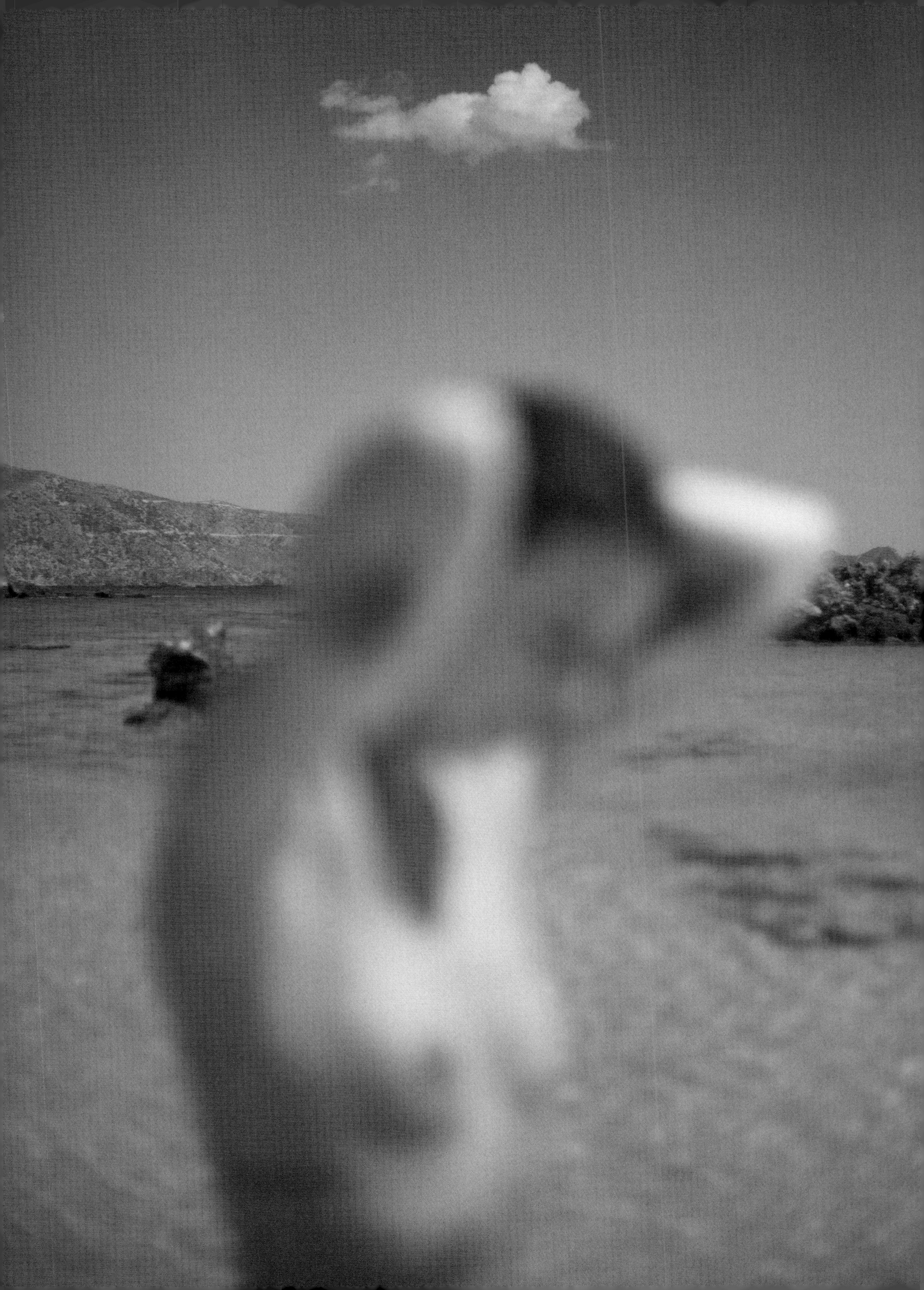

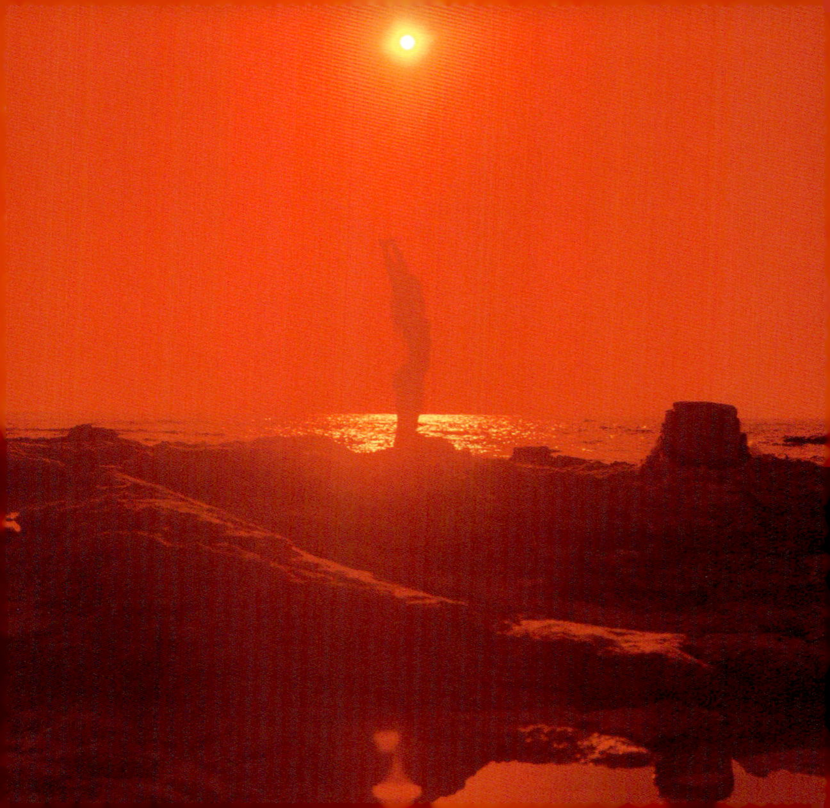

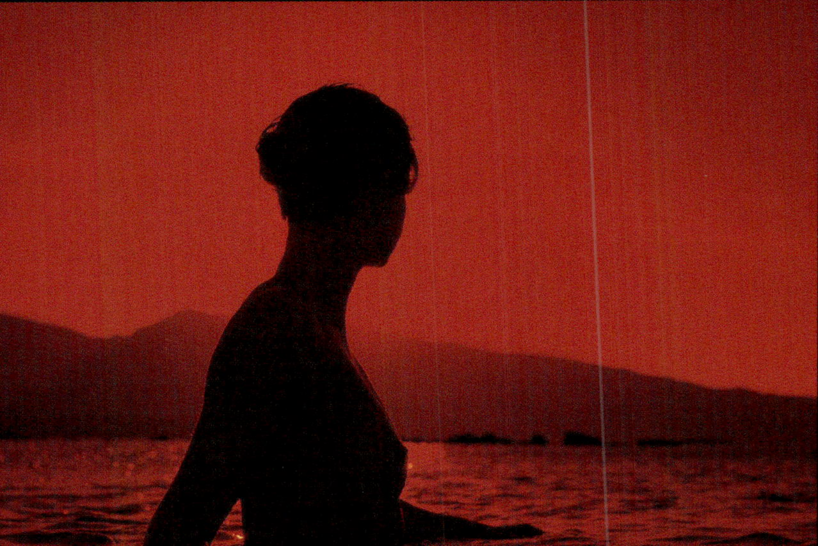

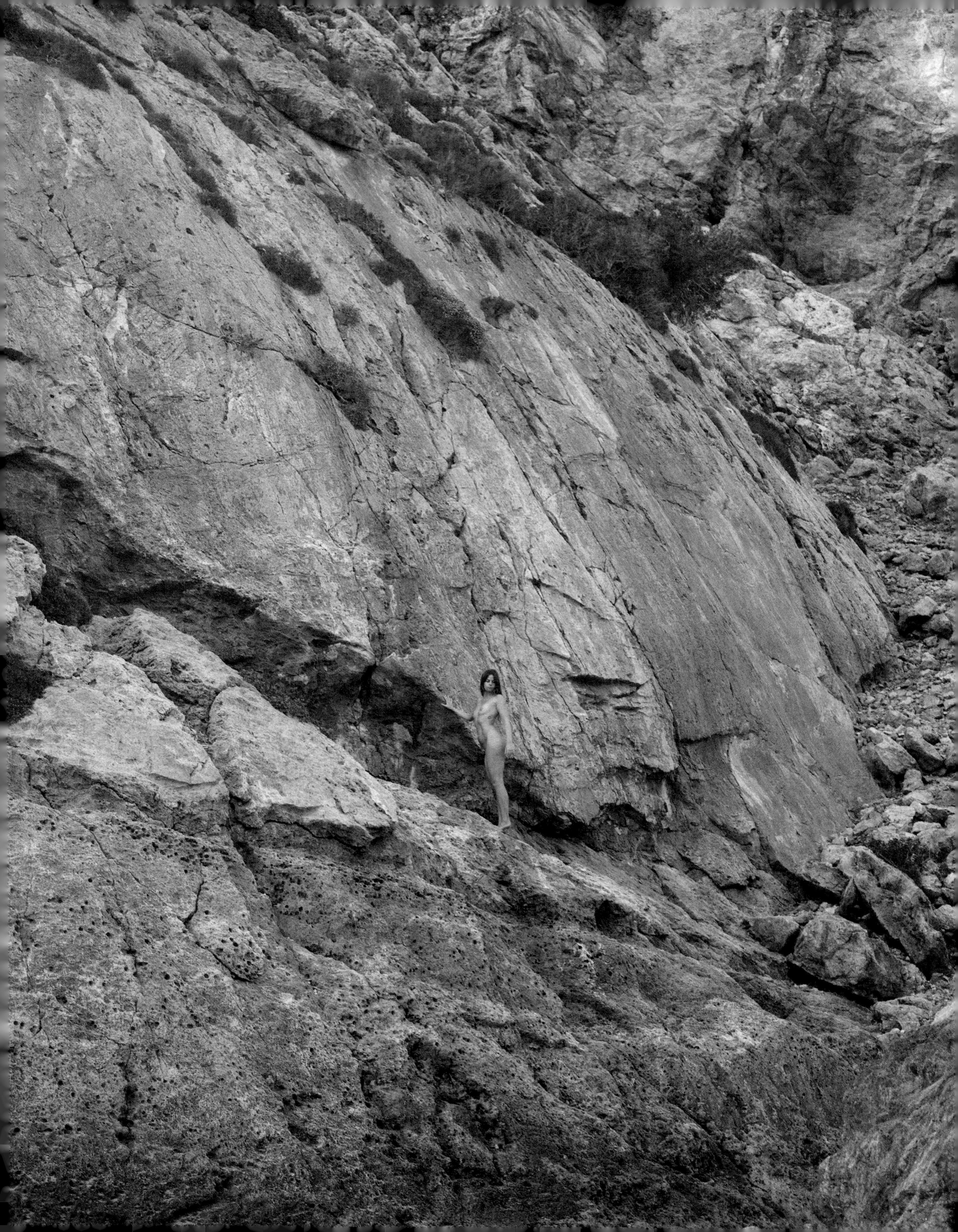

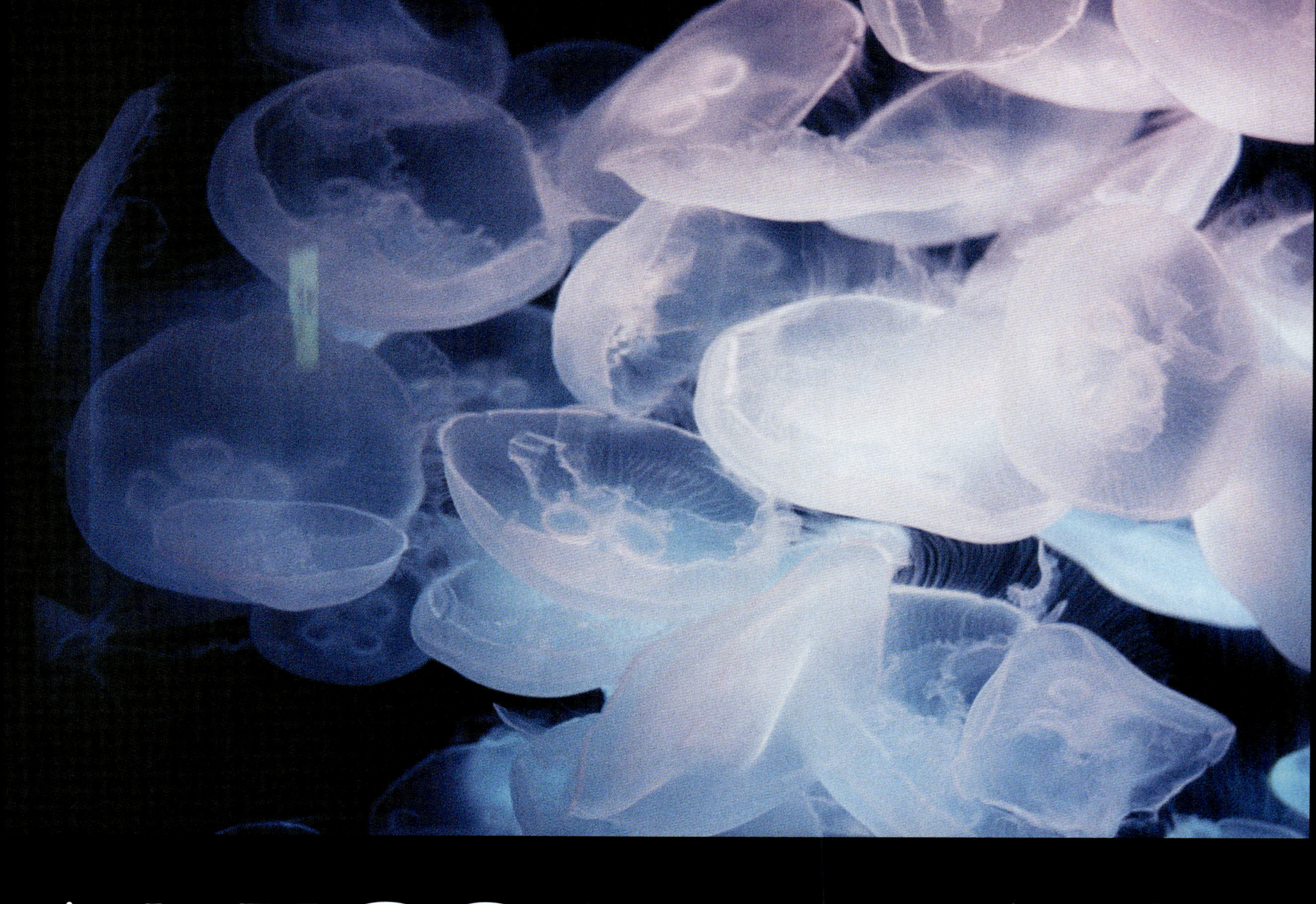

ALESSANDRO
CASAGRANDE

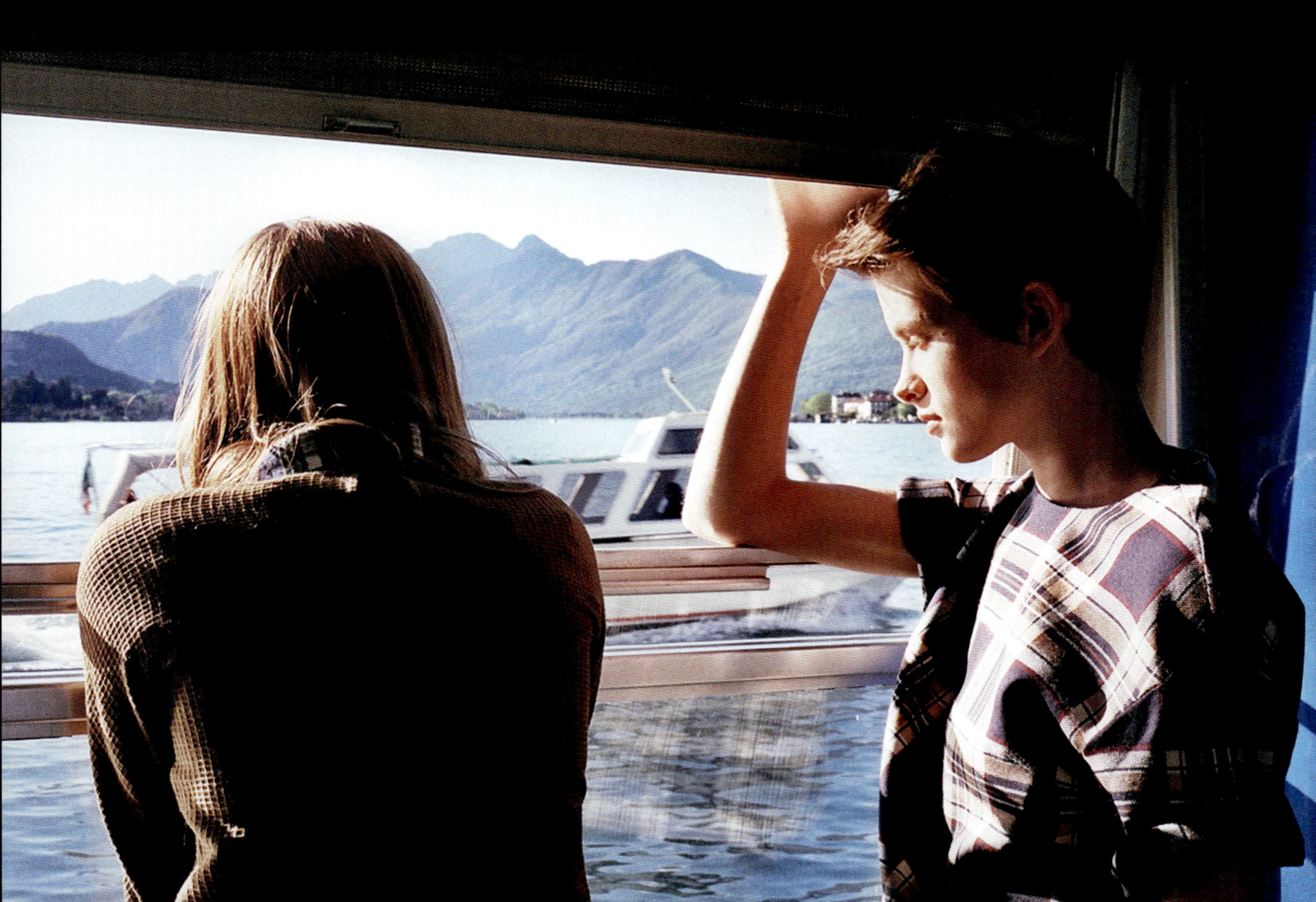

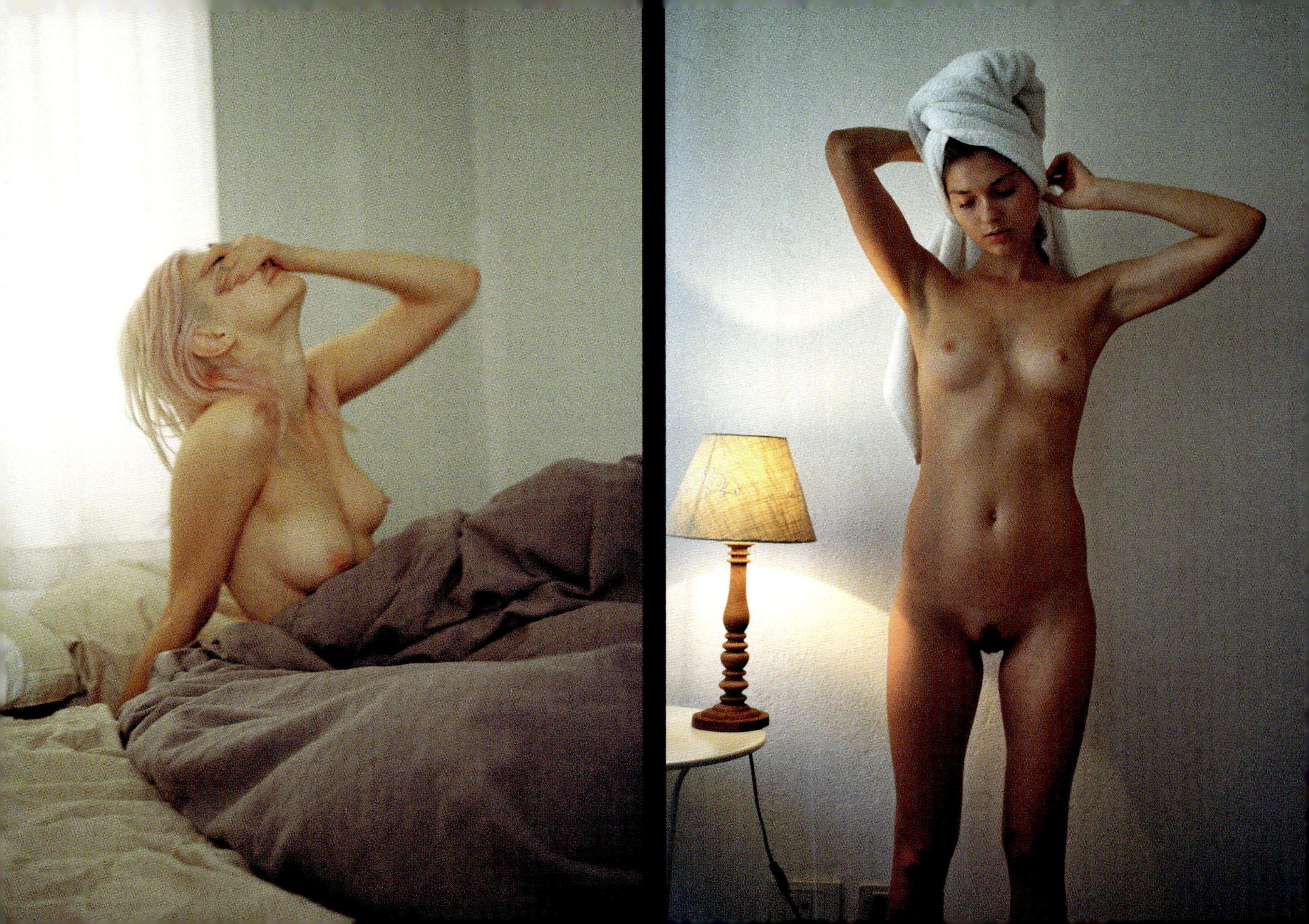

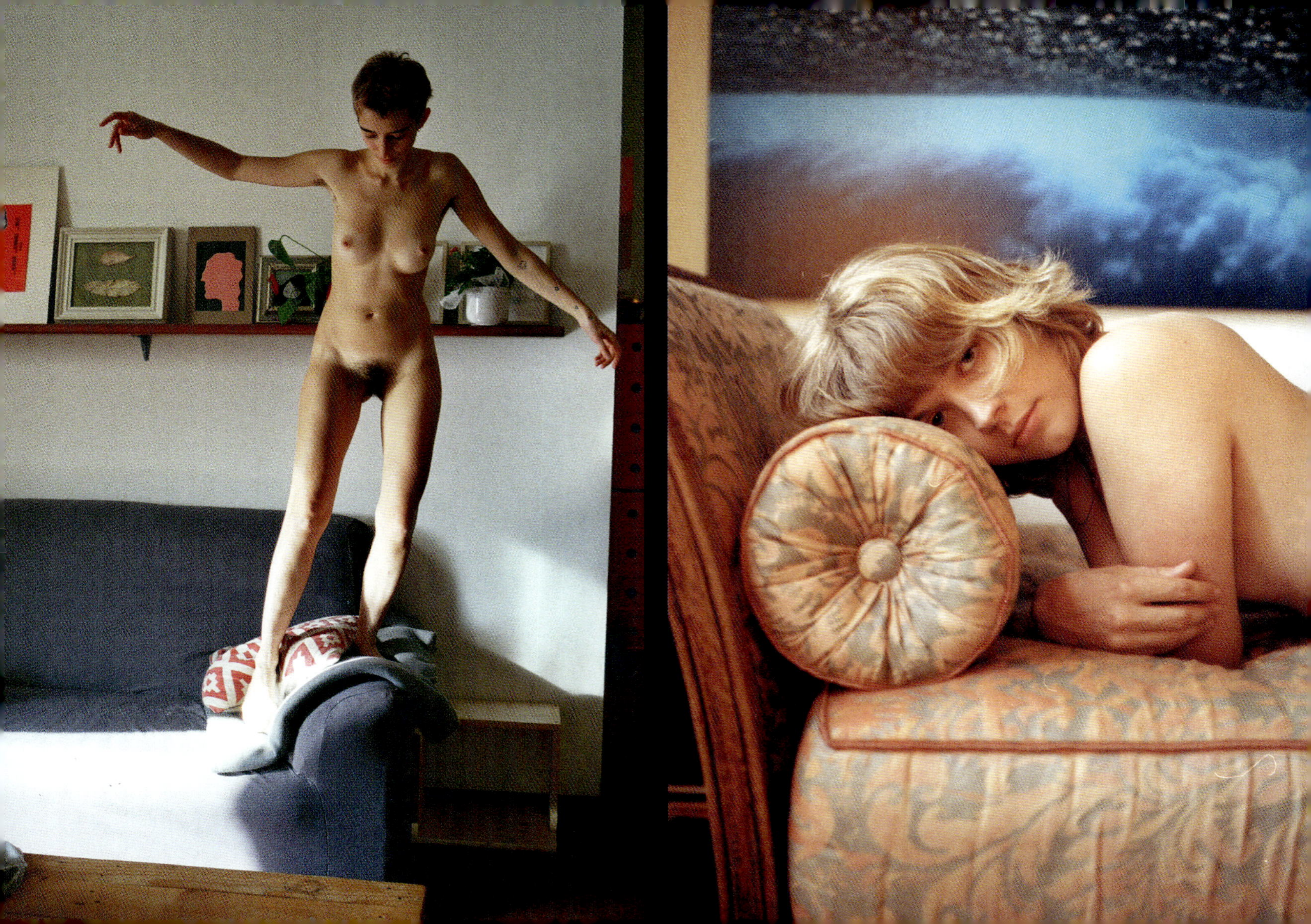

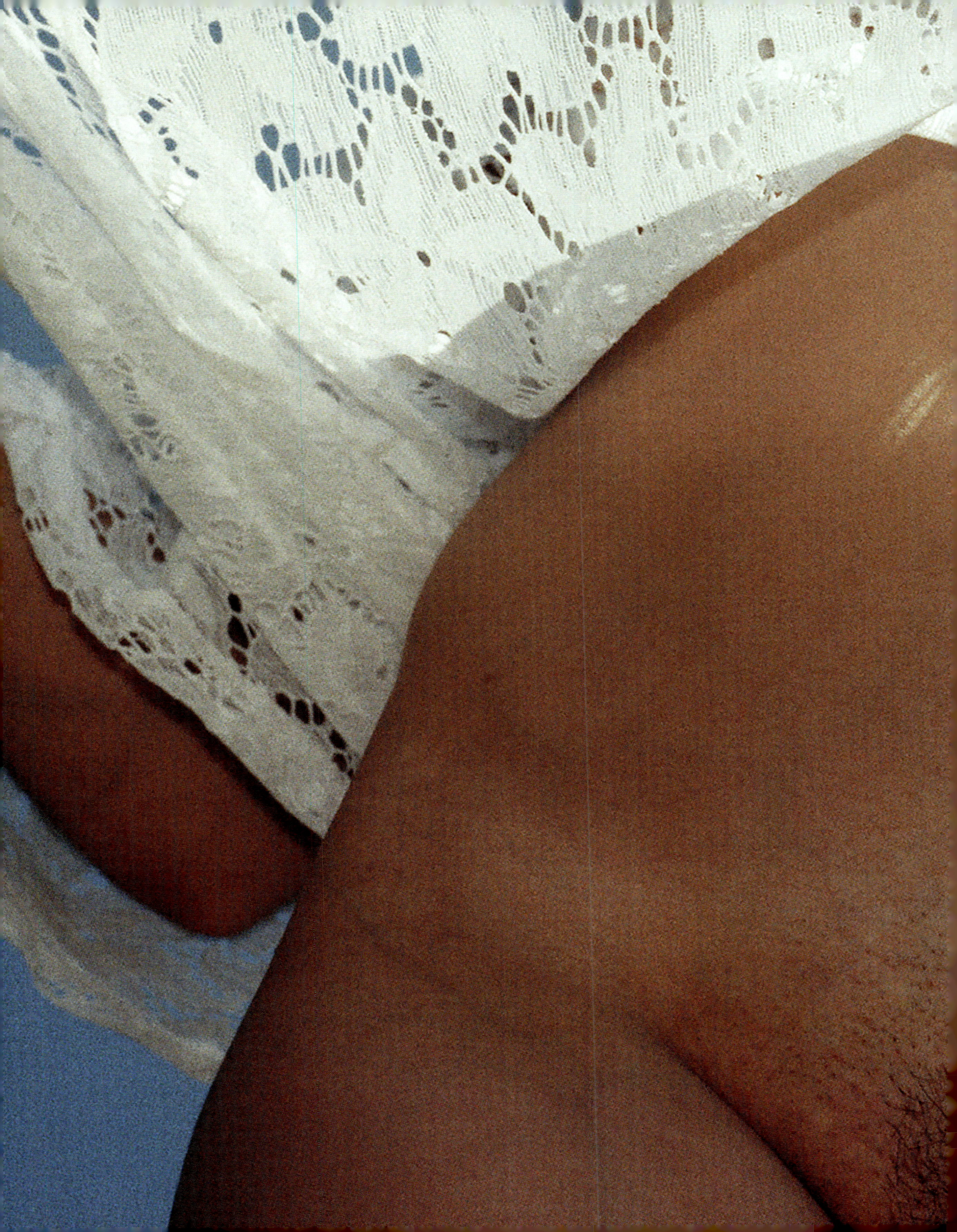

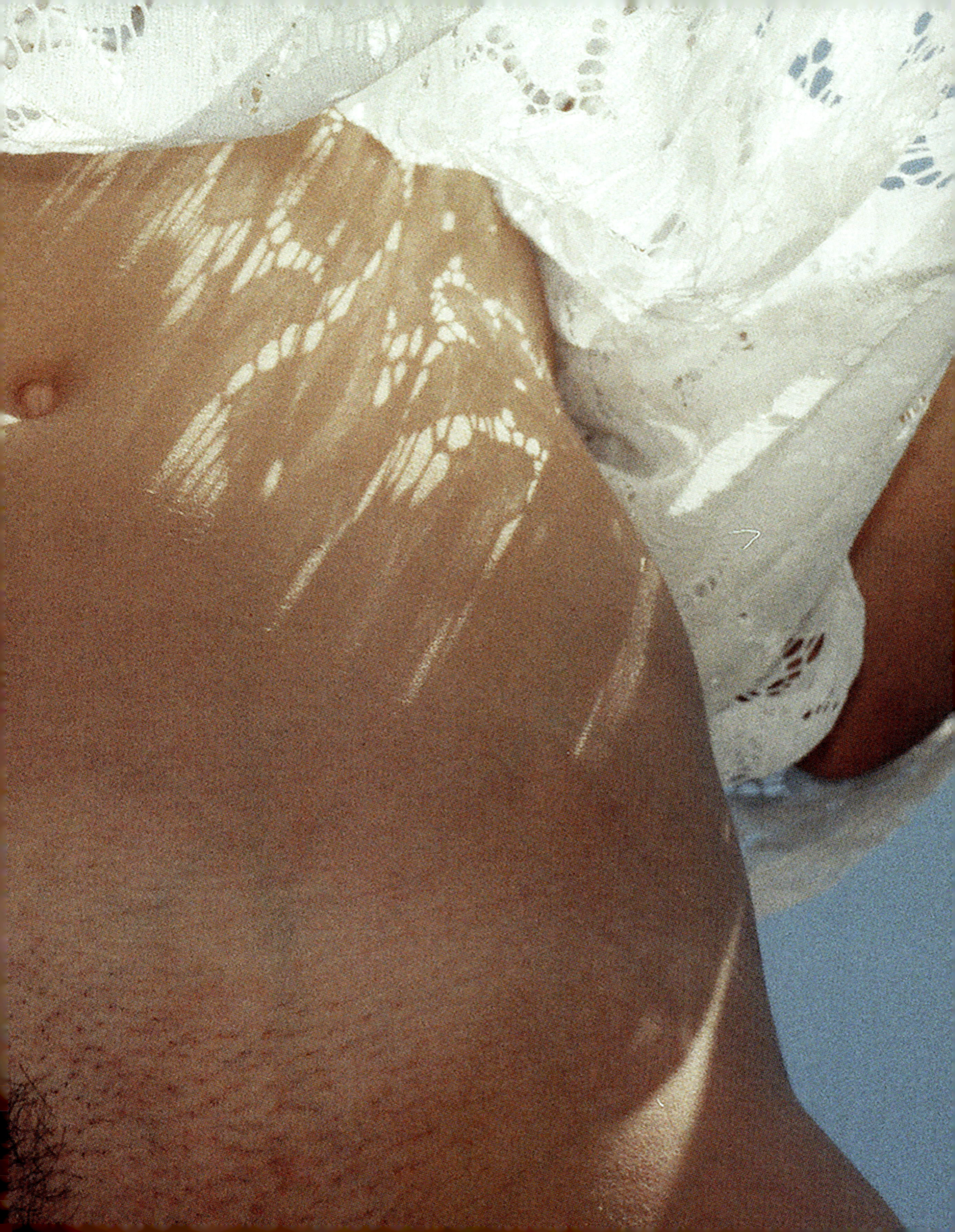

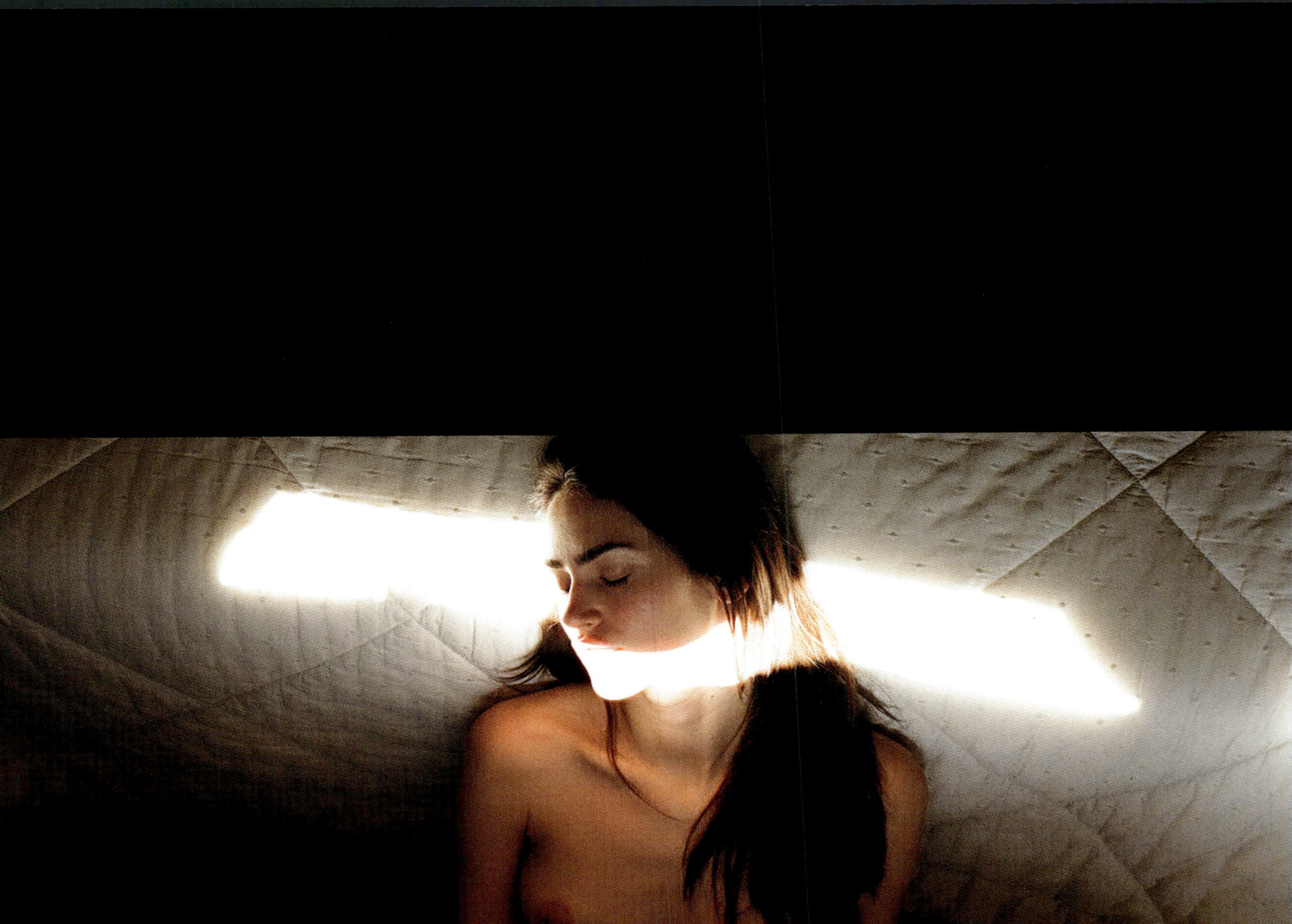

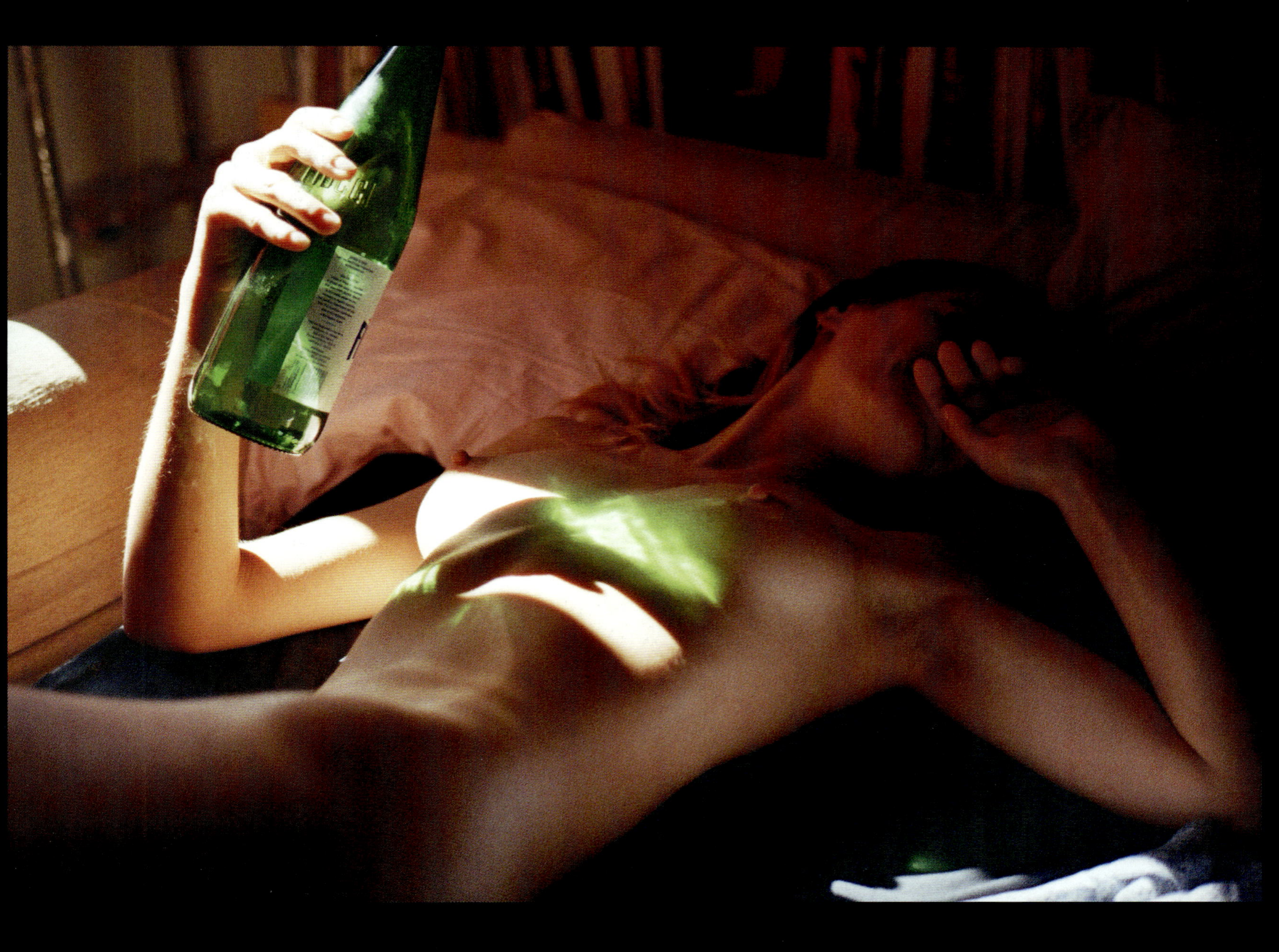

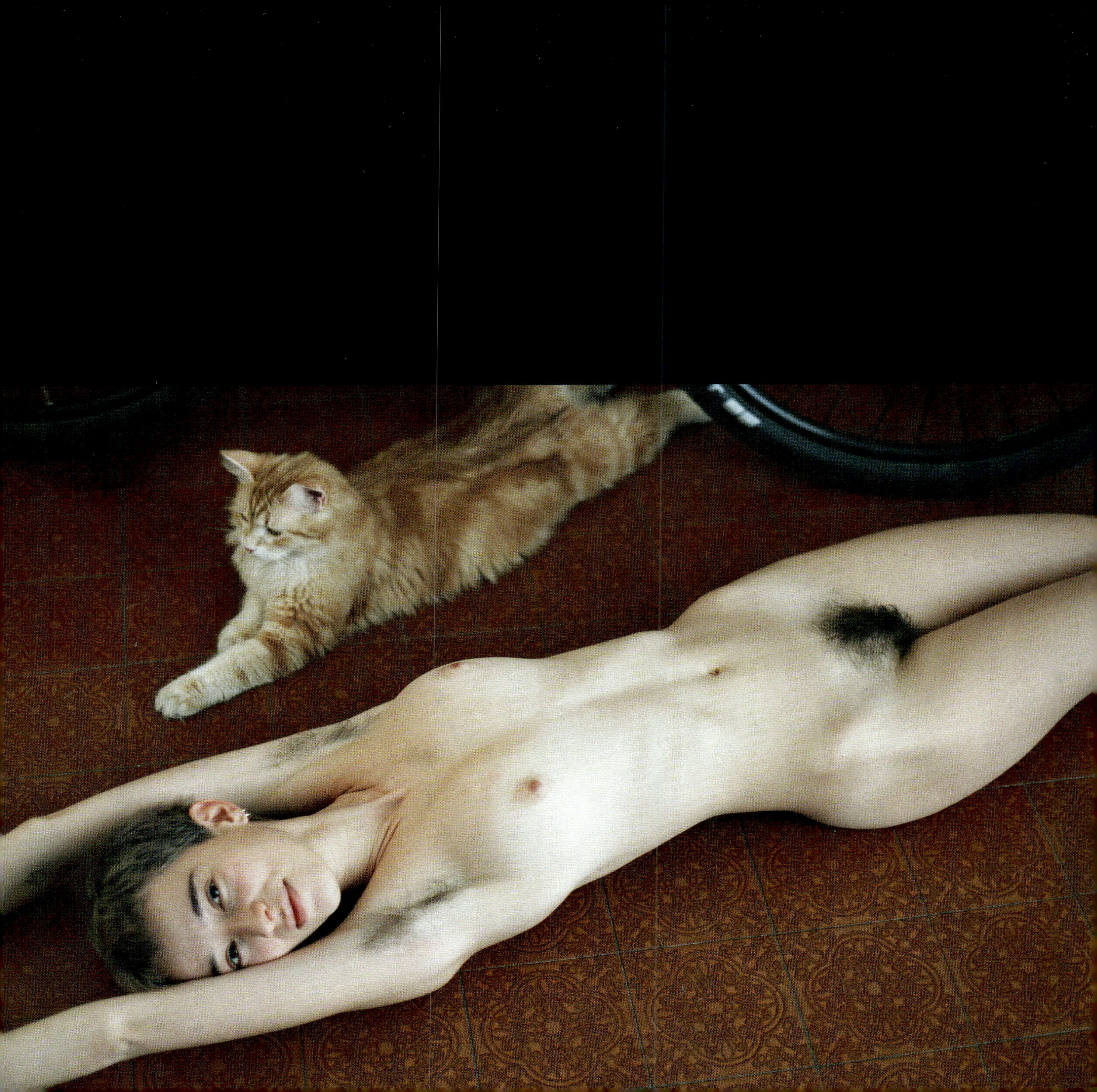

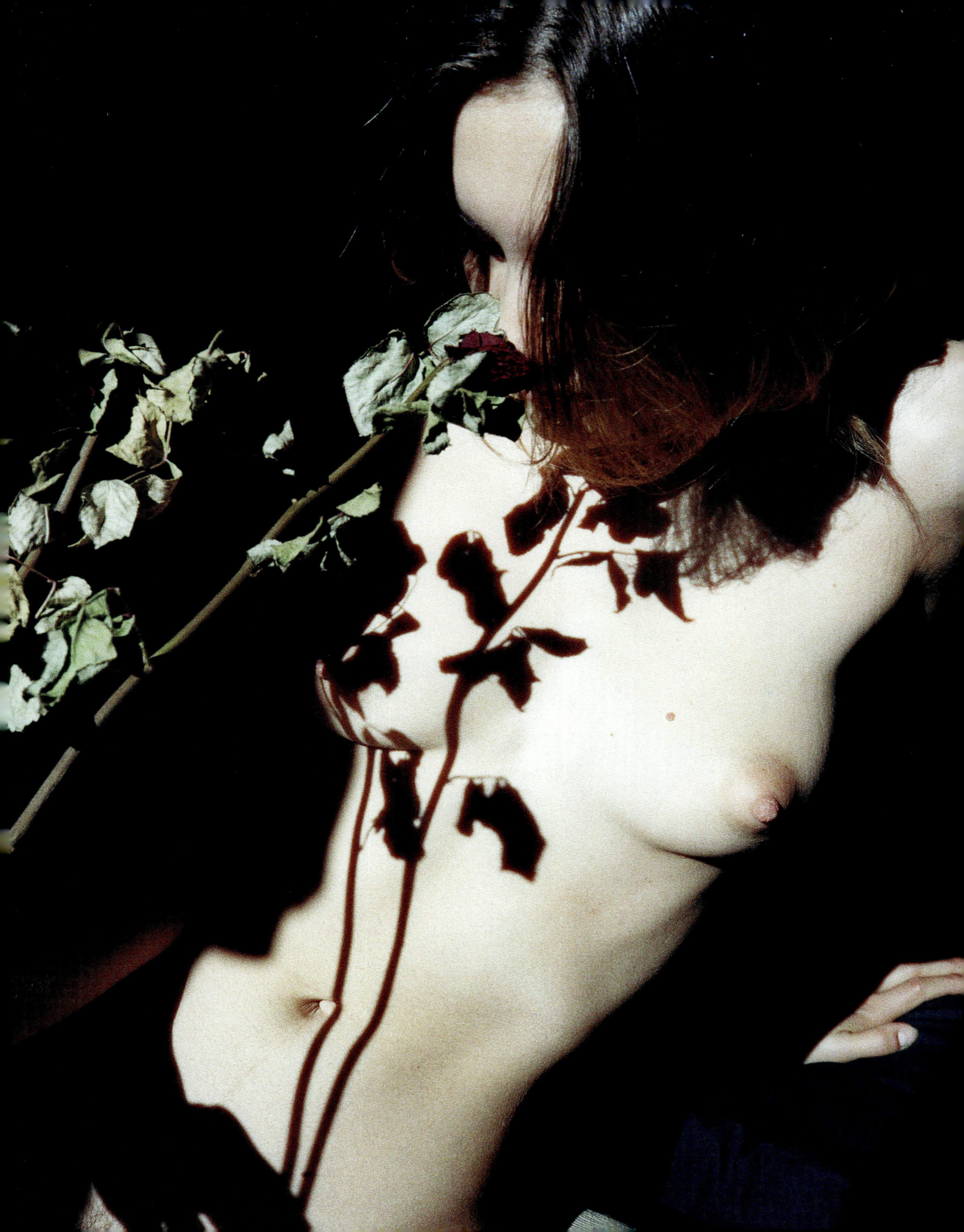

ANNE MARIA KLOSS

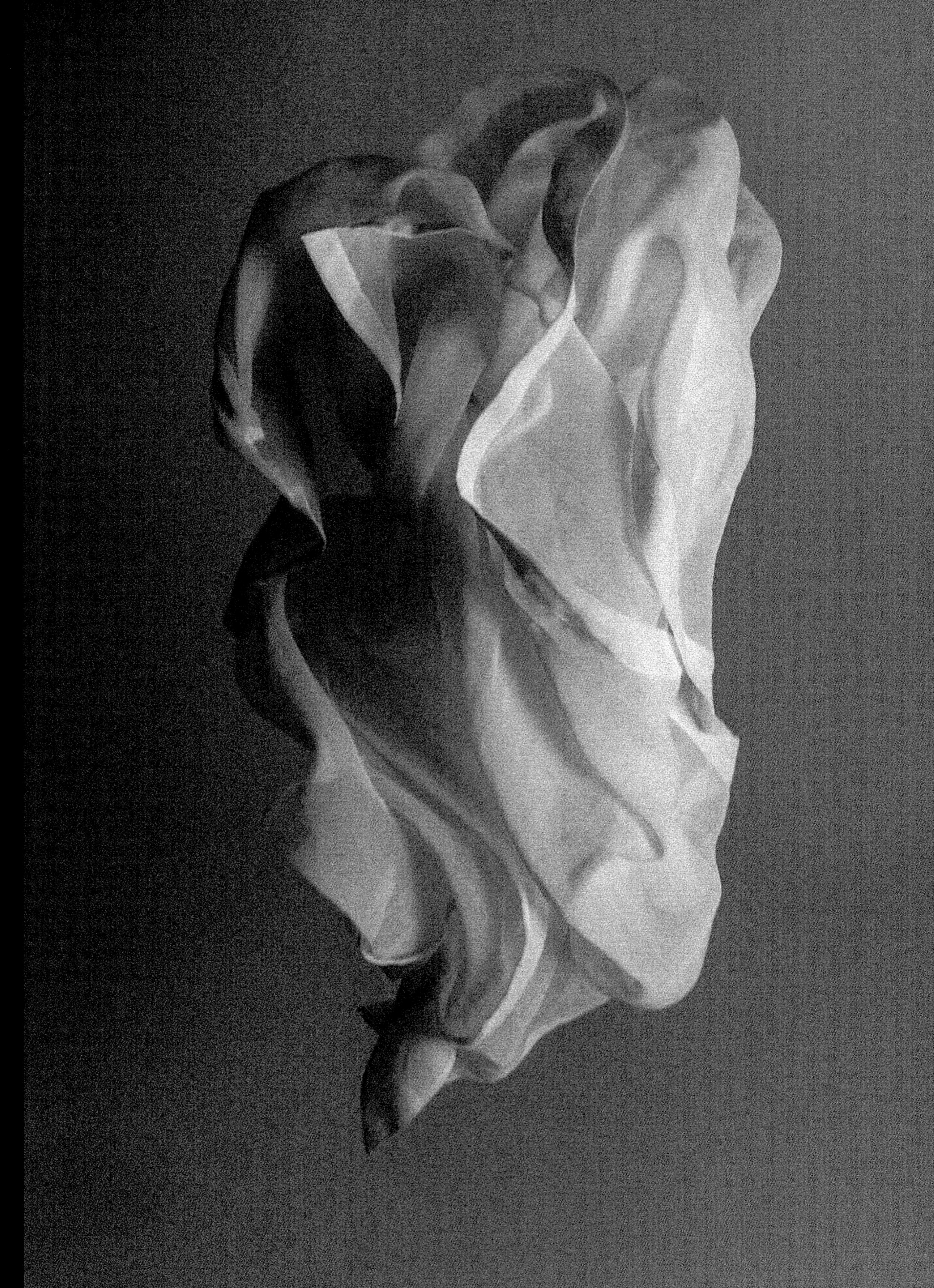

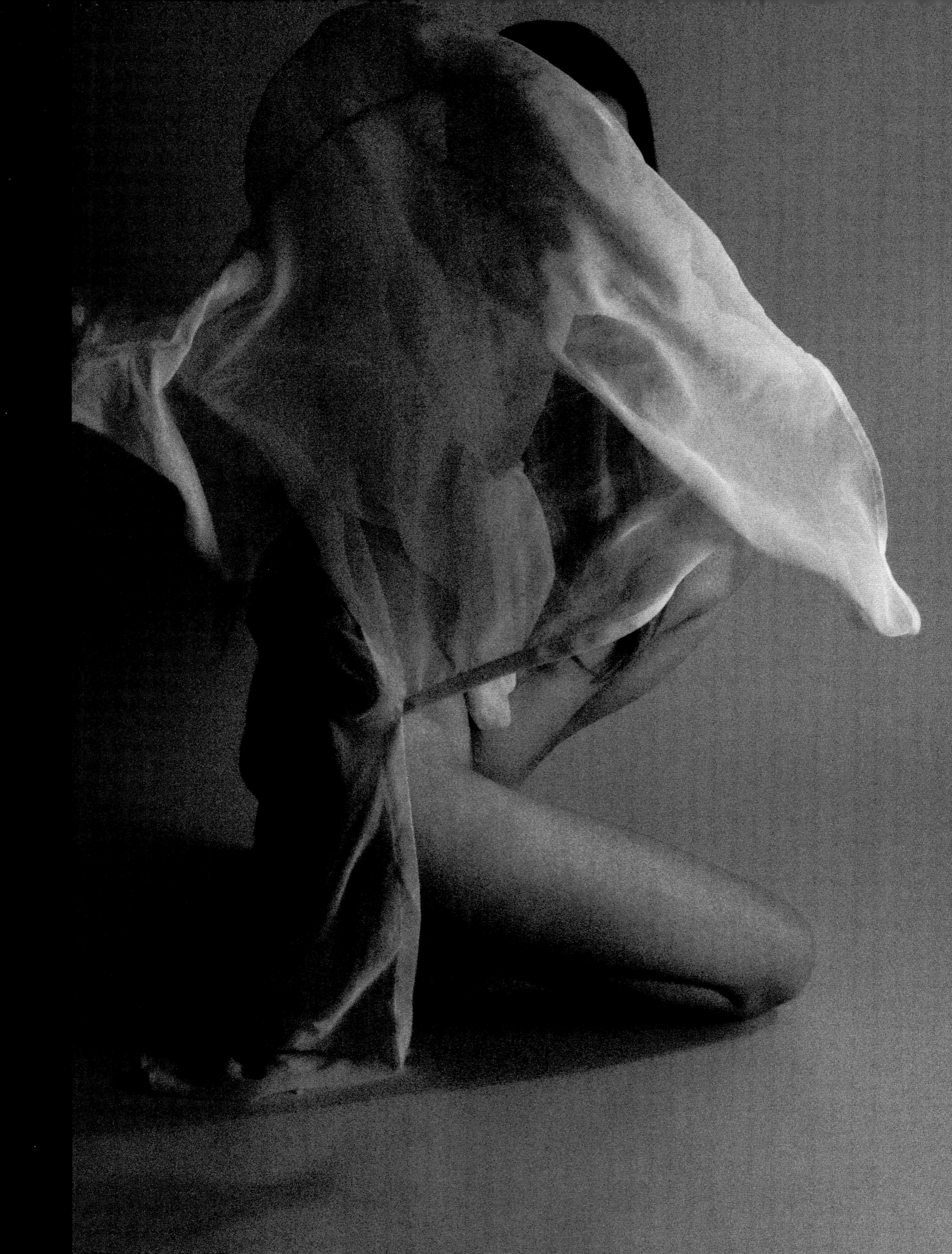

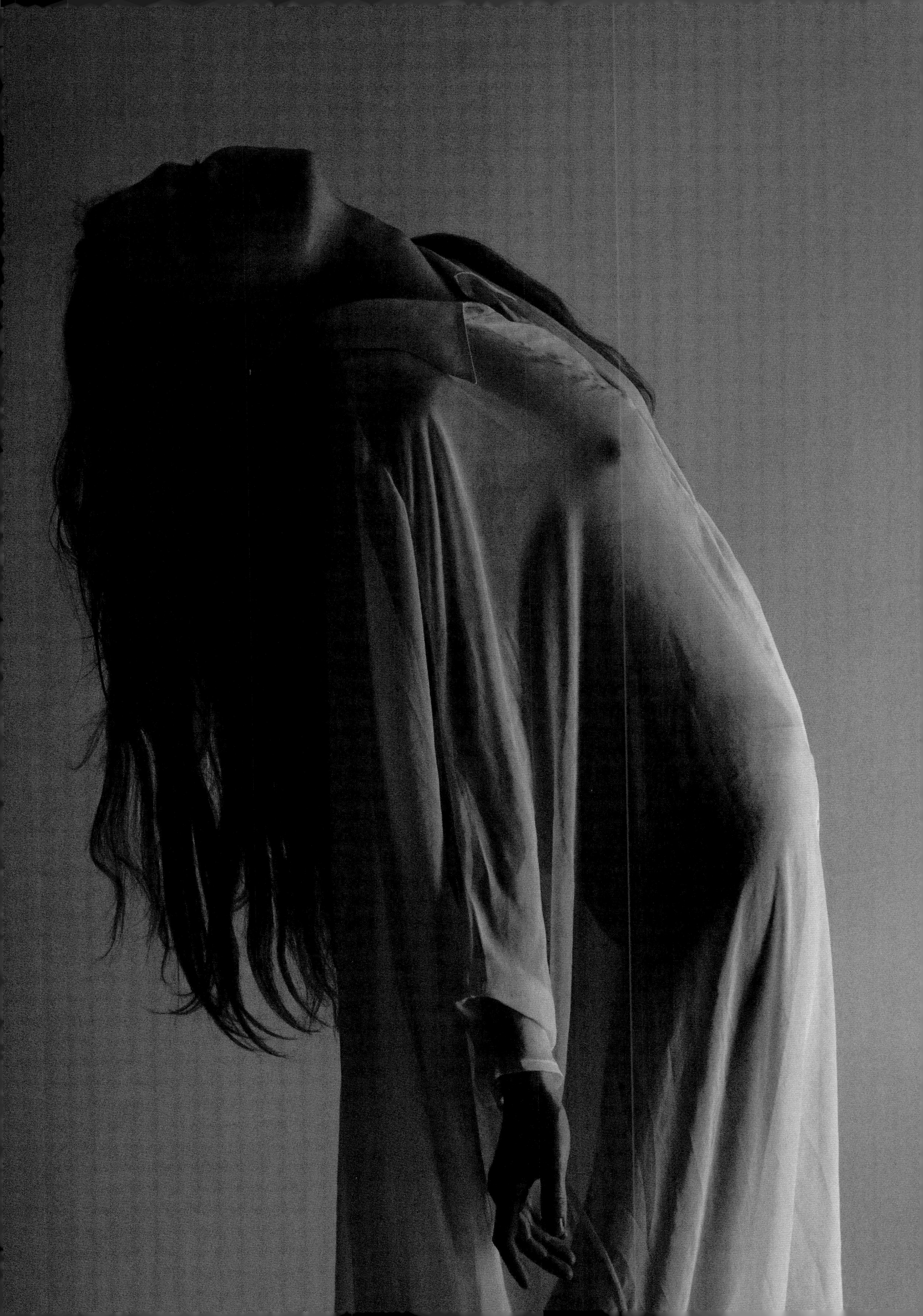

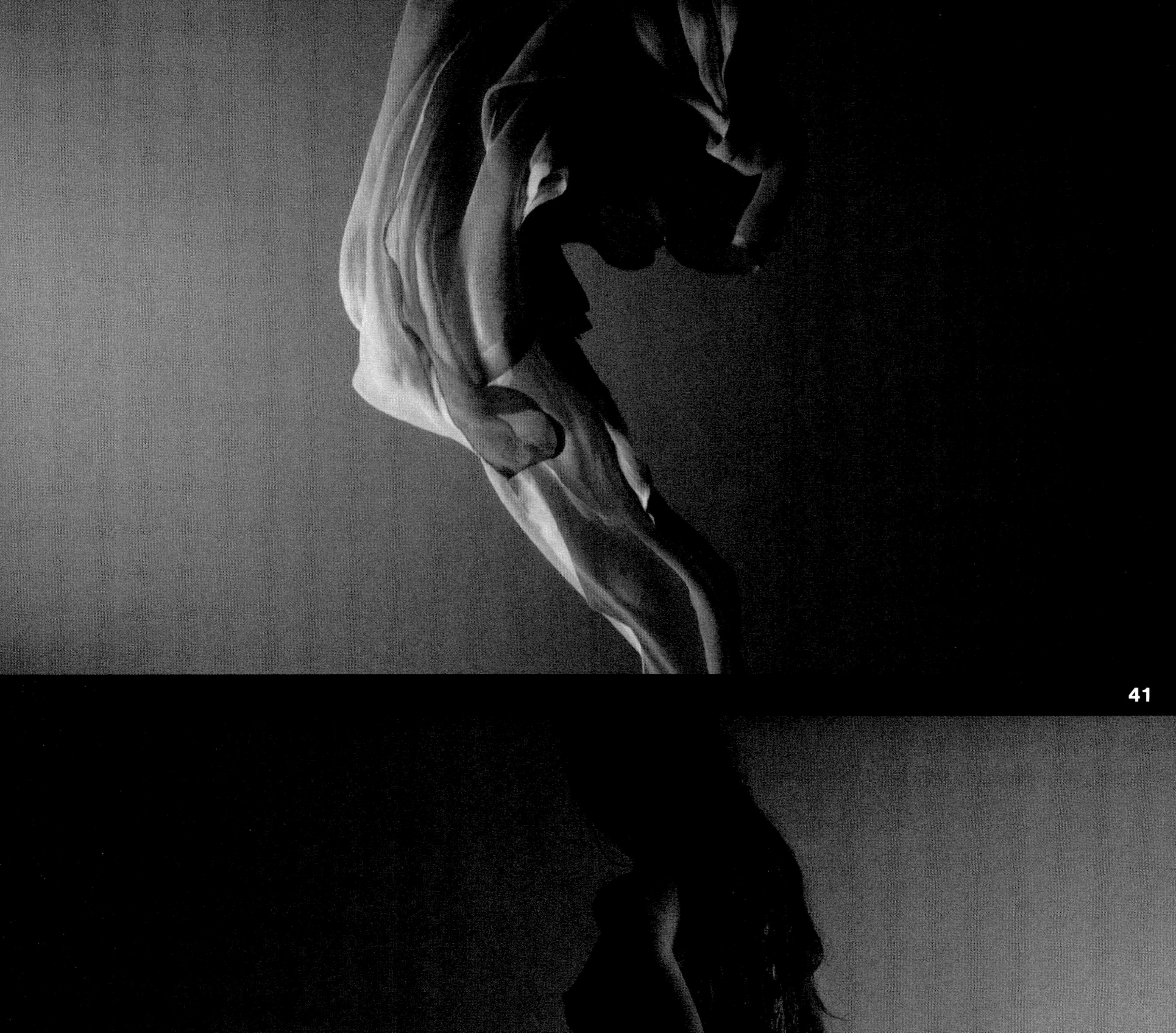

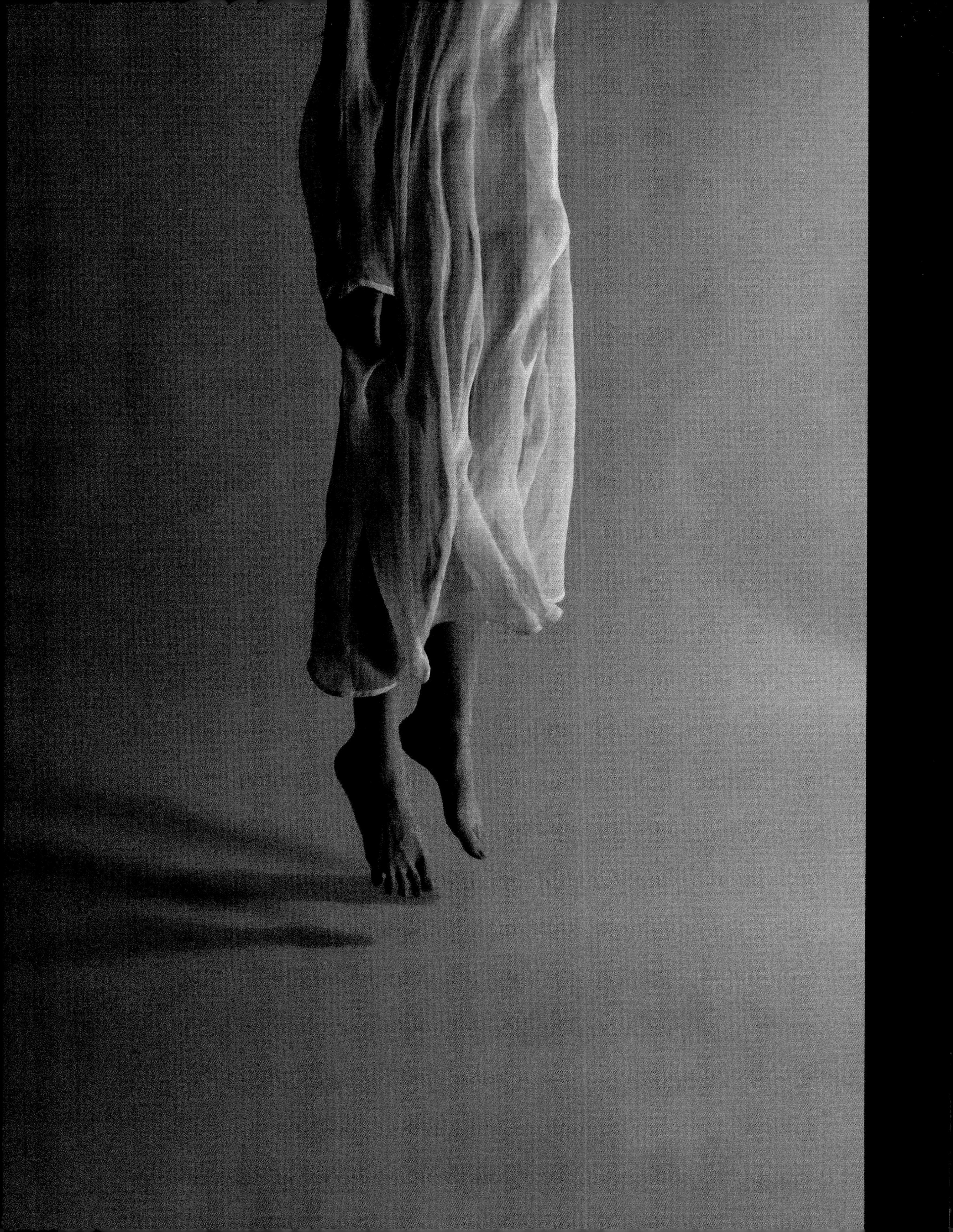

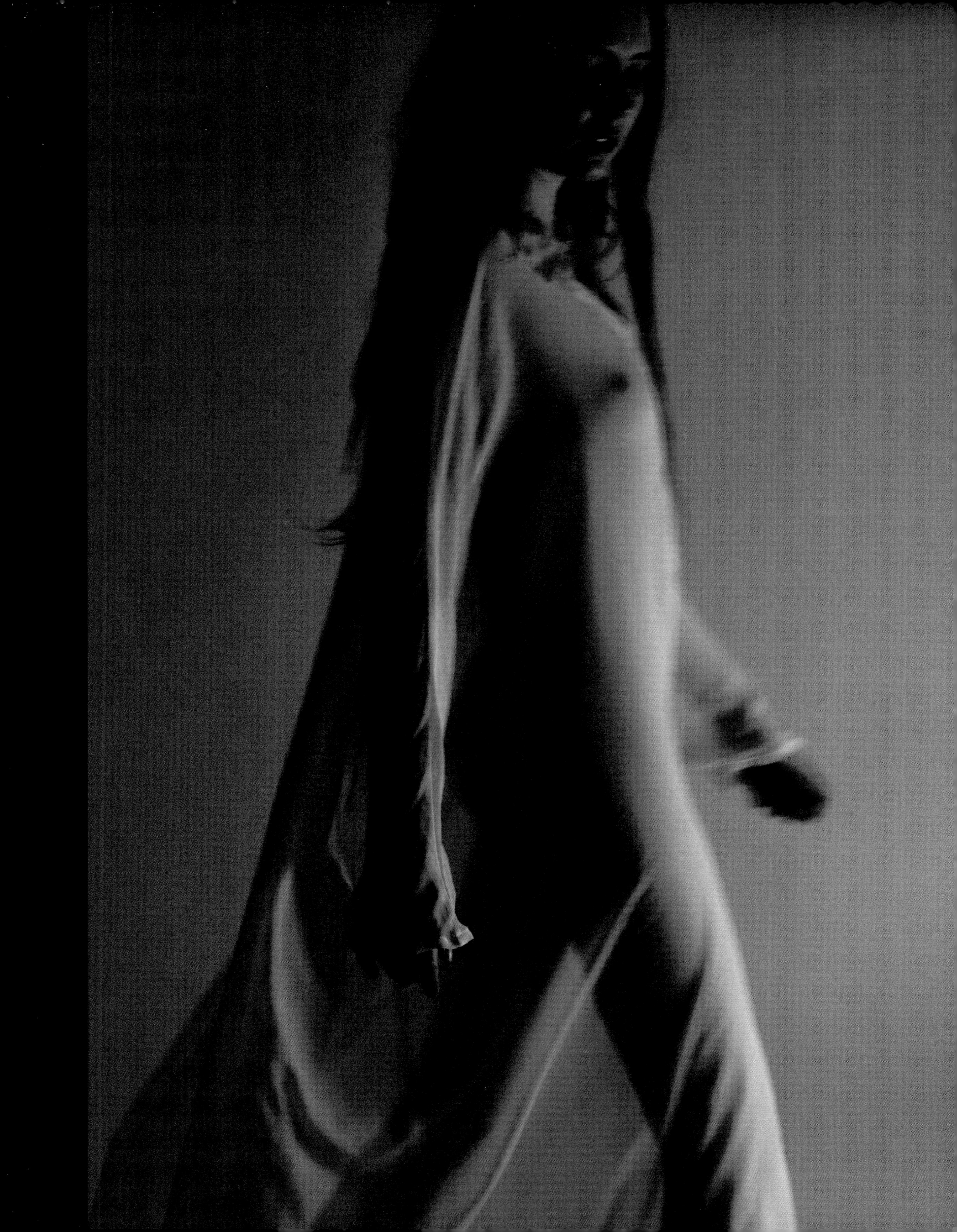

ARNE GRASHOFF

BODY TO BODY

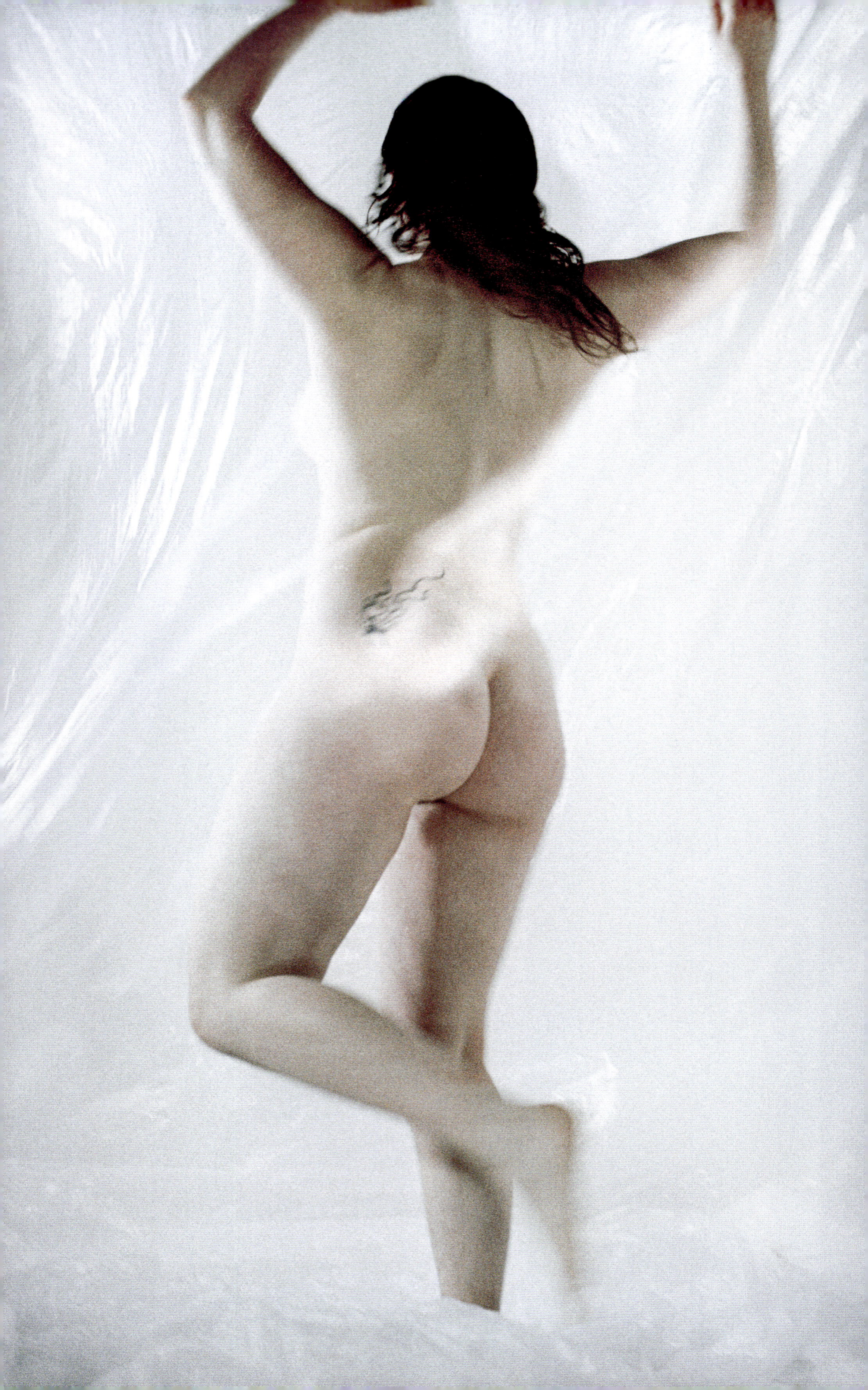

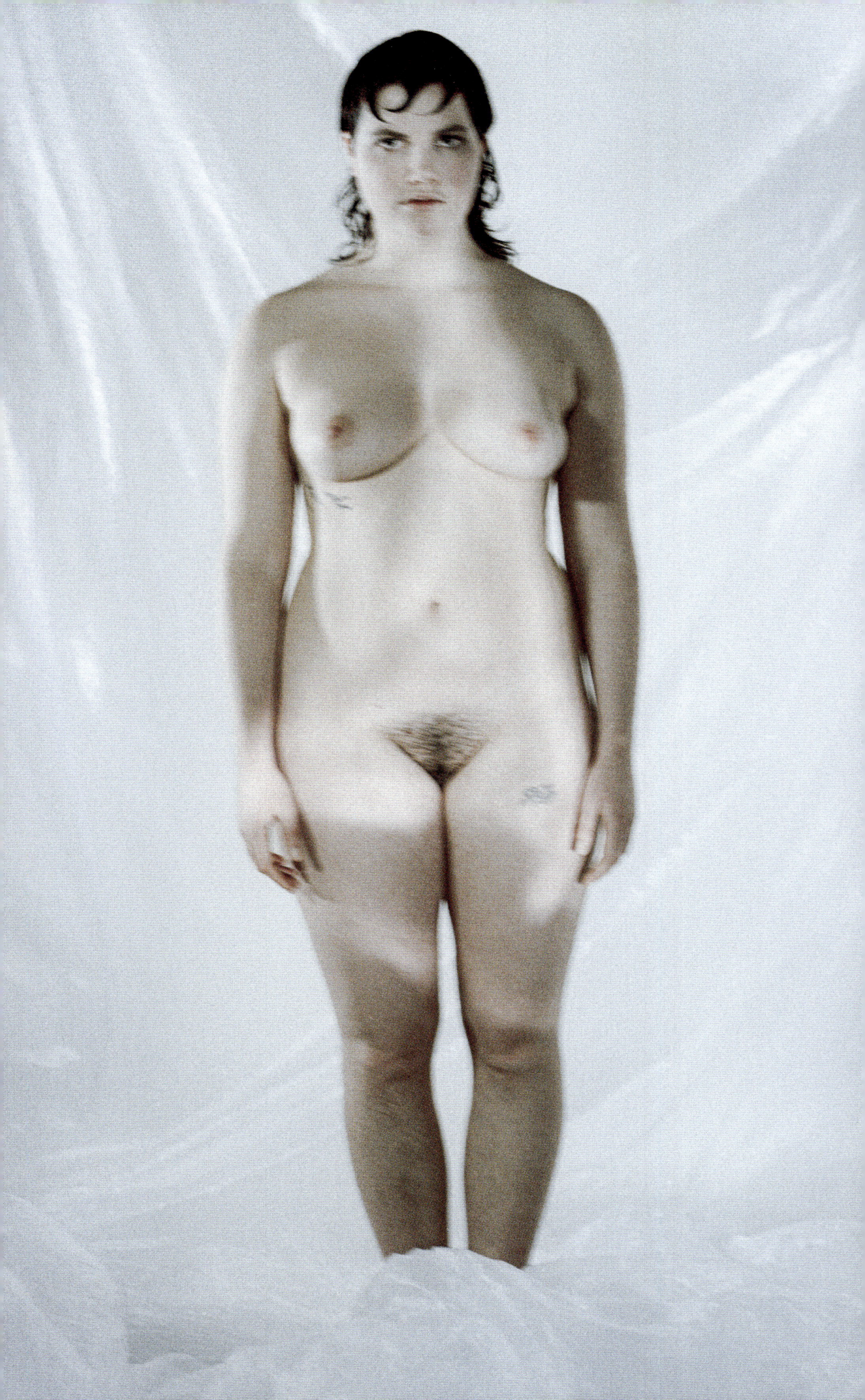

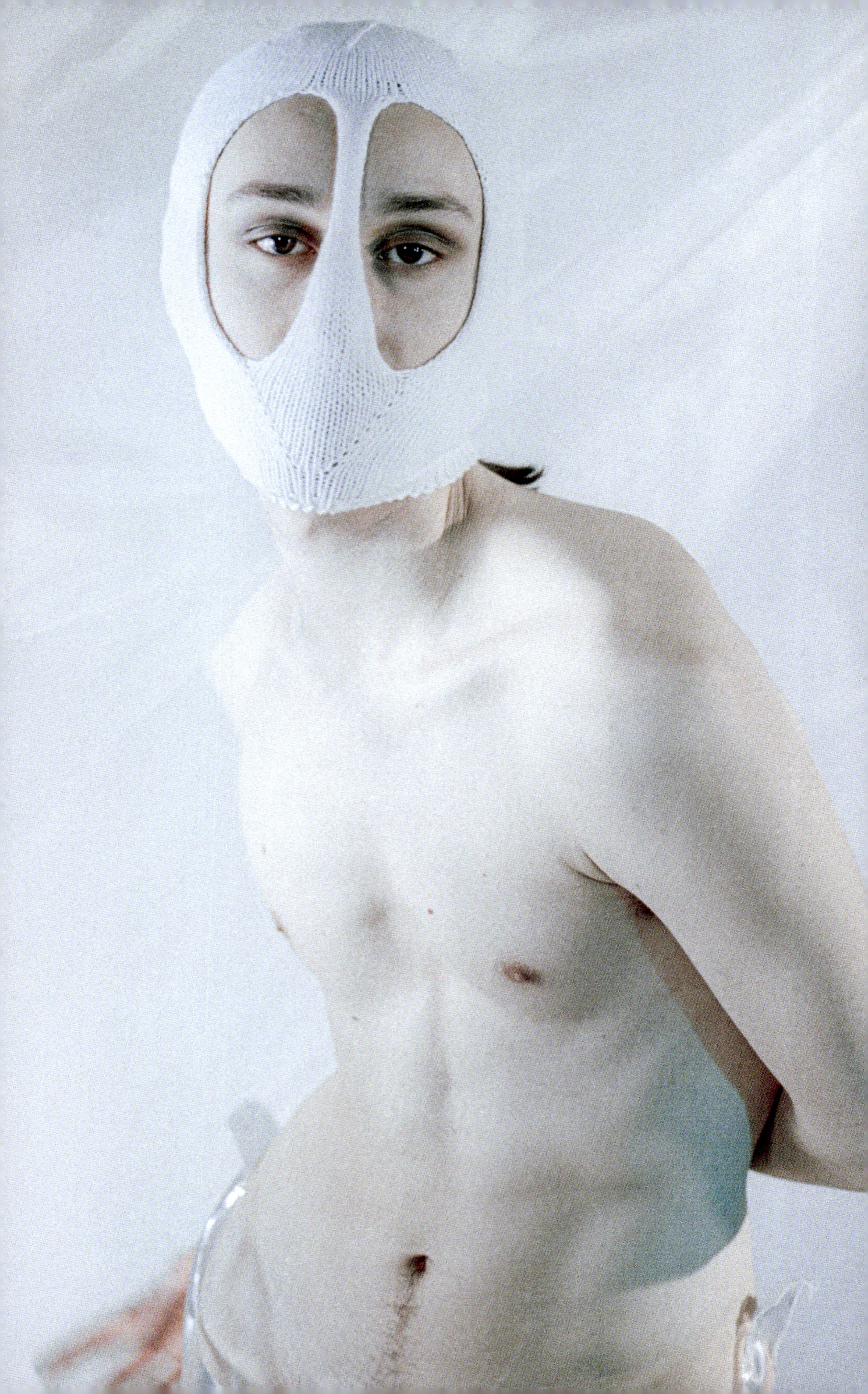

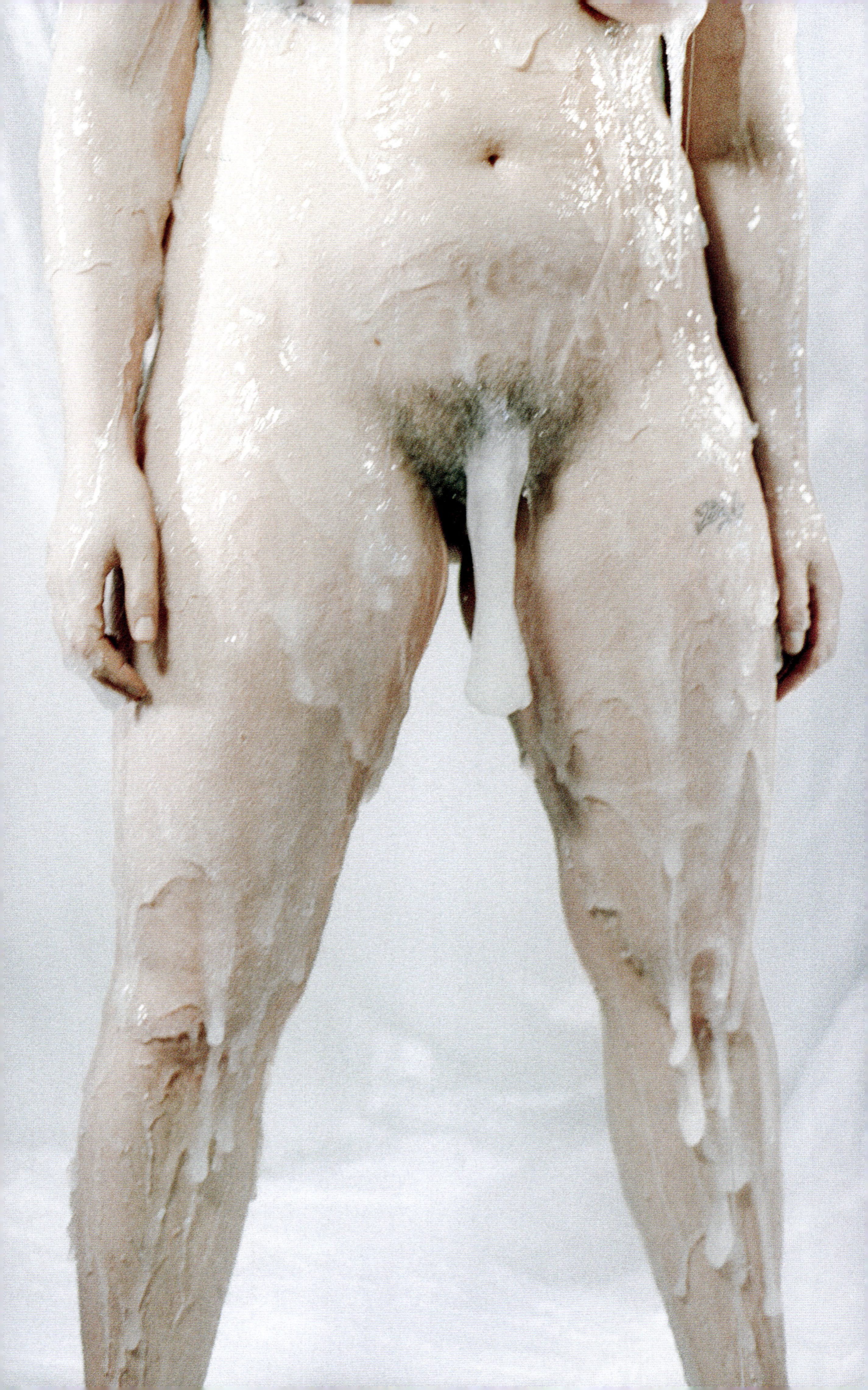

II.
HEROS

LEGENDARY FIGURES PERFORMING EXTRA-ORDINARY DEEDS AND EARN ETERNAL FAME BY EMBODYING VITAL ROLES, DEFYING FATE AND EMBODY-ING STRENGTH, WISDOM, OR TRAGIC BEAUTY.

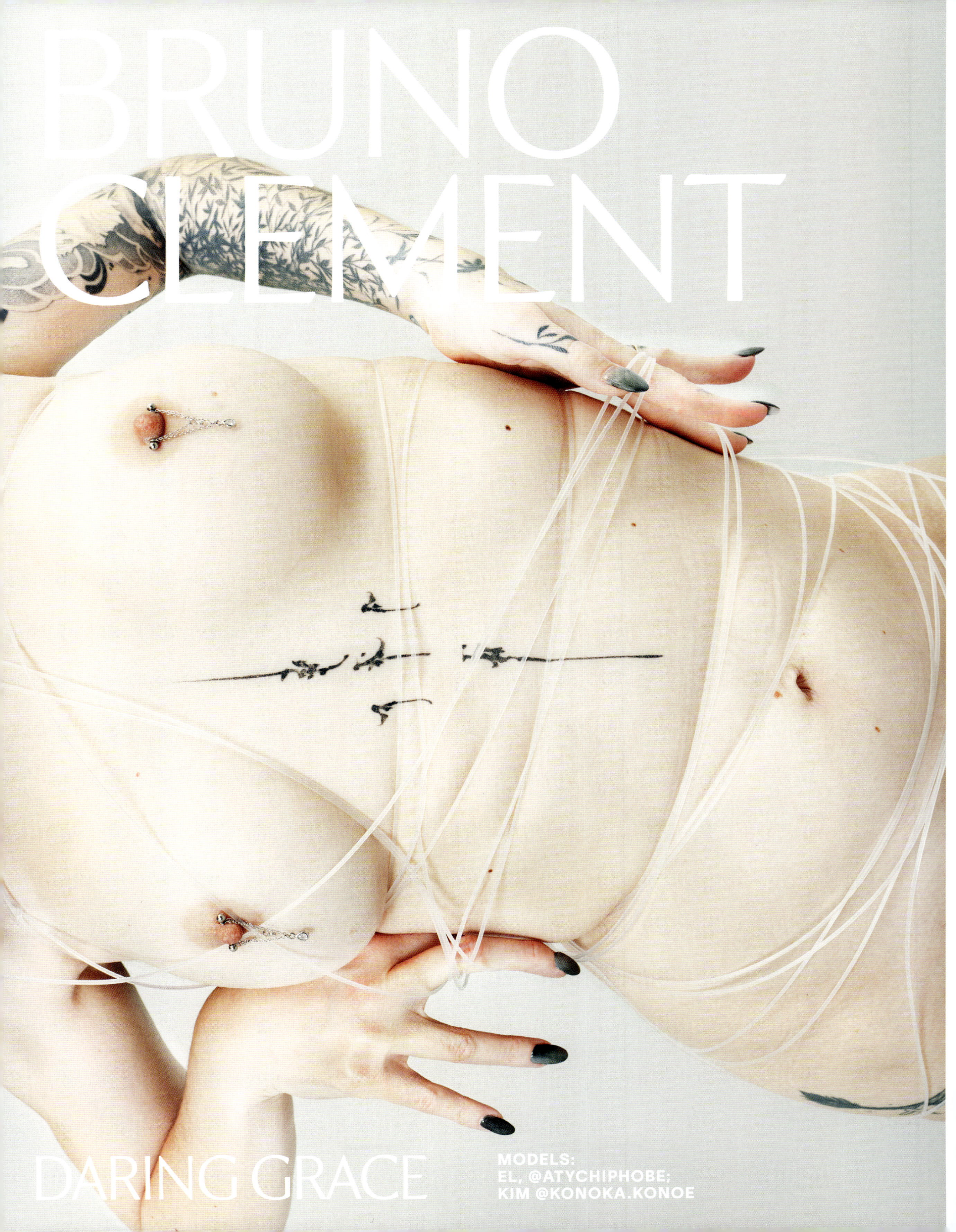
BRUNO
CLEMENT
DARING GRACE
MODELS:
EL, @ATYCHIPHOBE:
KIM @KONOKA.KONOE

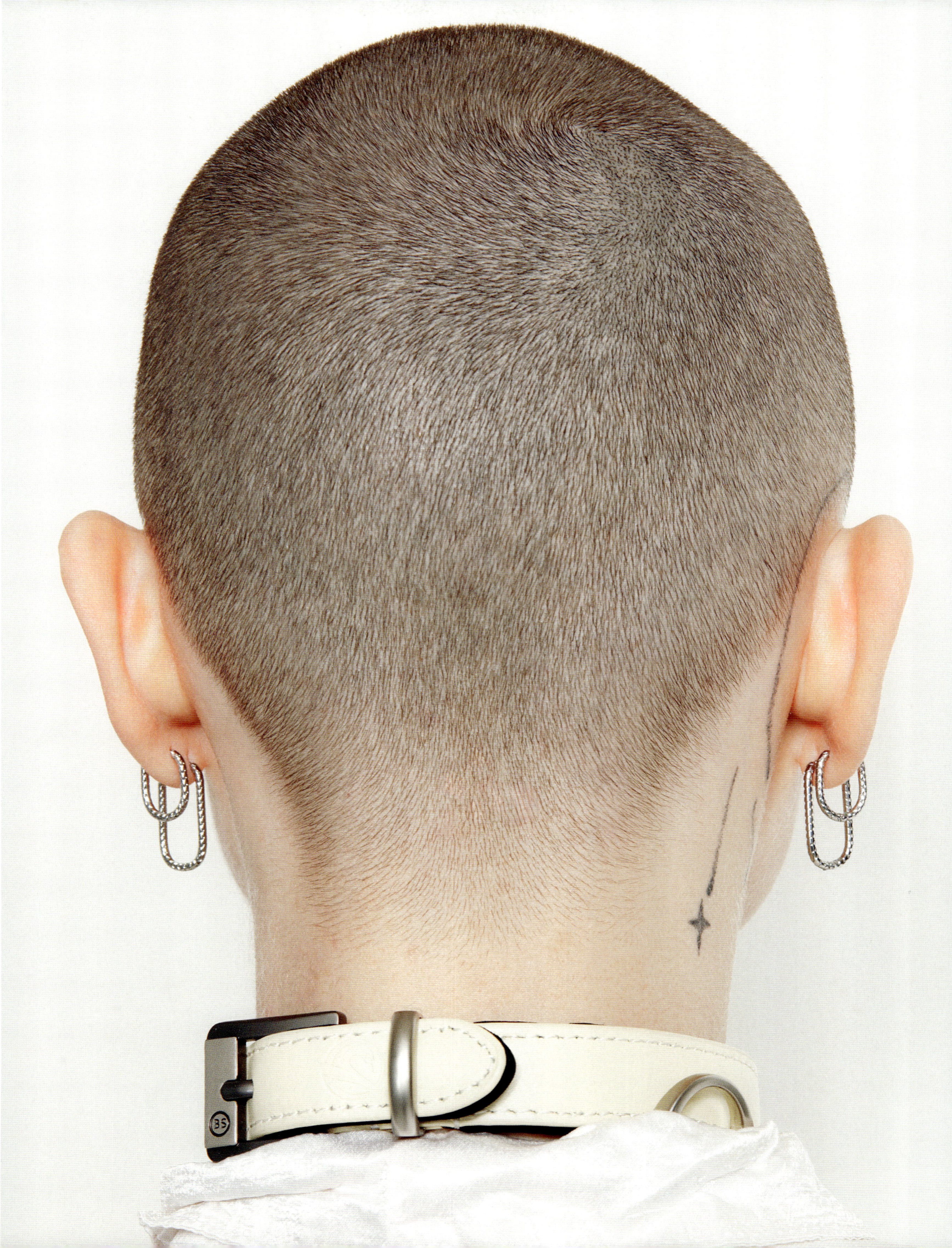

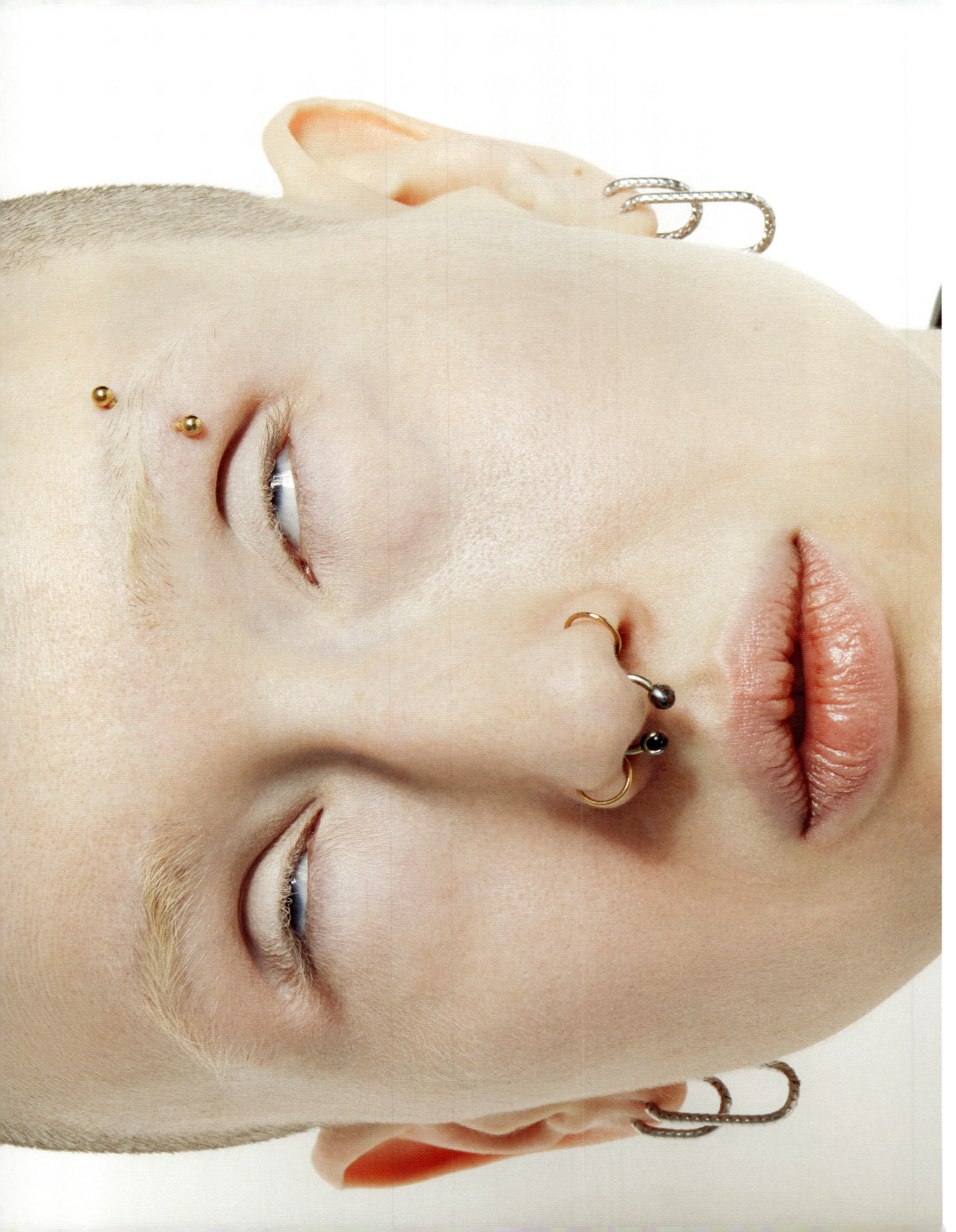

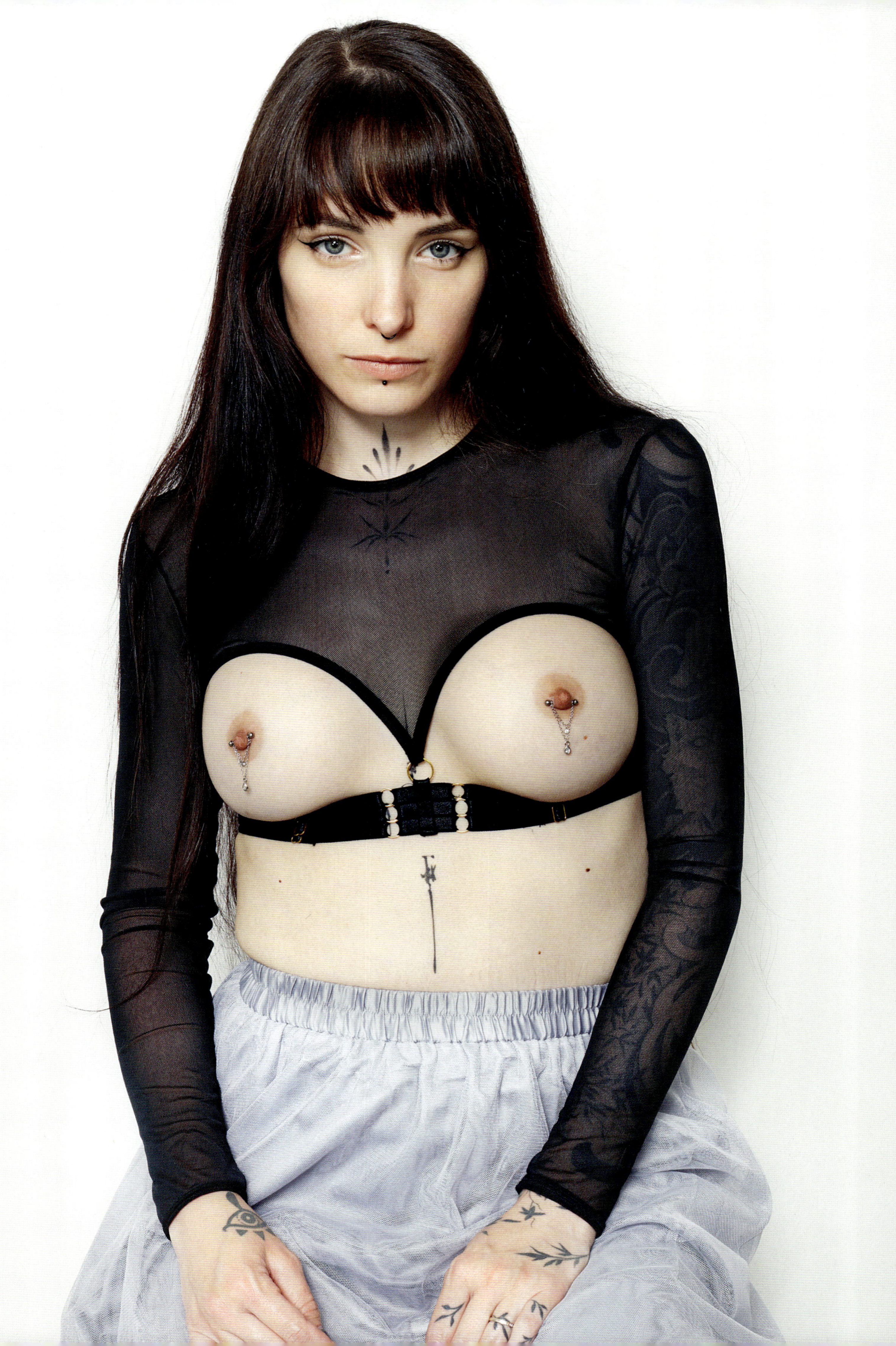

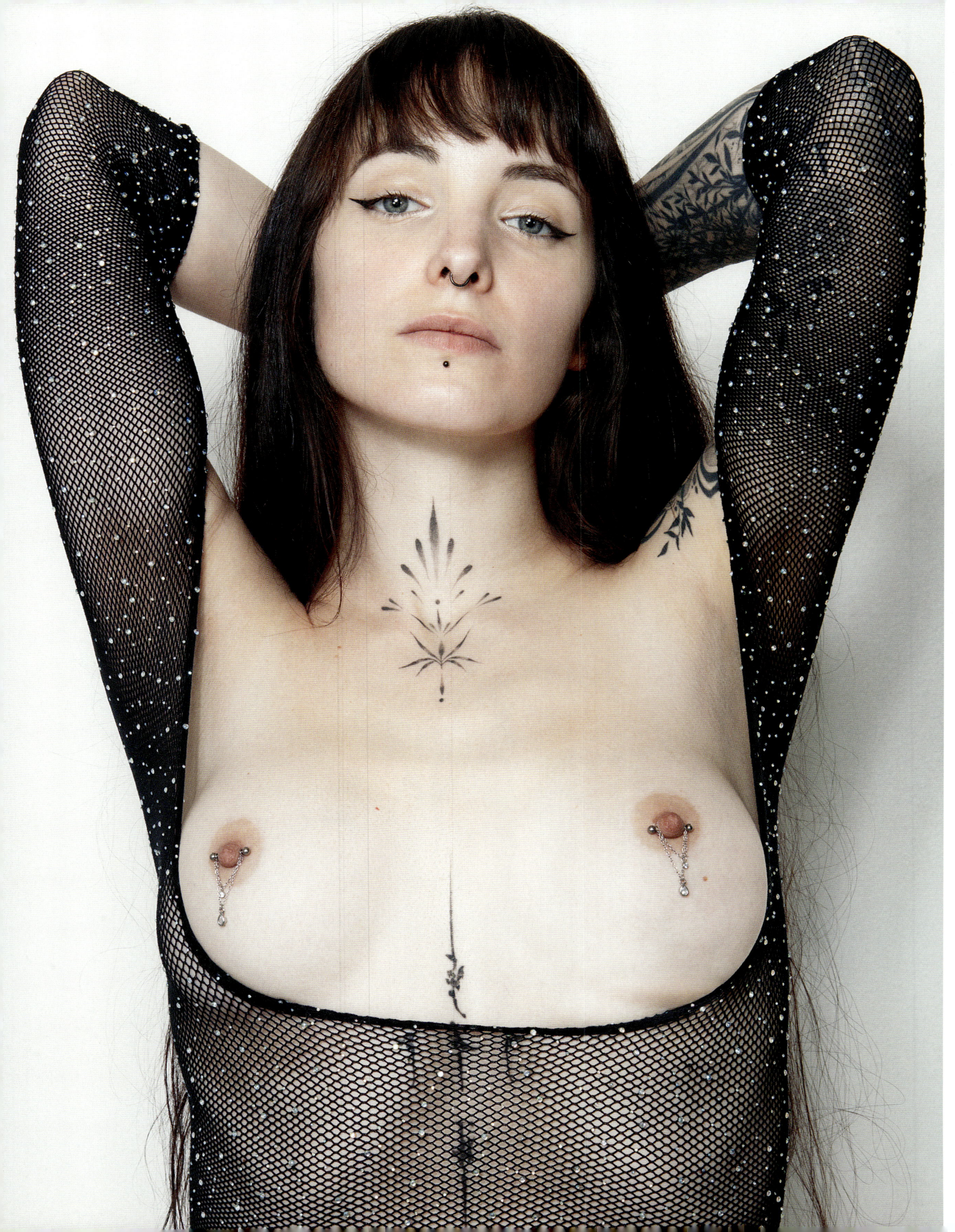

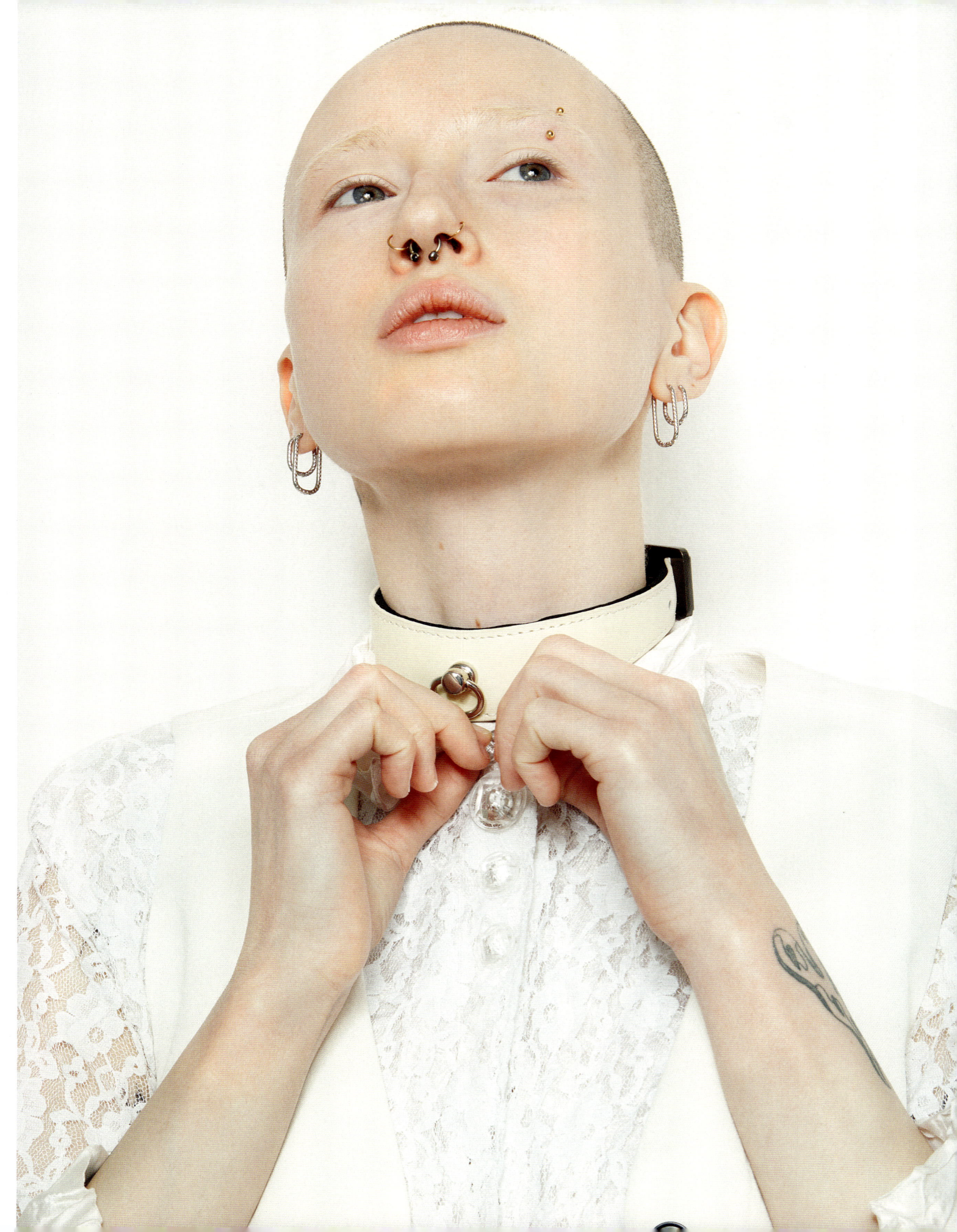

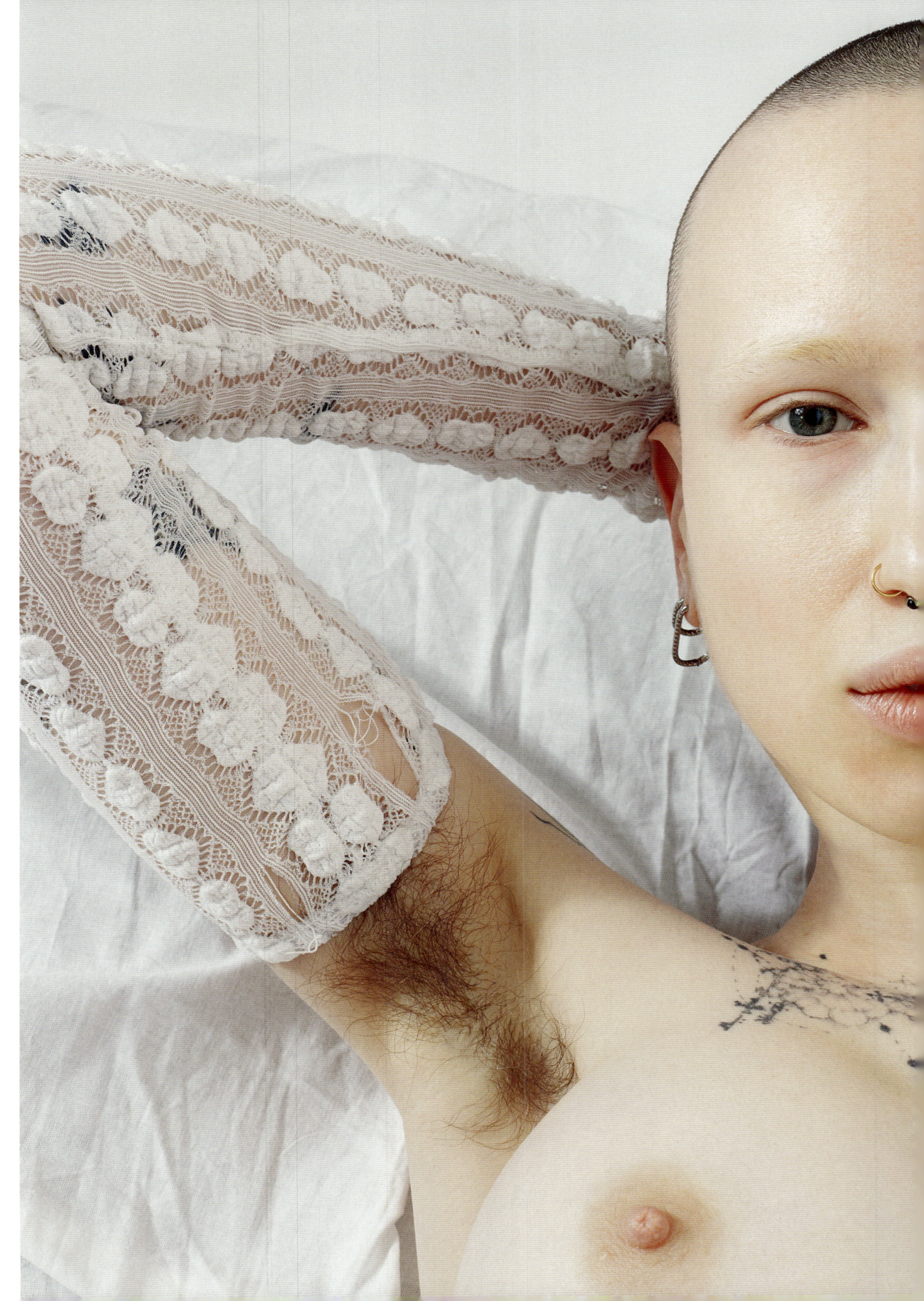

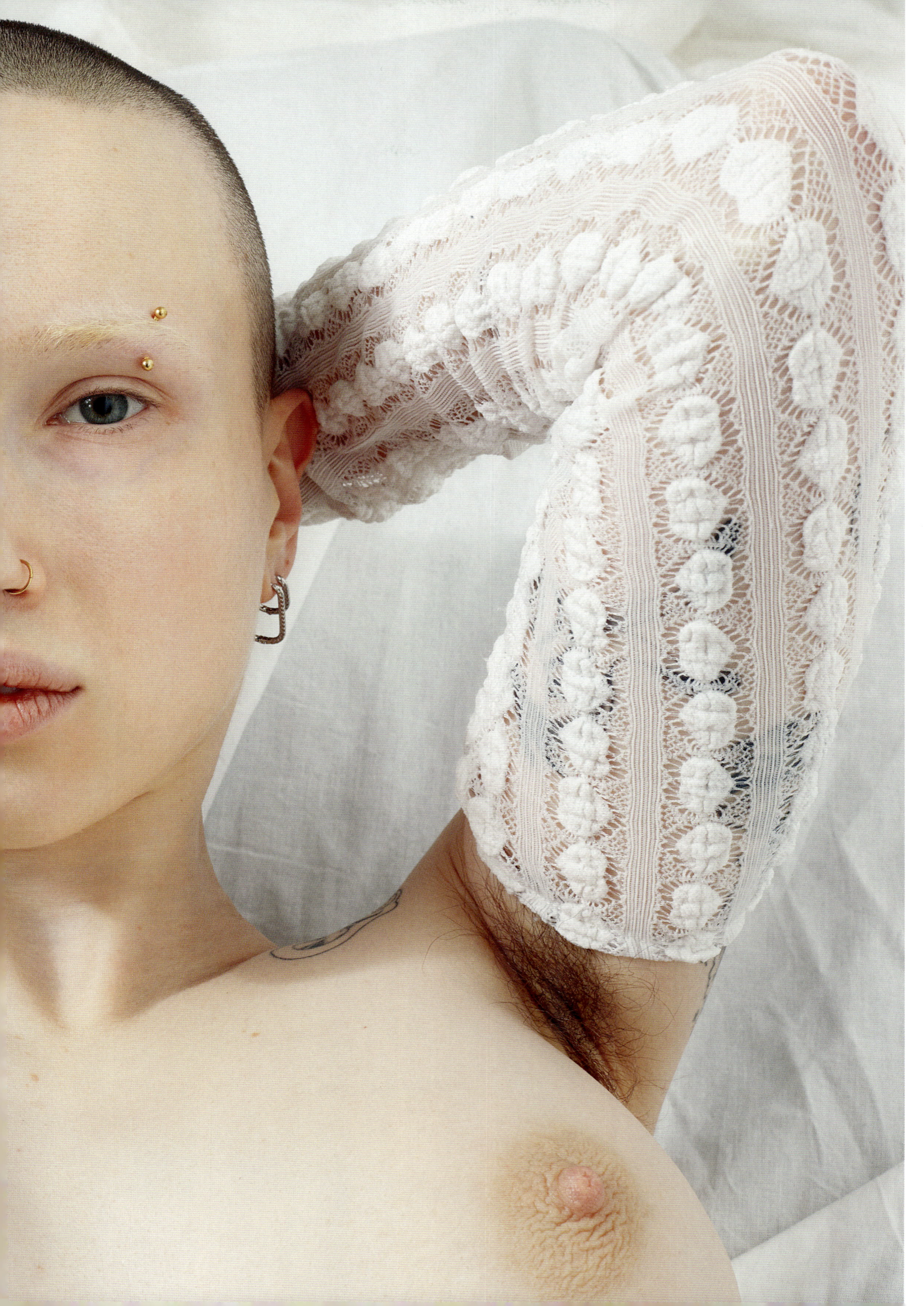

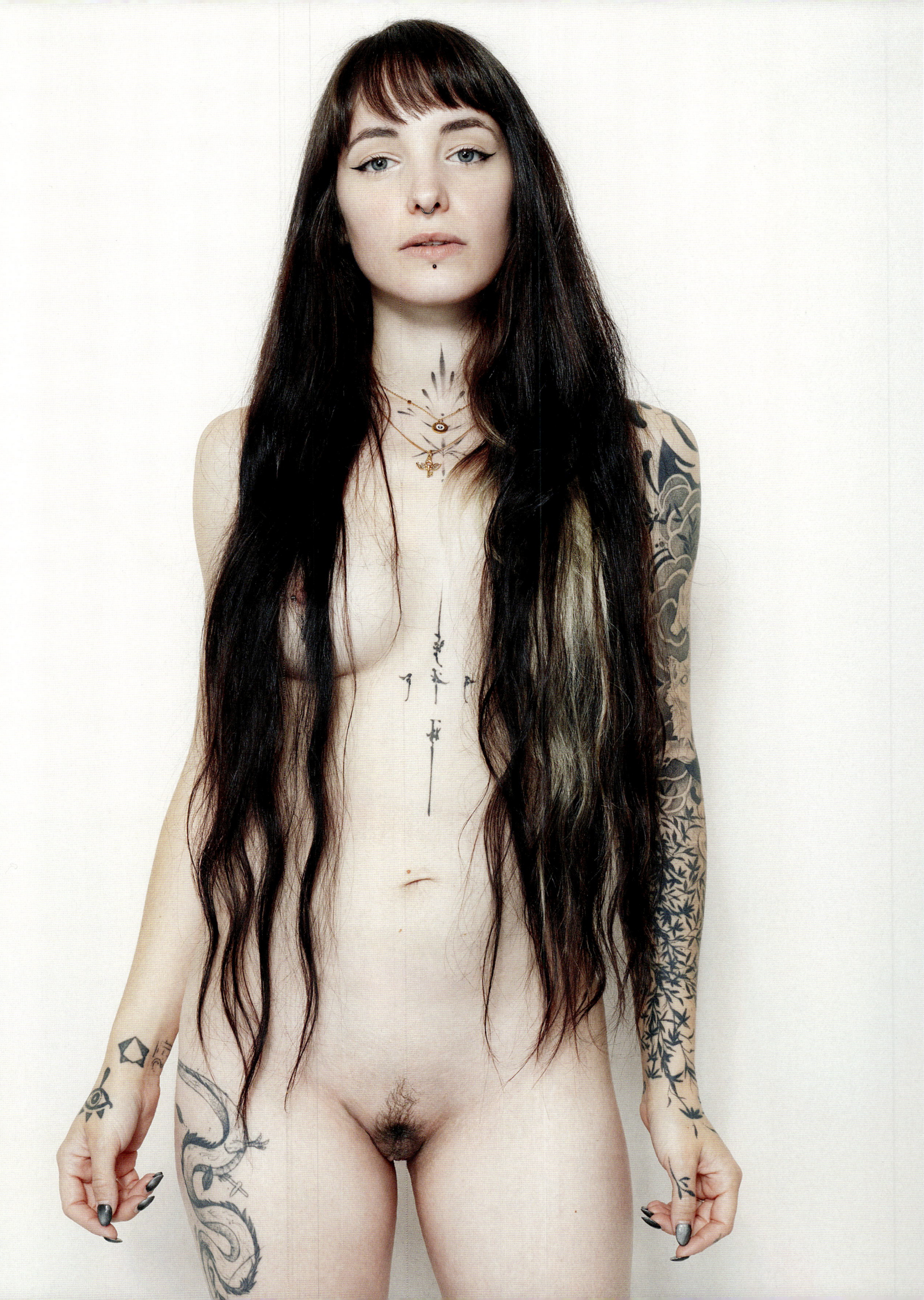

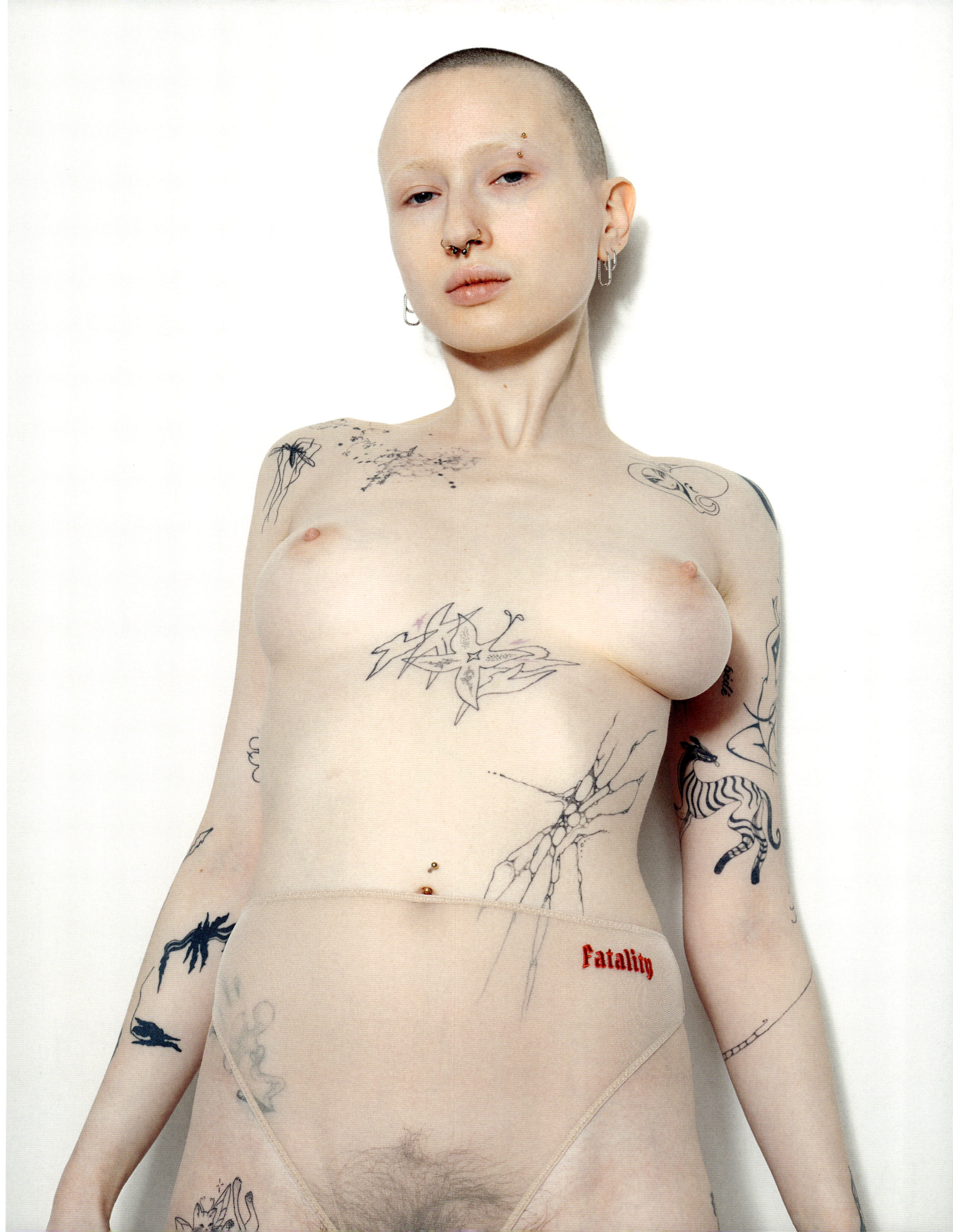
Fatality

NINA CLAUDIA LUCIE

TAO

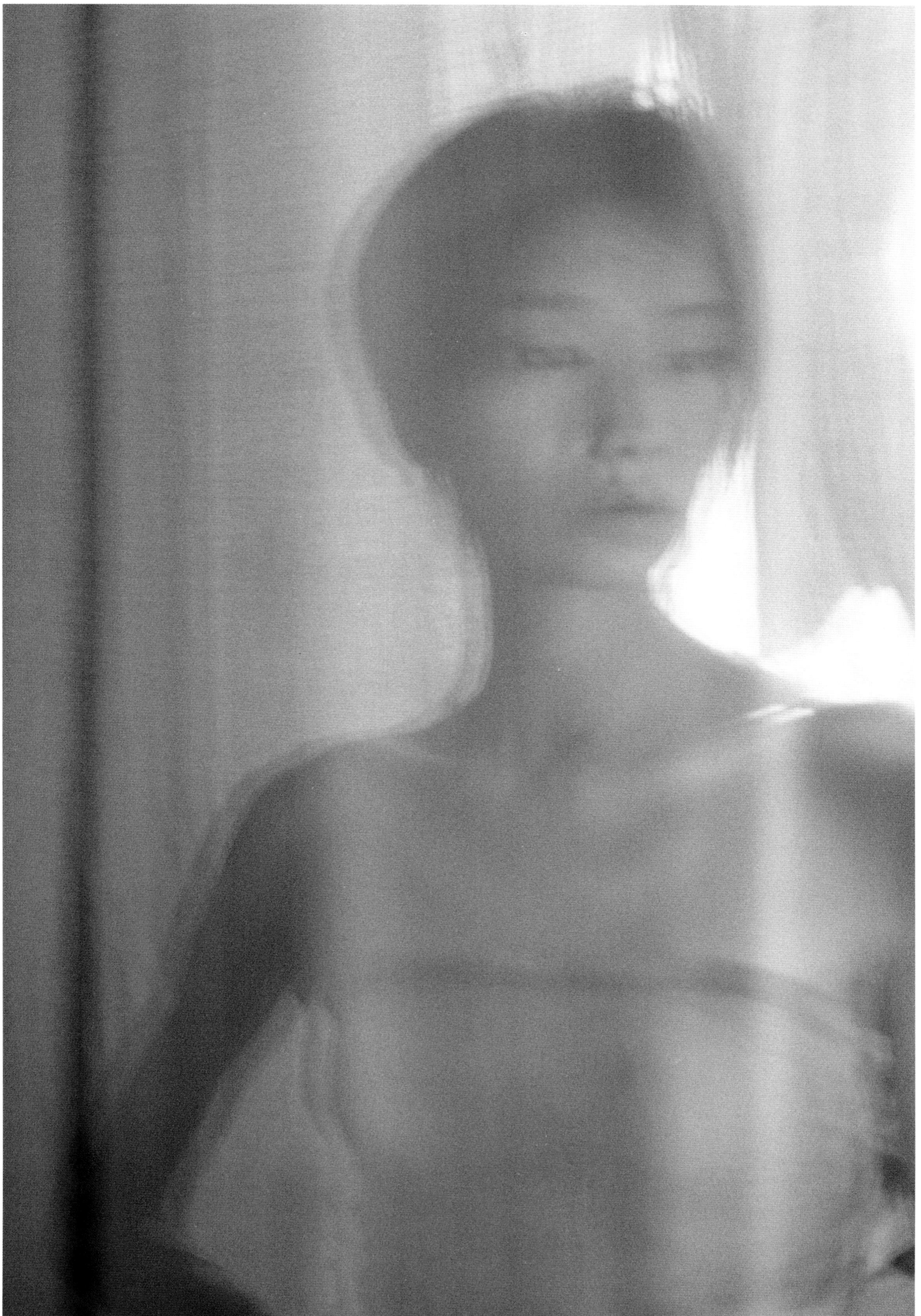

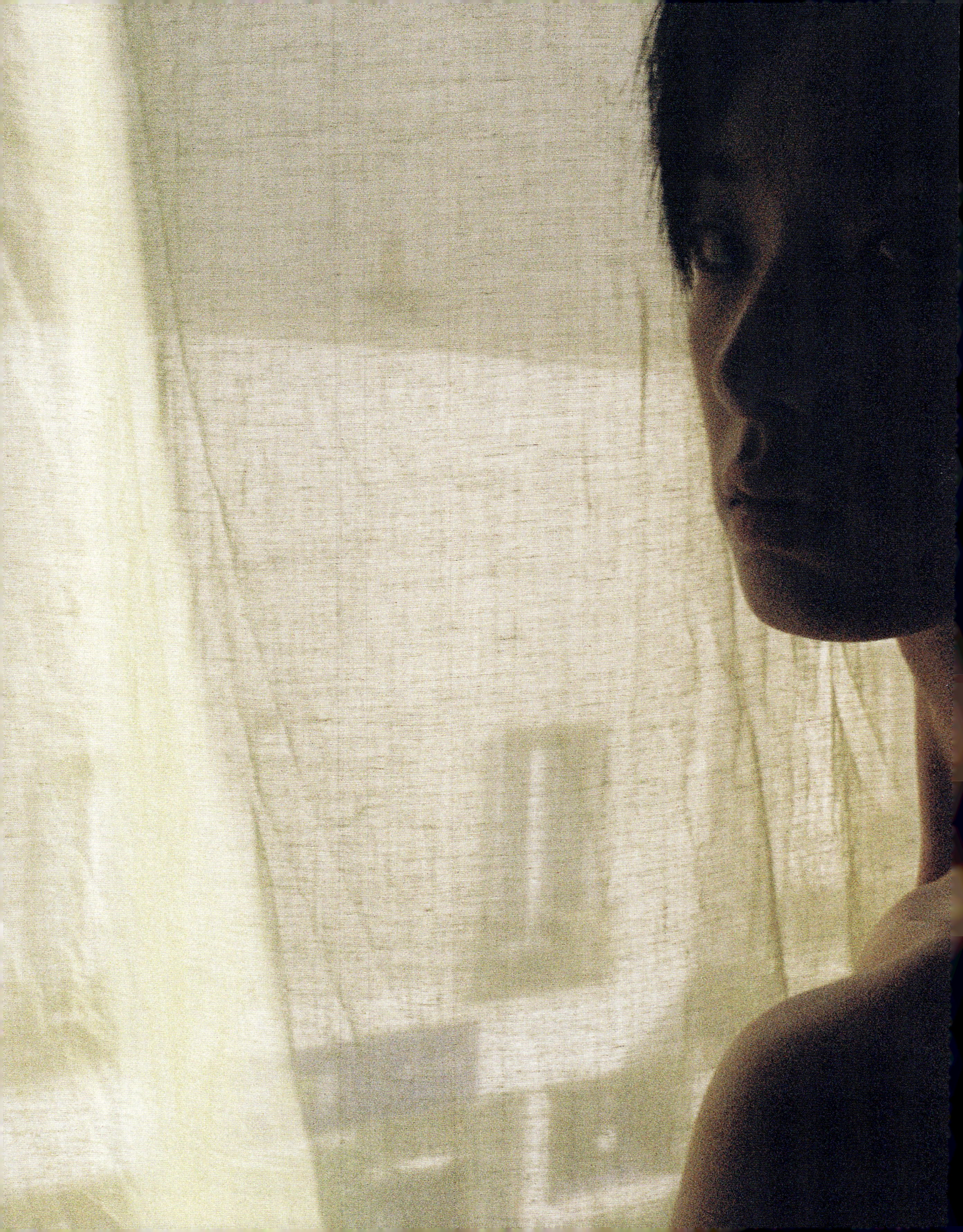

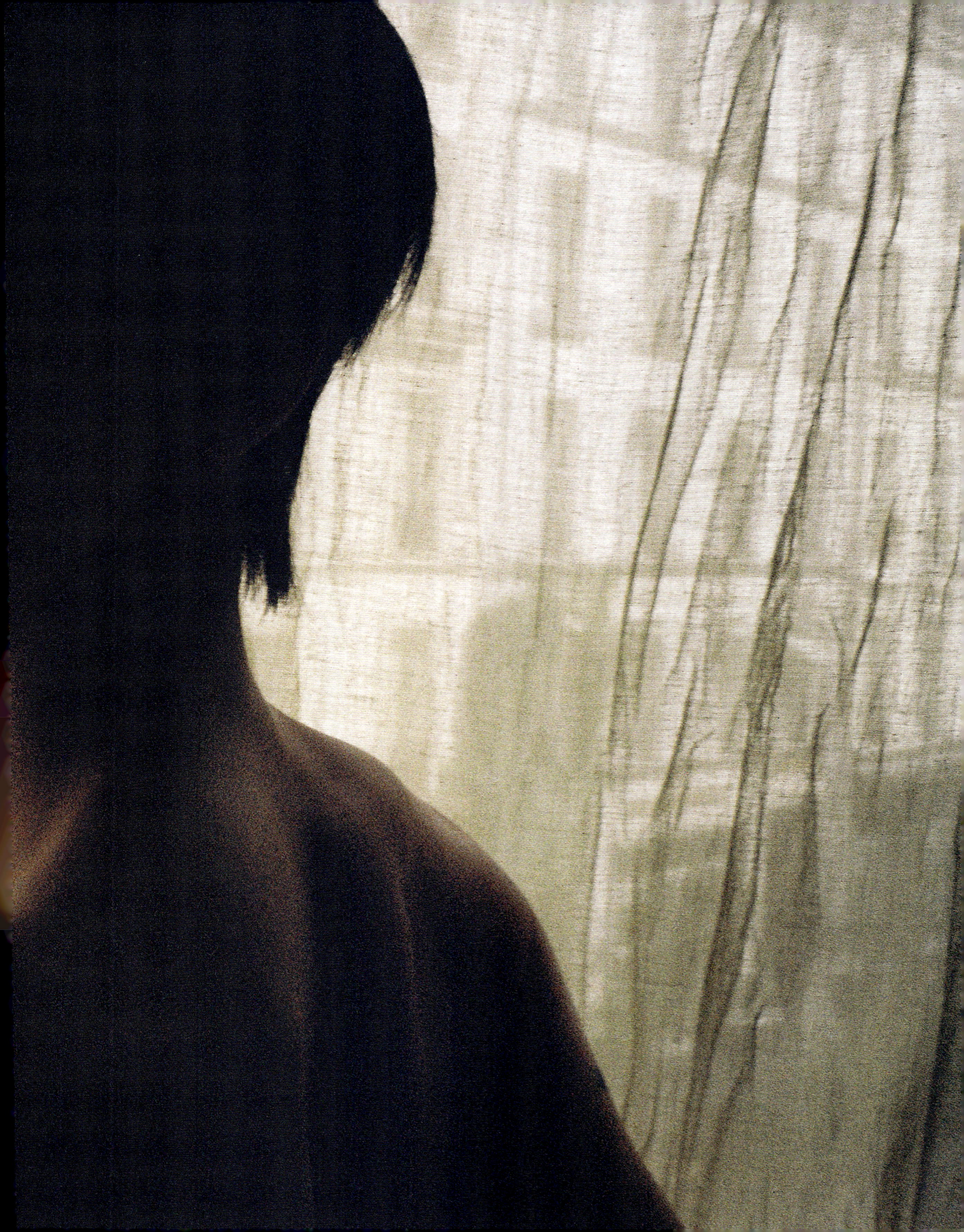

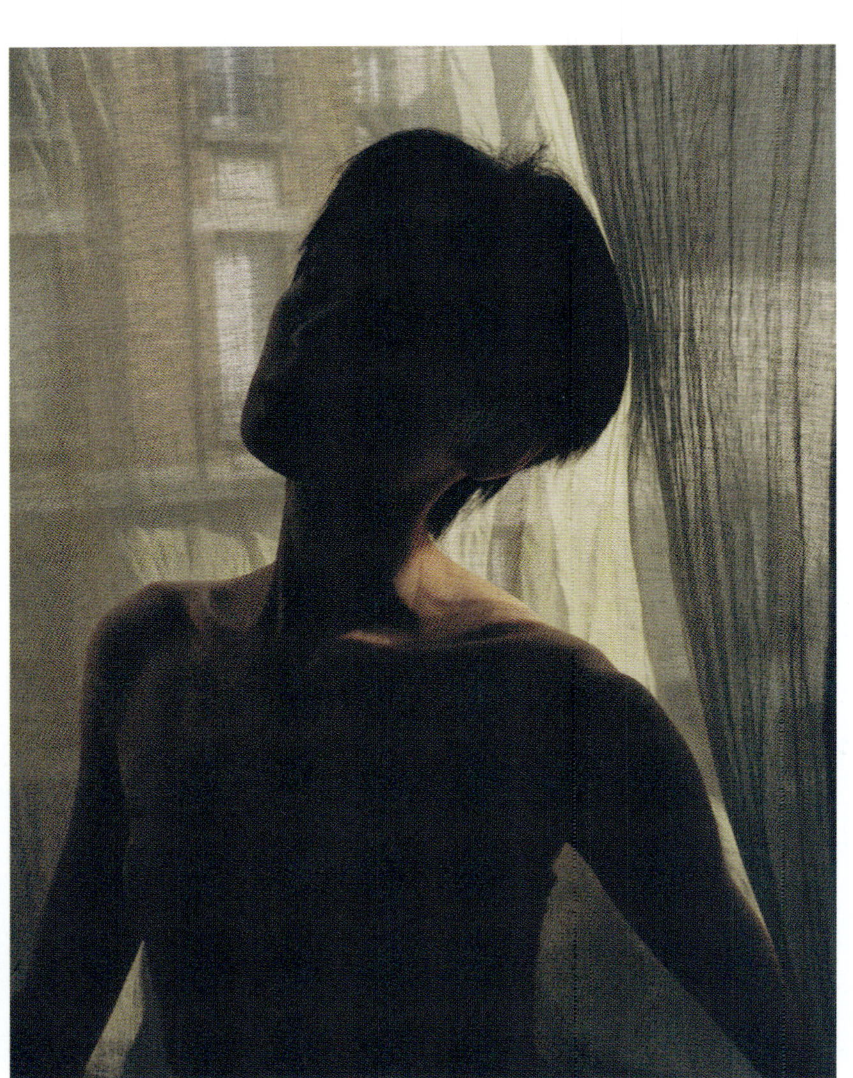

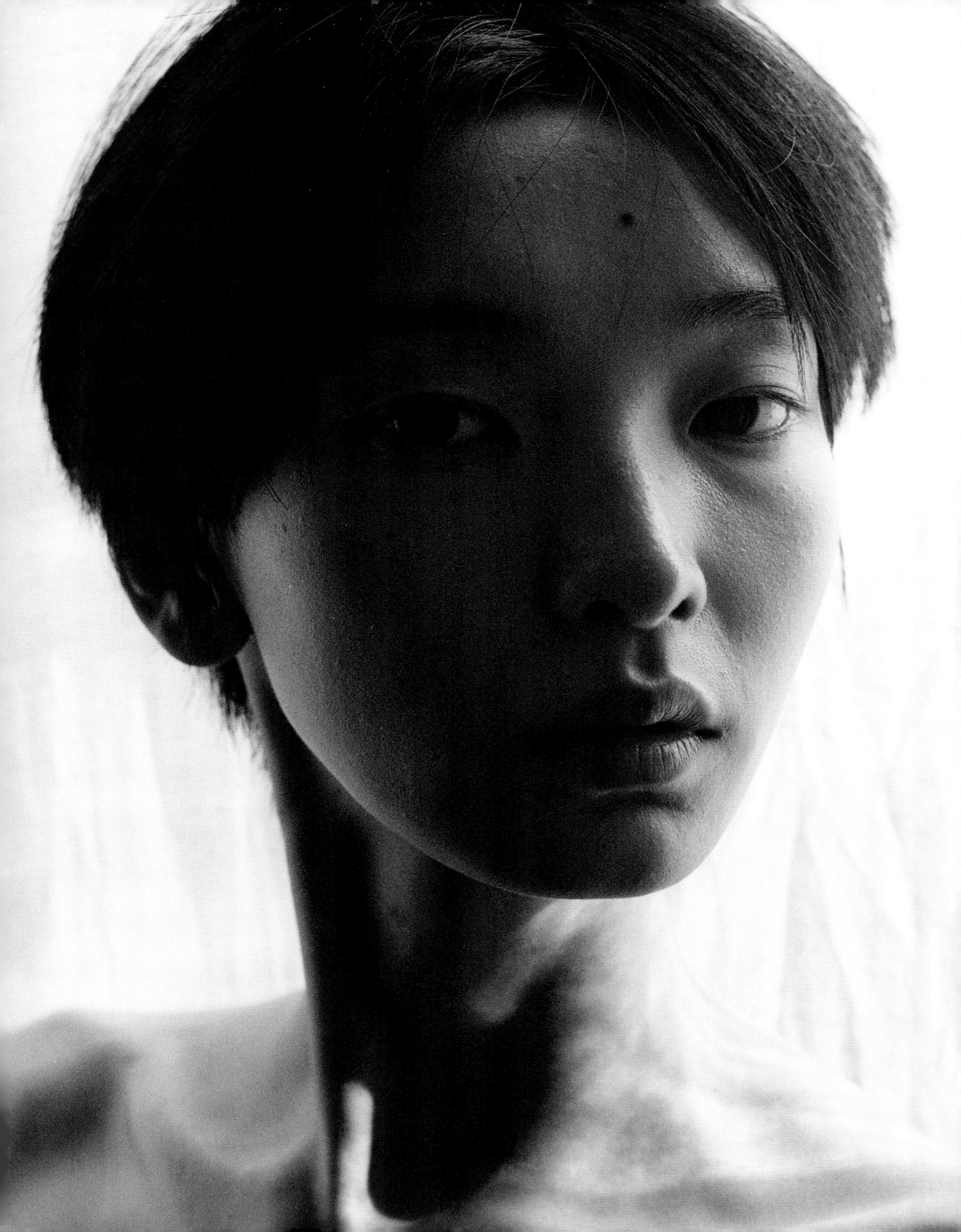

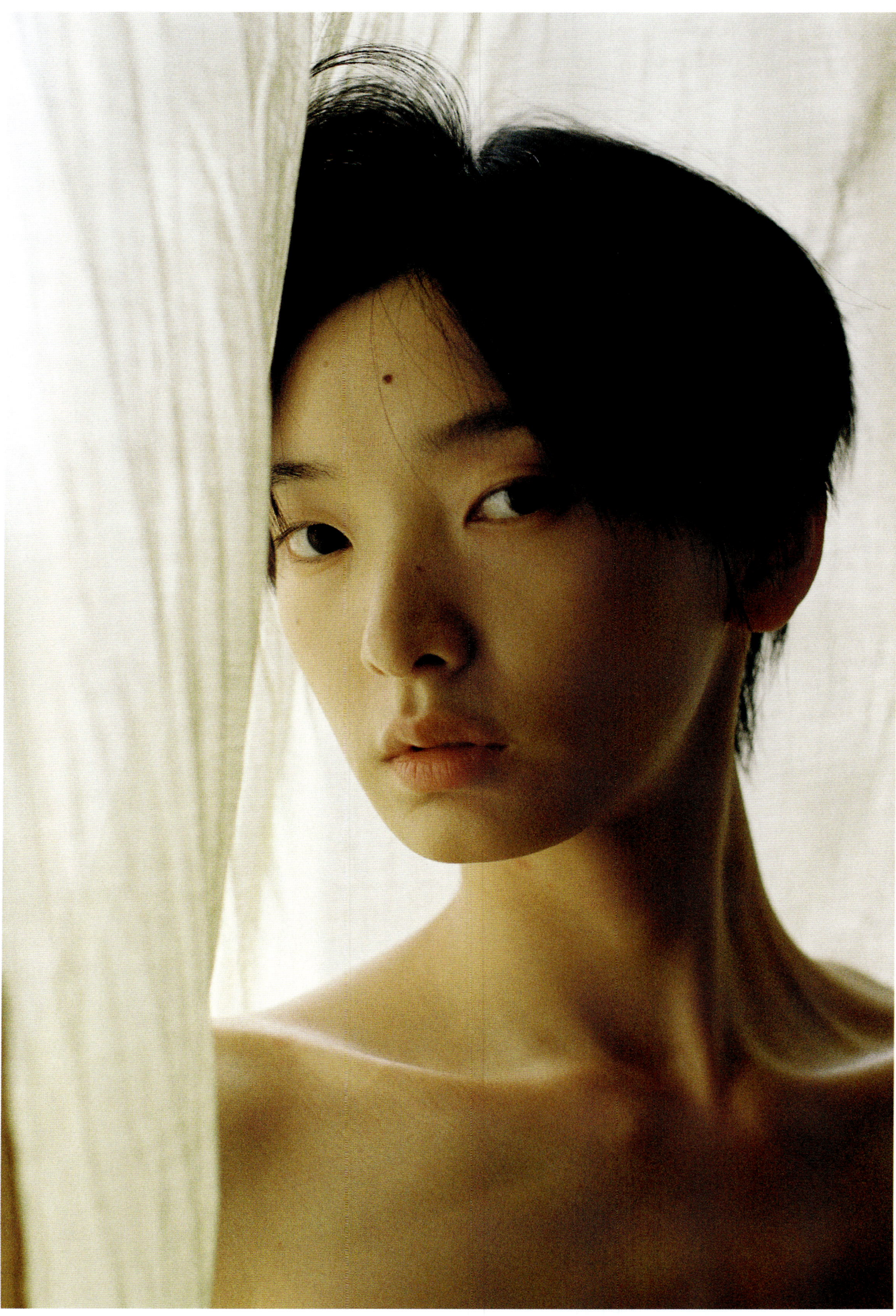

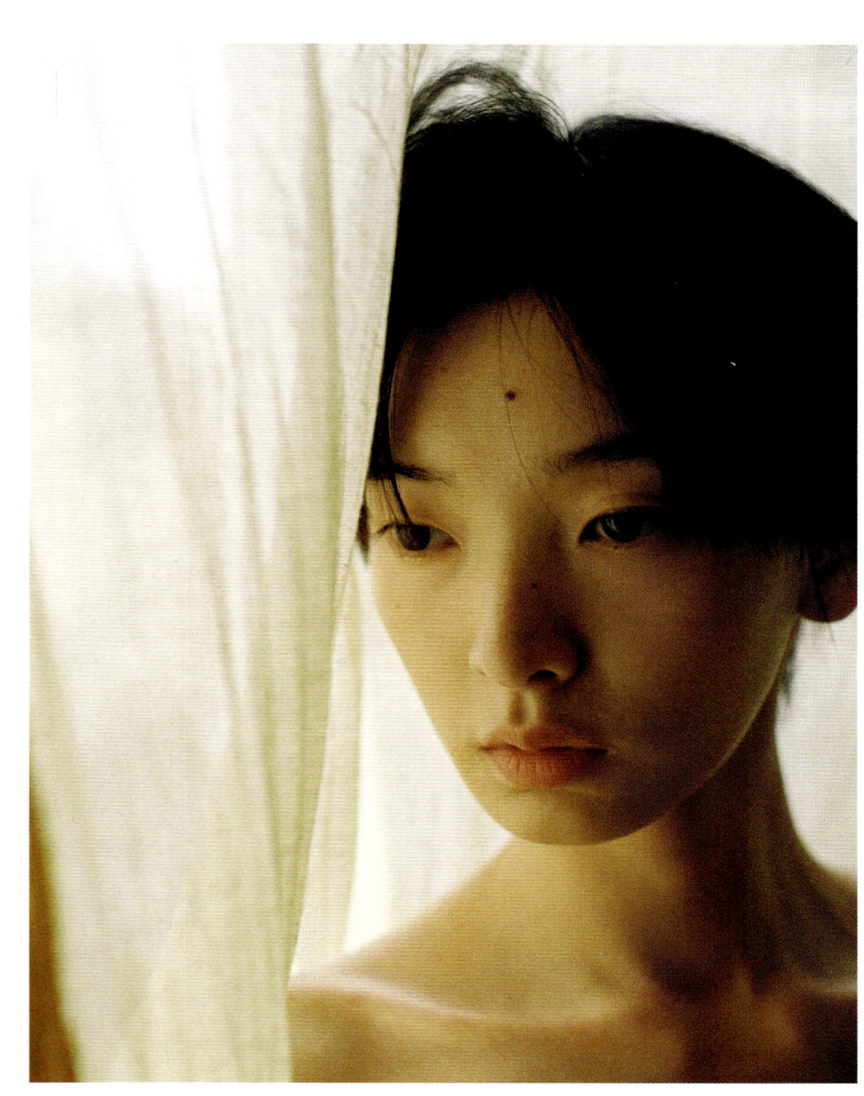

FLUIDUM

KATJA HEINEMANN

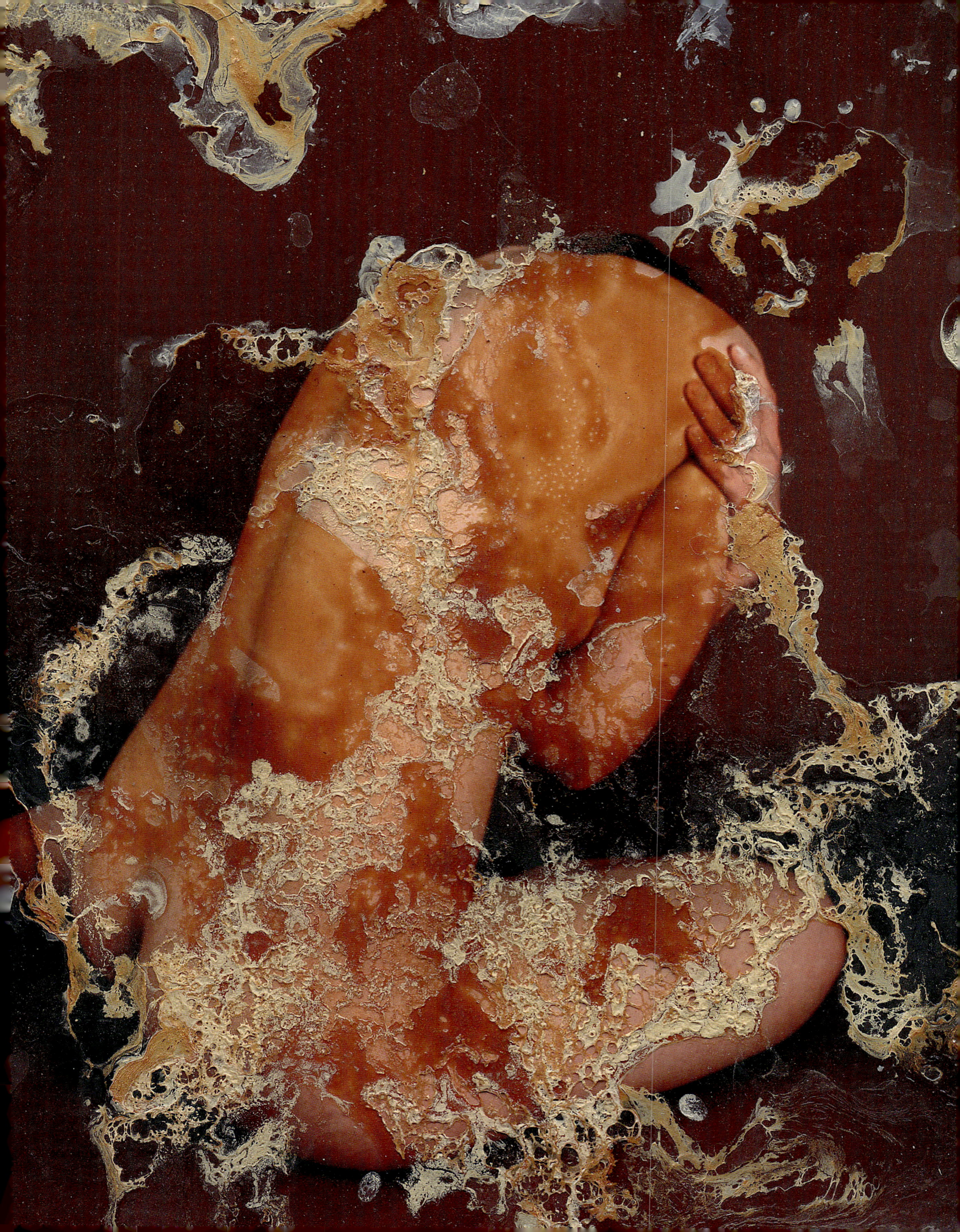

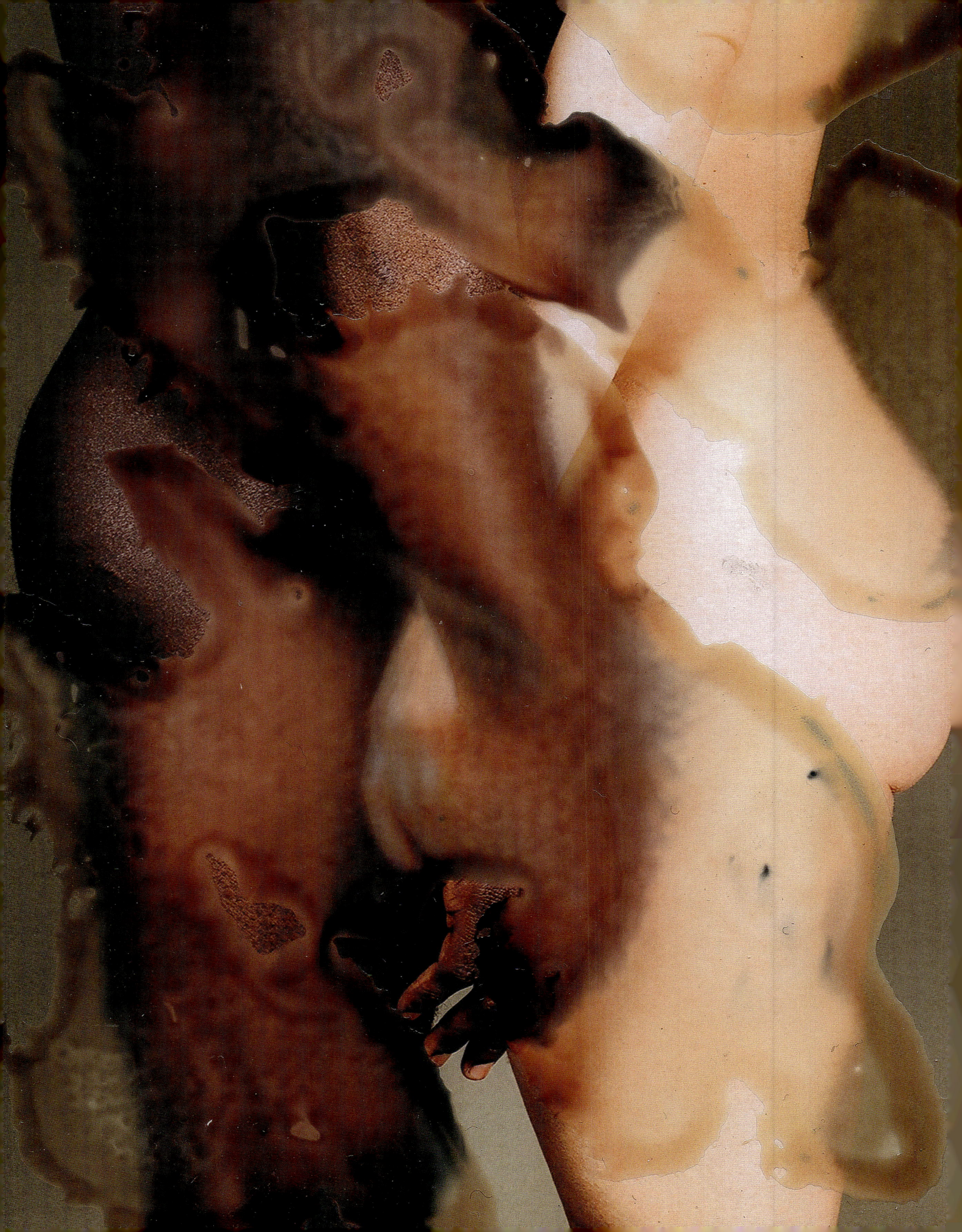

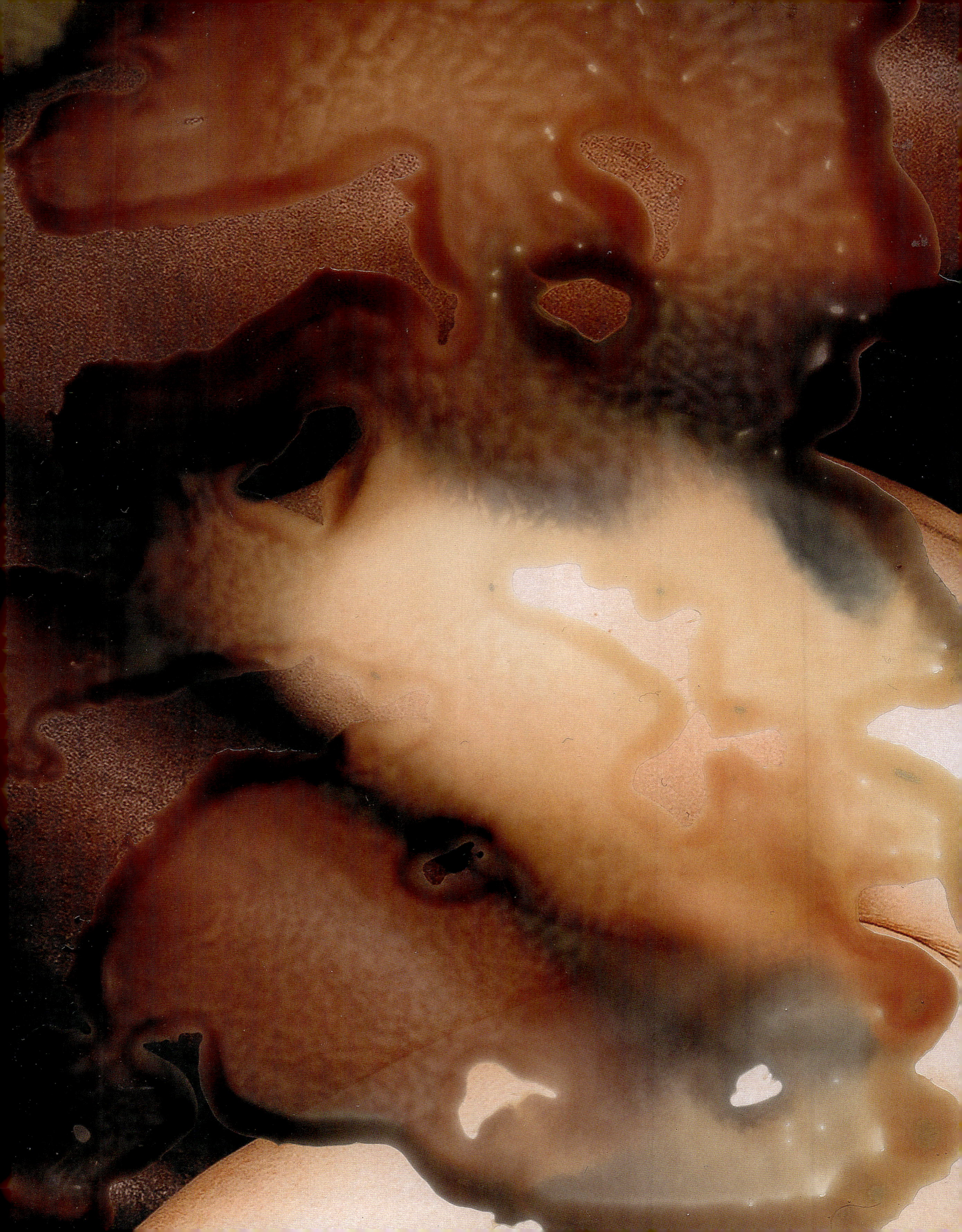

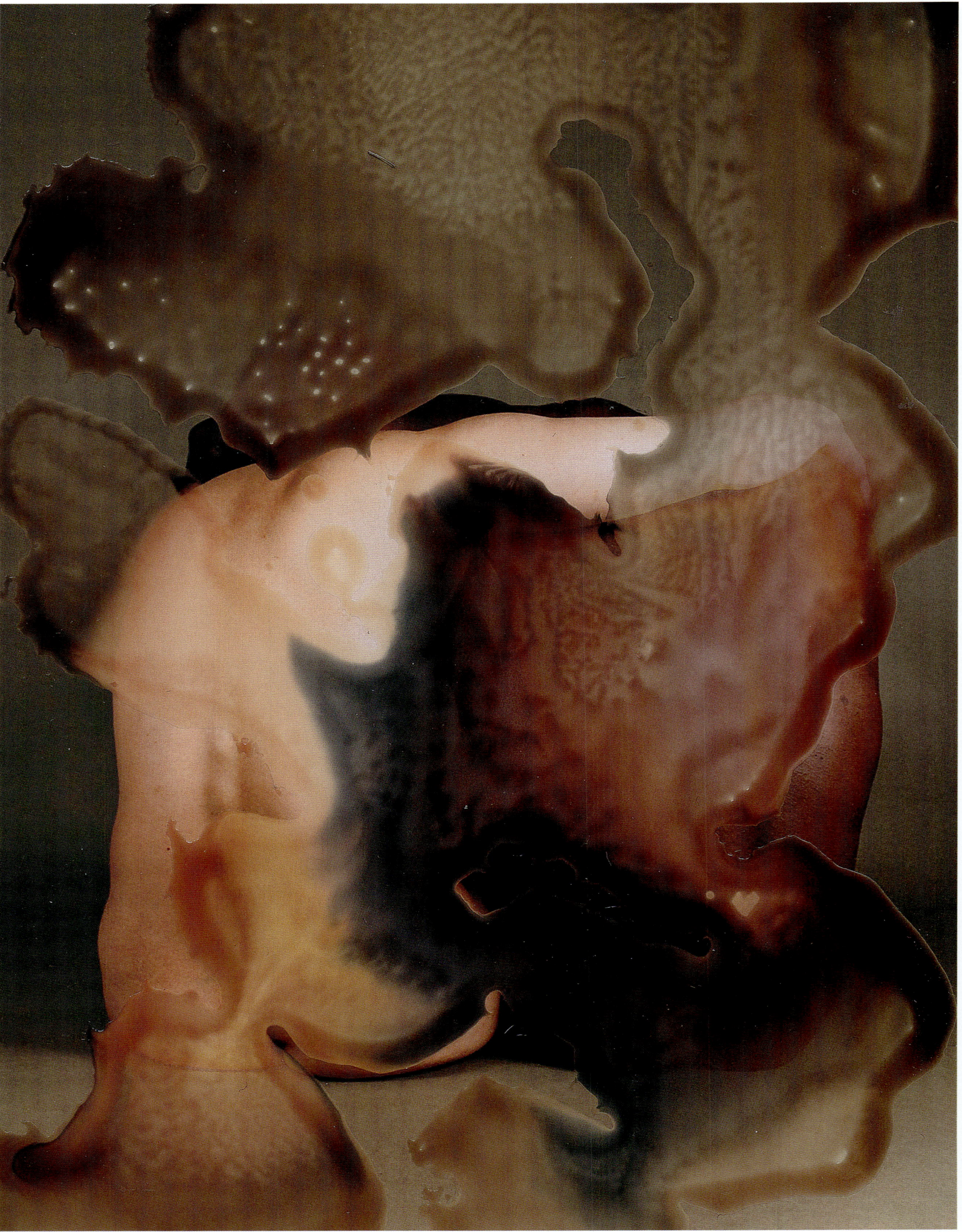

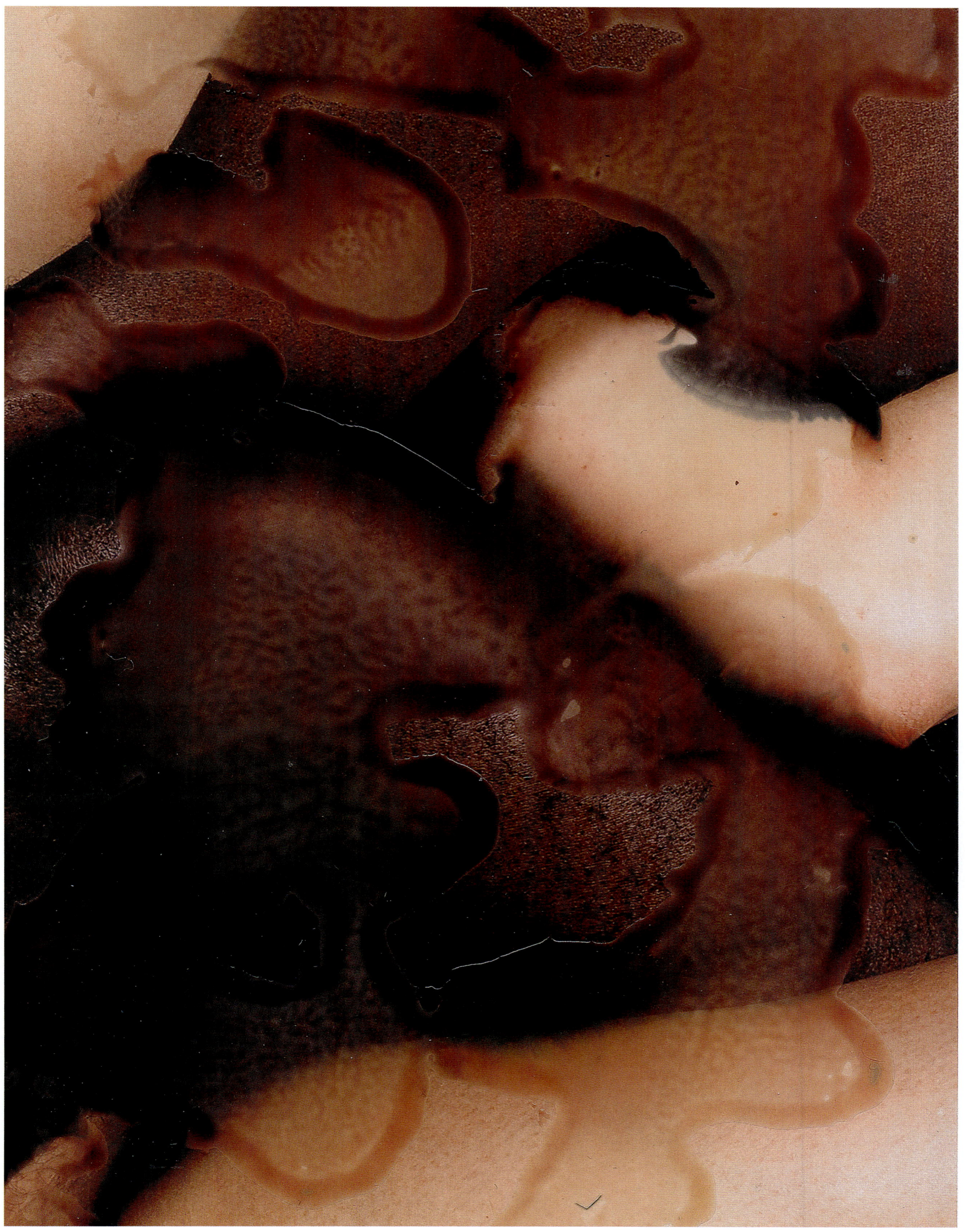

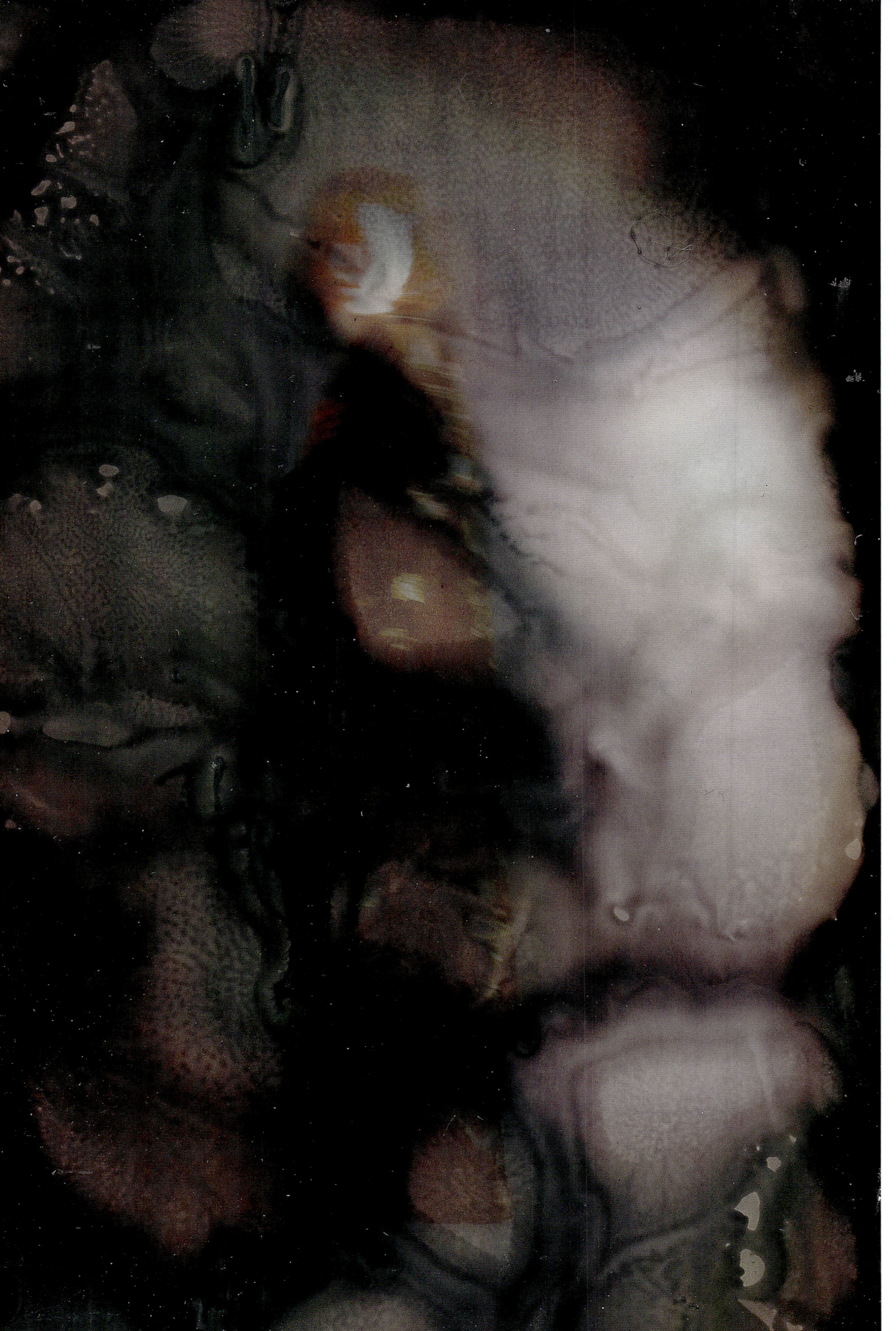

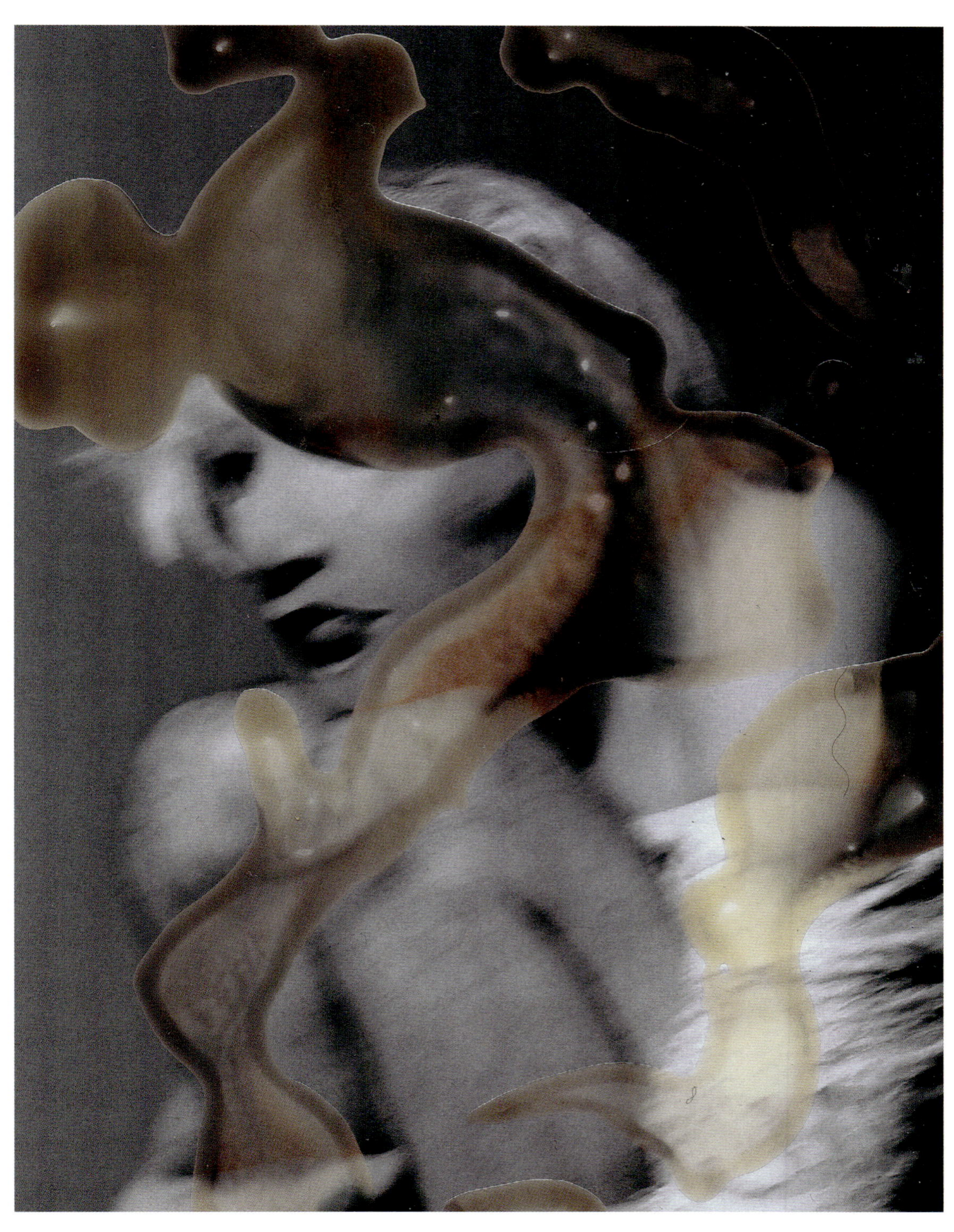

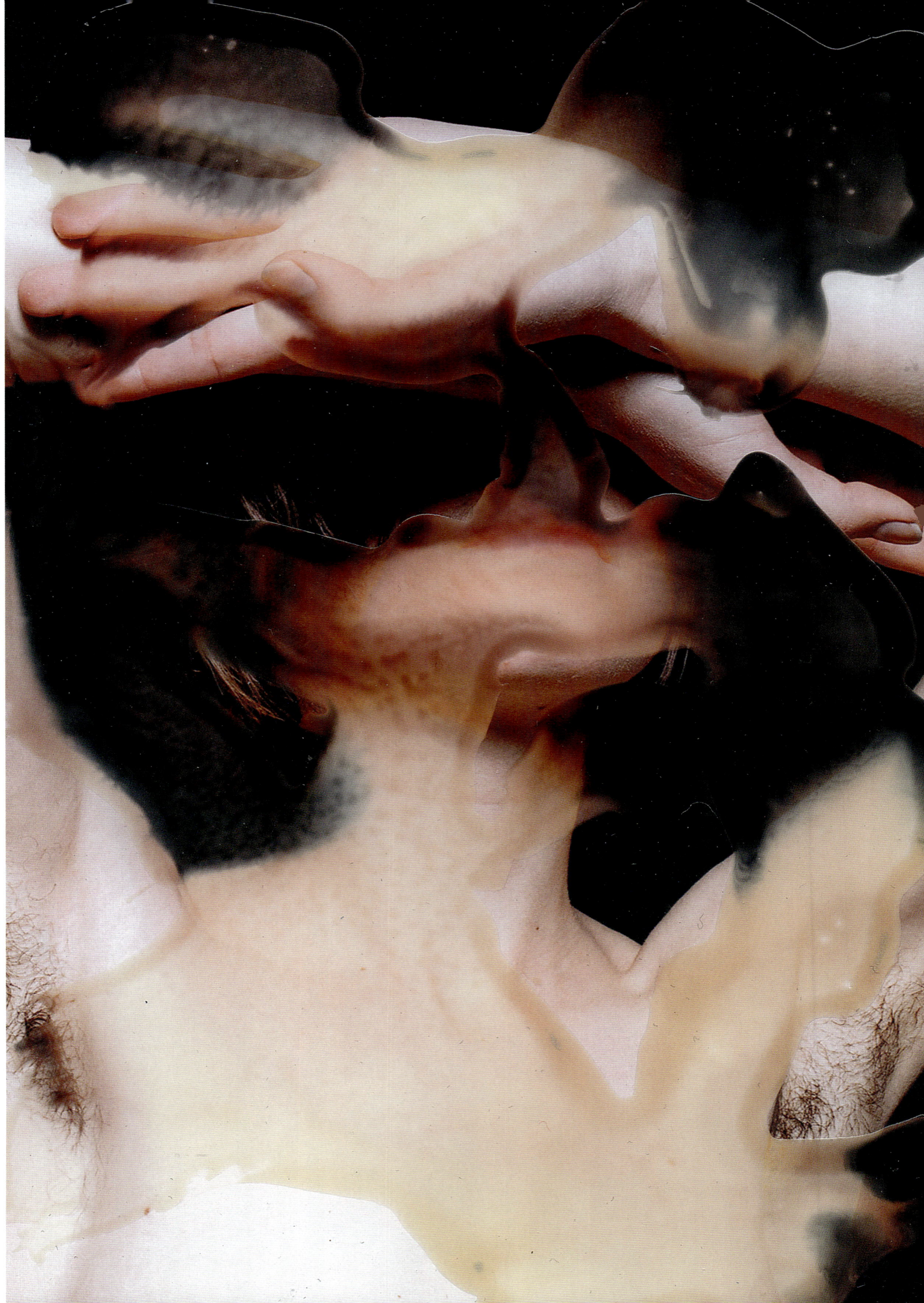

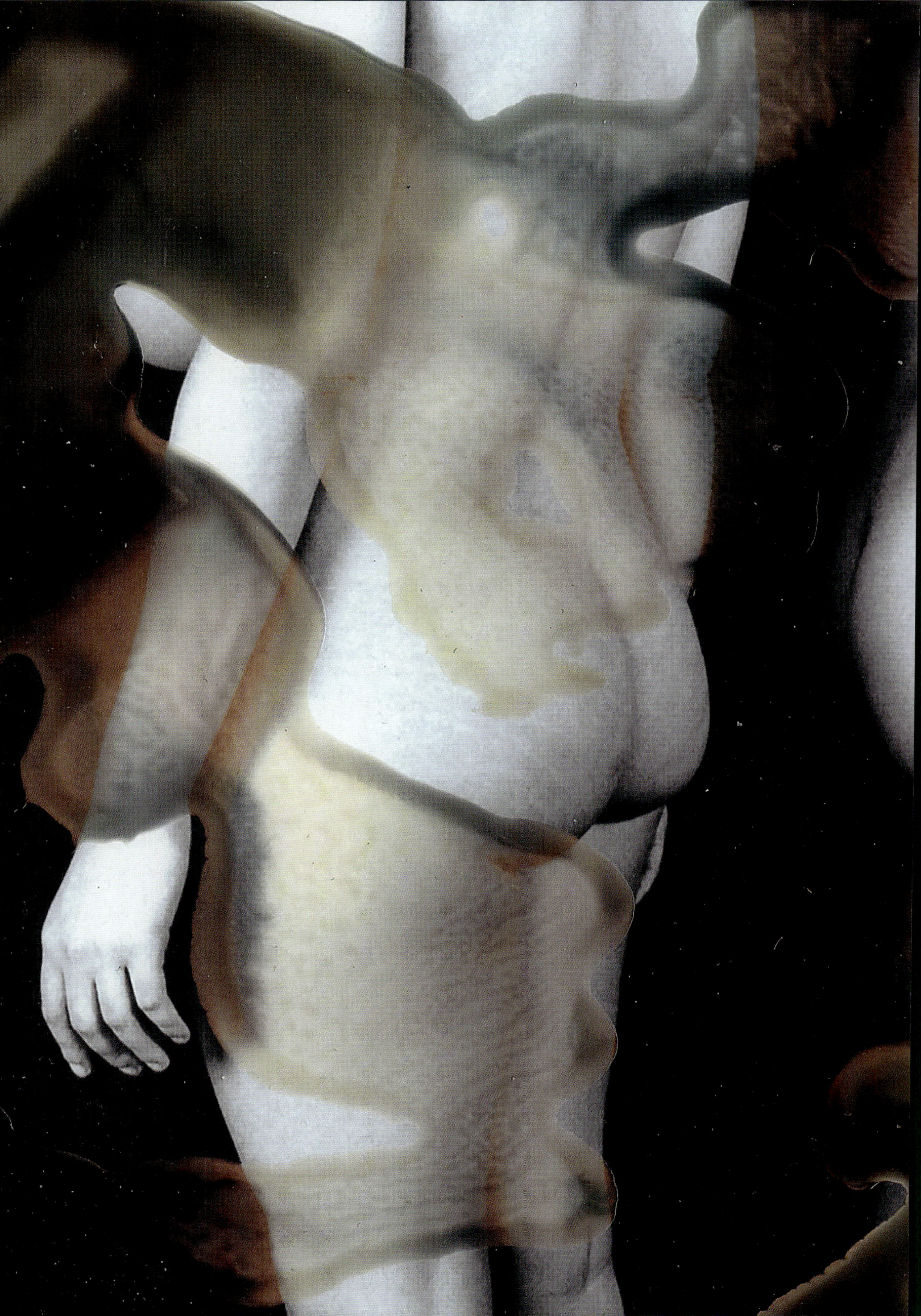

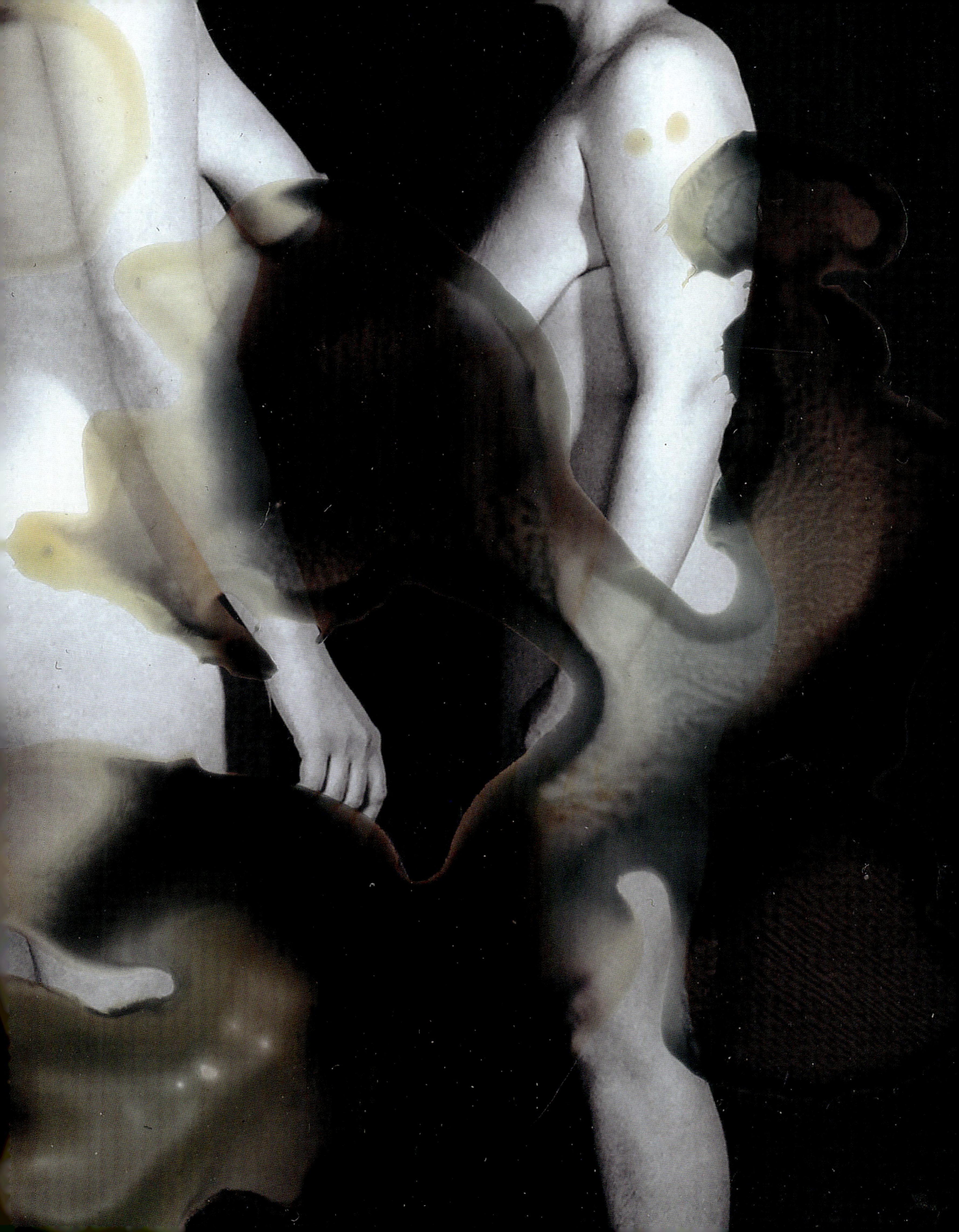

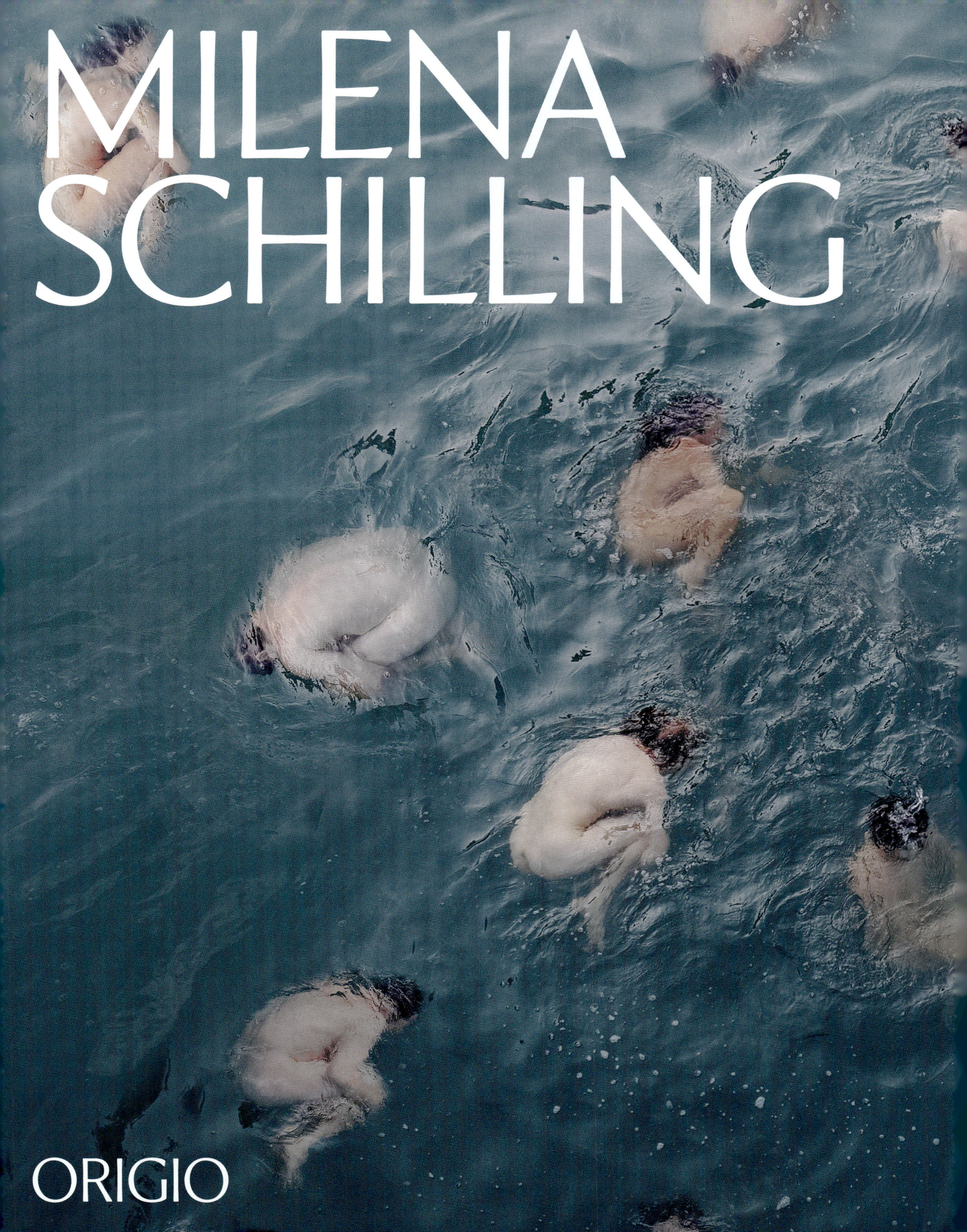

MILENA
SCHILLING
ORIGIO

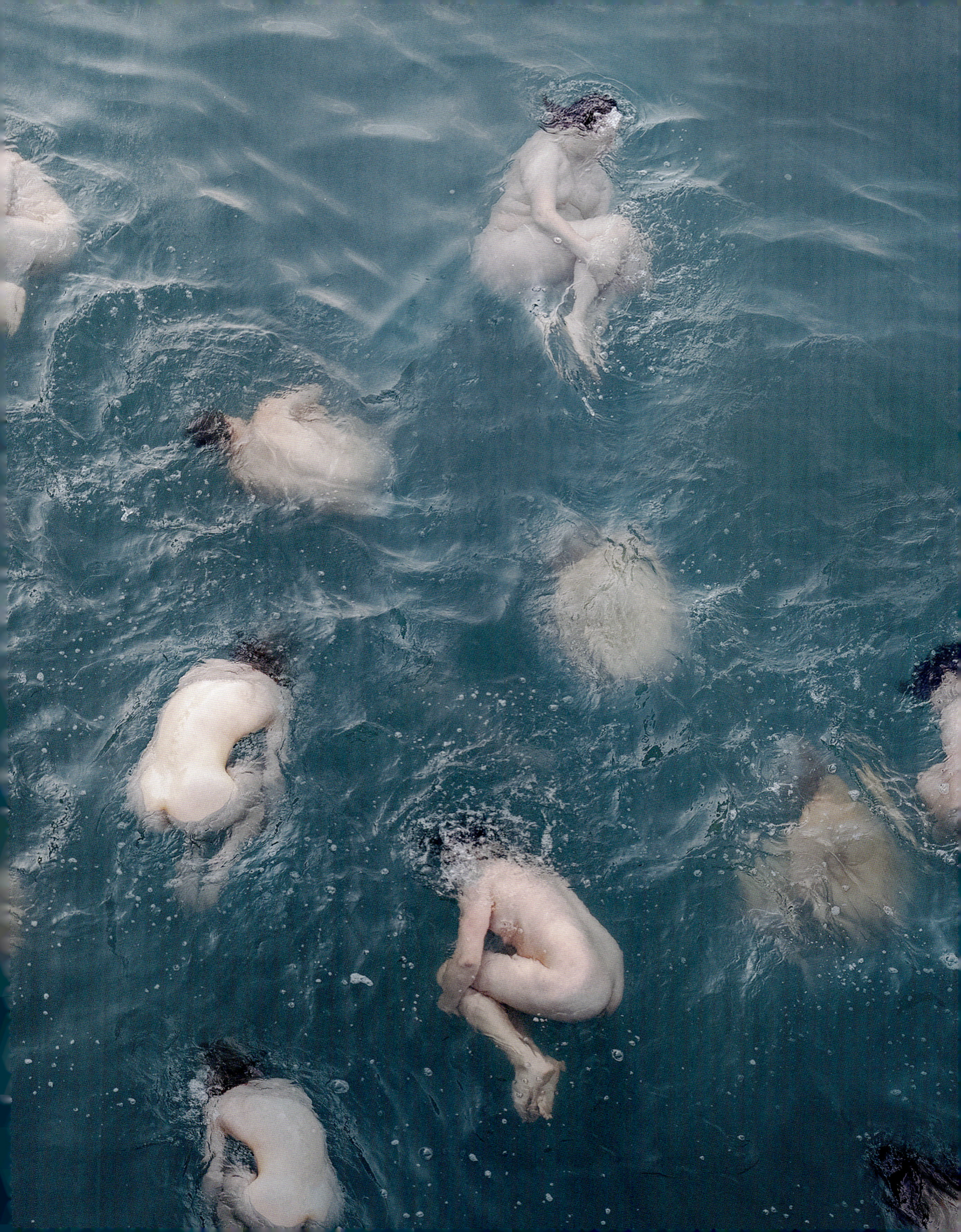

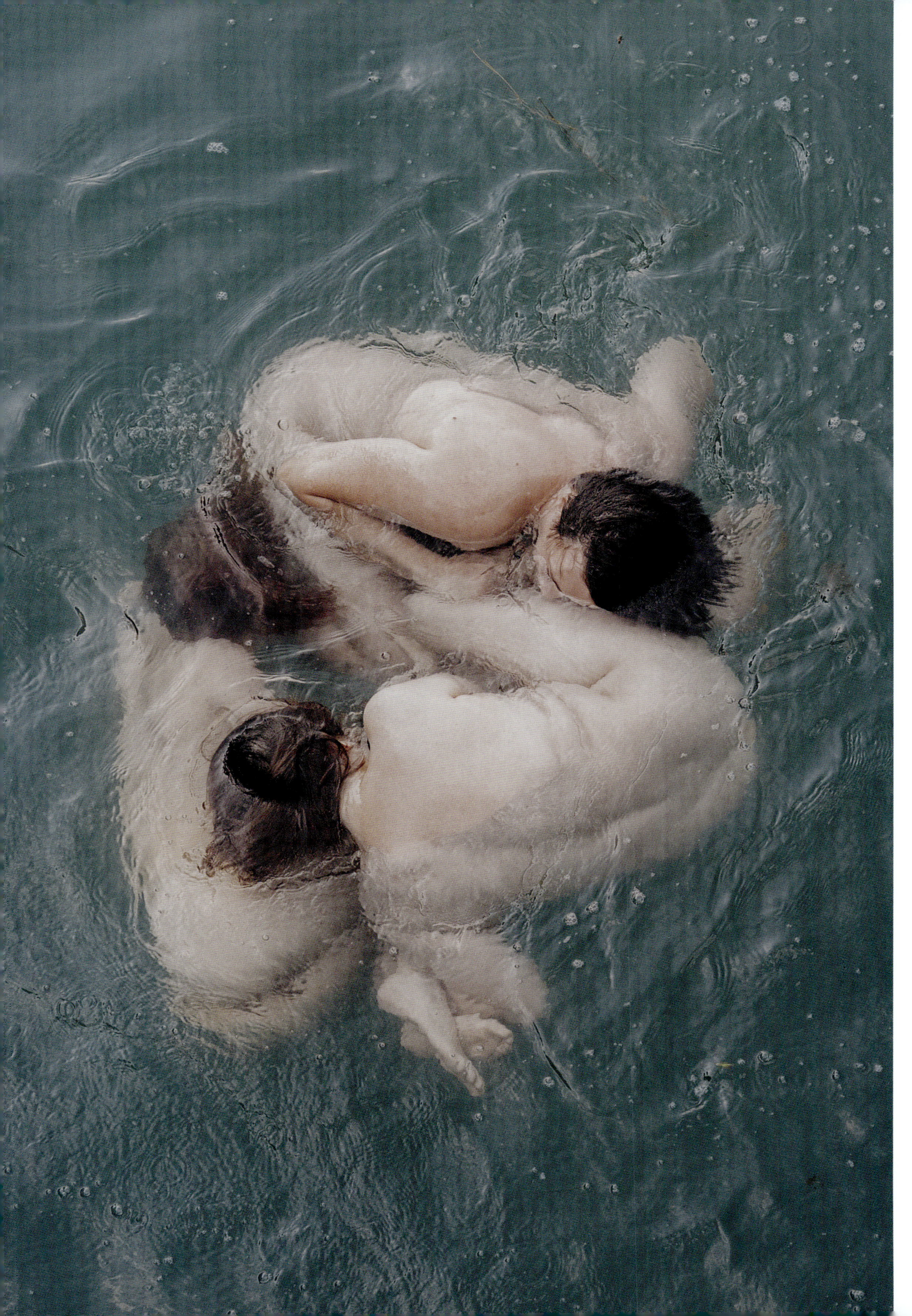

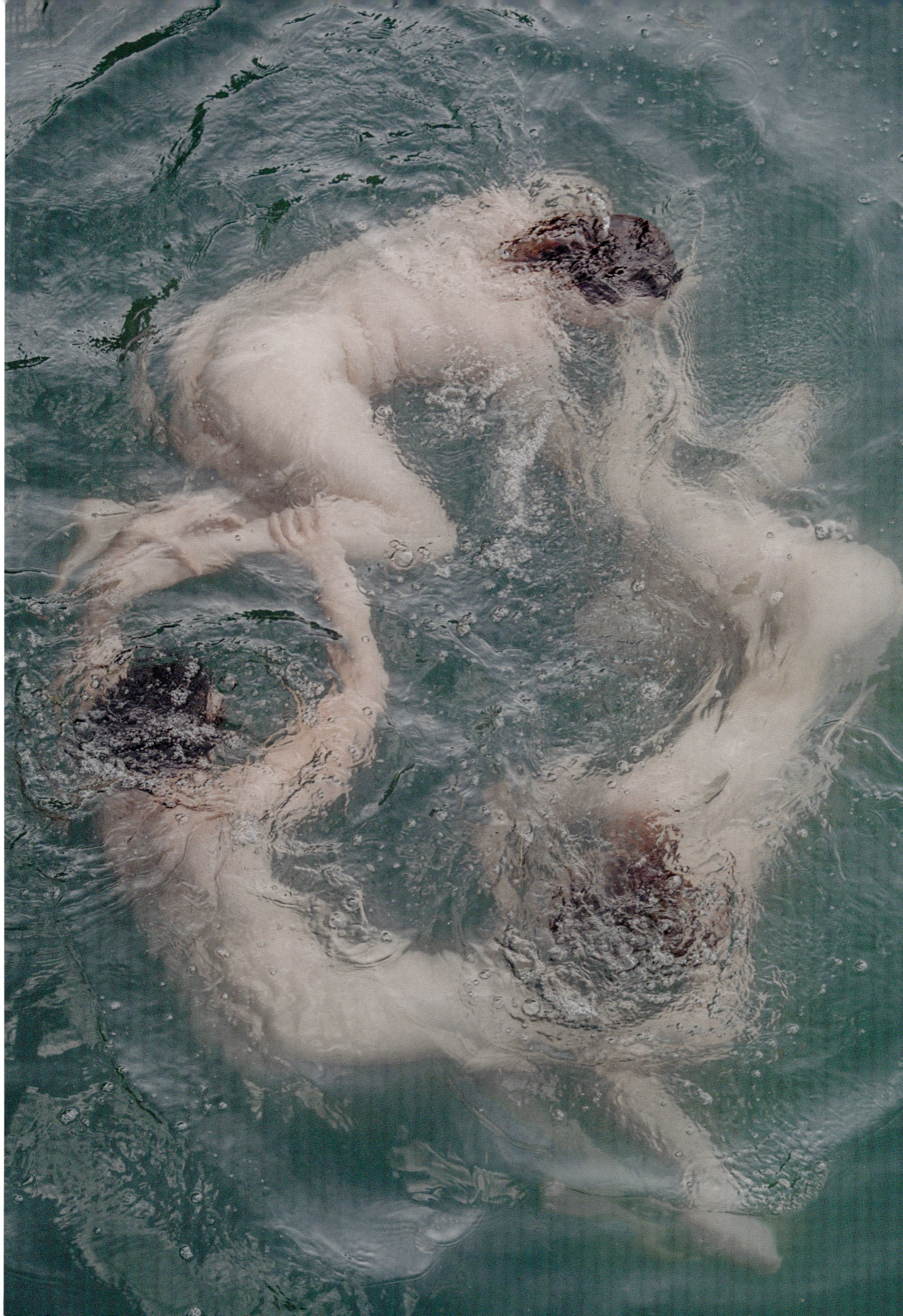

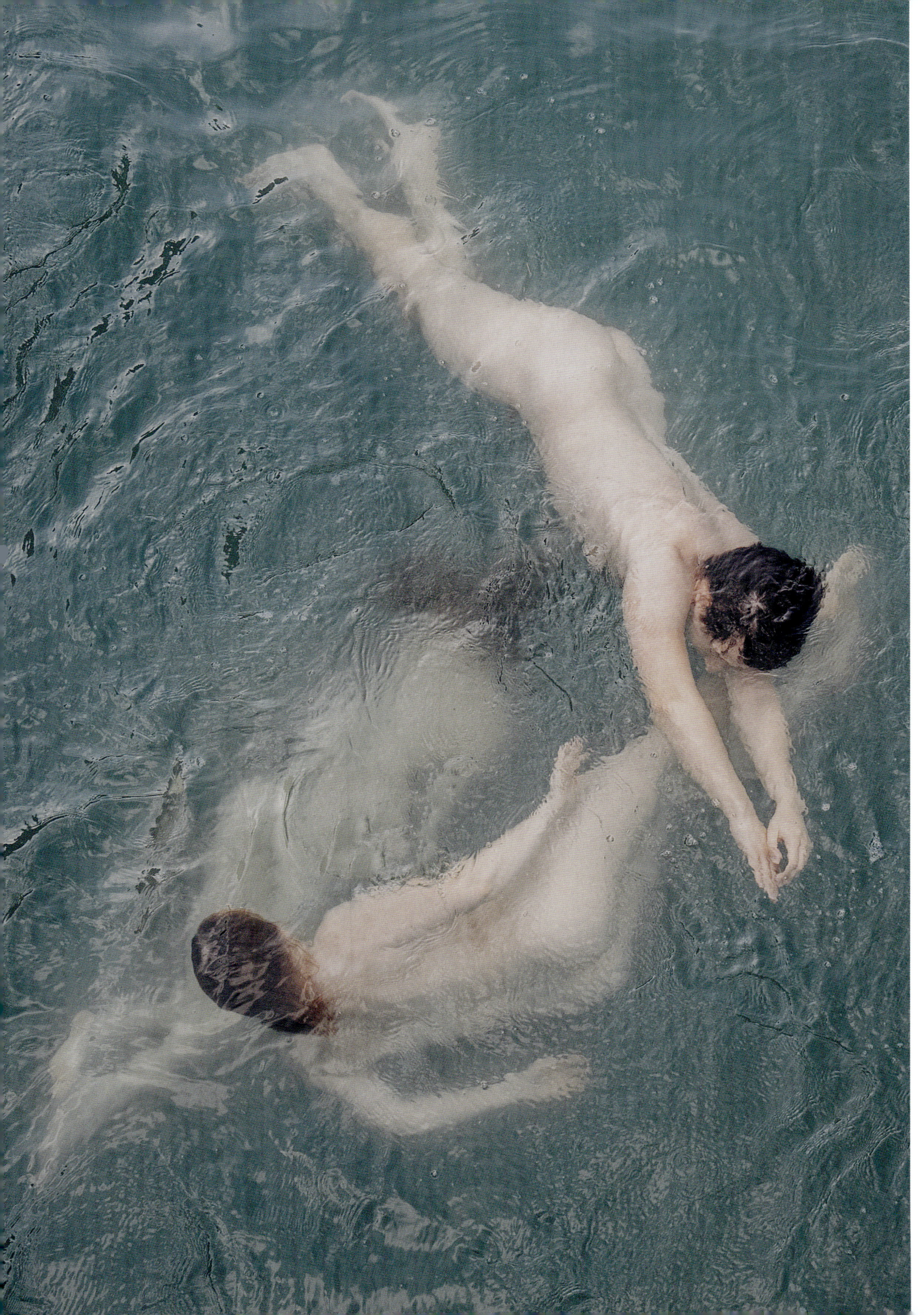

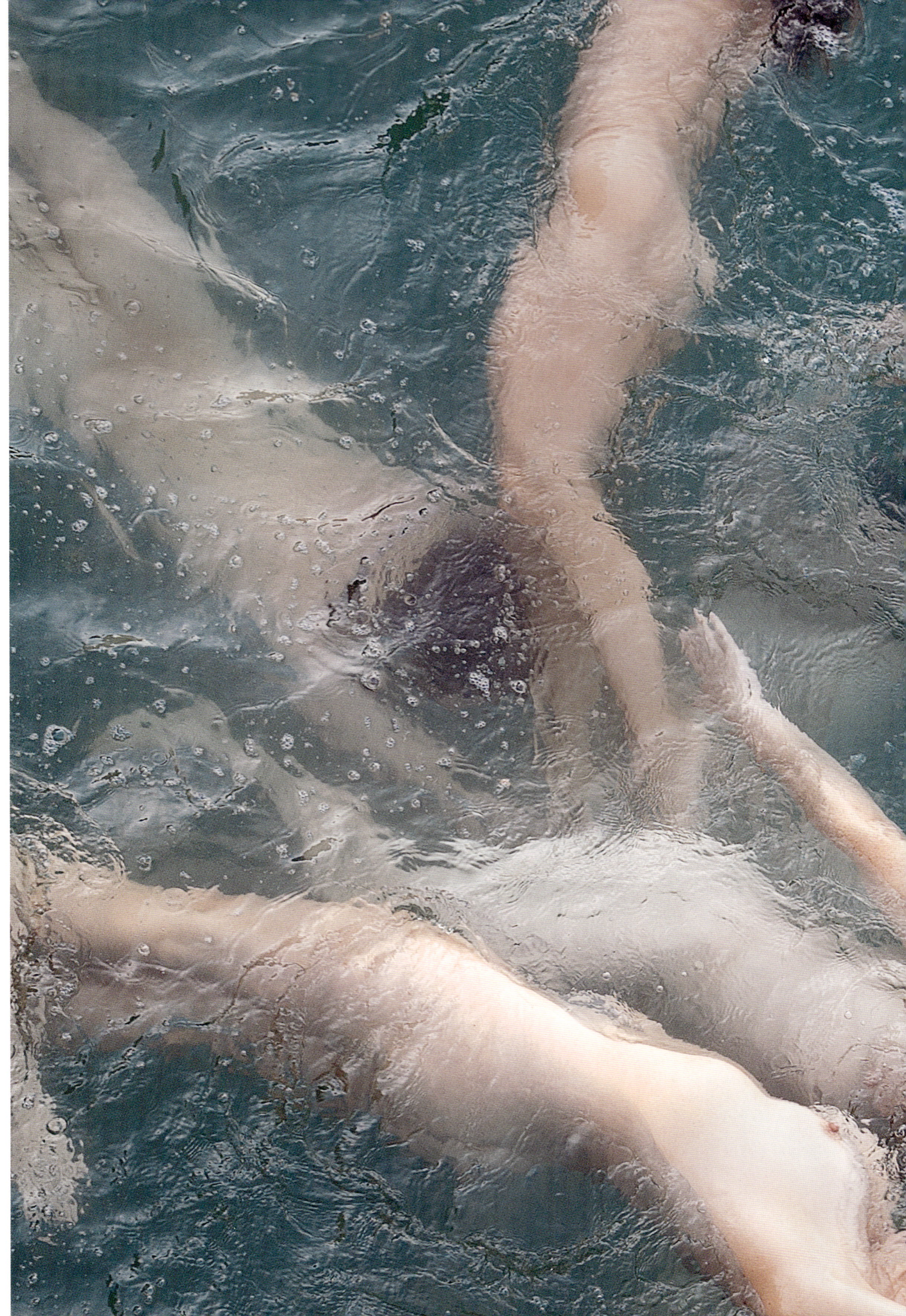

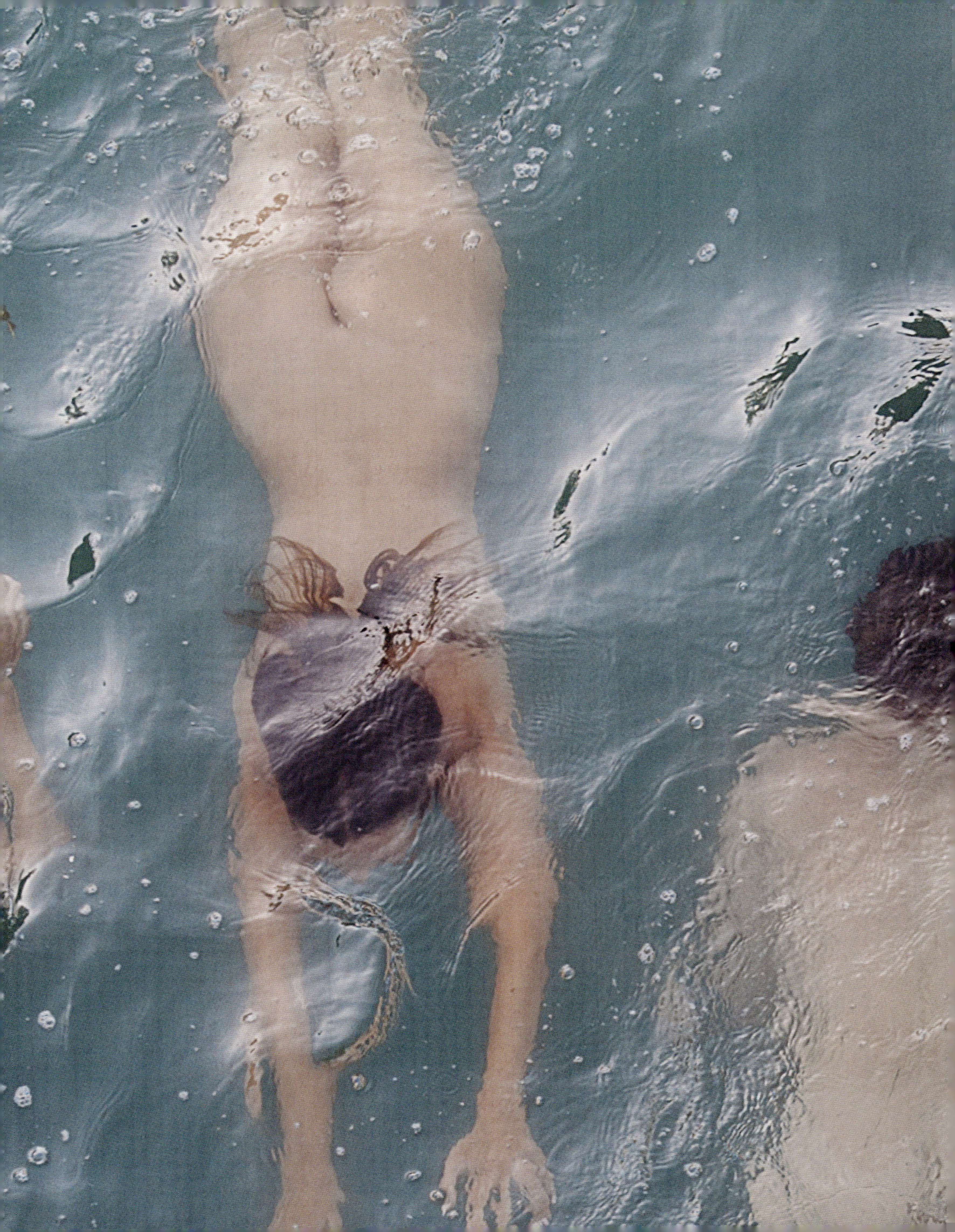

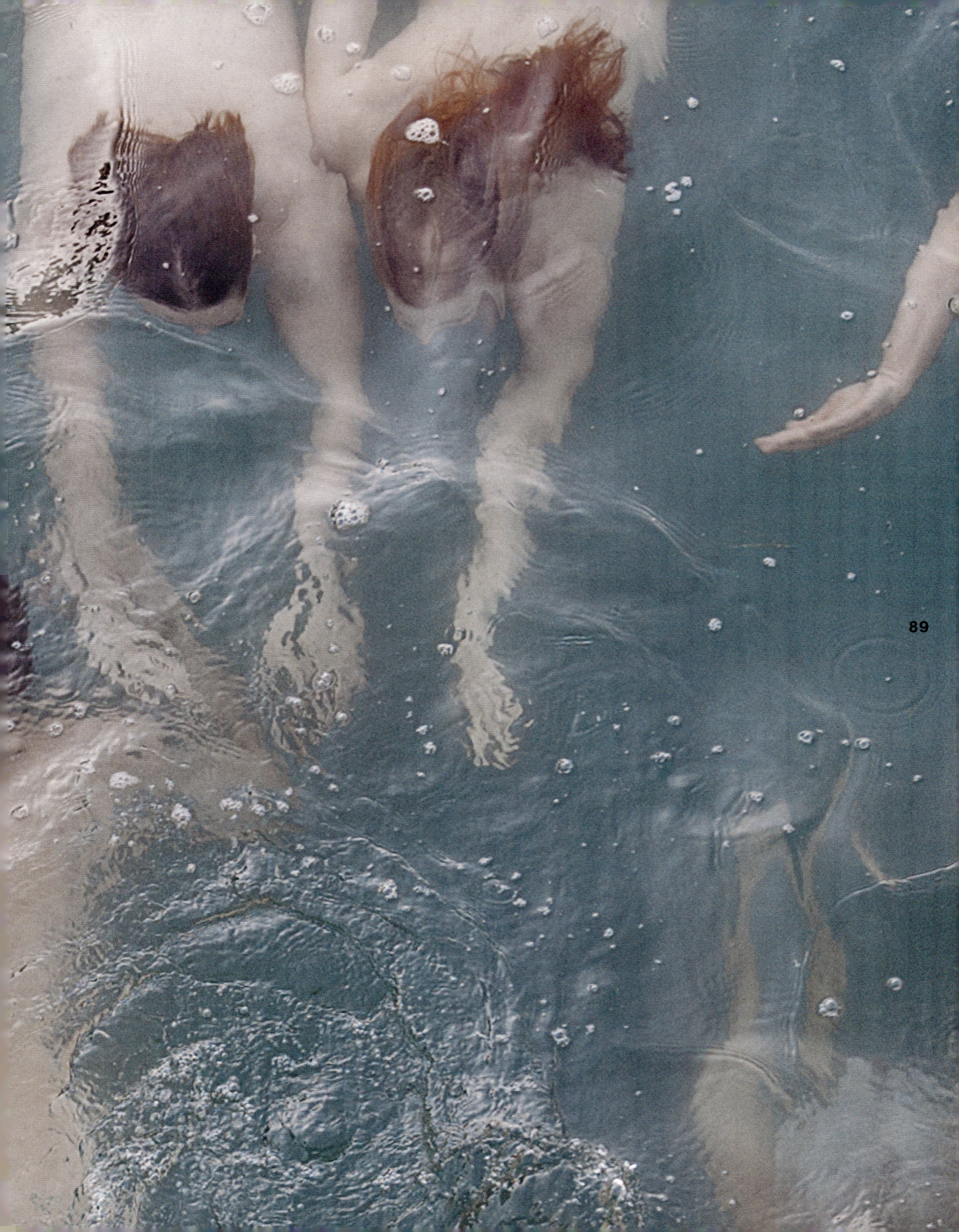

III.
PHYSIS

THE MANIFESTATION OF MATTER BASED ON PHYSICAL LAWS AND EVOLUTION. VISIBLE AND HAPTIC OBJECTS, BEINGS, INTERACTIONS AND LIFE FORMS IN A NATURAL ORDER.

AYLINE
OLUKMAN

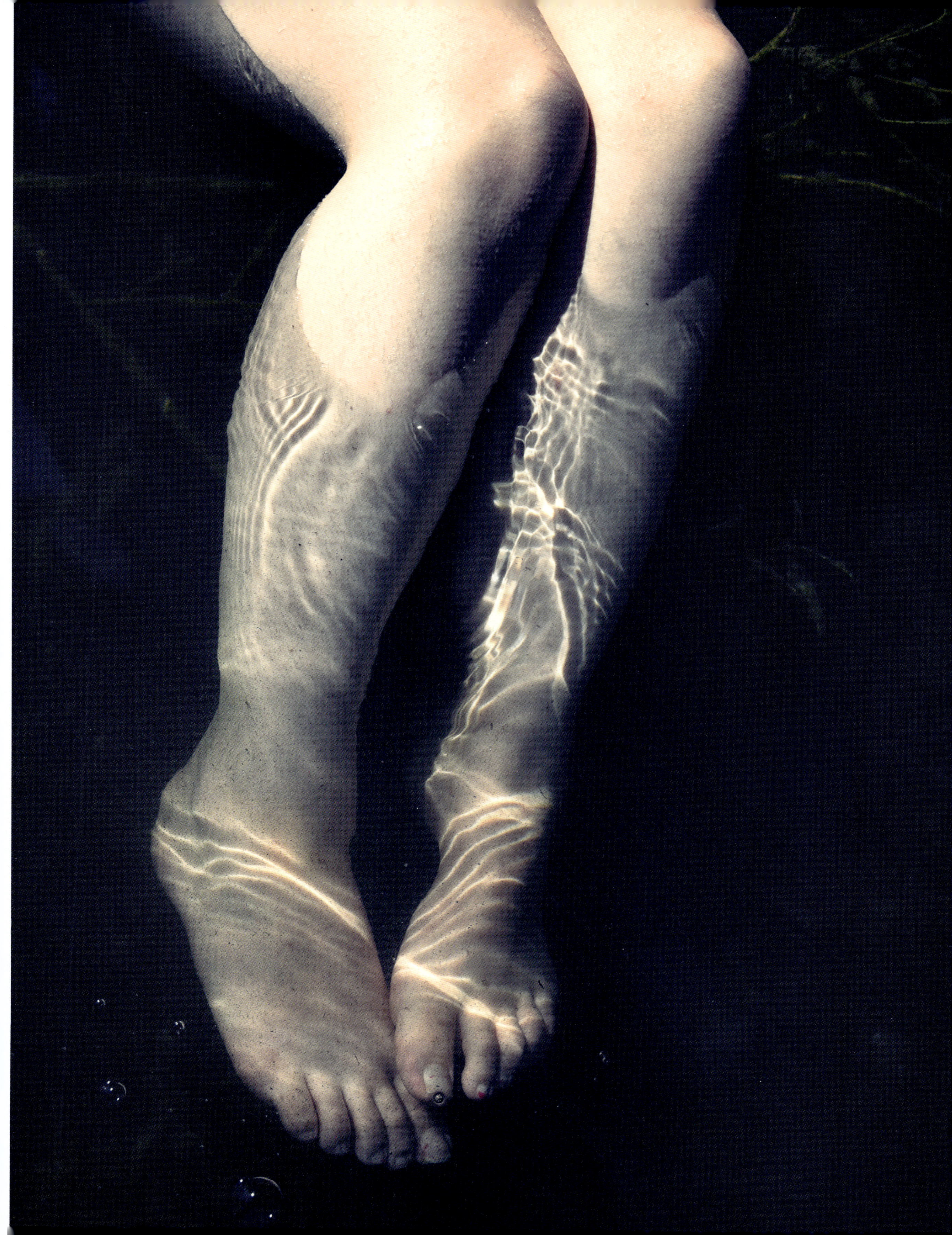

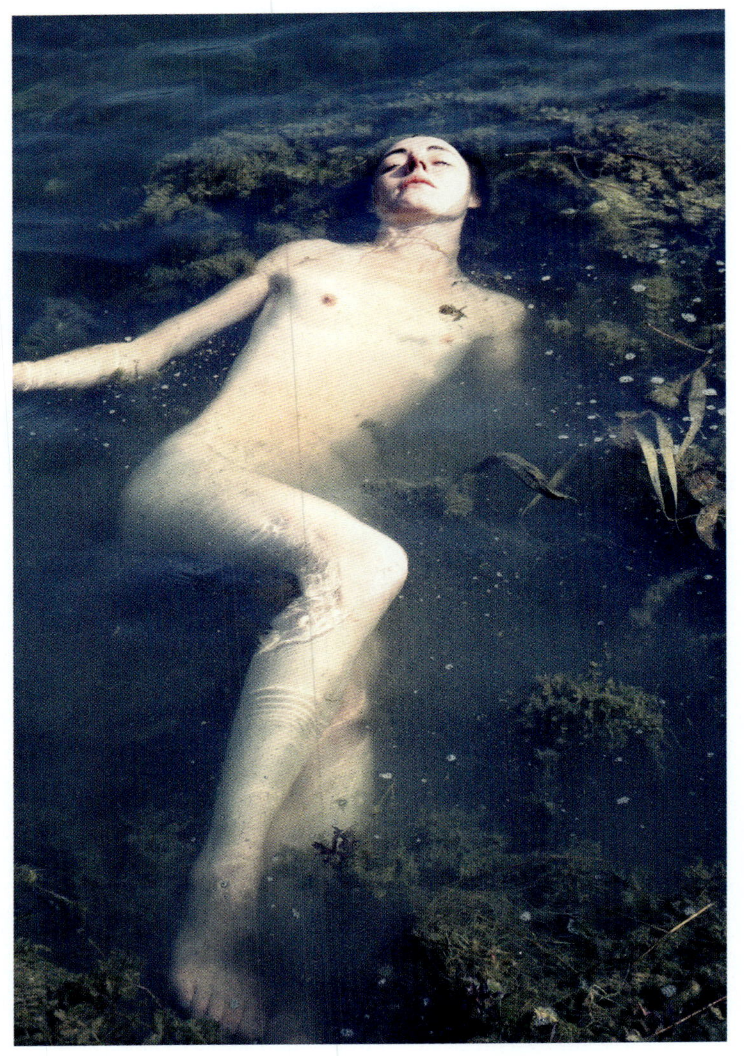

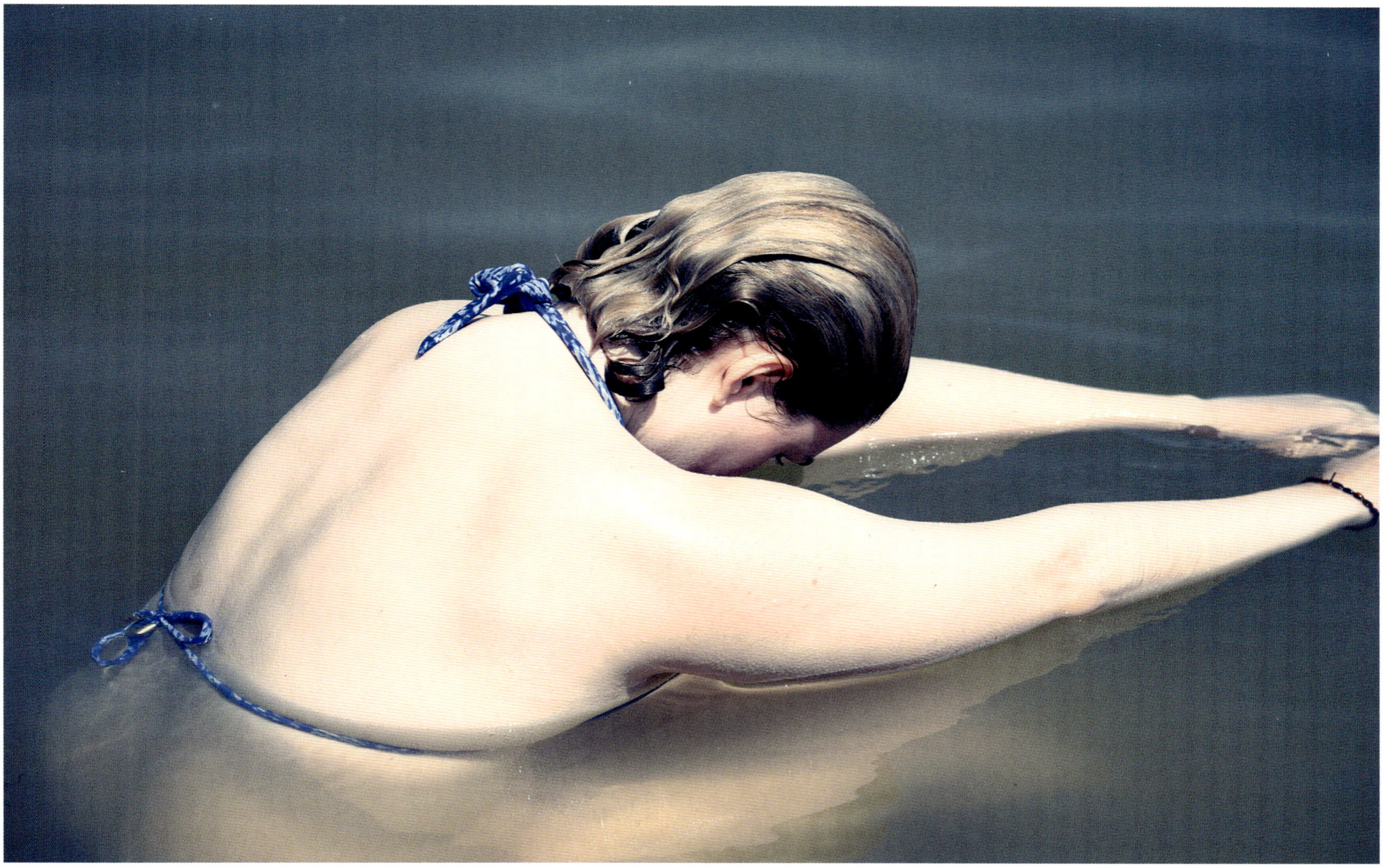

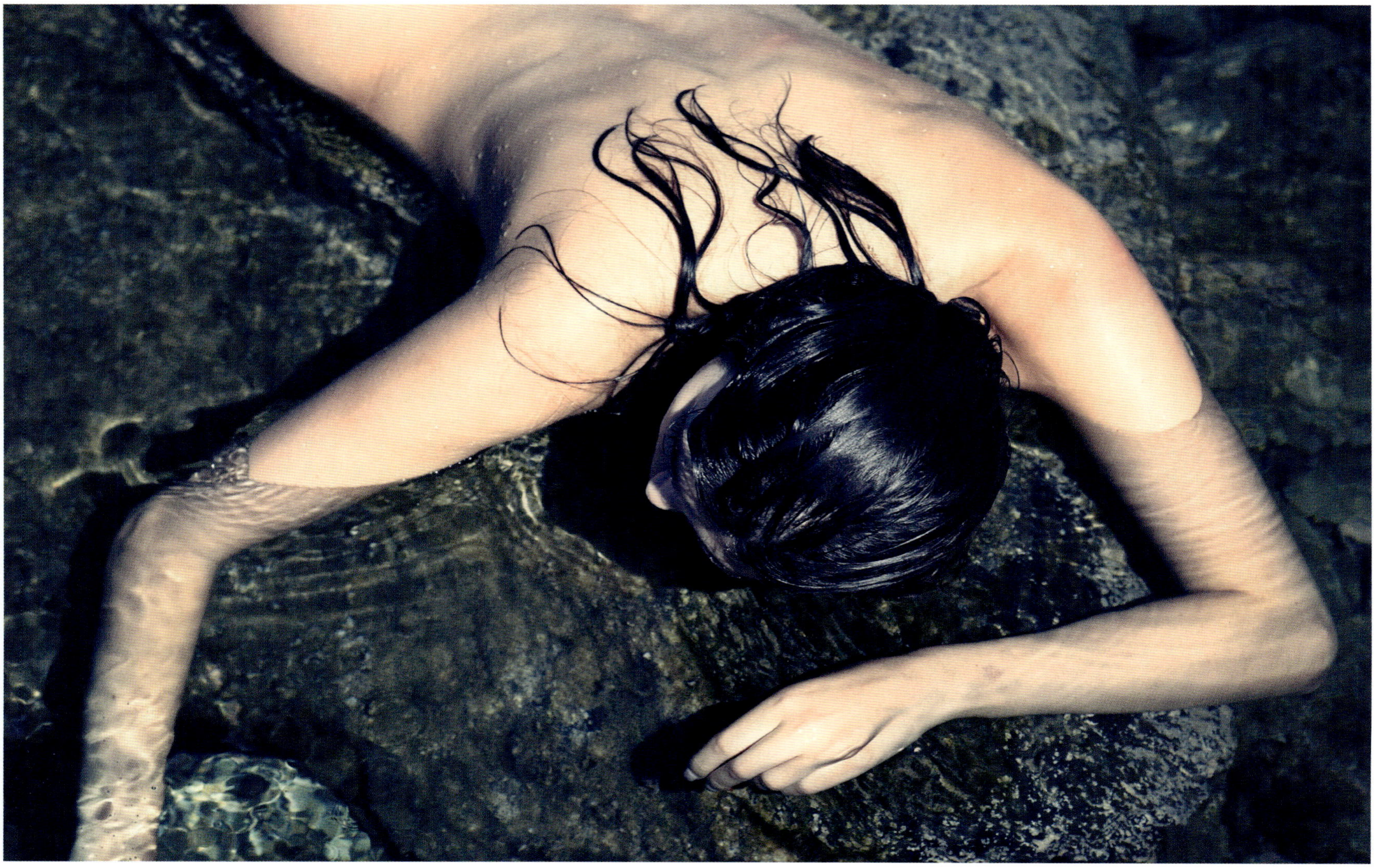

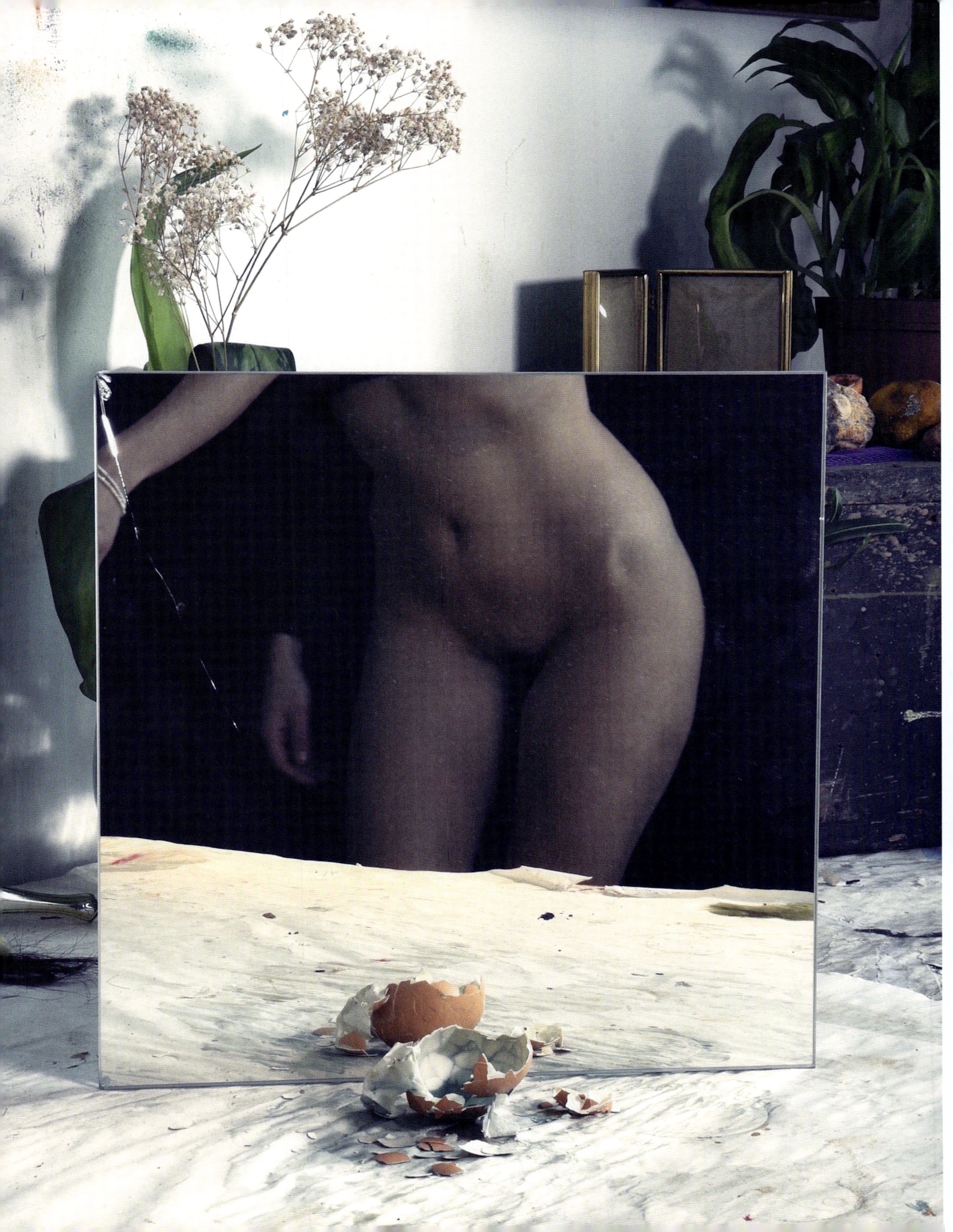

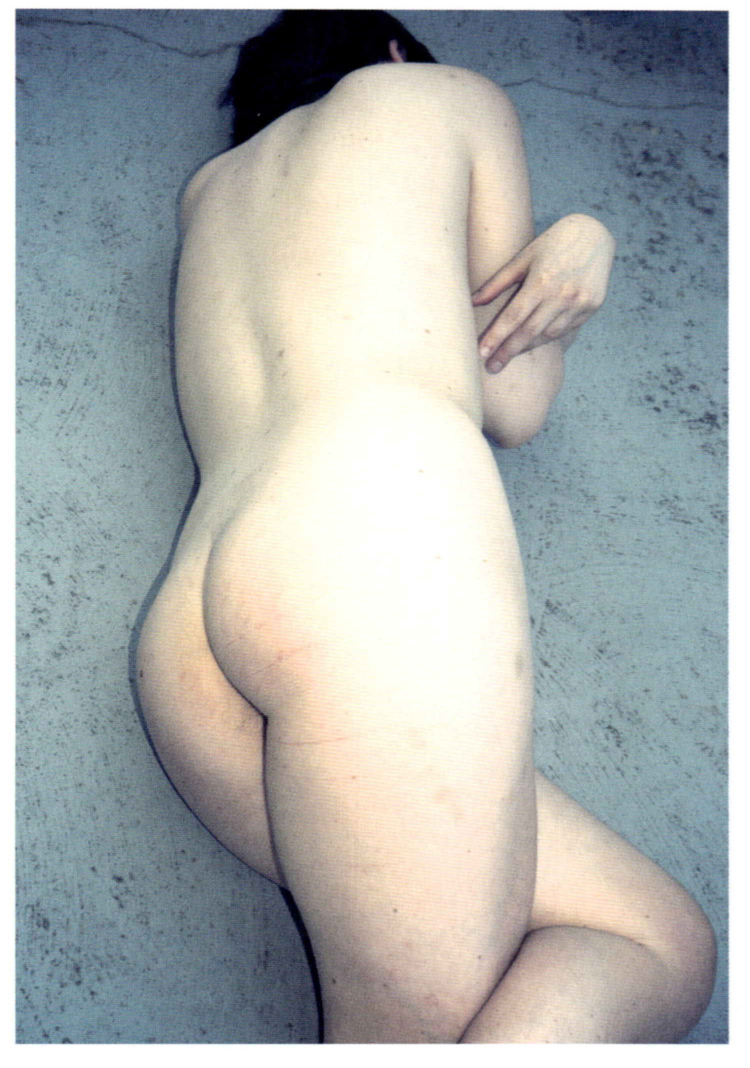

97

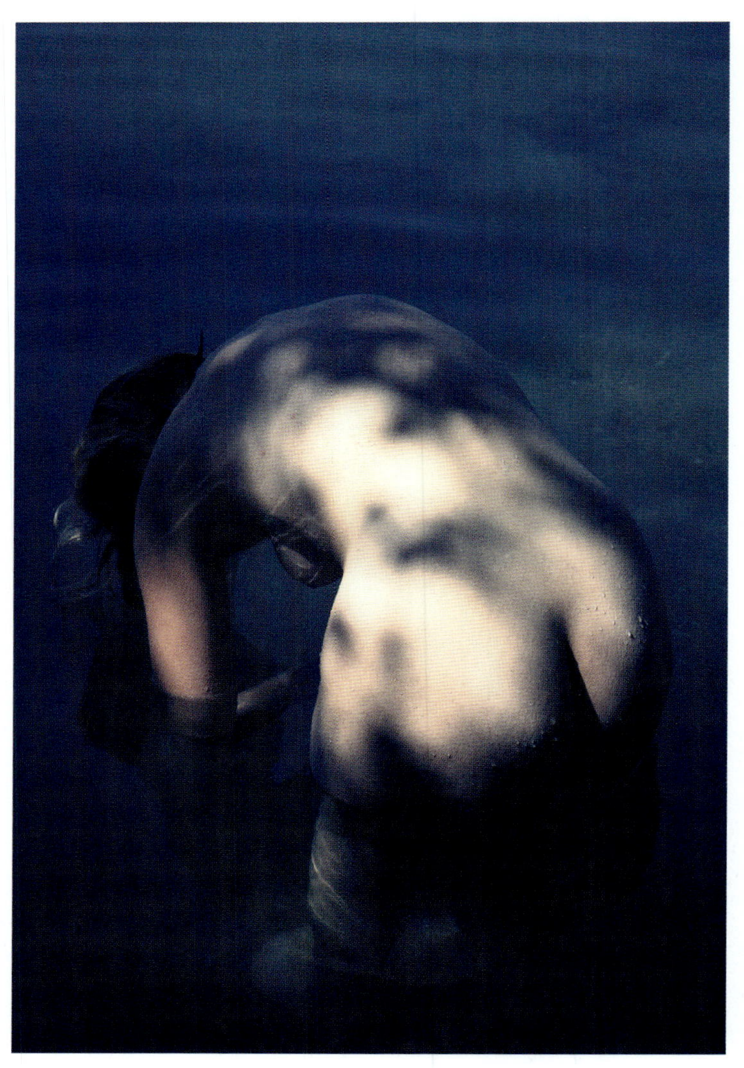

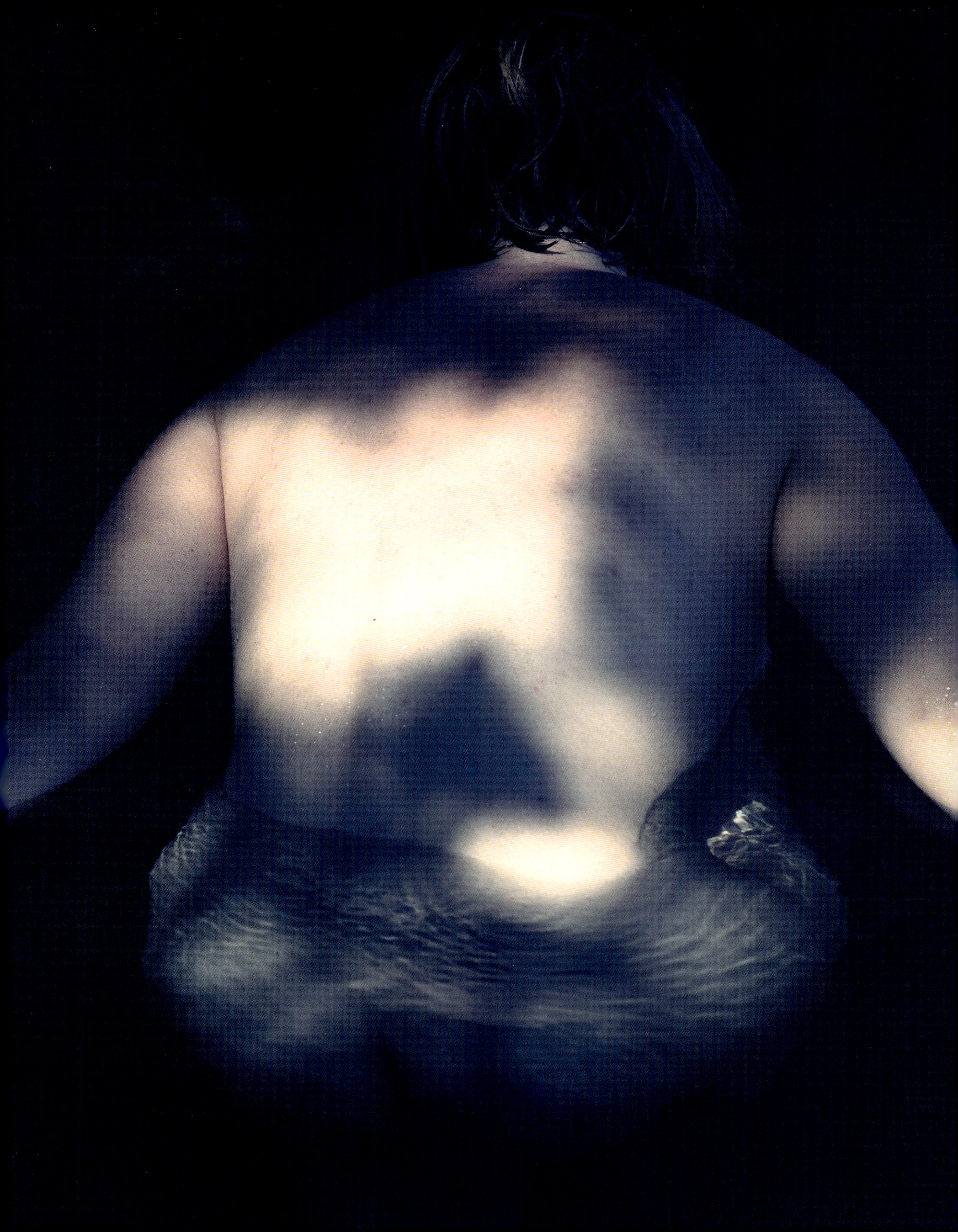

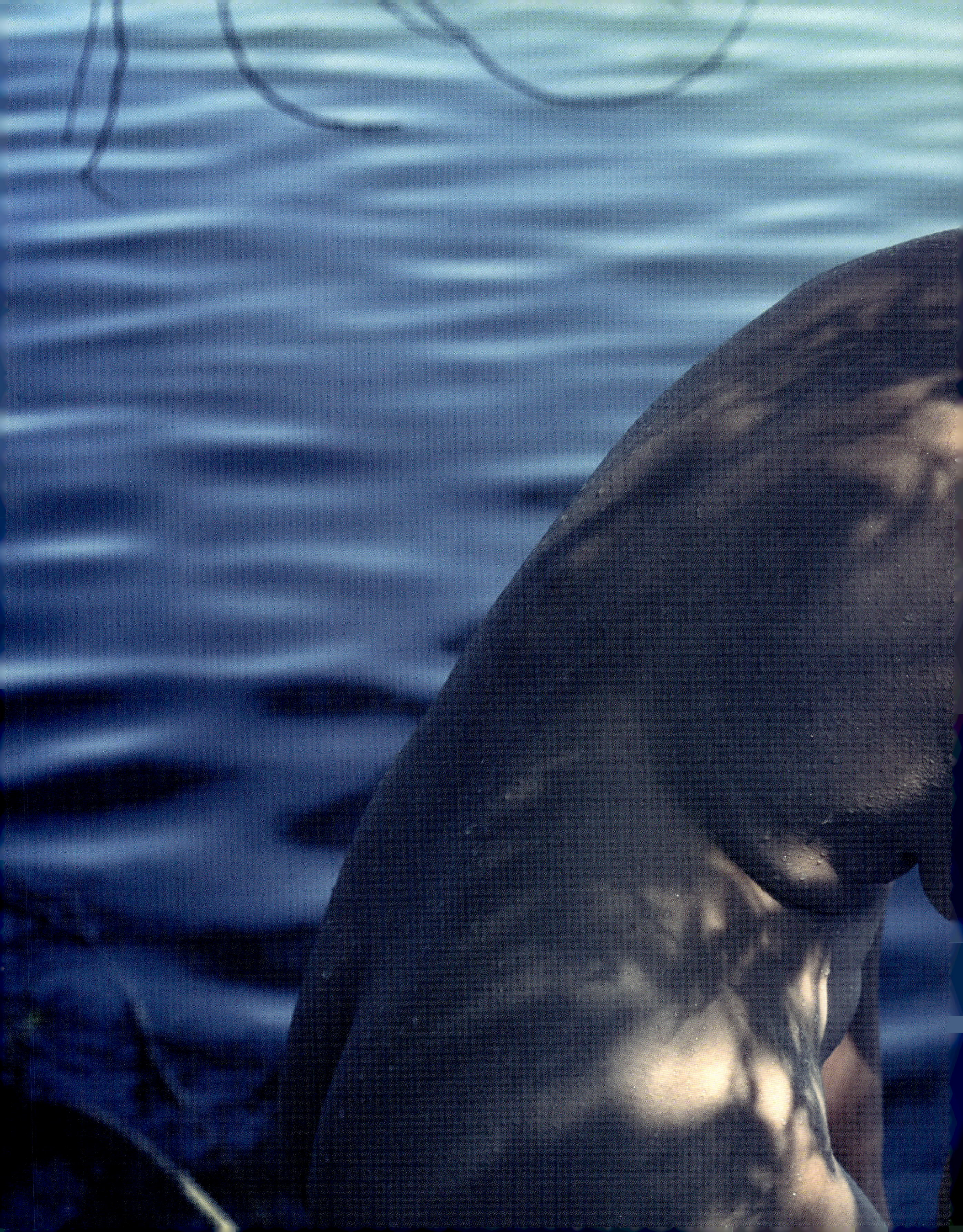

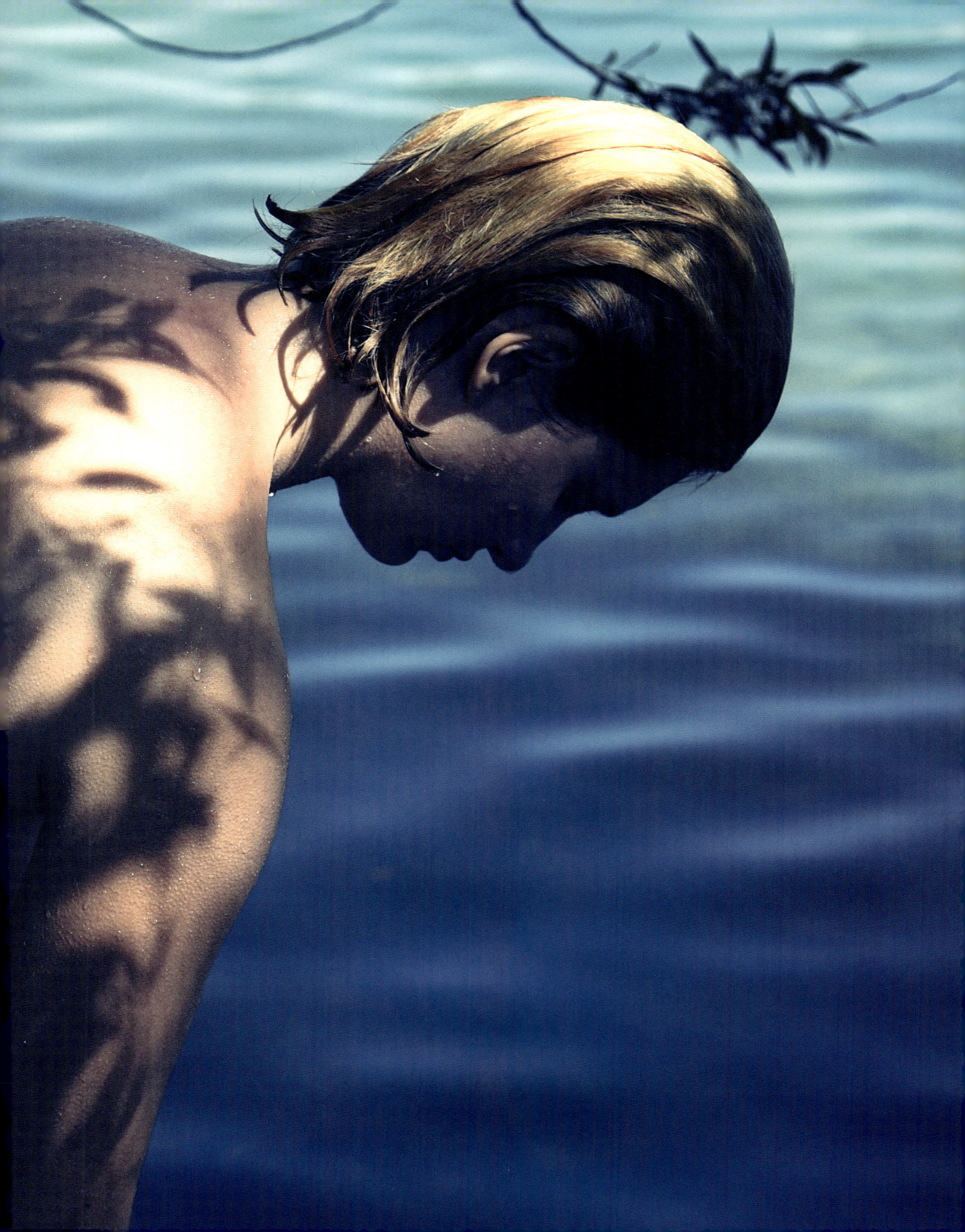

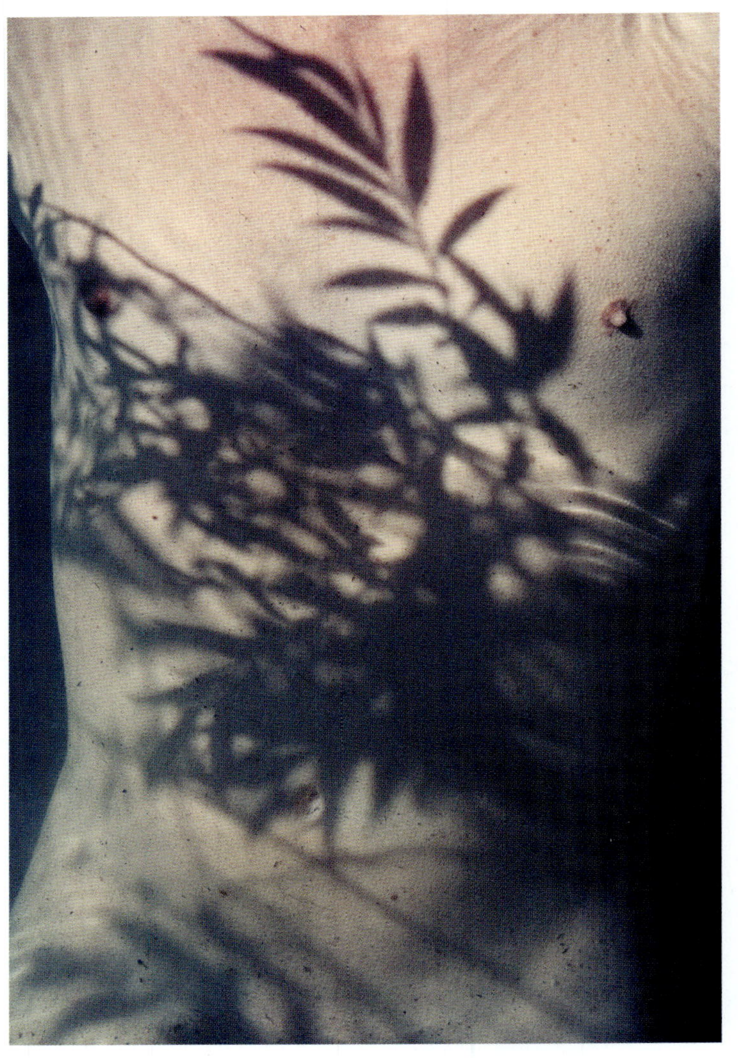

102

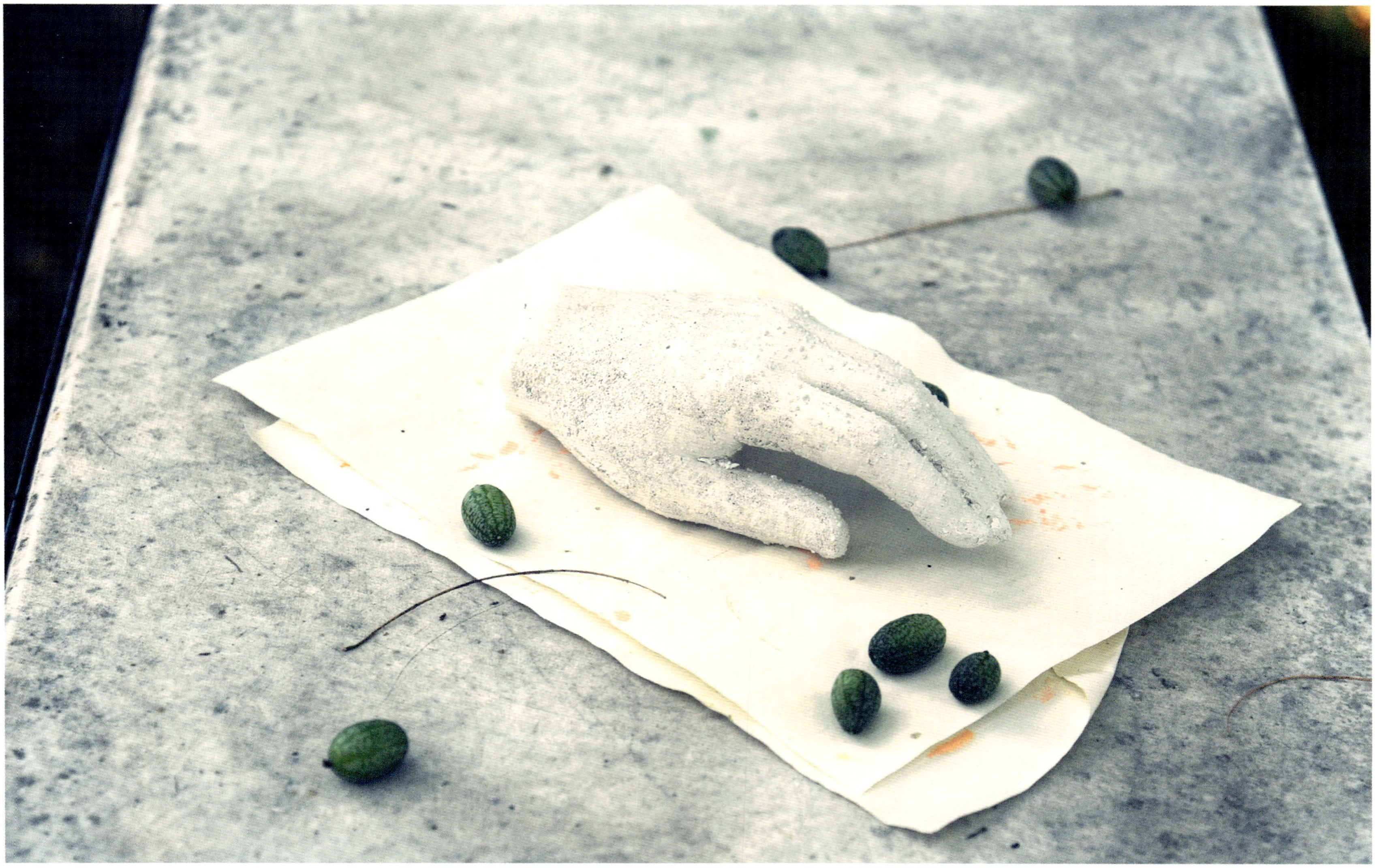

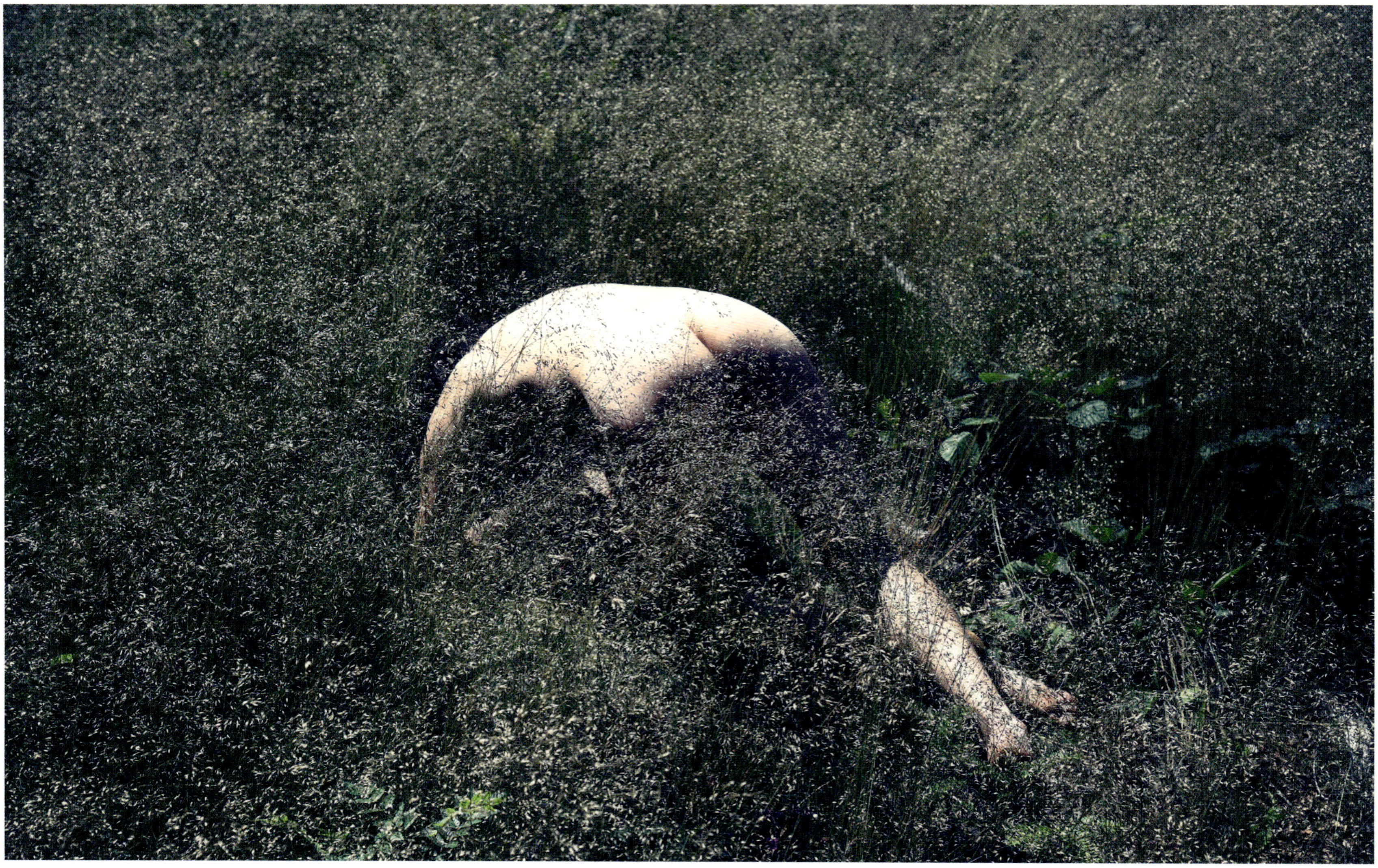

NEELTJE DE VRIES

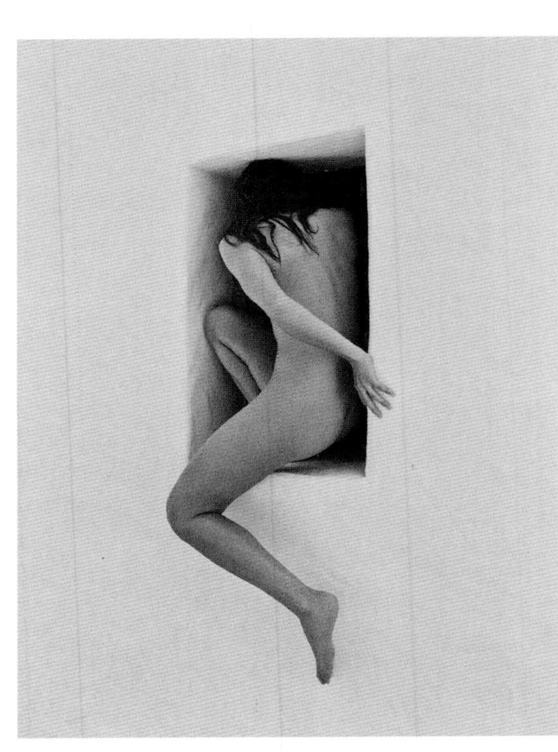

FREE OF FORM

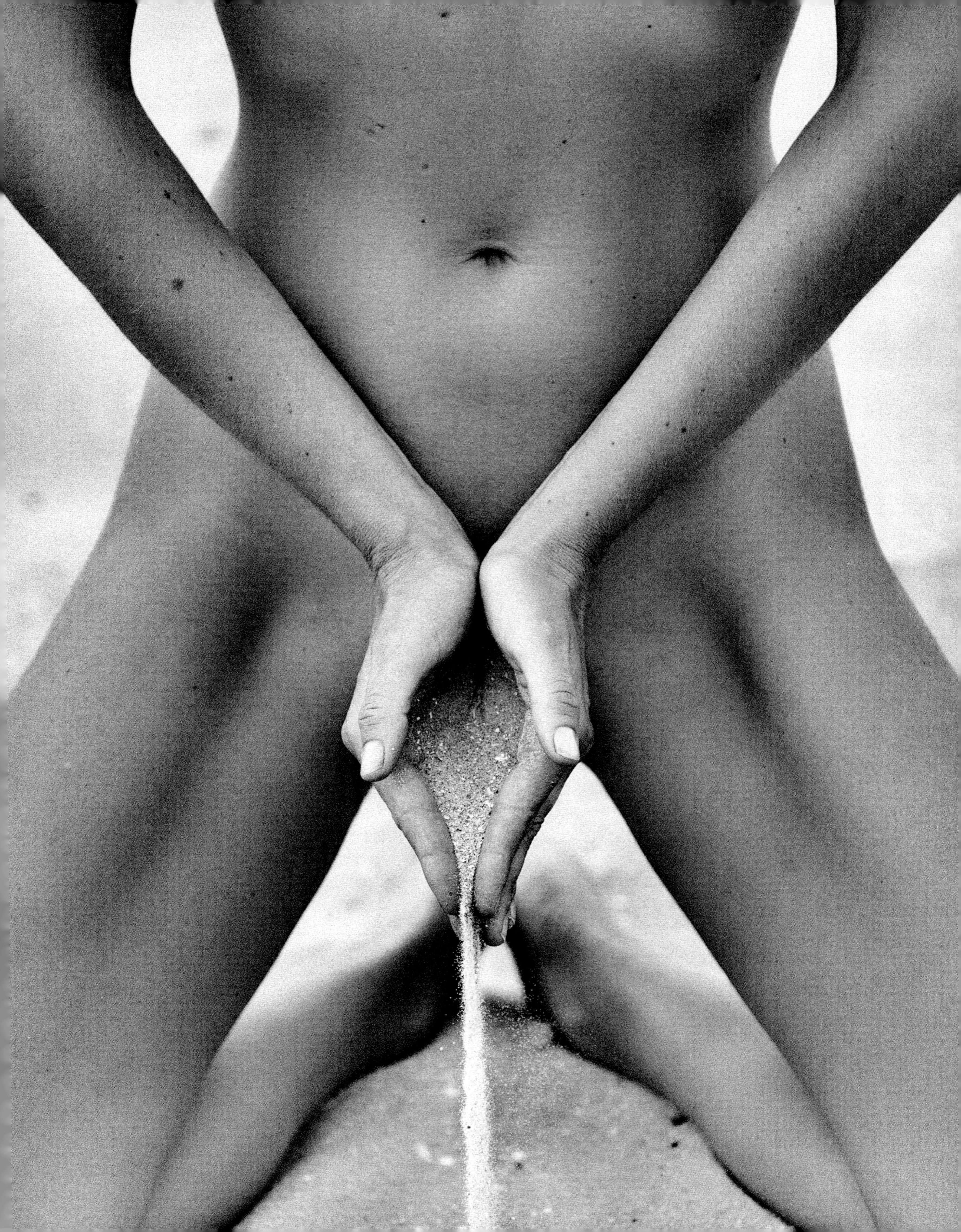

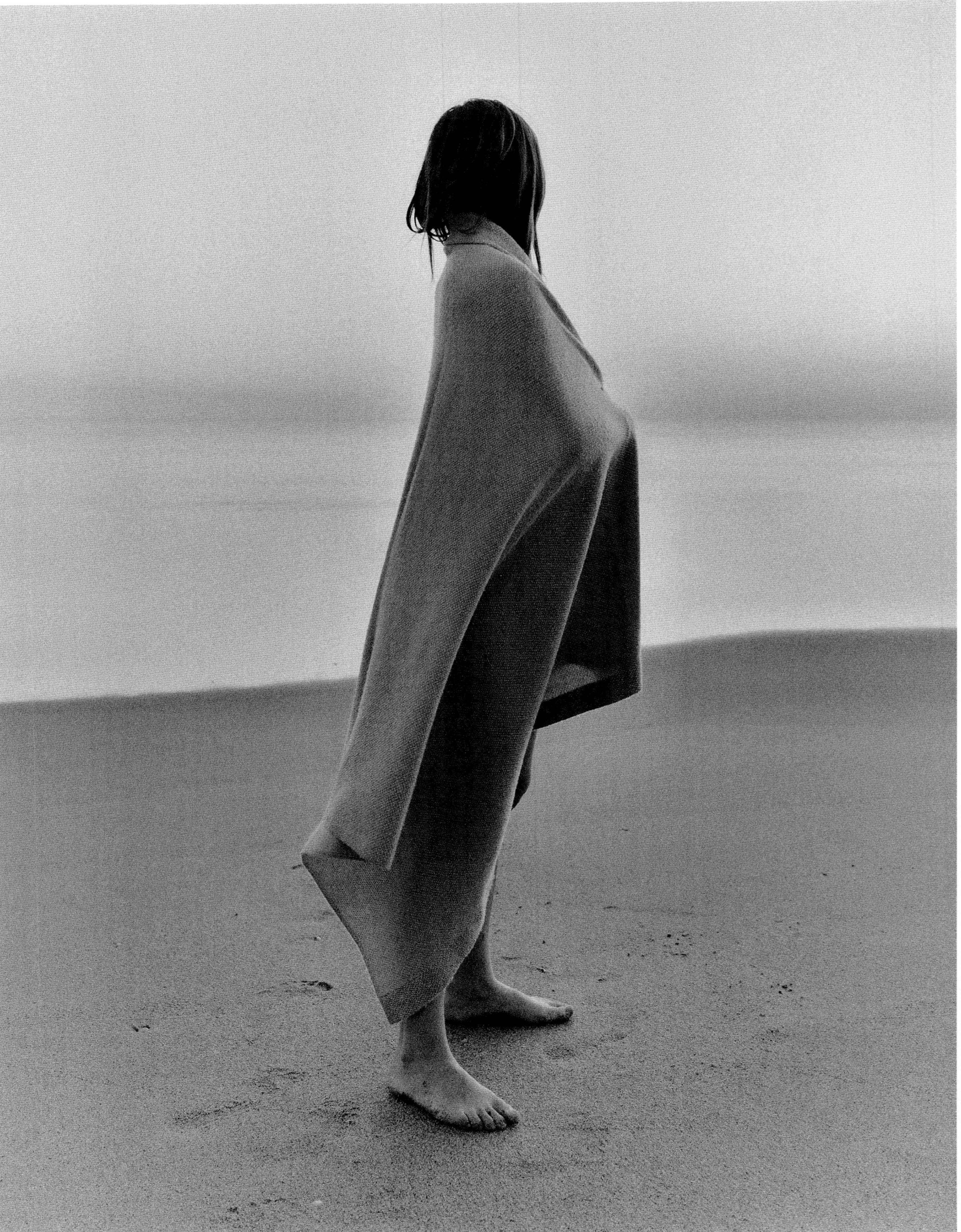

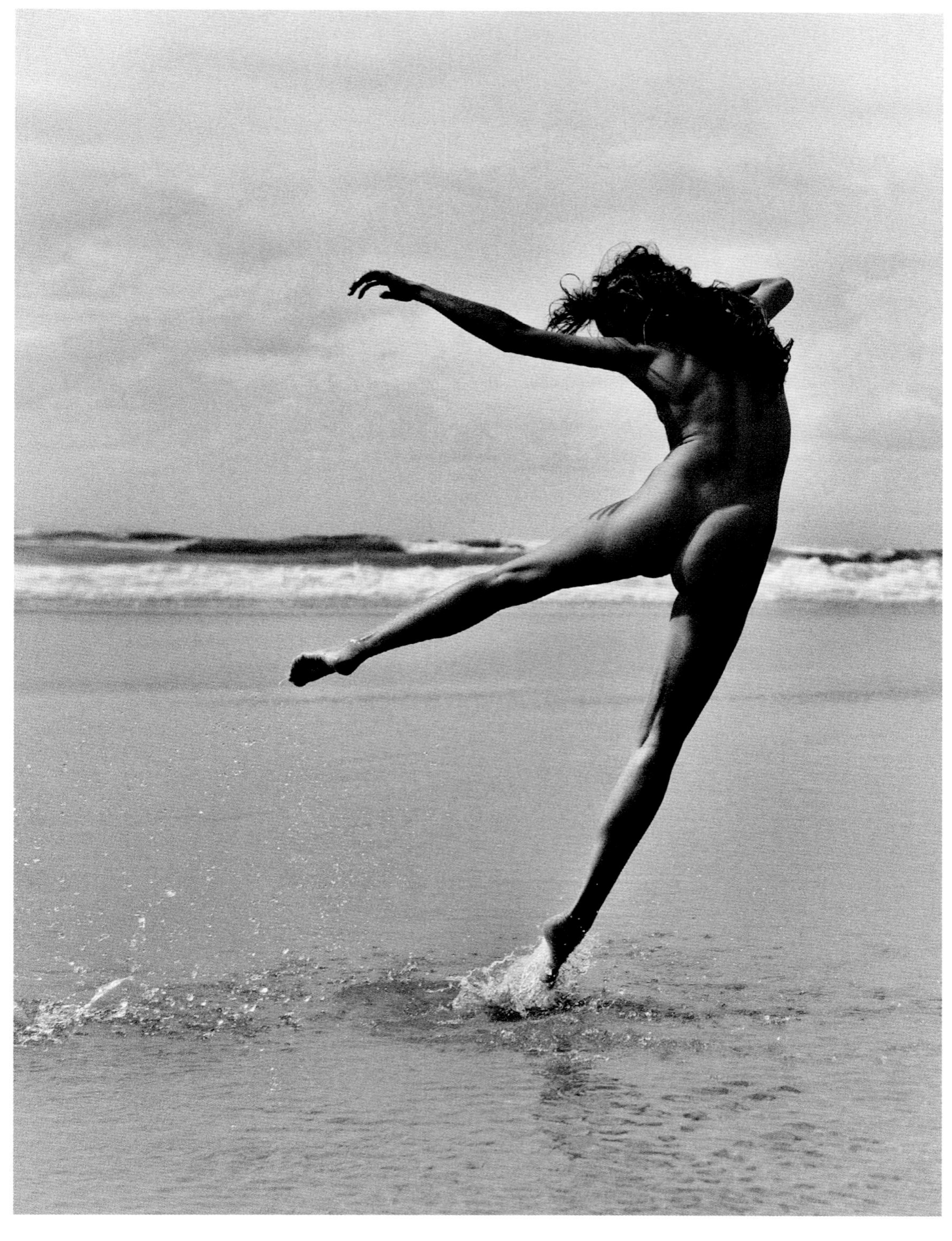

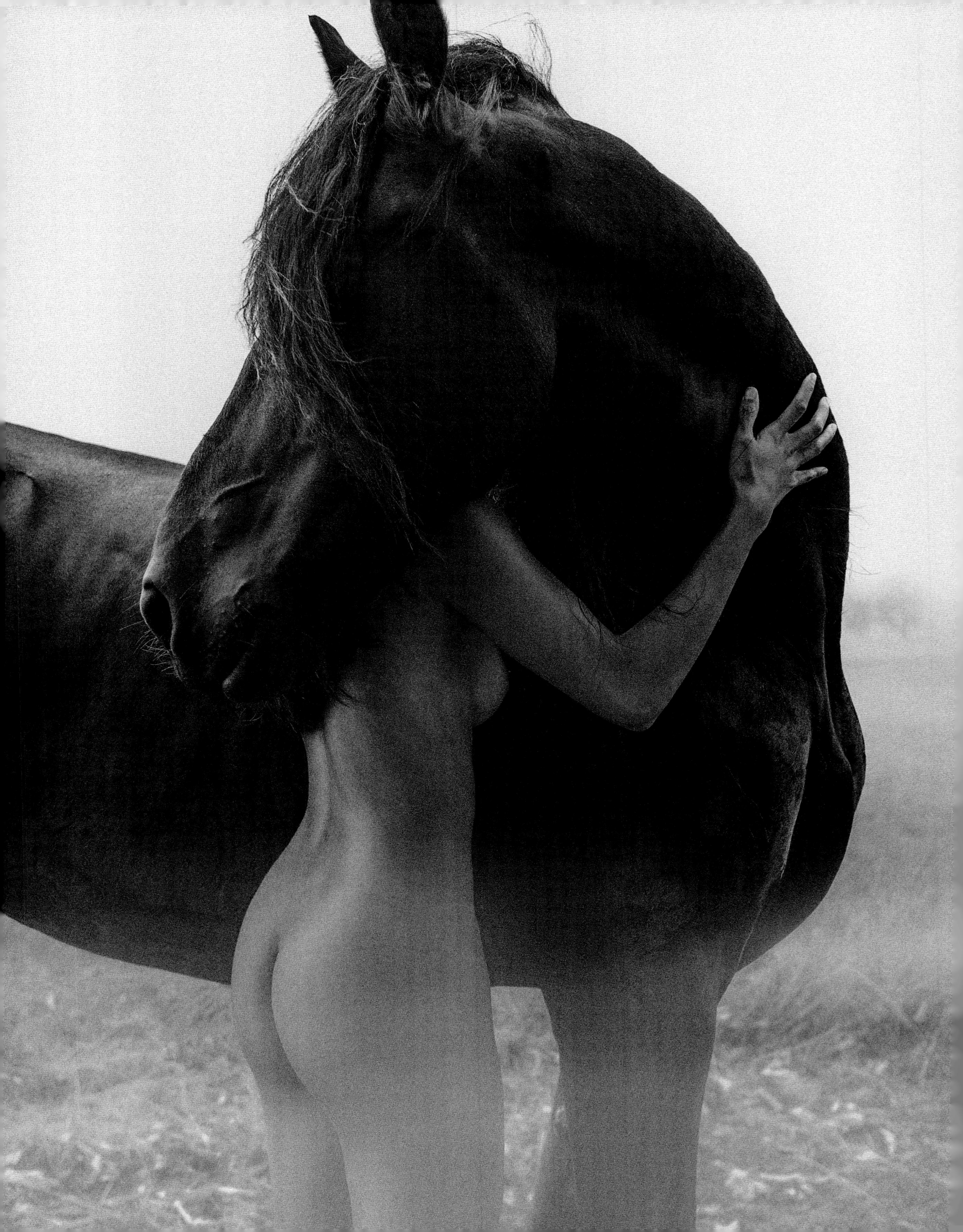

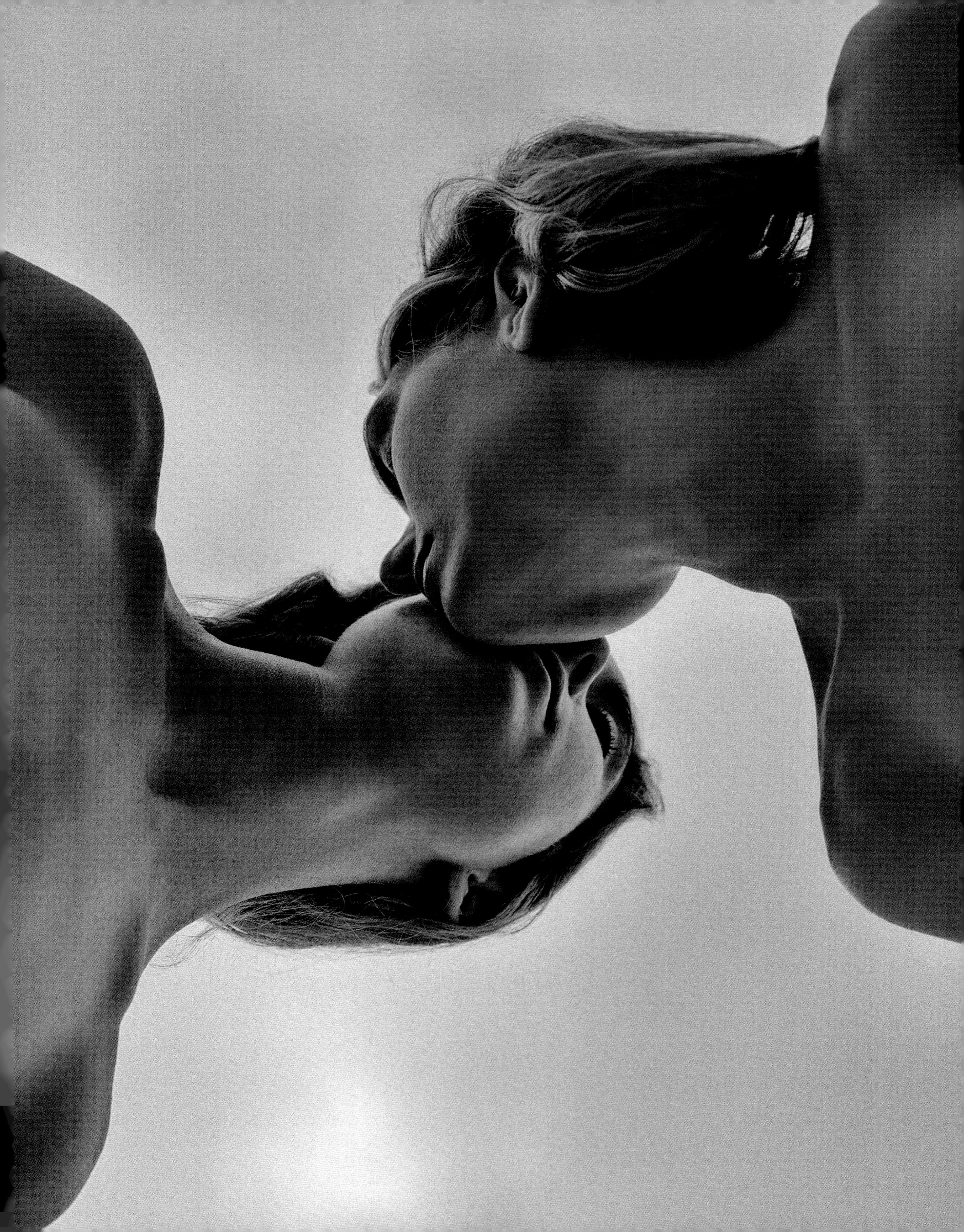

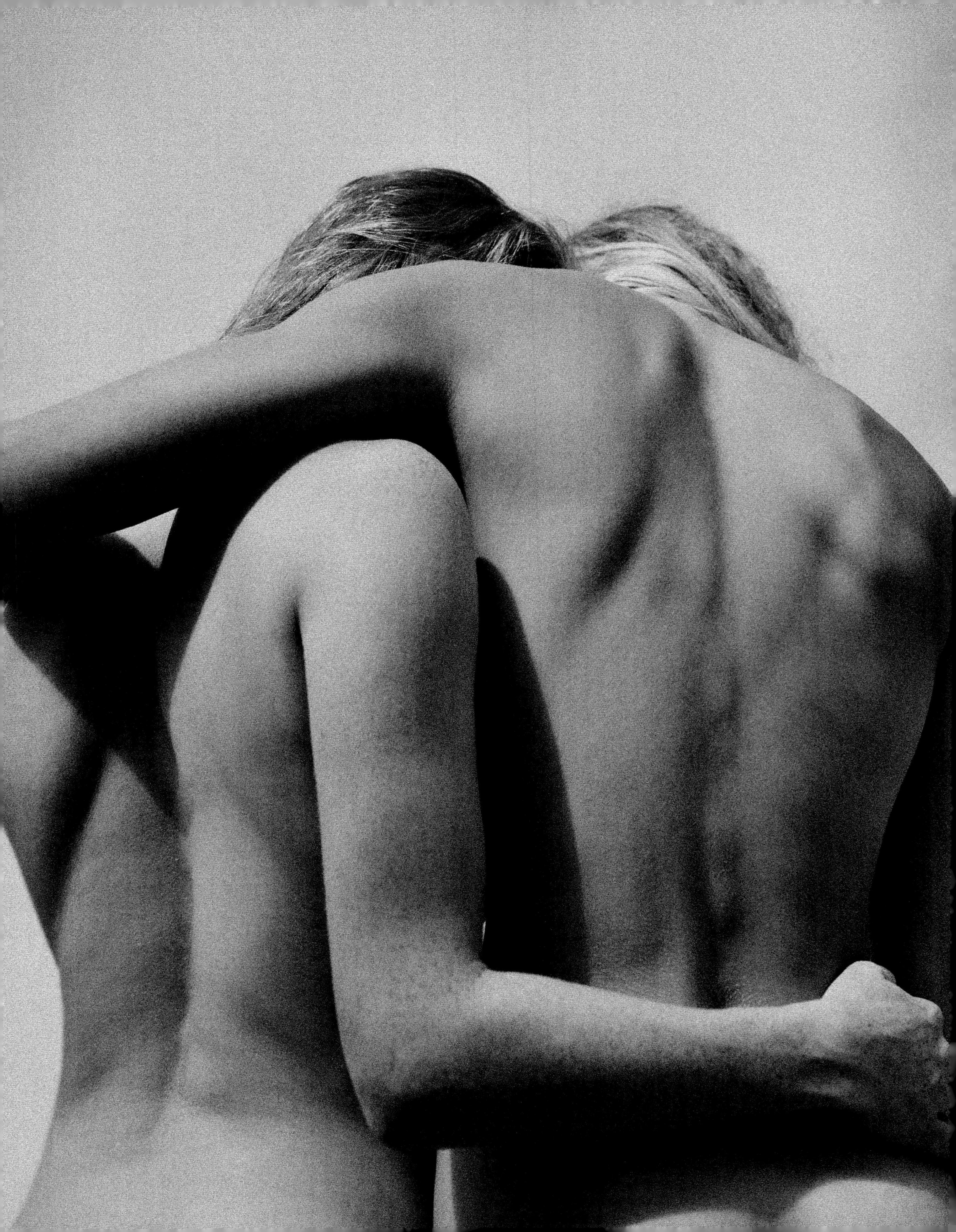

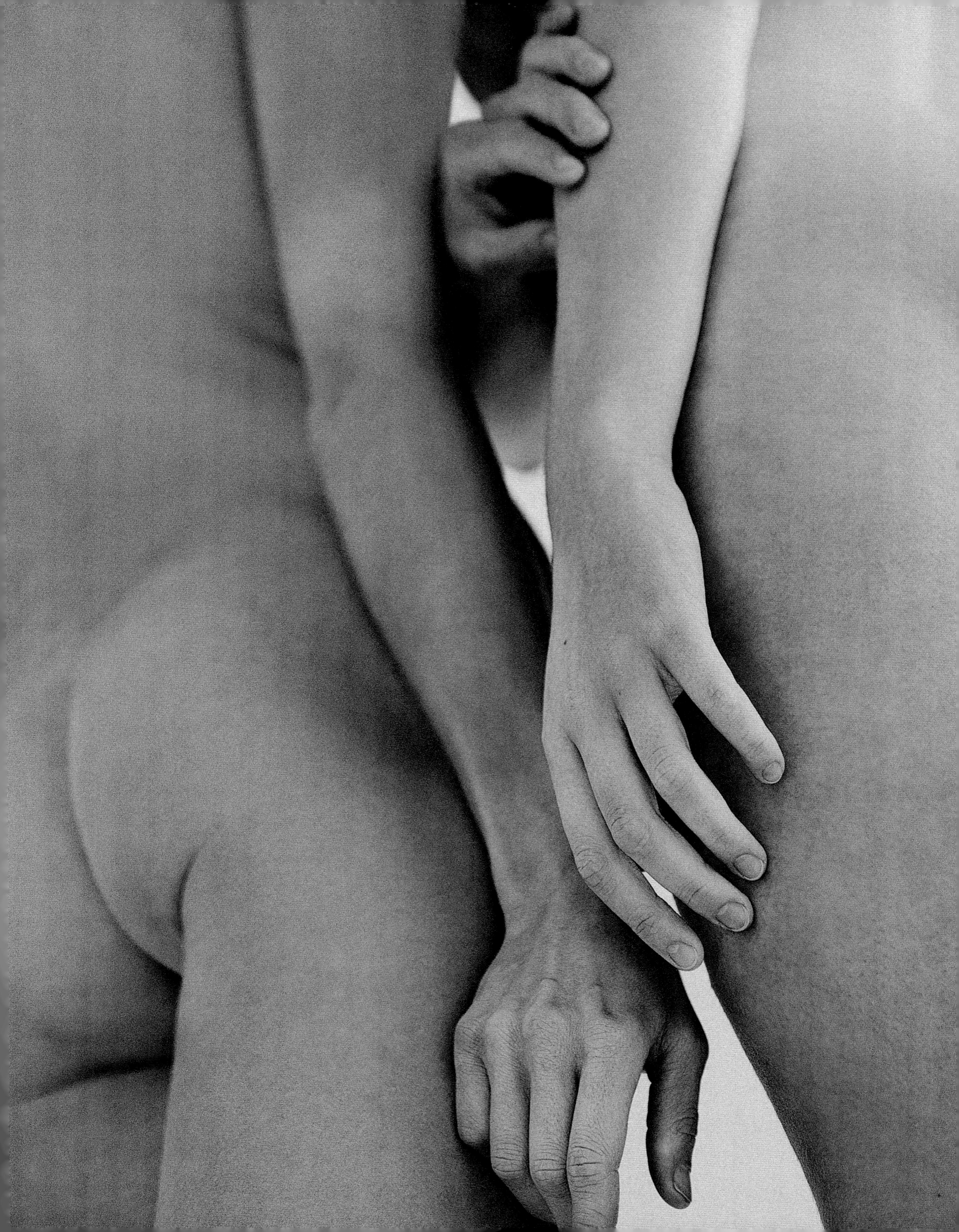

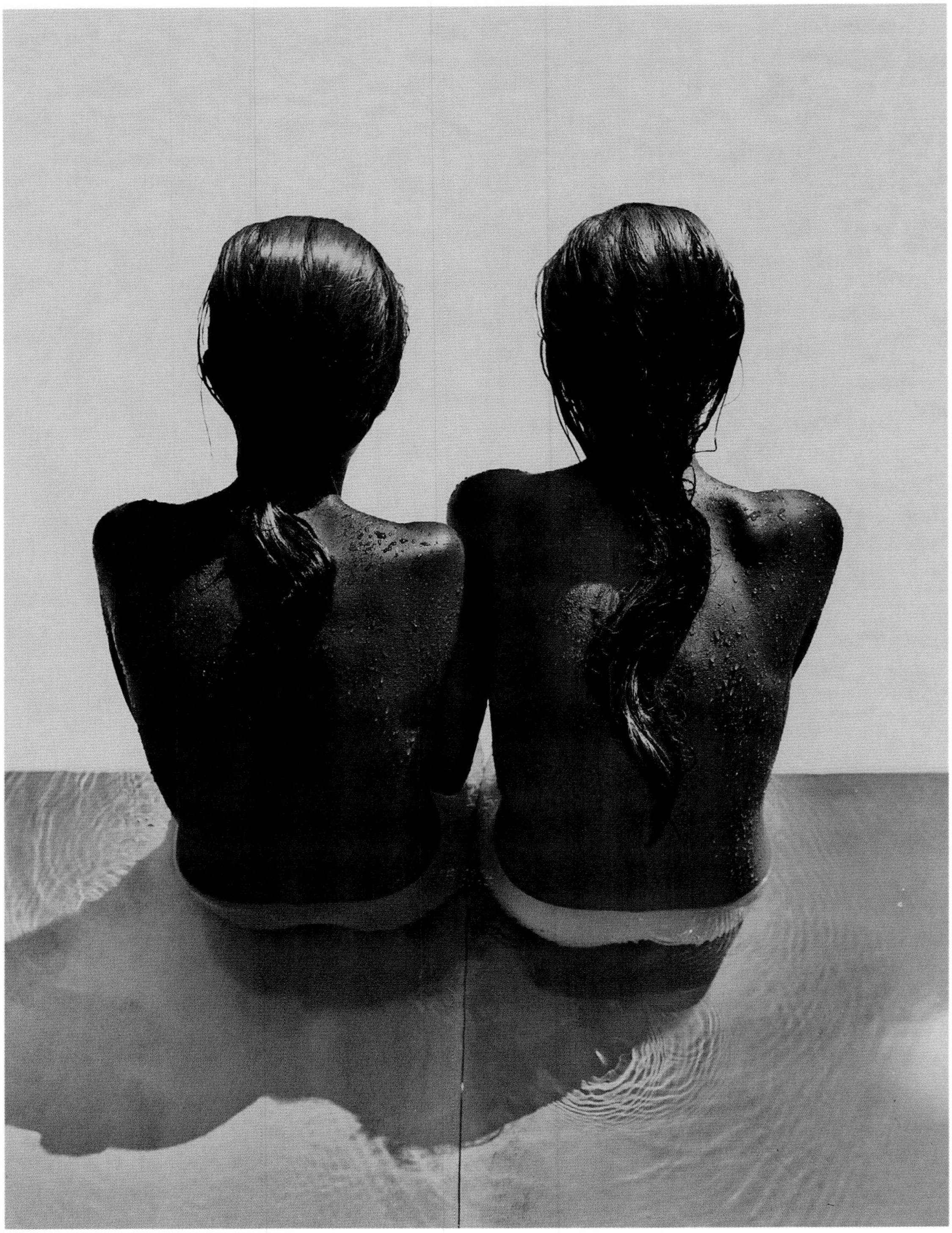

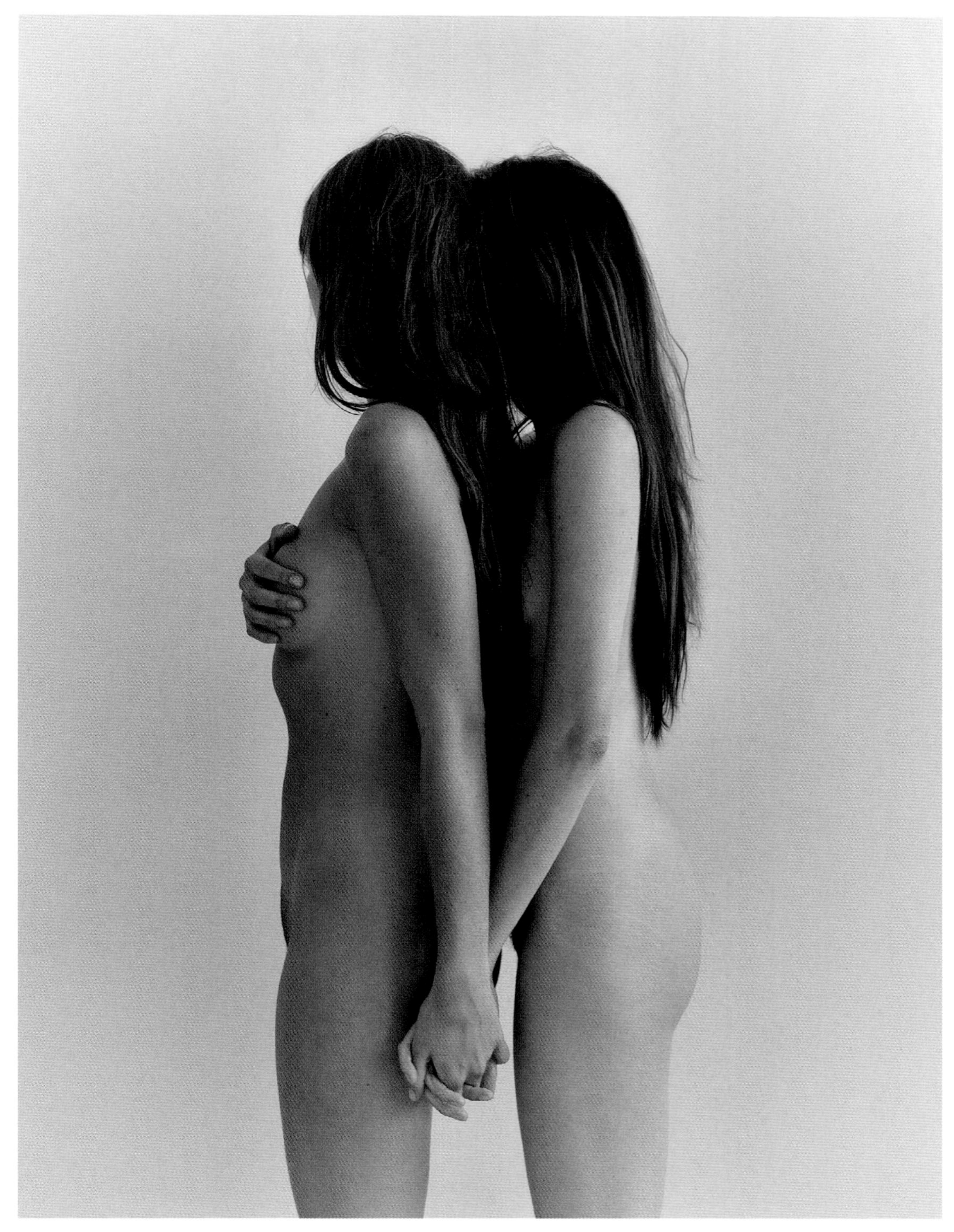

ALWIN MAIGLER

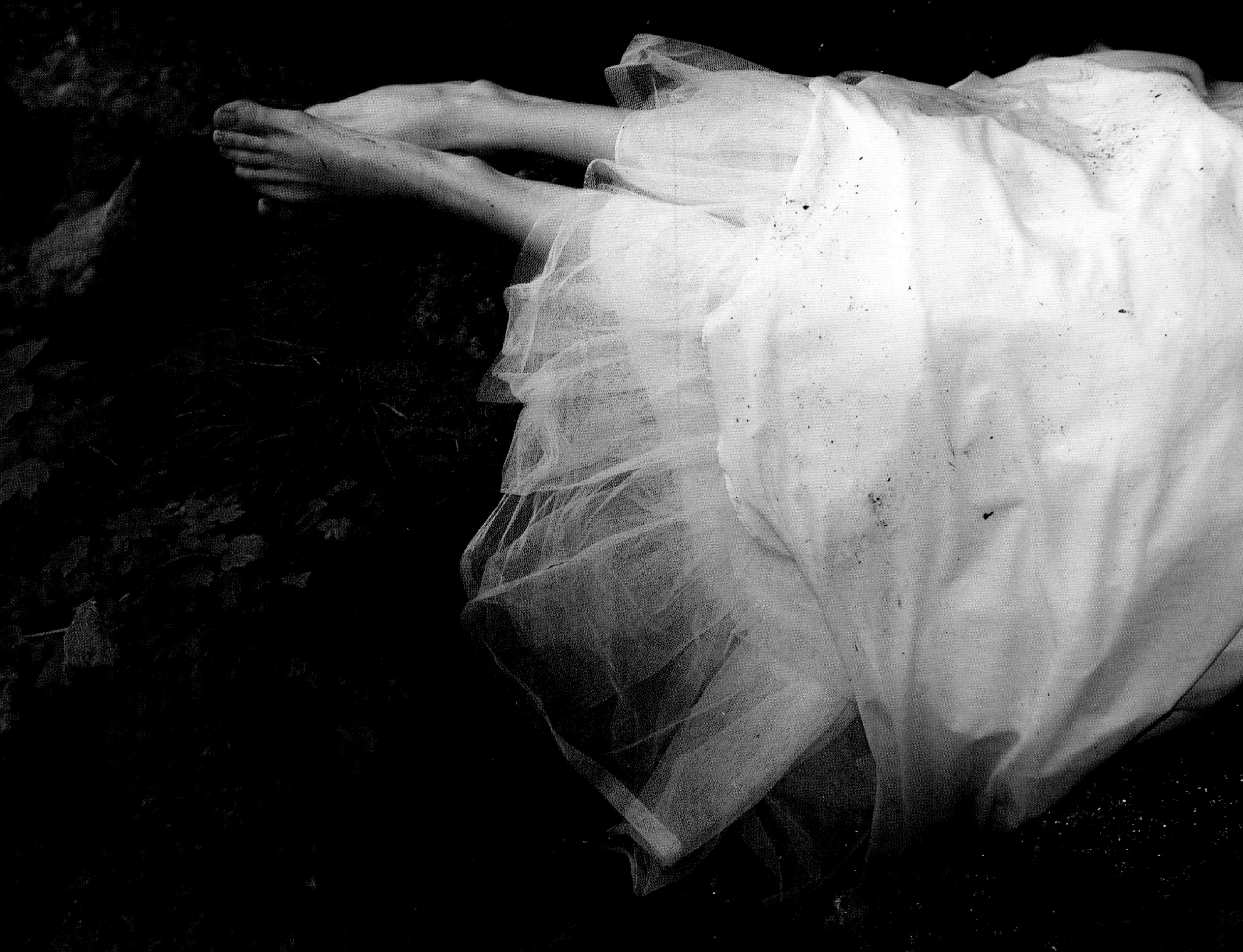

PANTA RHEI

MODEL:
ANASTASIIA IUSUPOVA

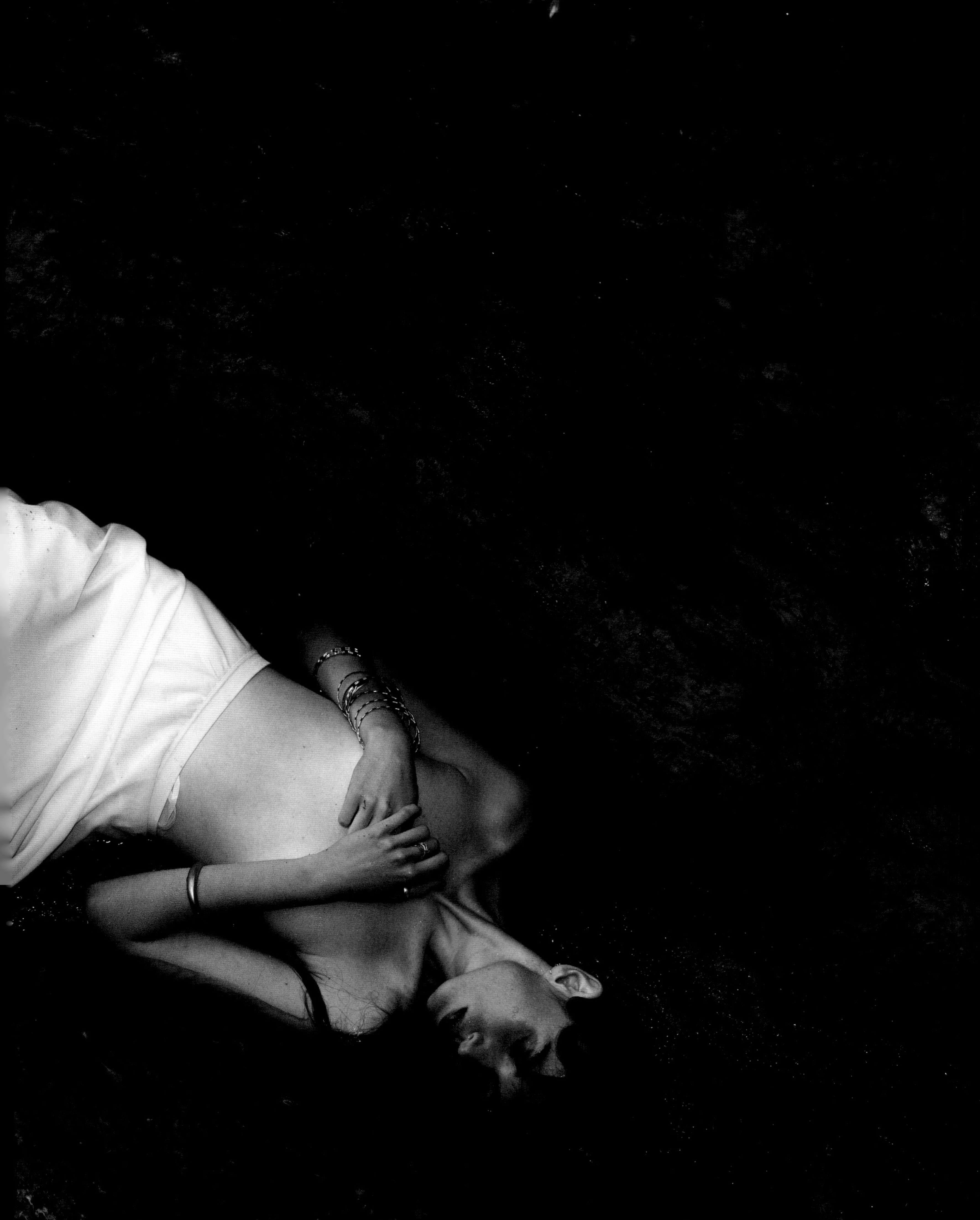

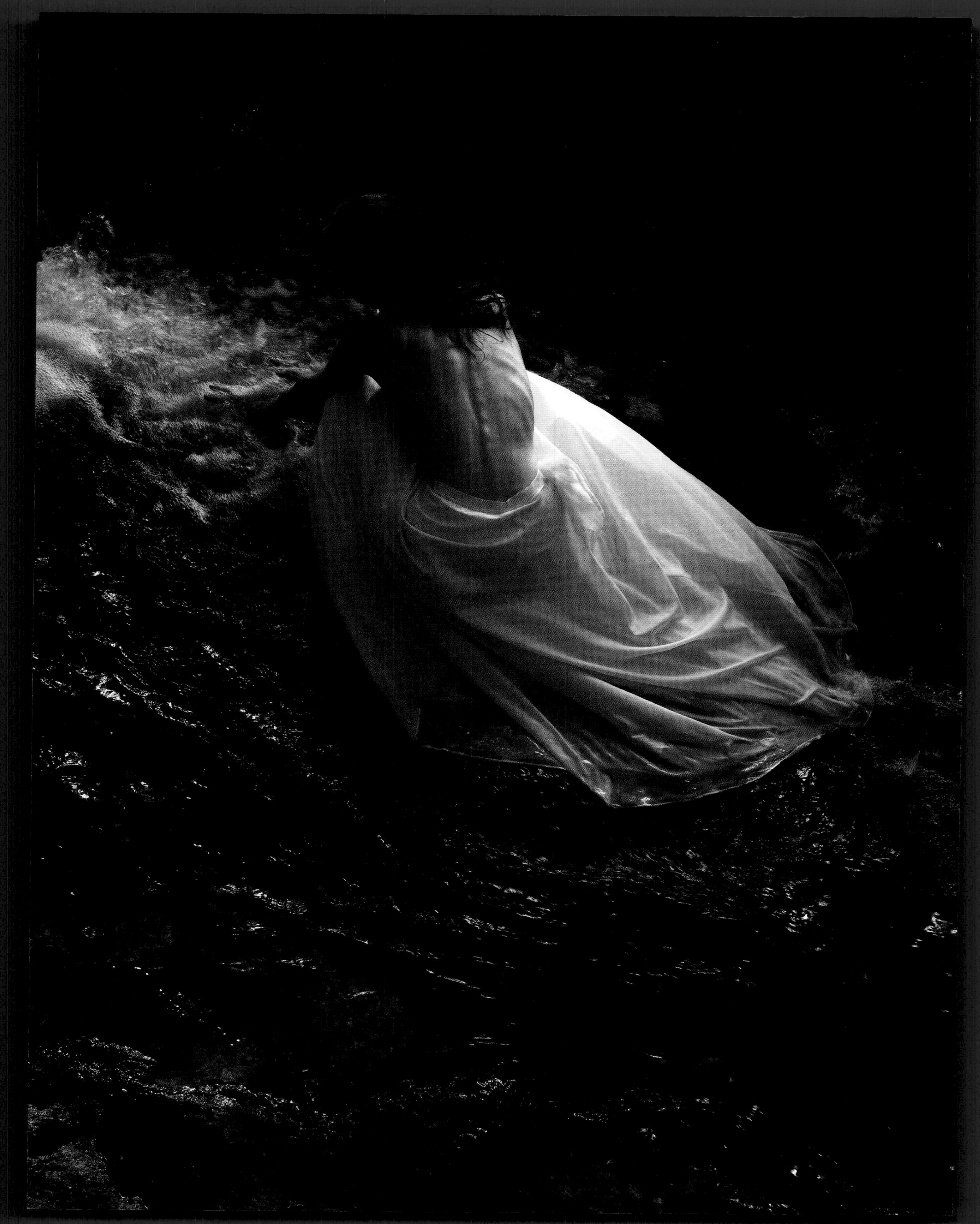

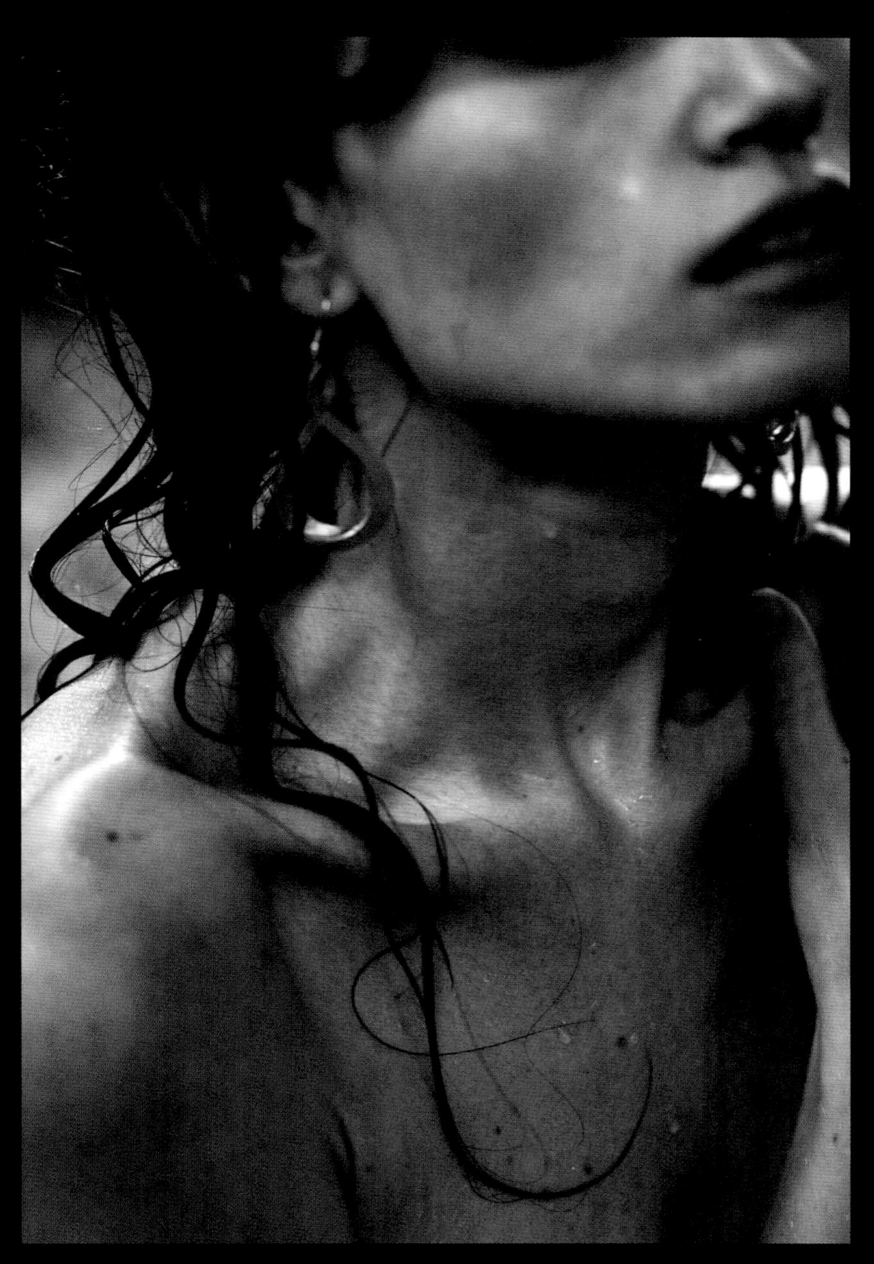

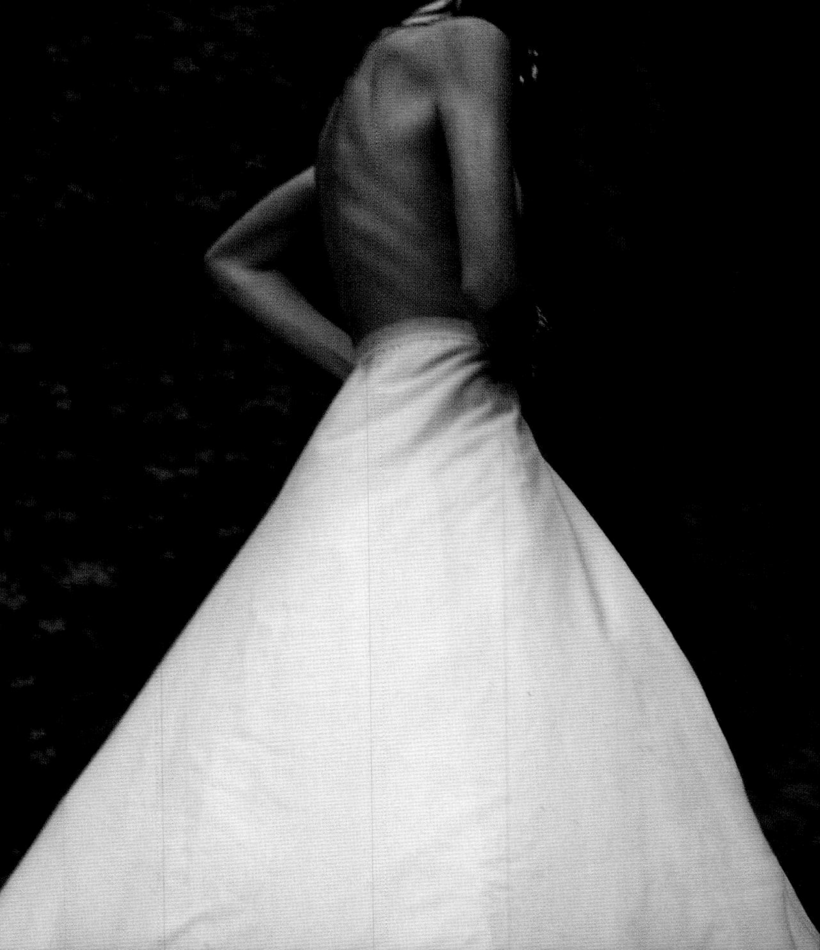

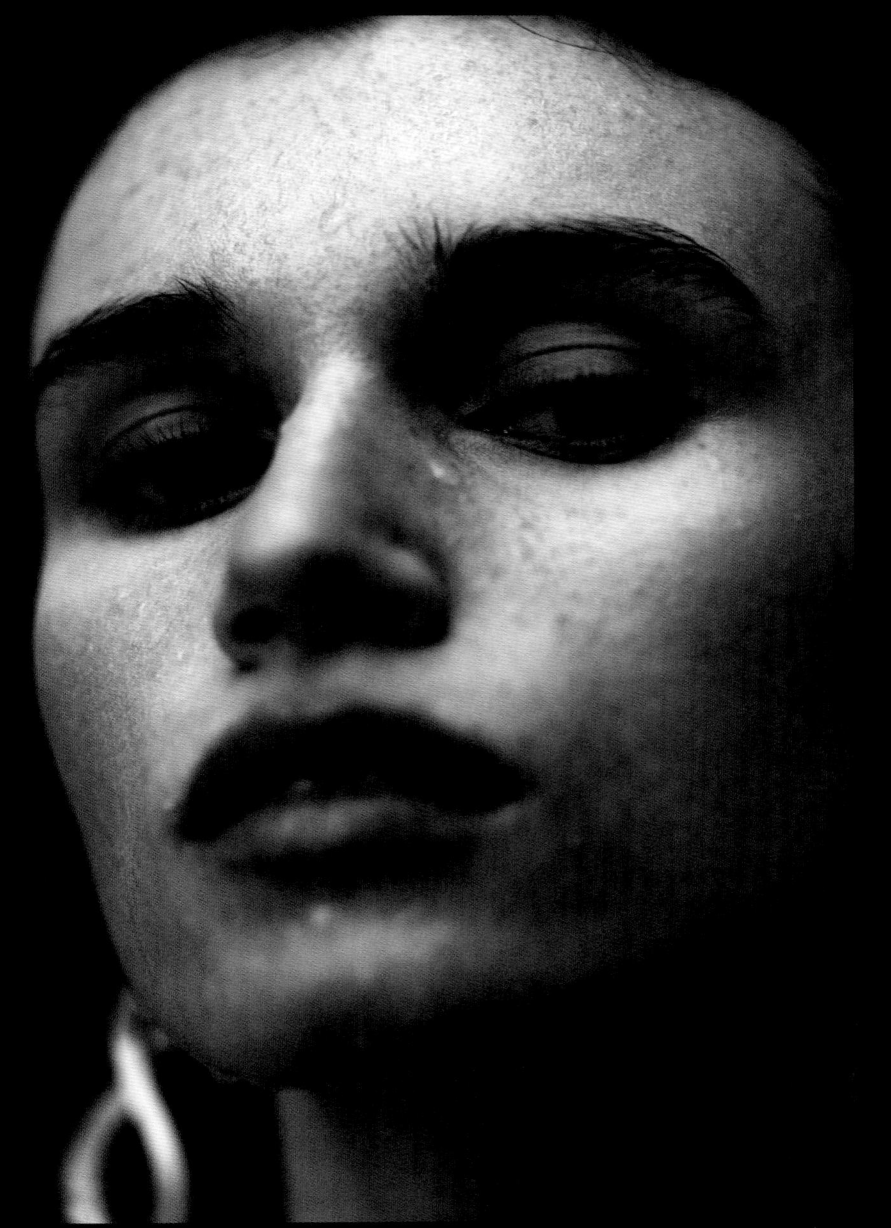

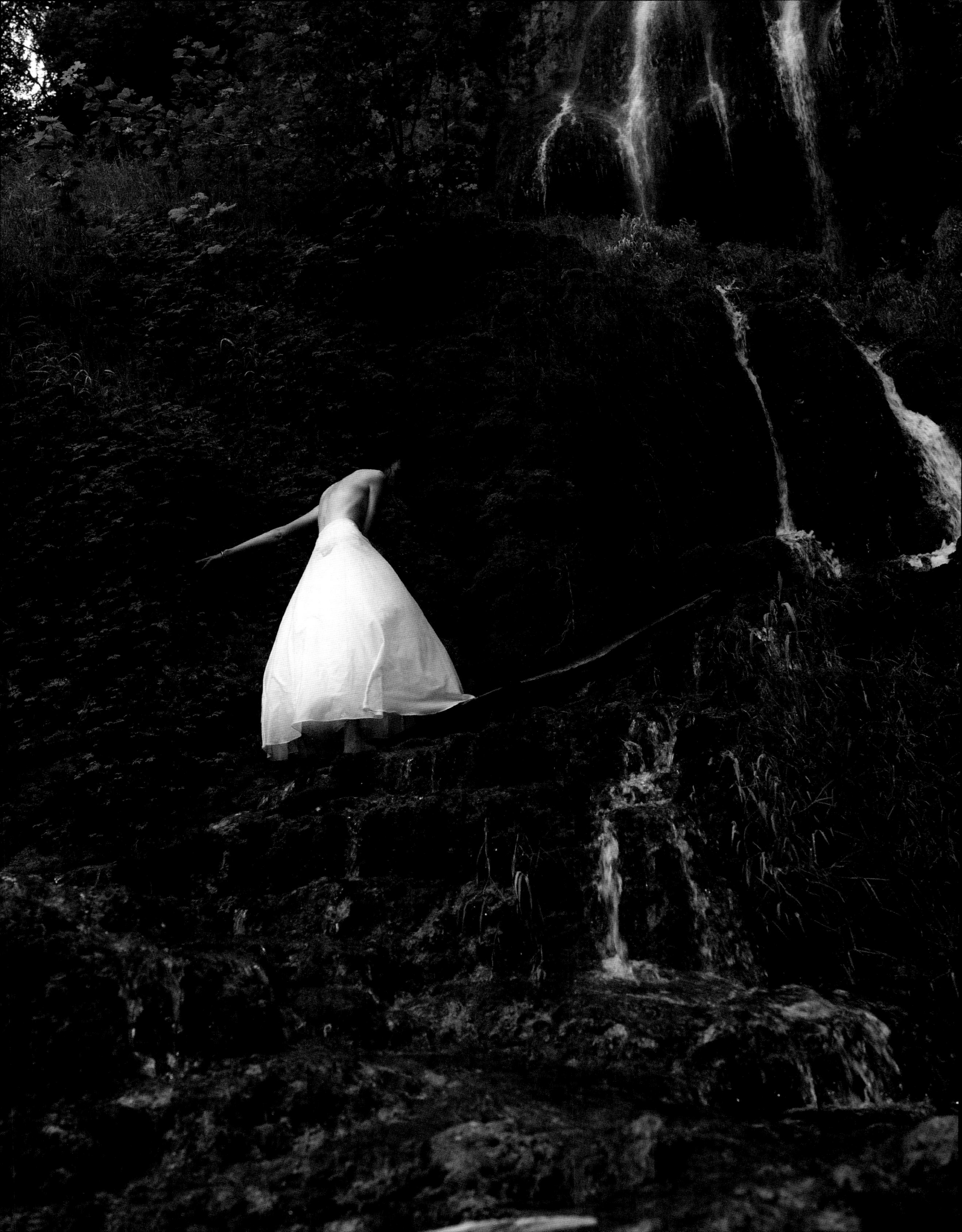

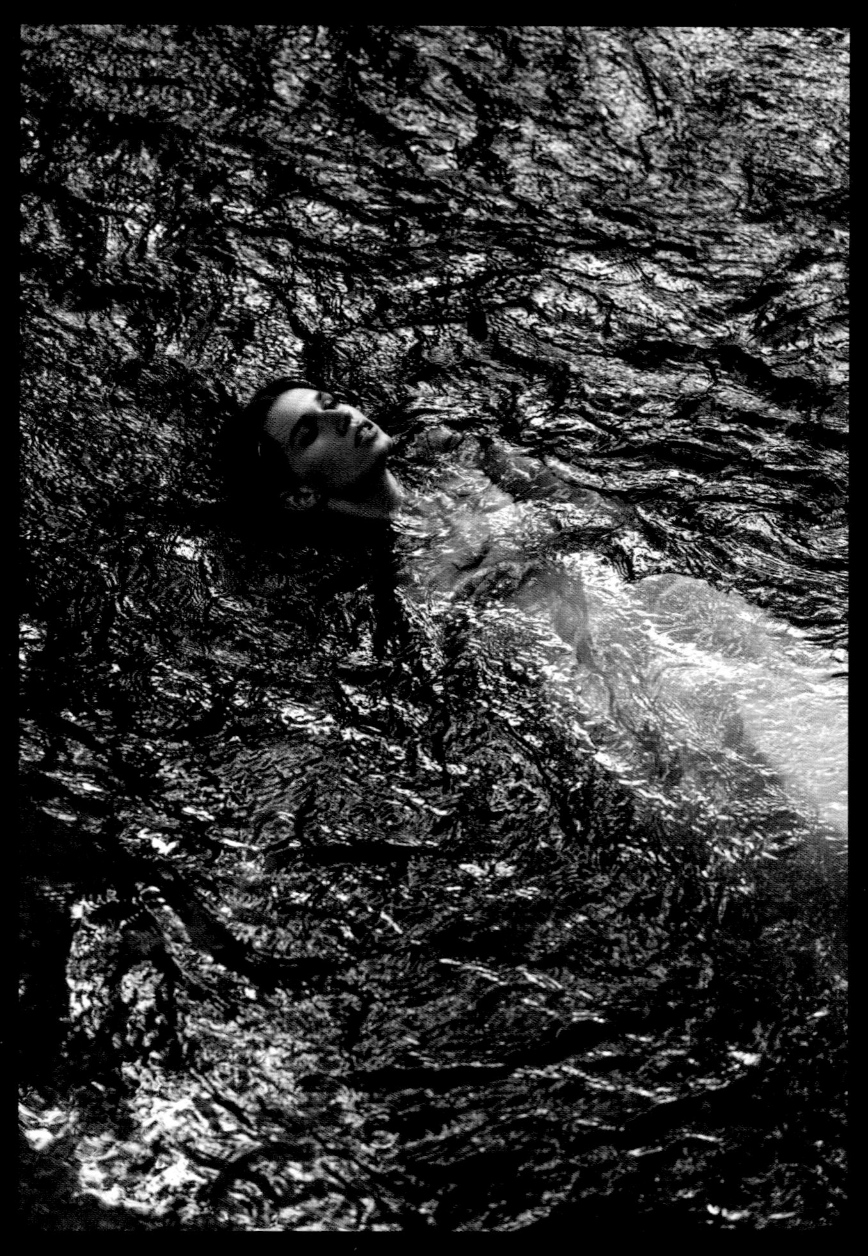

NANDA HAGENAARS

122

BONA
FORTUNA

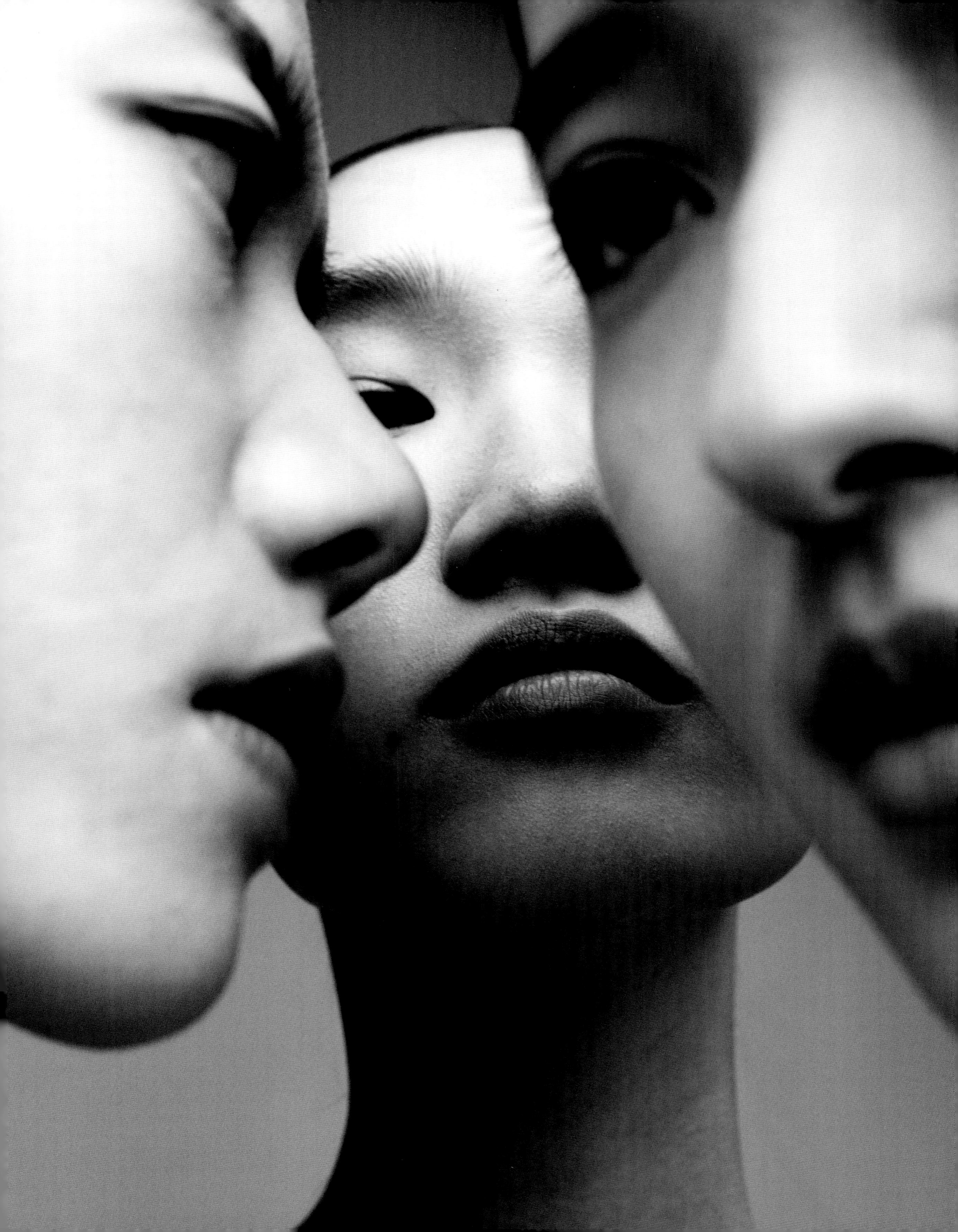

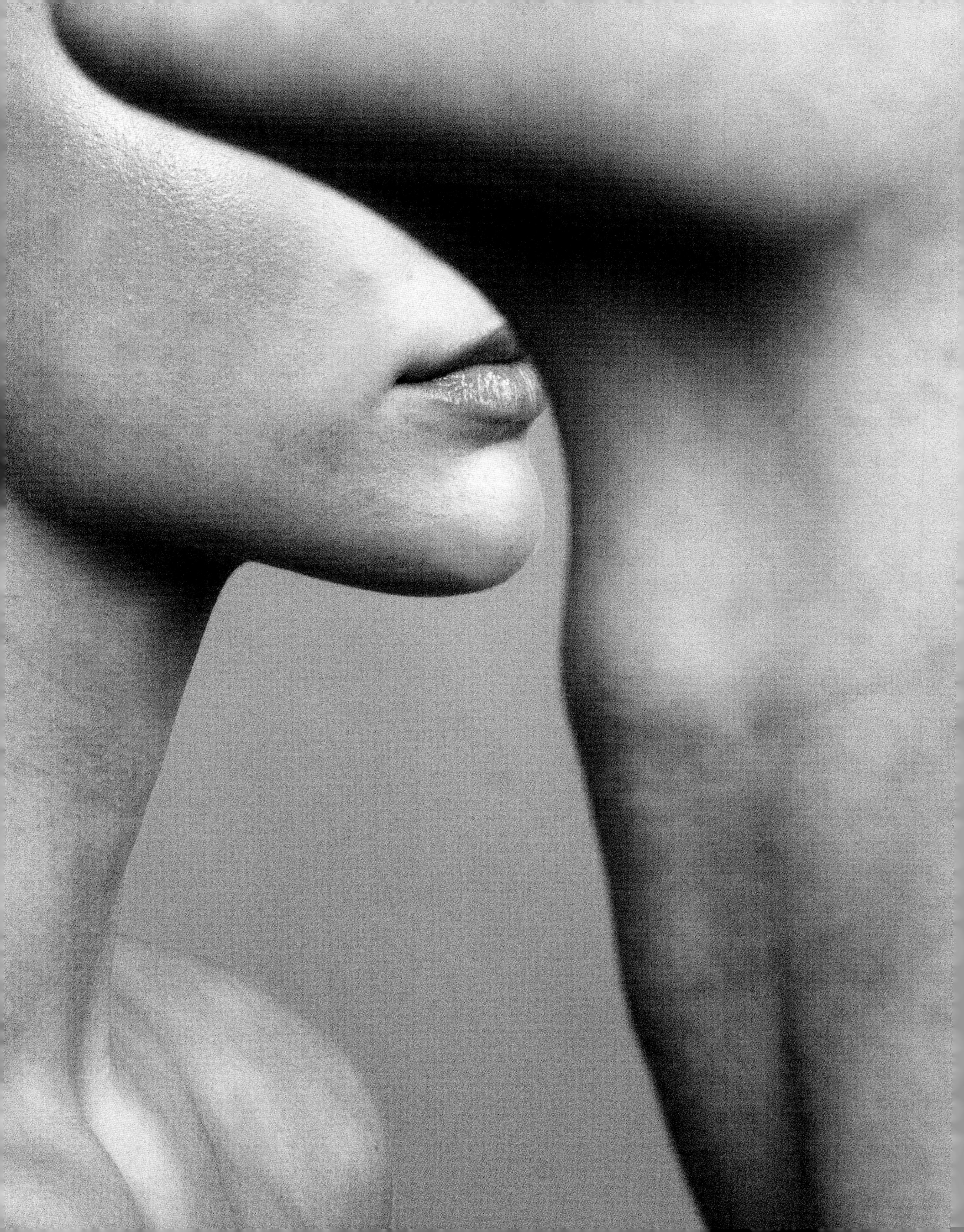

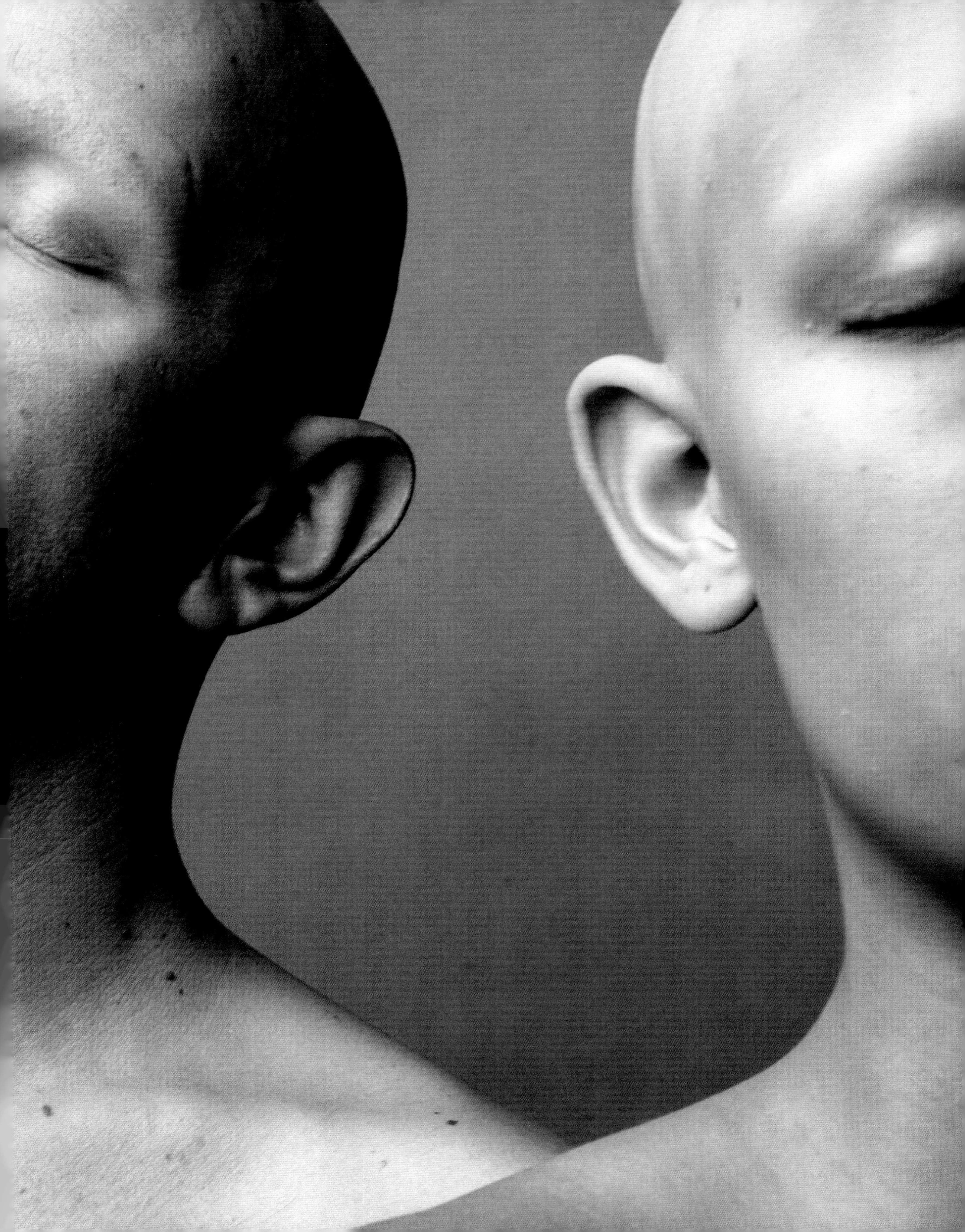

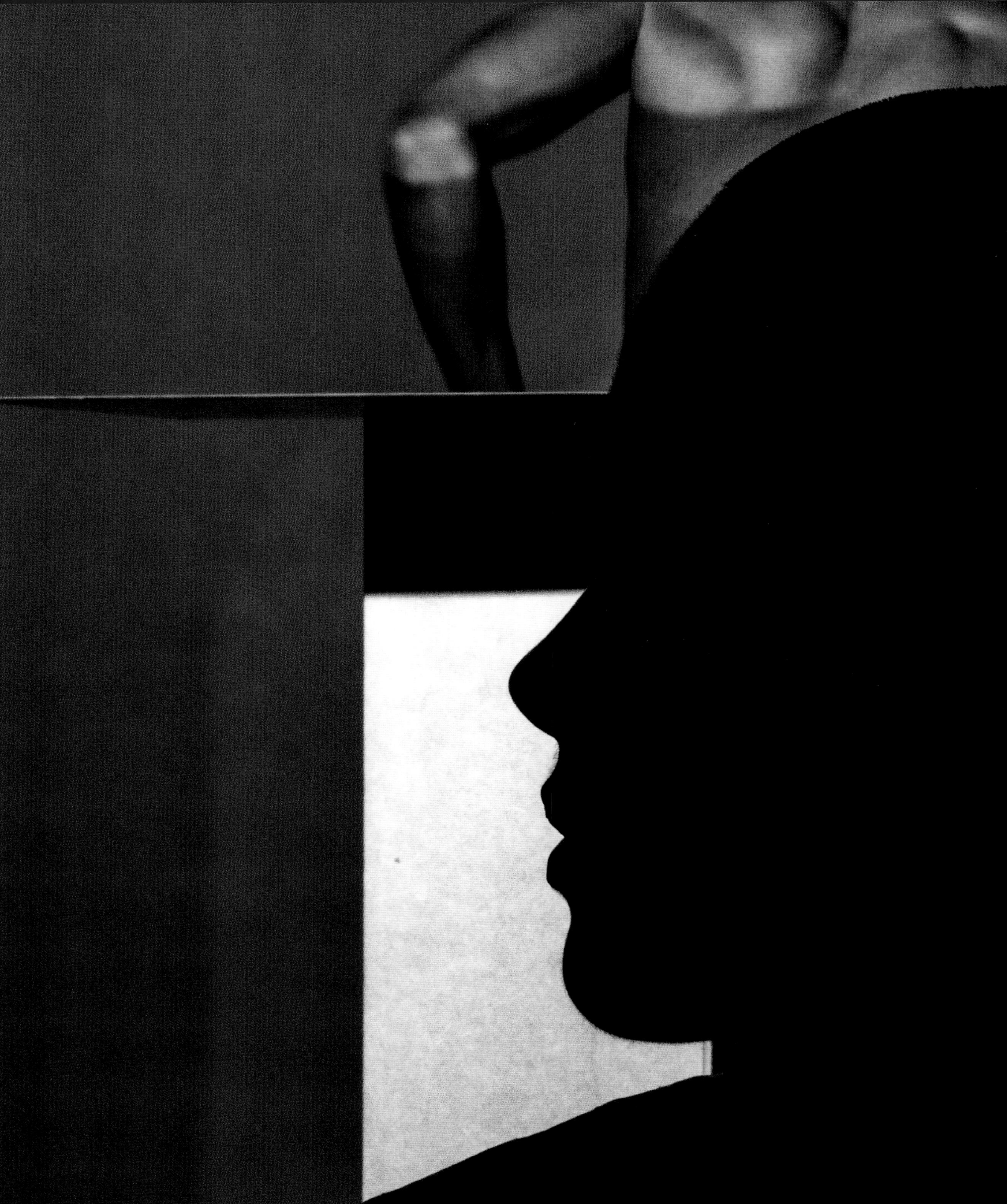

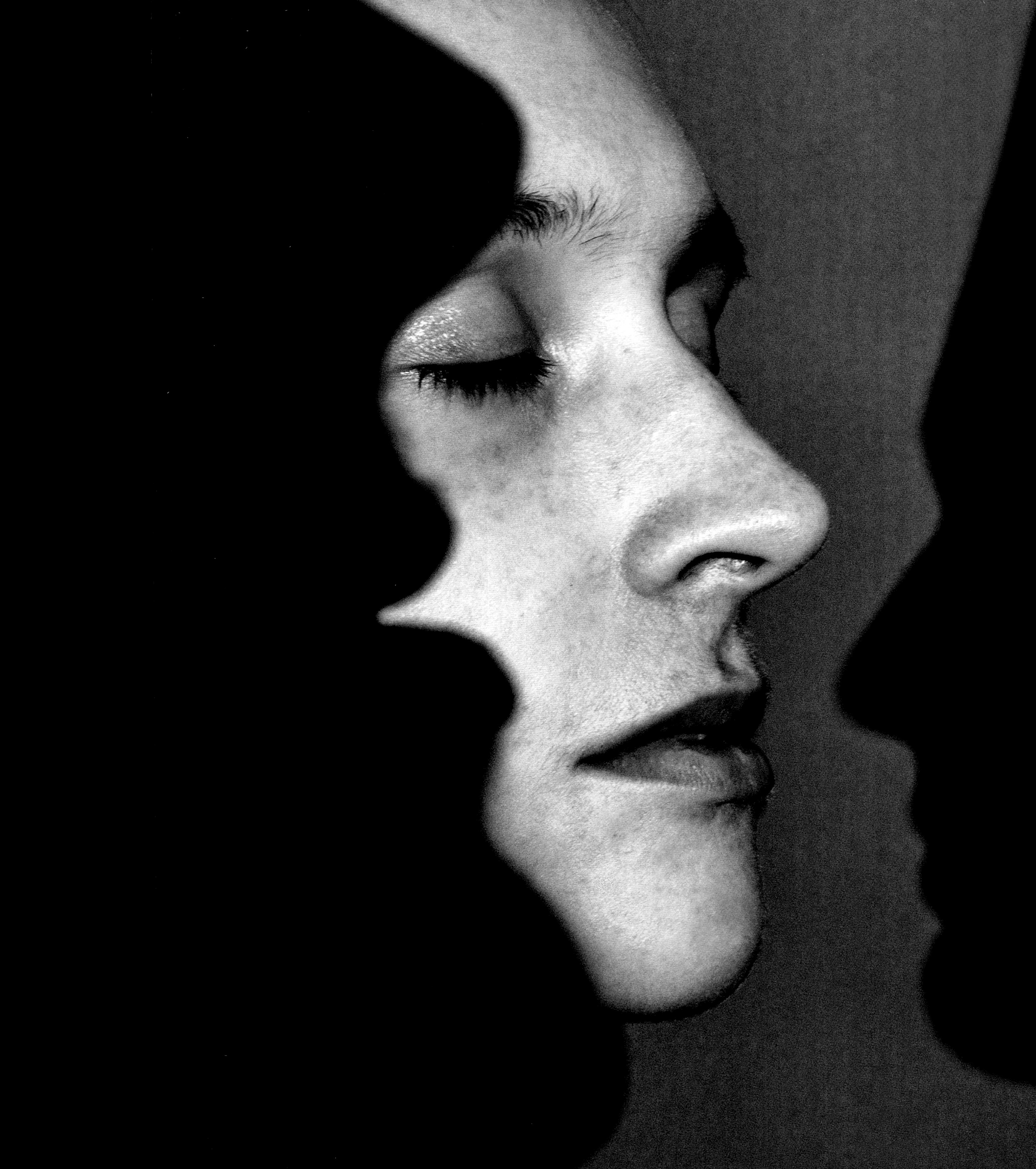

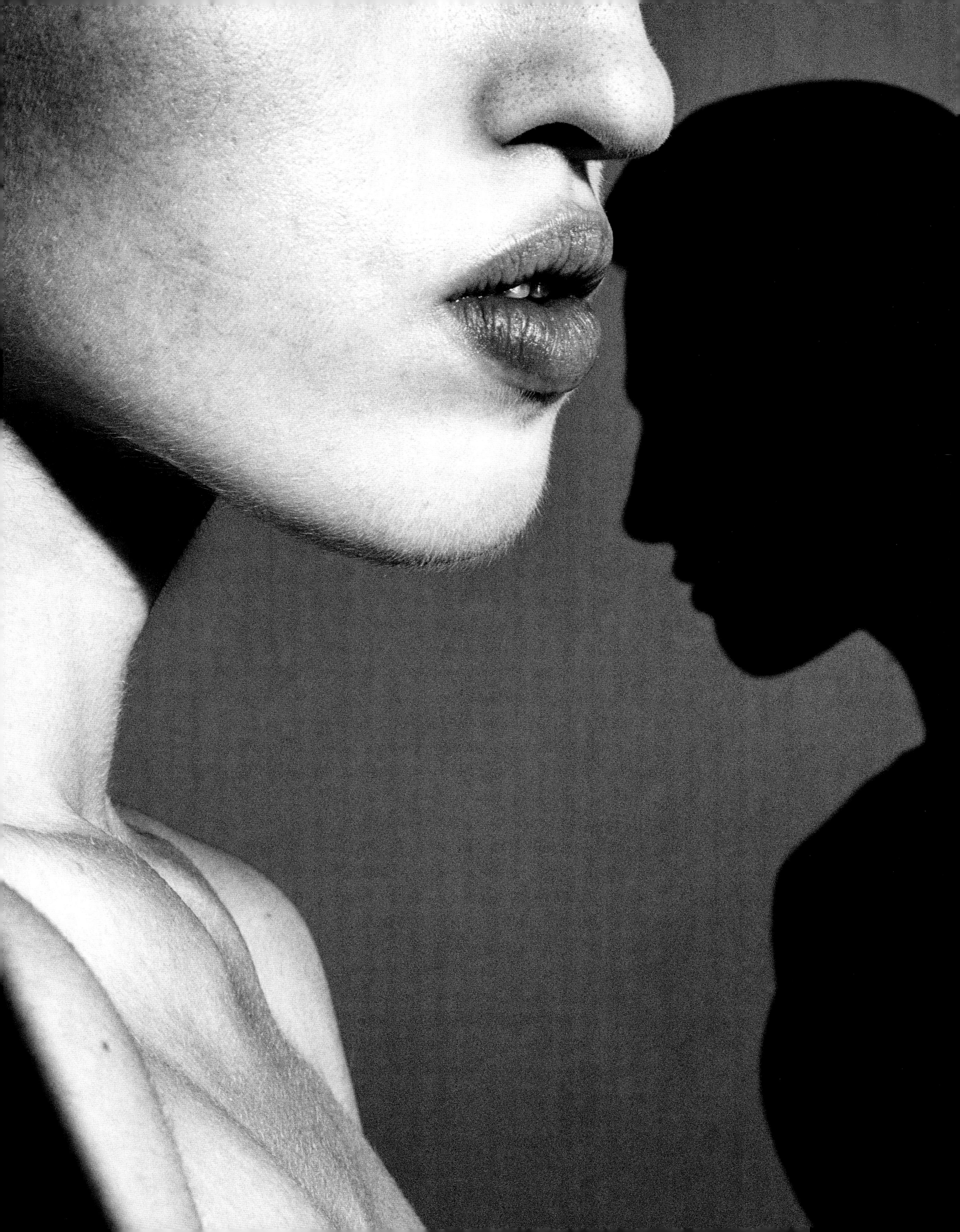

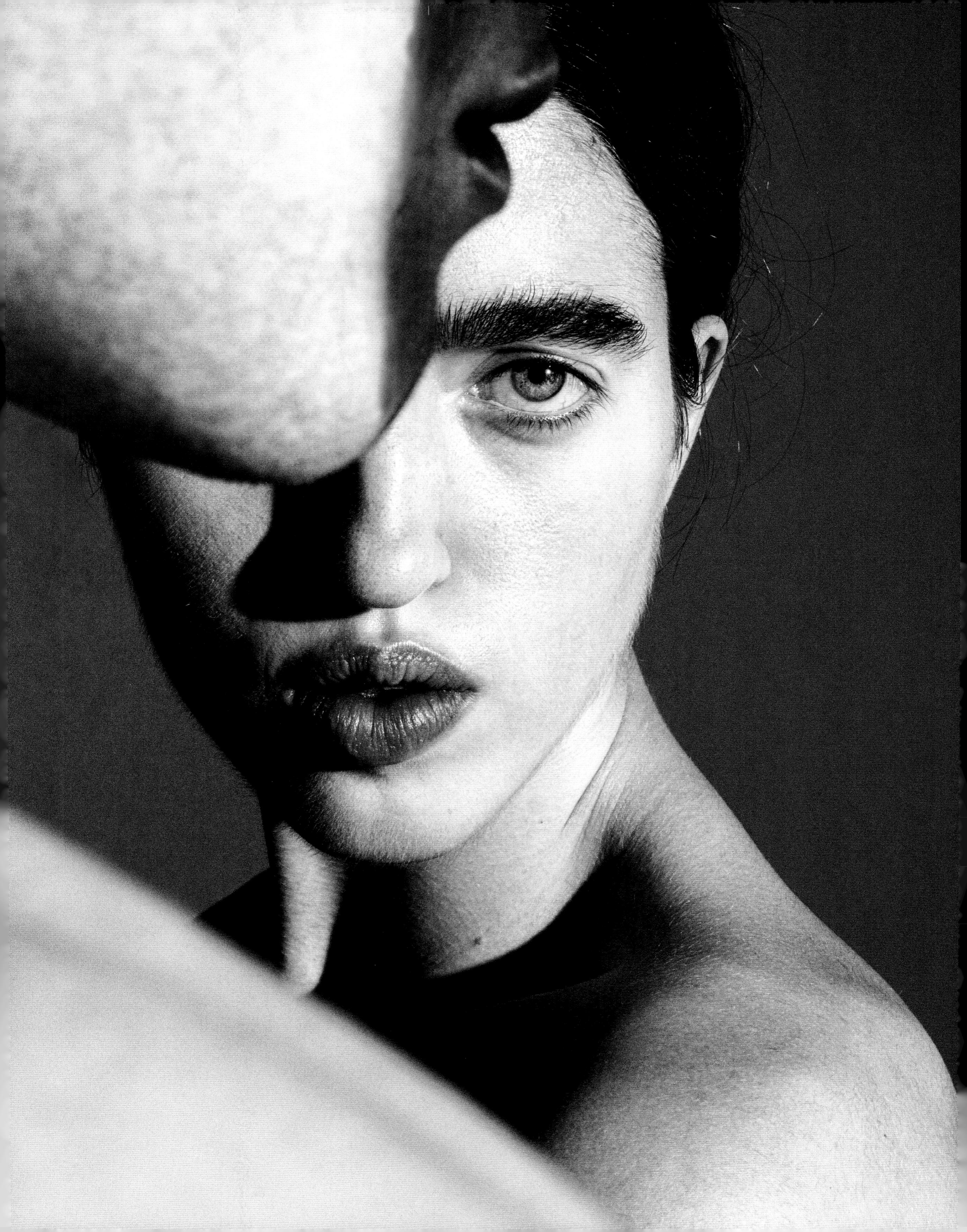

IV. THEOS

MYTHS CENTERED ON THE GODS AND THEIR DIVINE REALMS. THESE STORIES REVEAL THE POWERS, PERSONALITIES, AND COSMIC ROLES OF DEITIES WHO GOVERN NATURE, FATE, AND HUMAN DESTINY.

ANASTASIA MIHAYLOVA

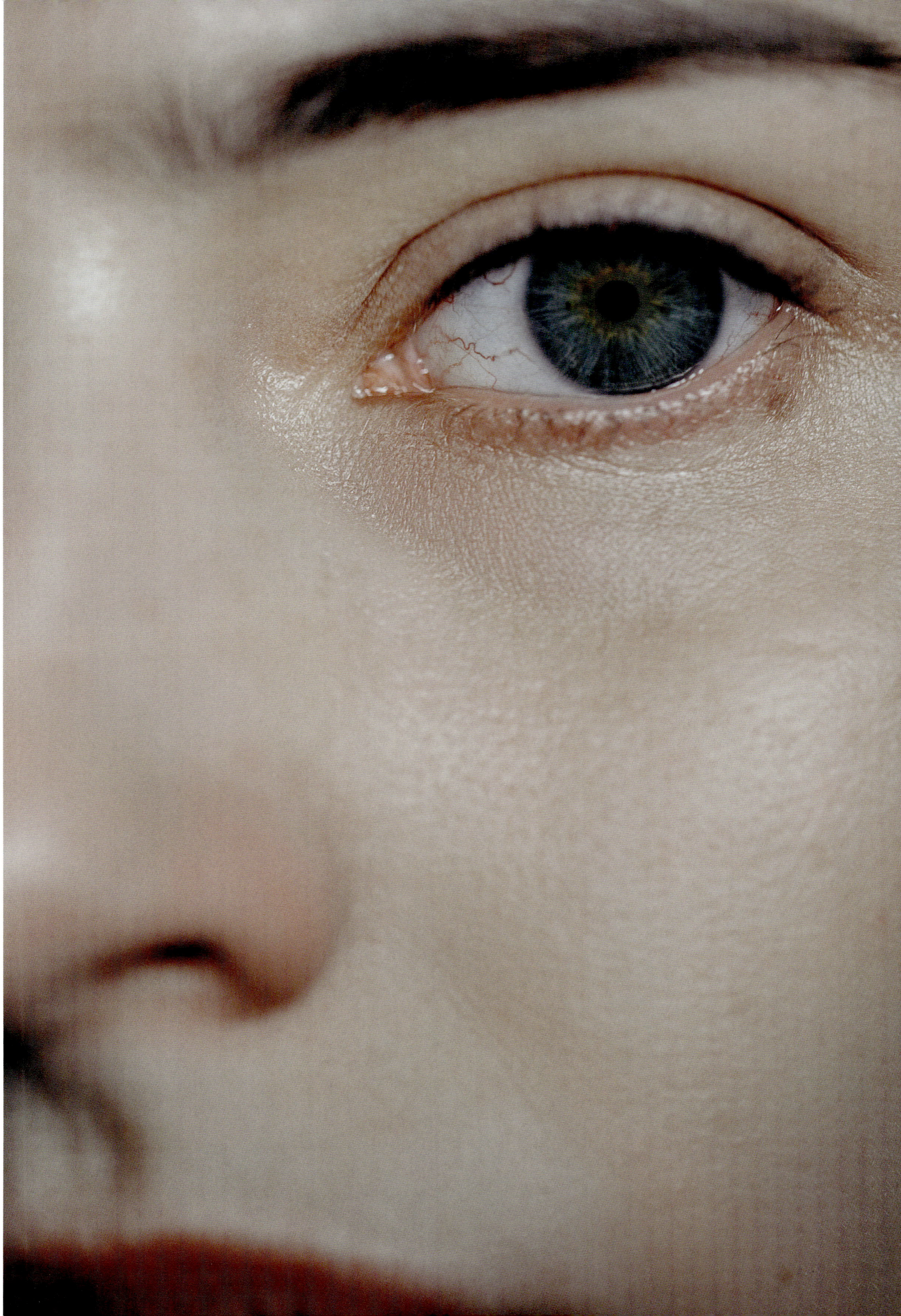

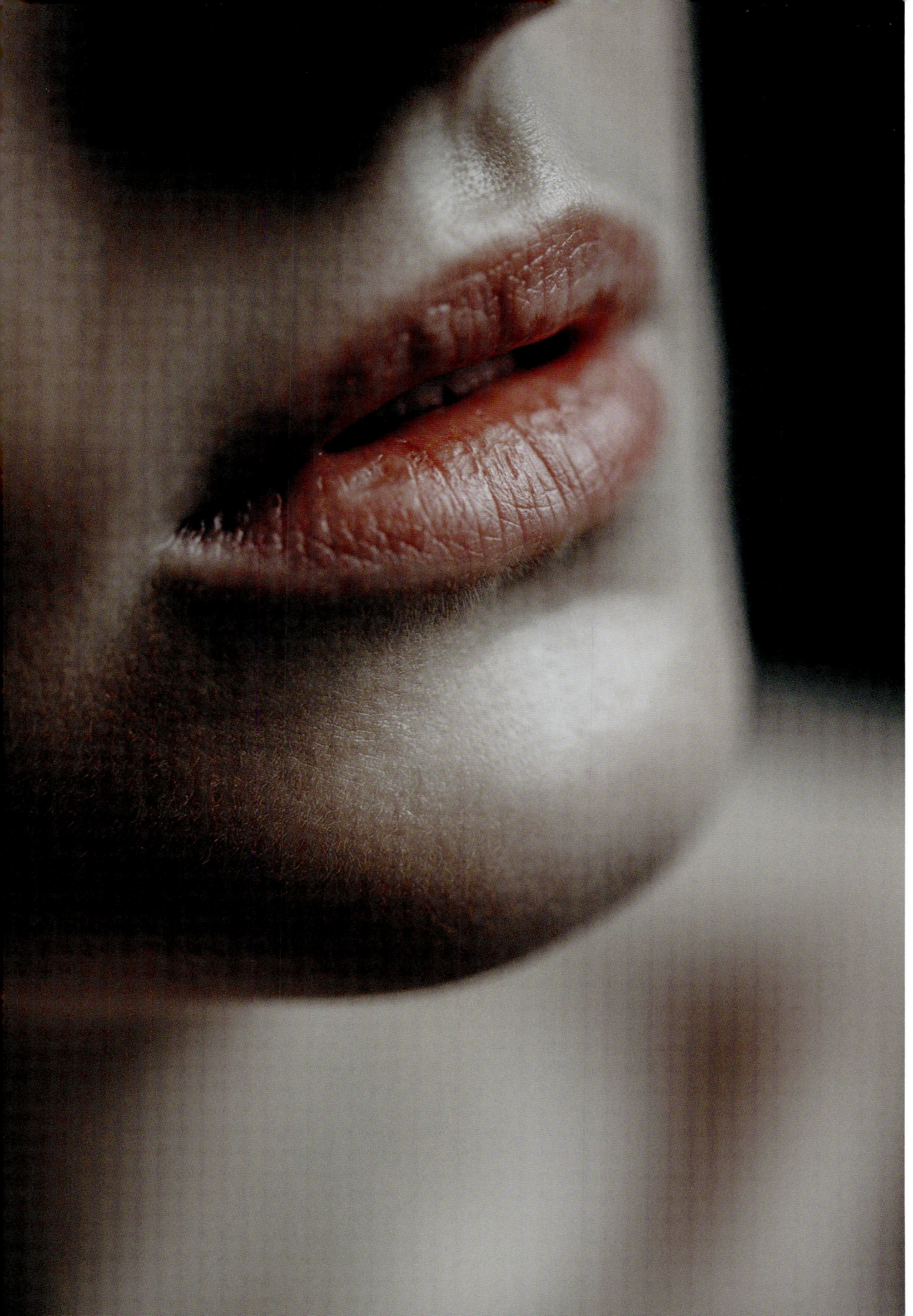

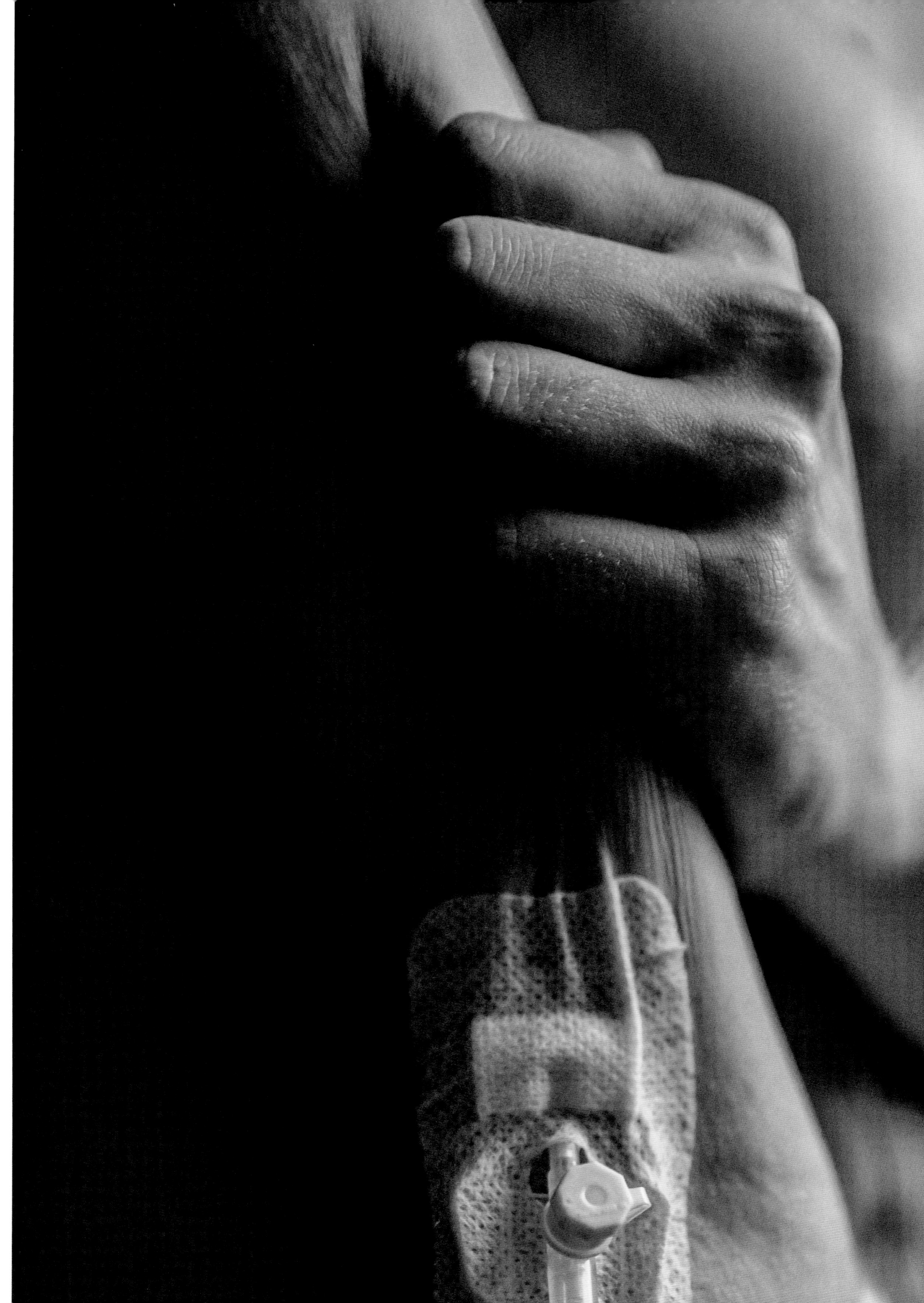

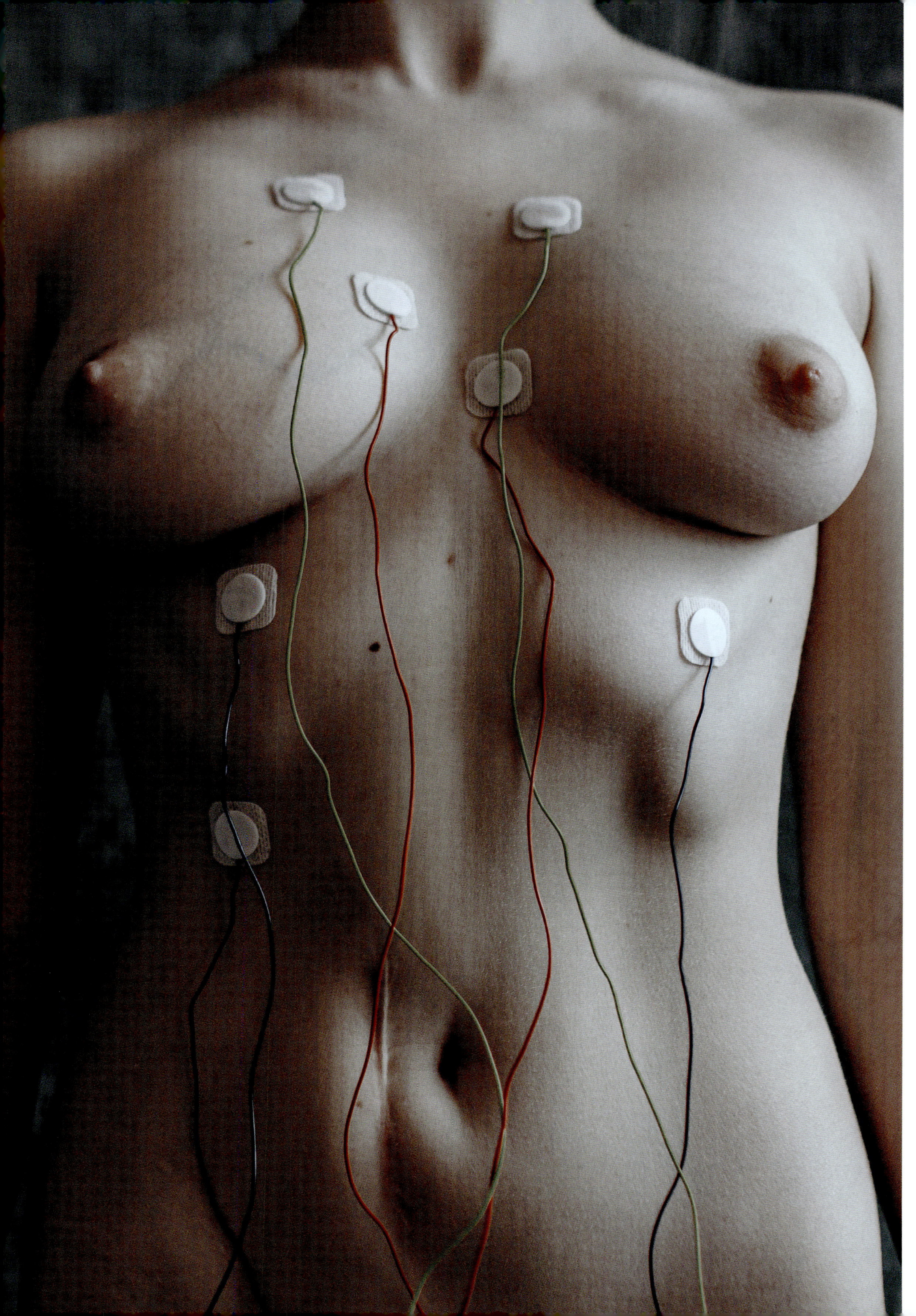

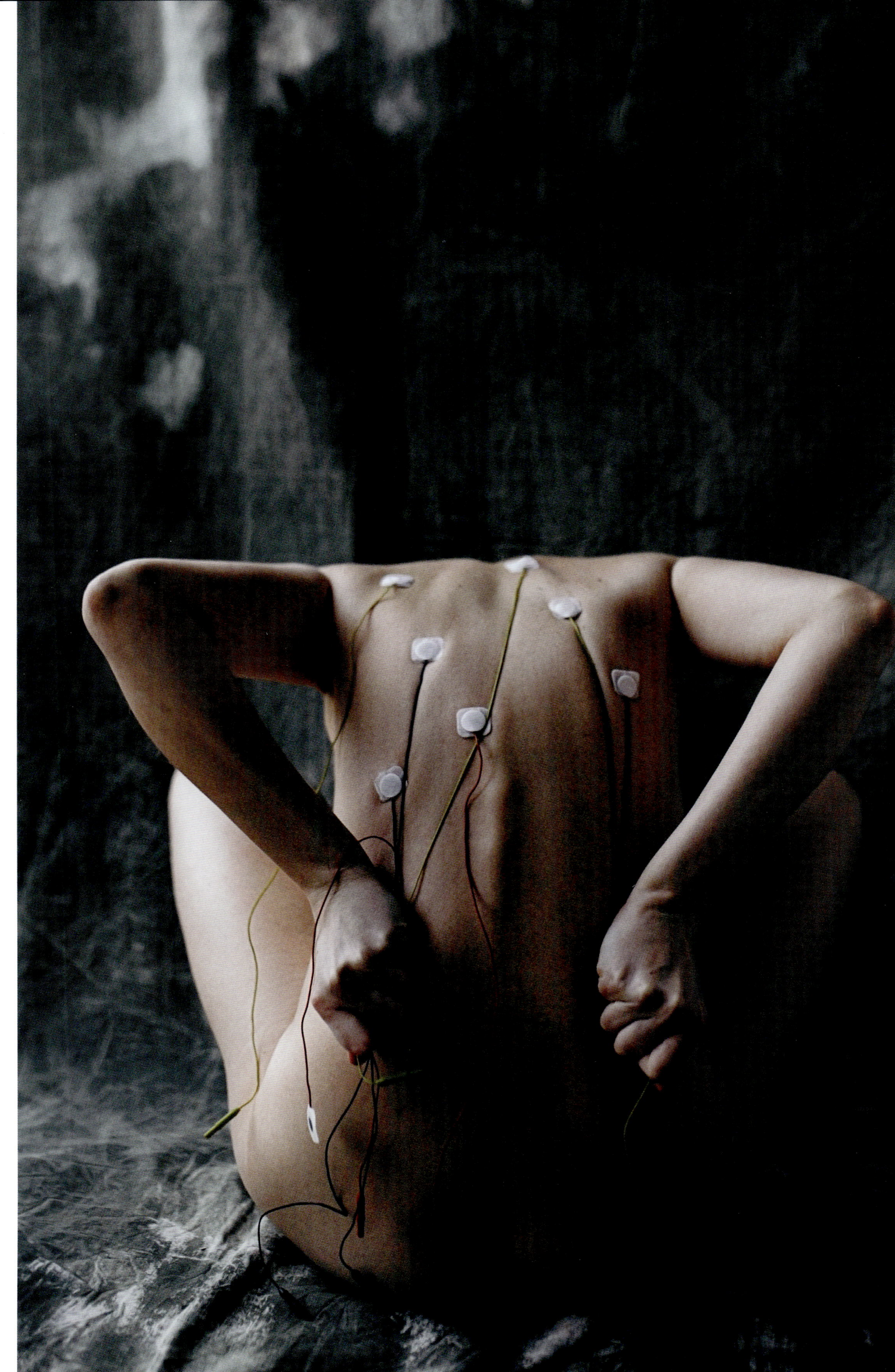

138

DARIA
GAIDUK

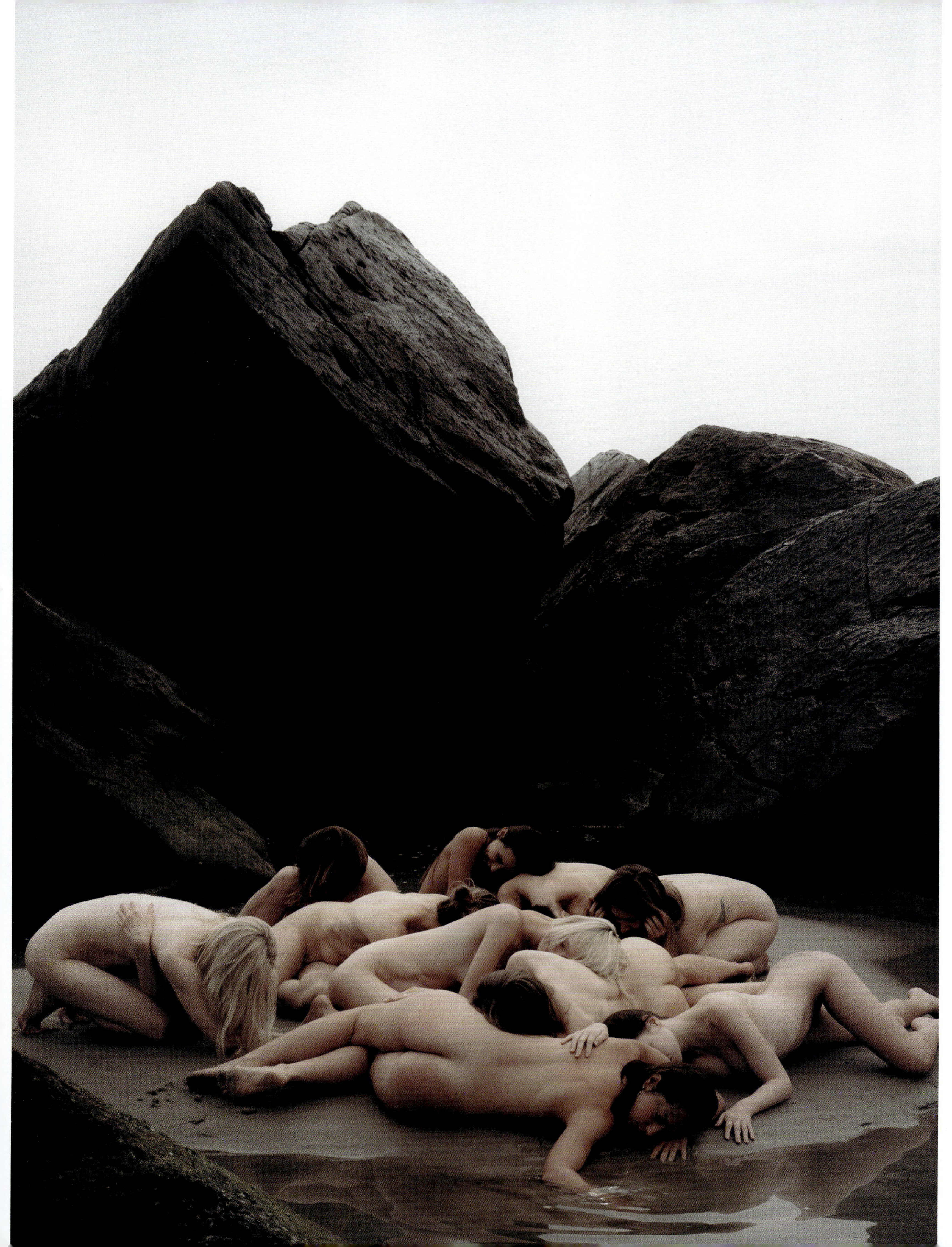

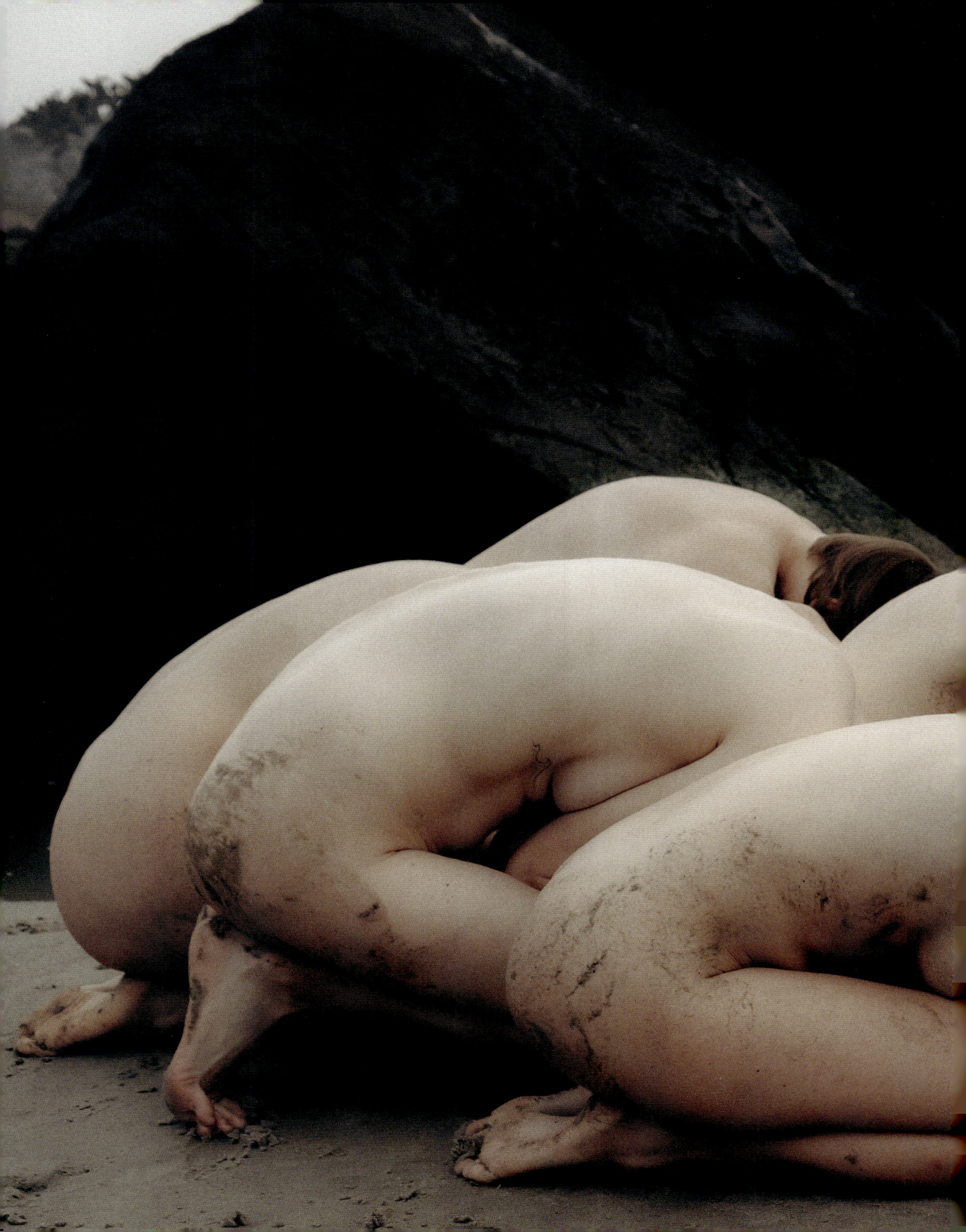

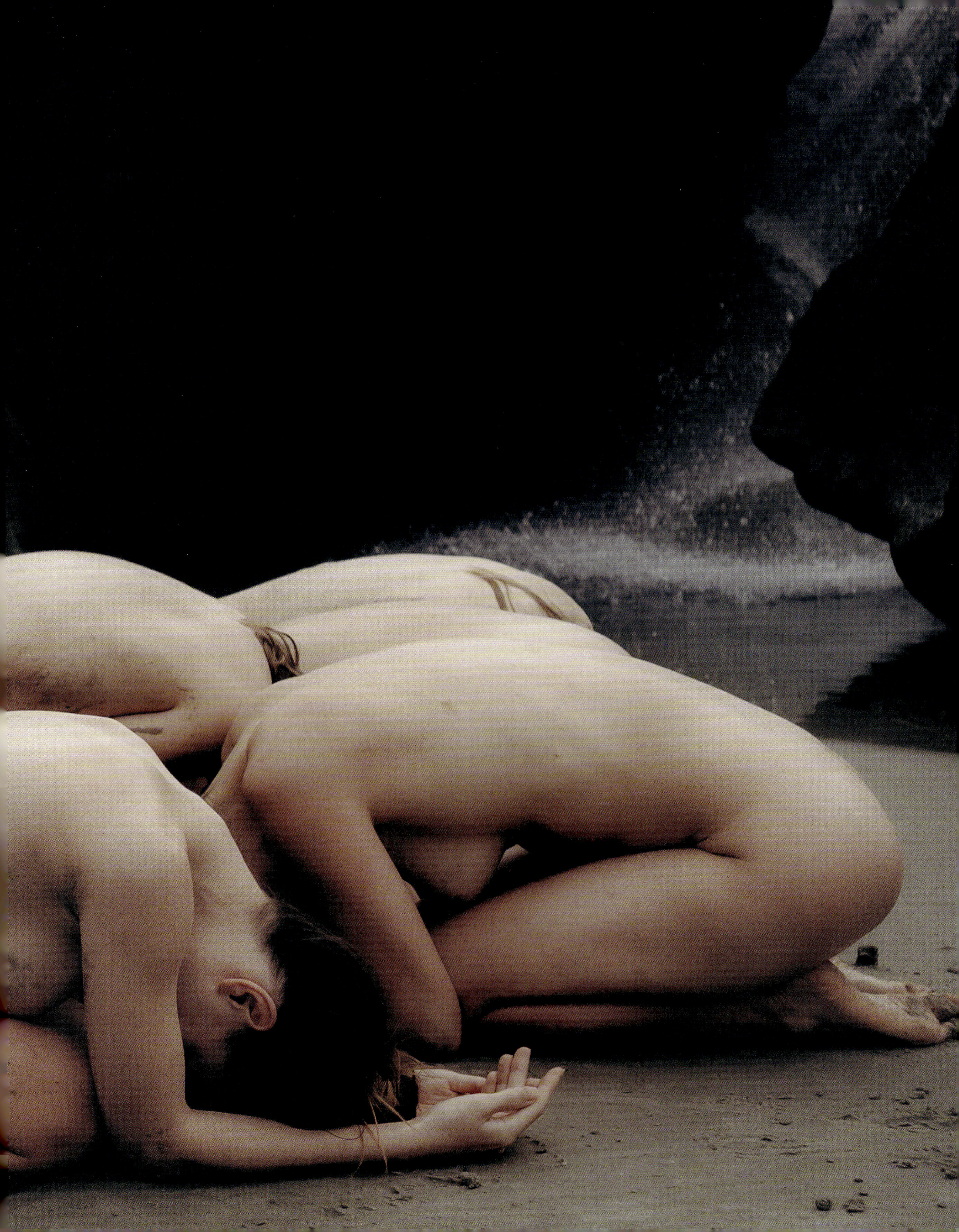

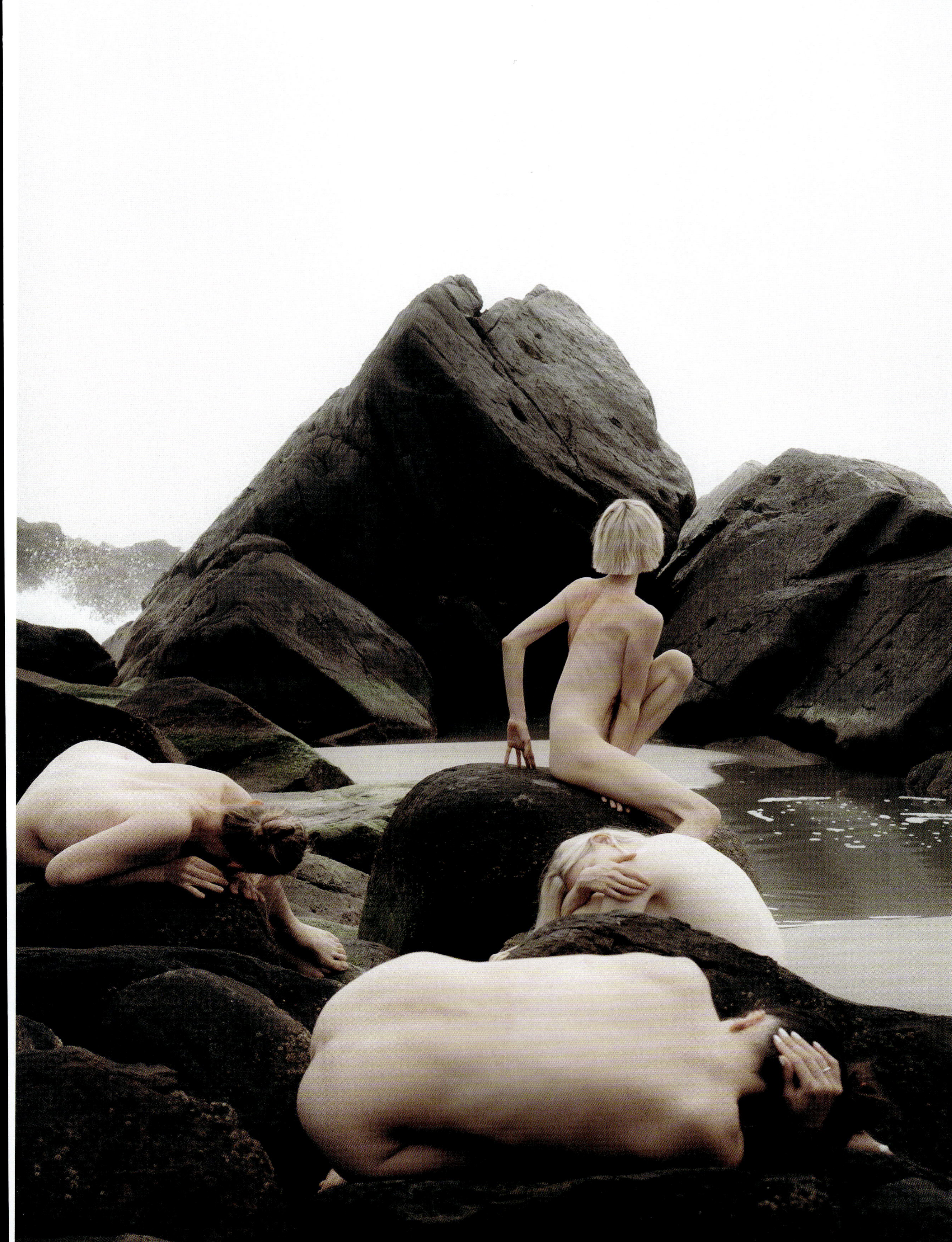

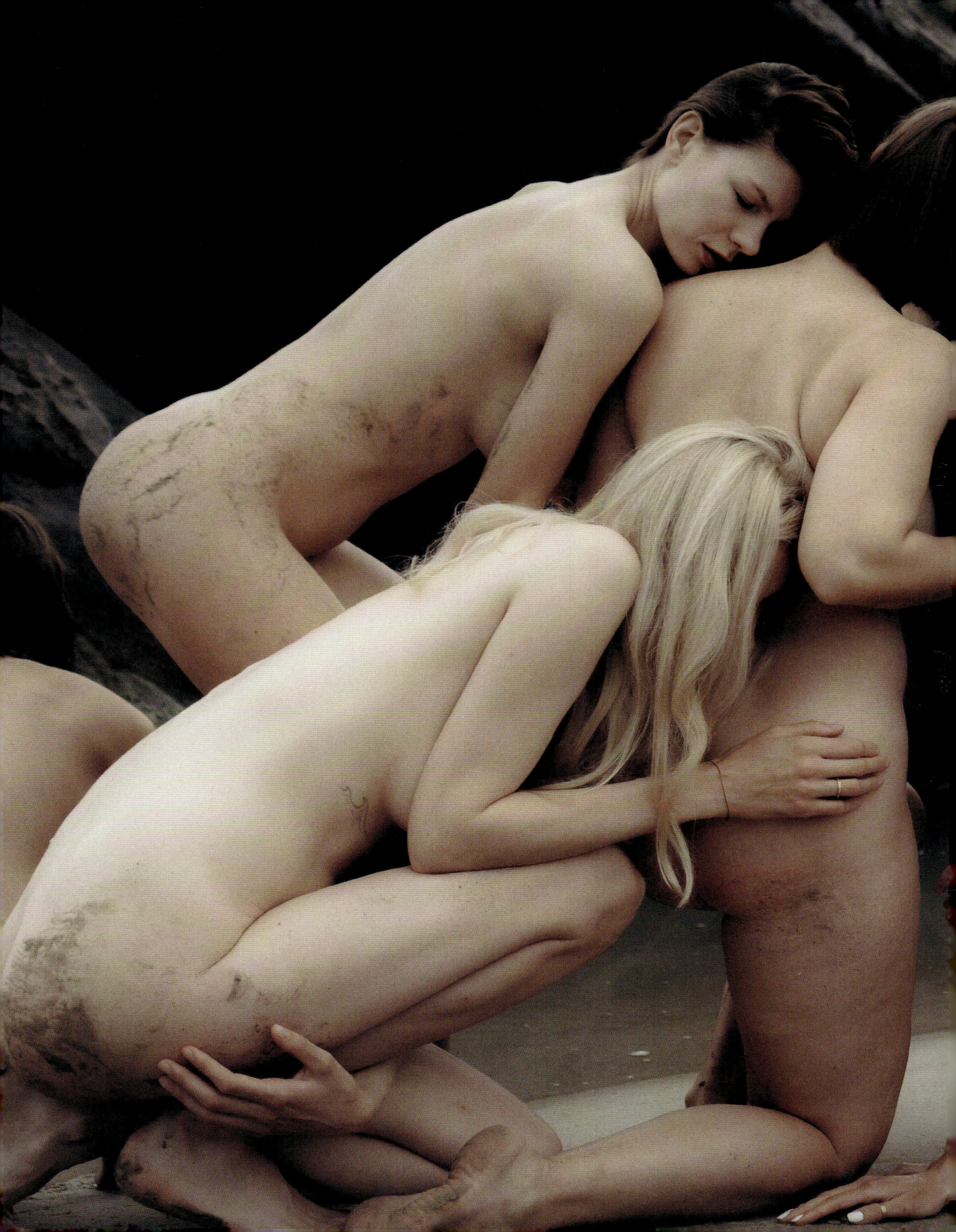

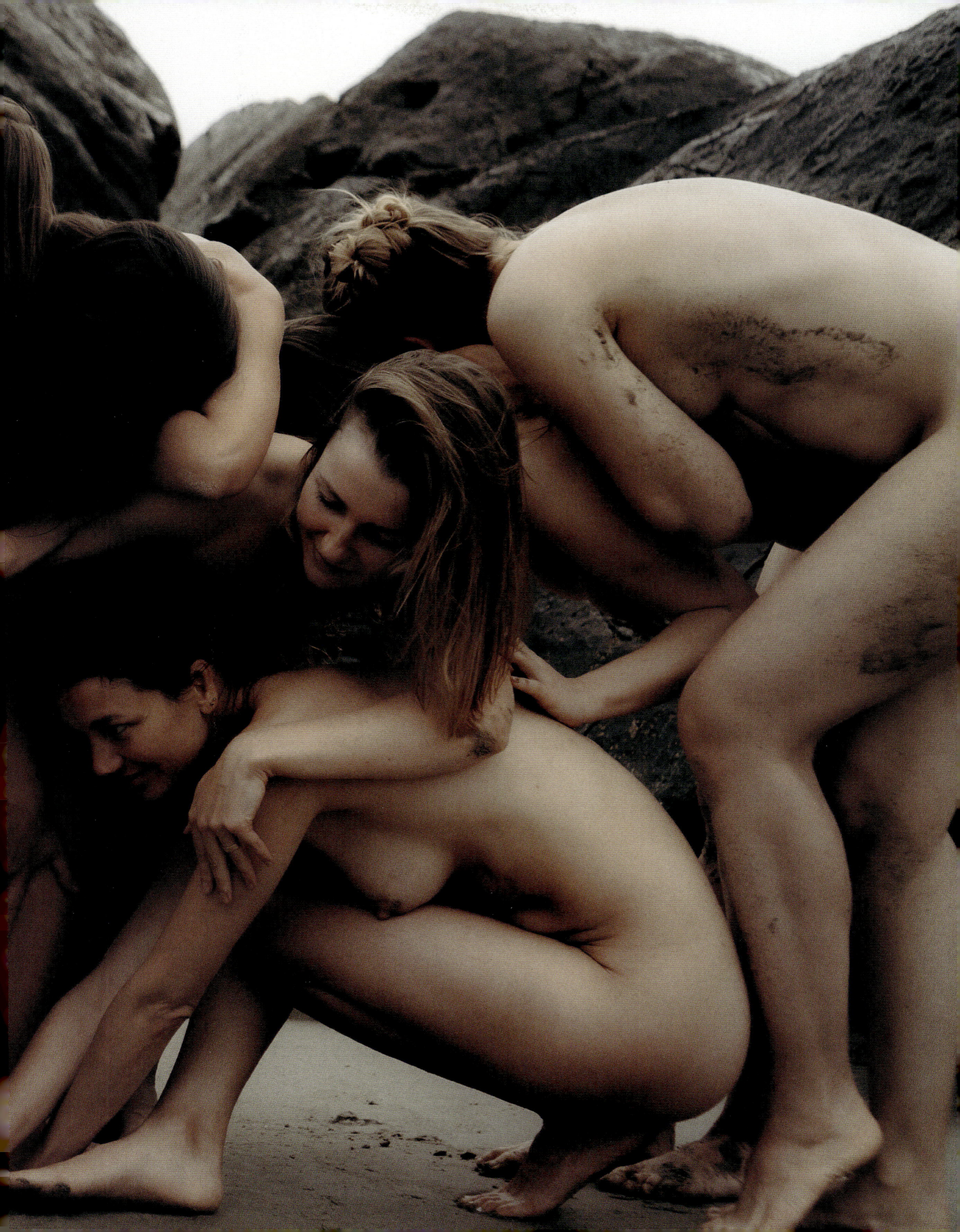

NANANANO

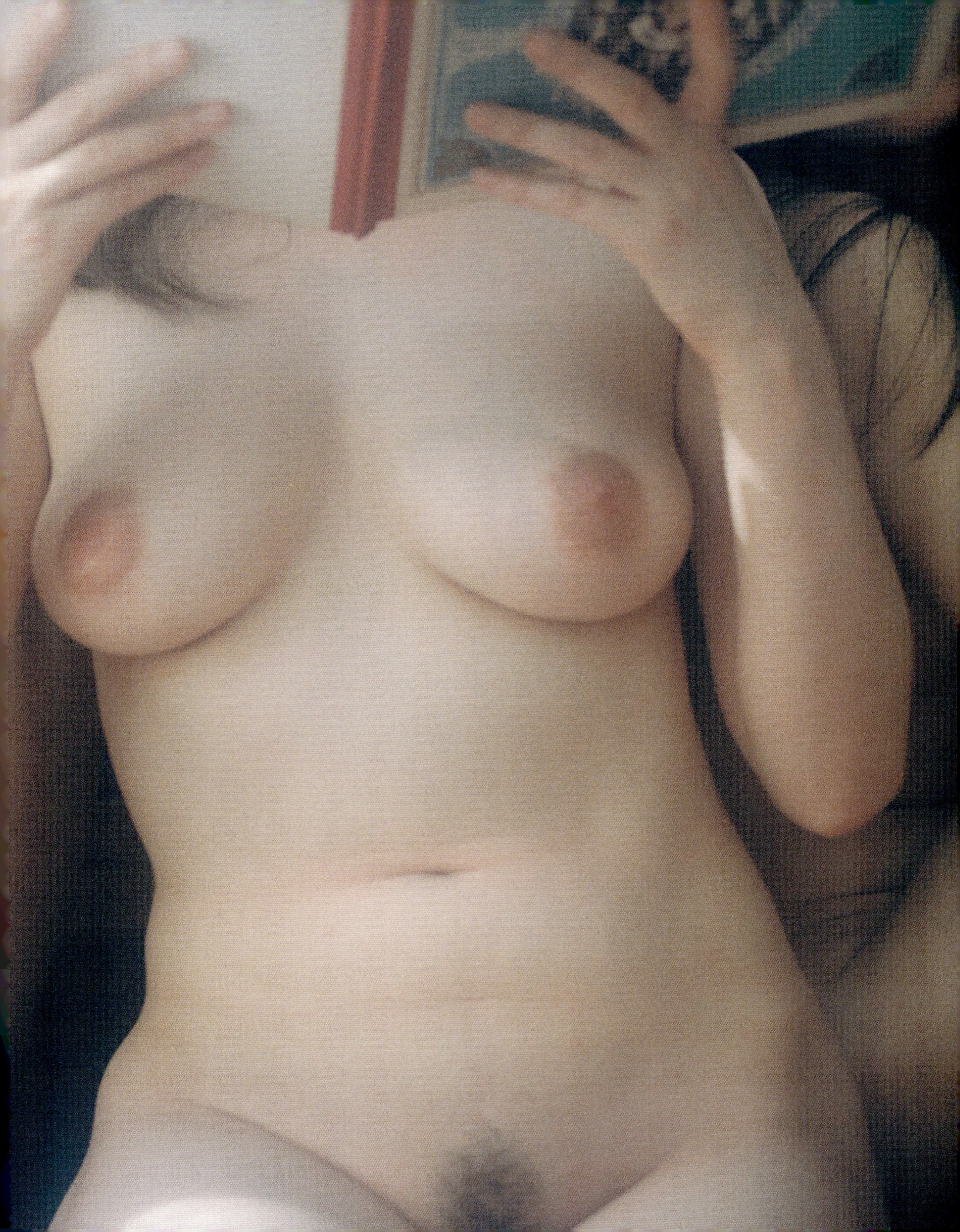

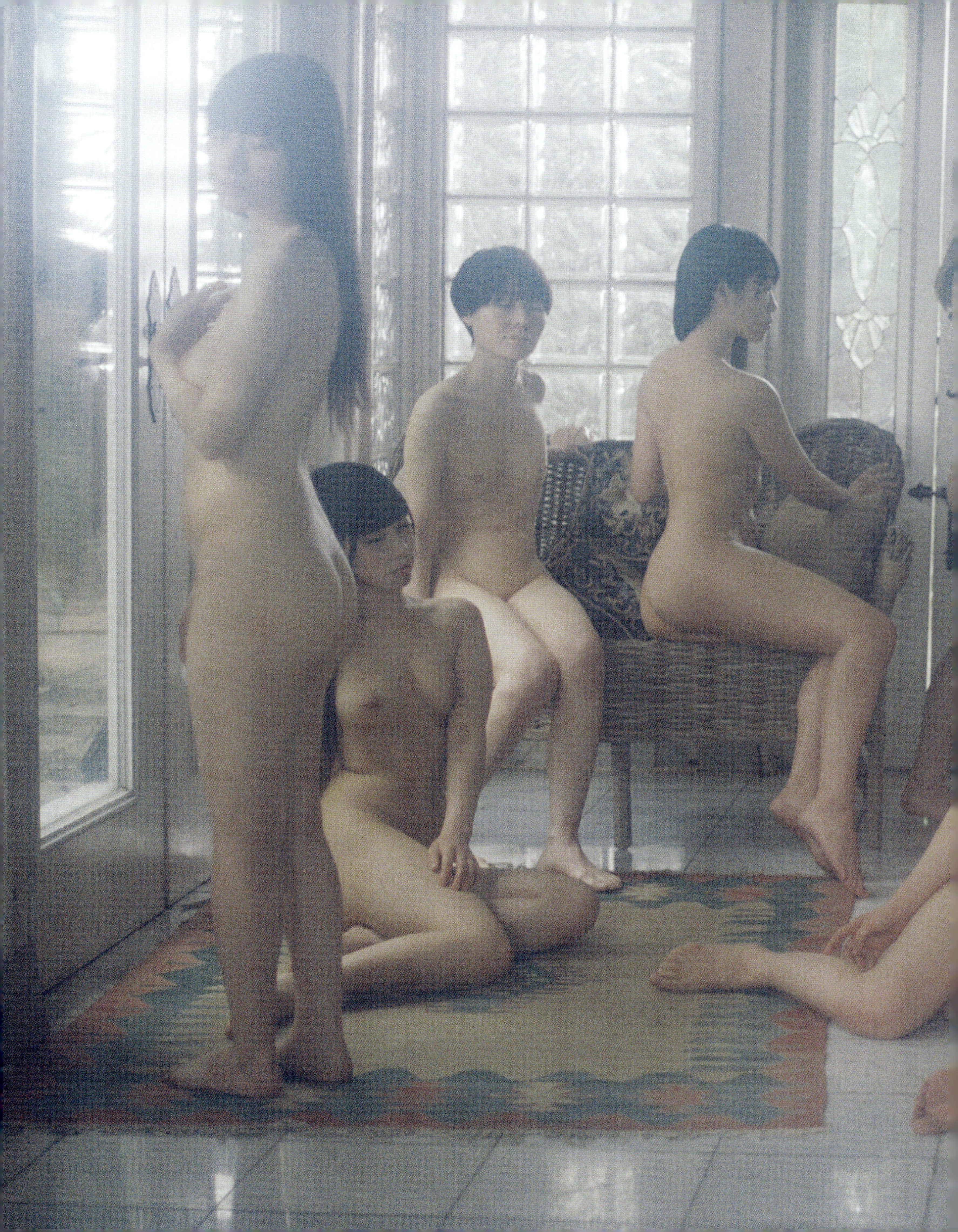

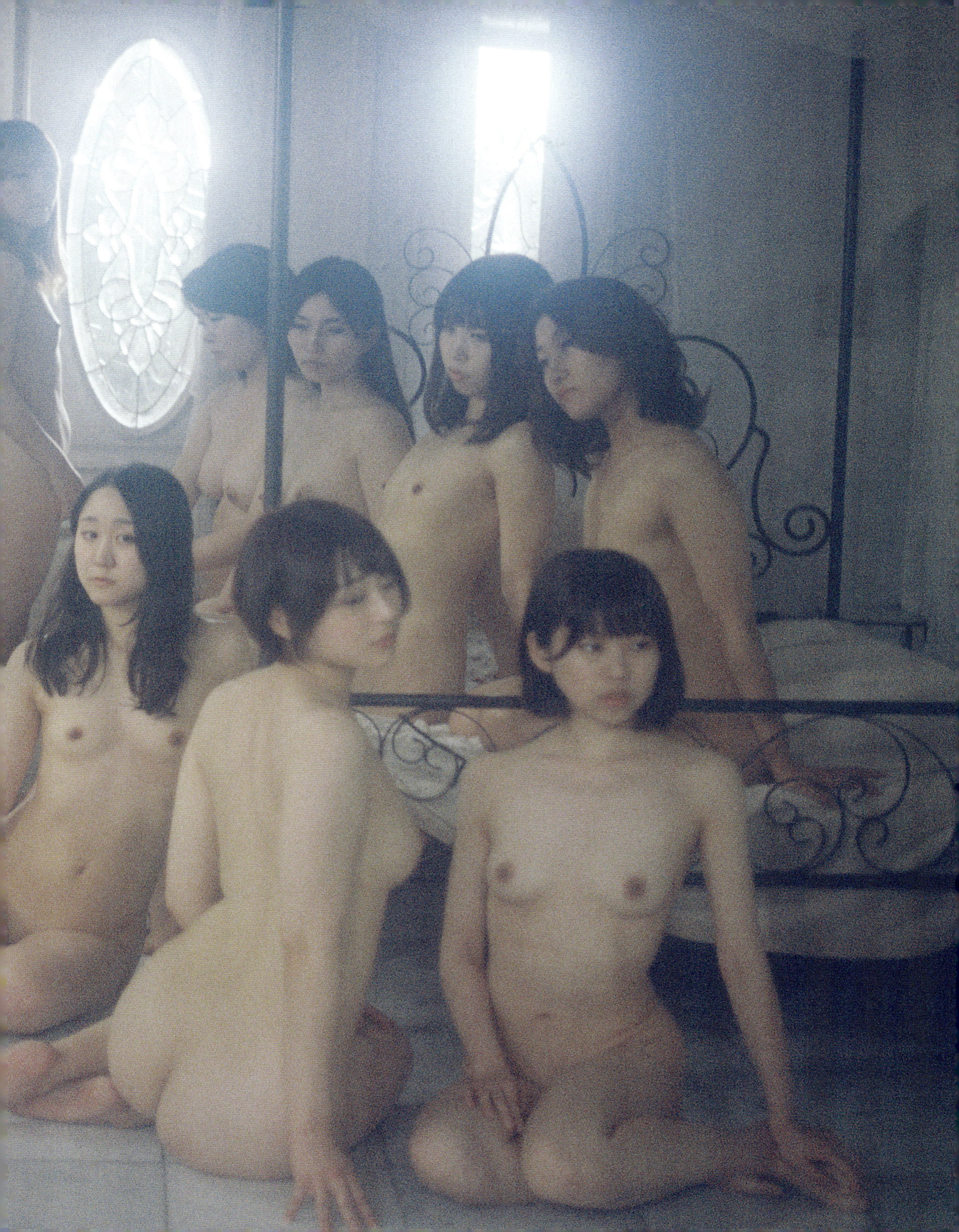

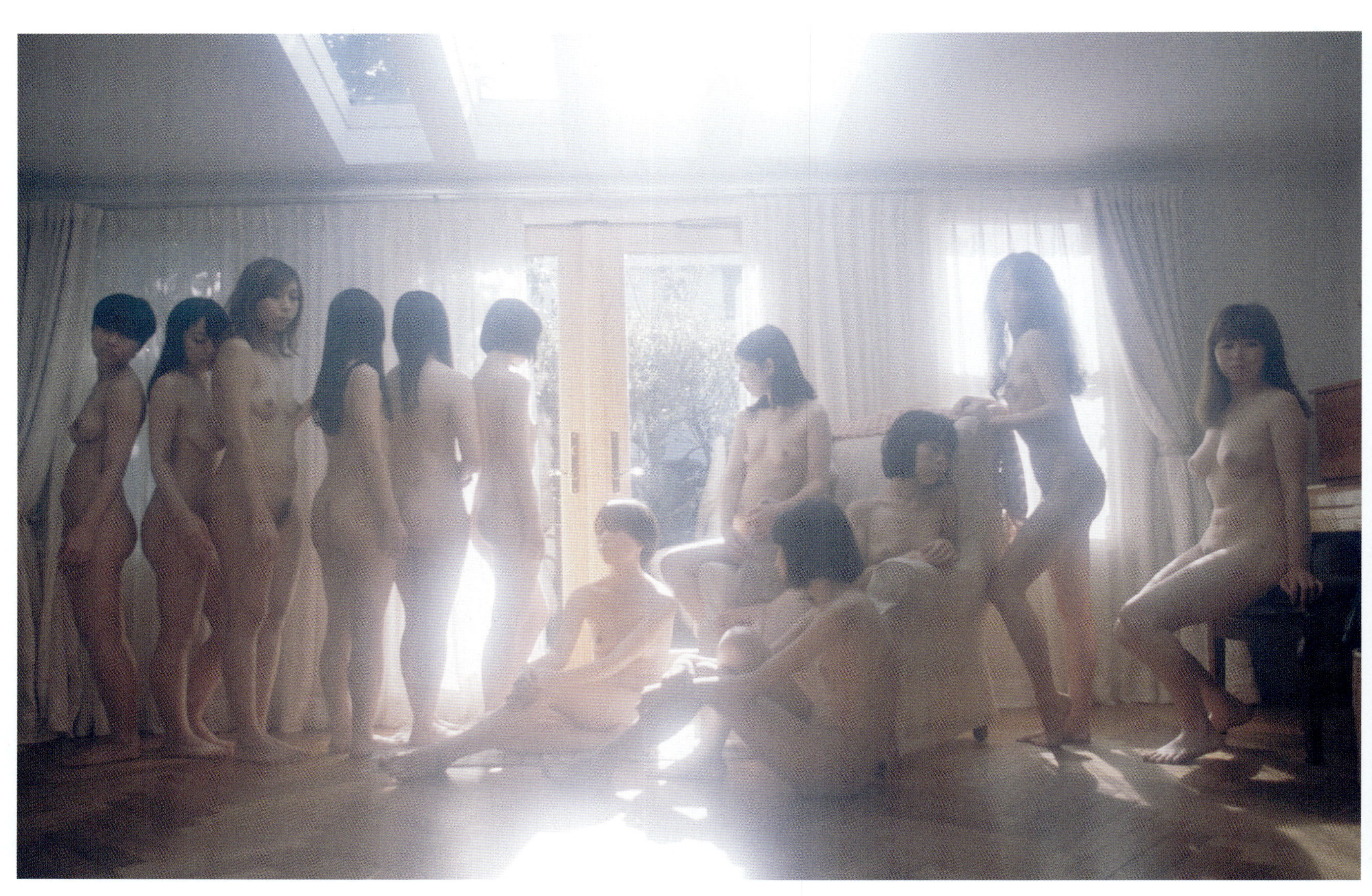

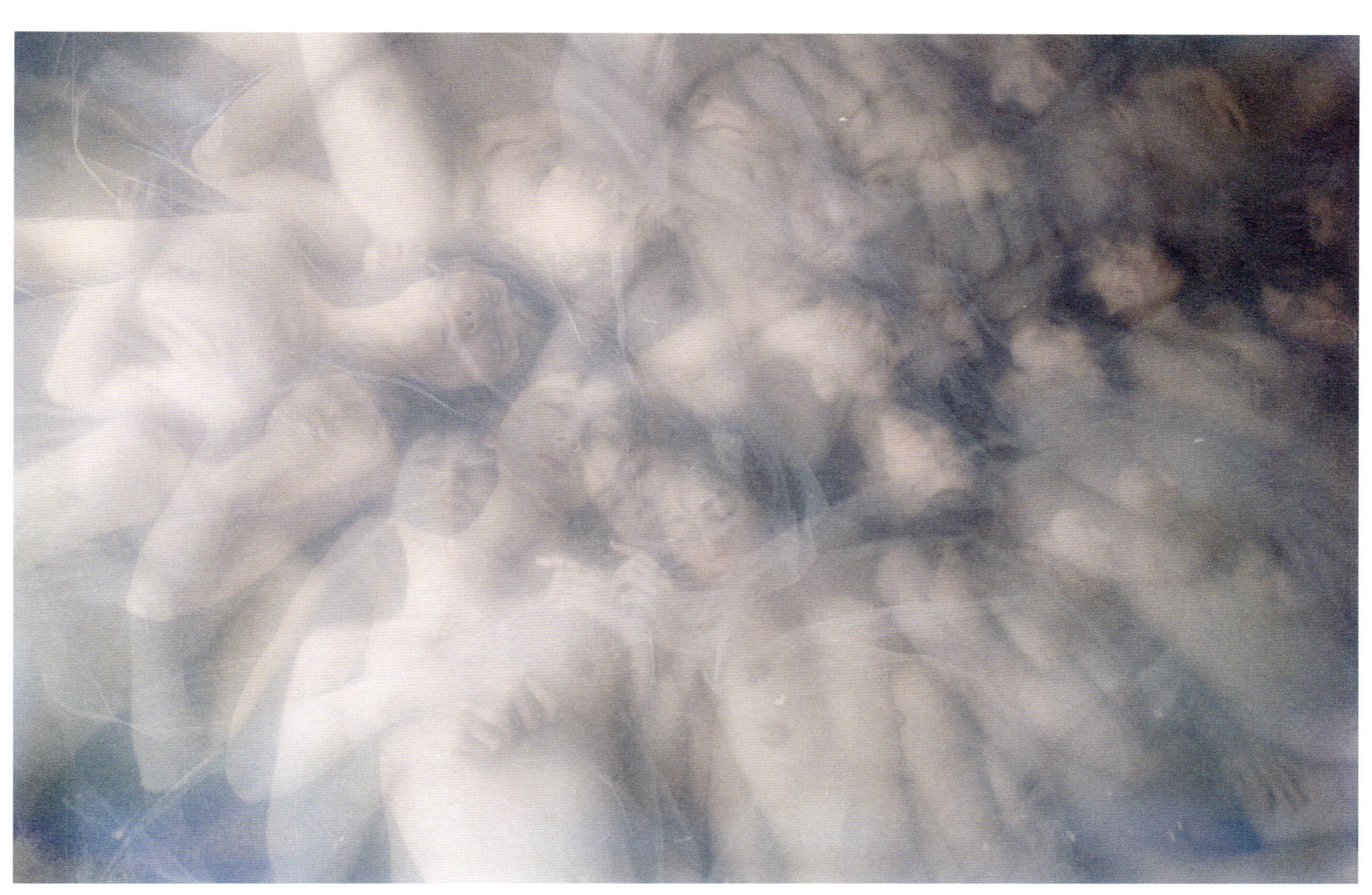

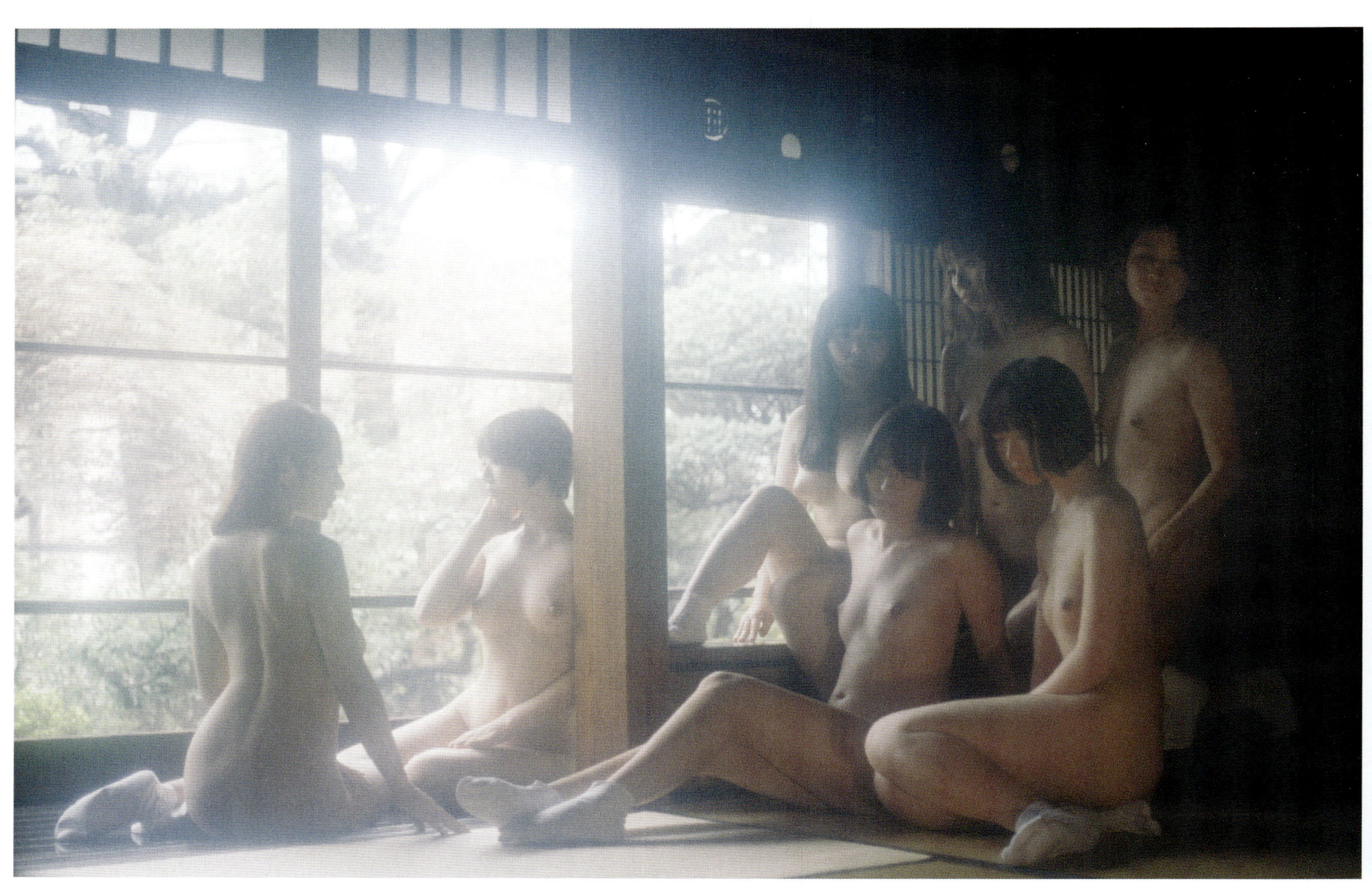

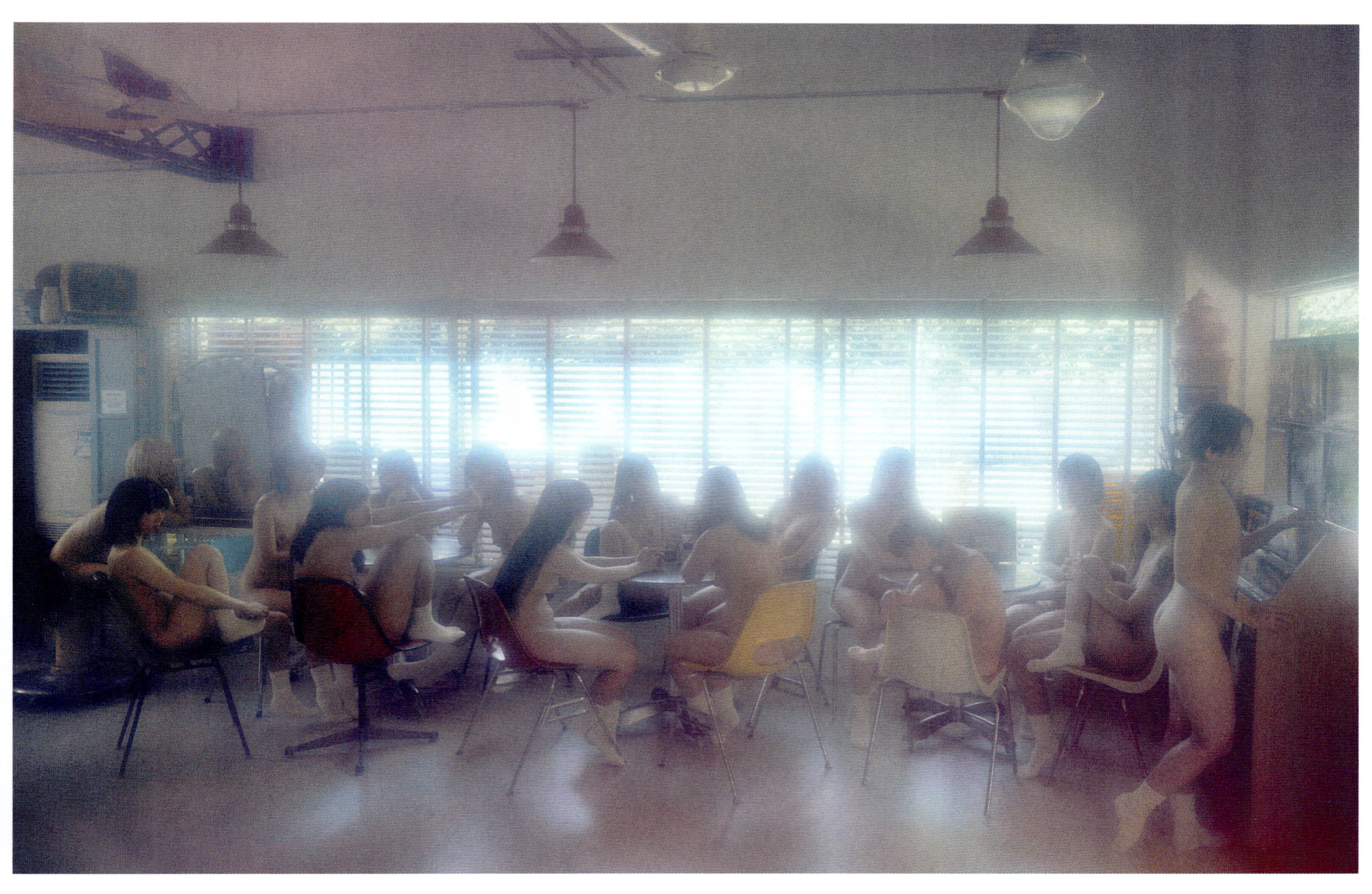

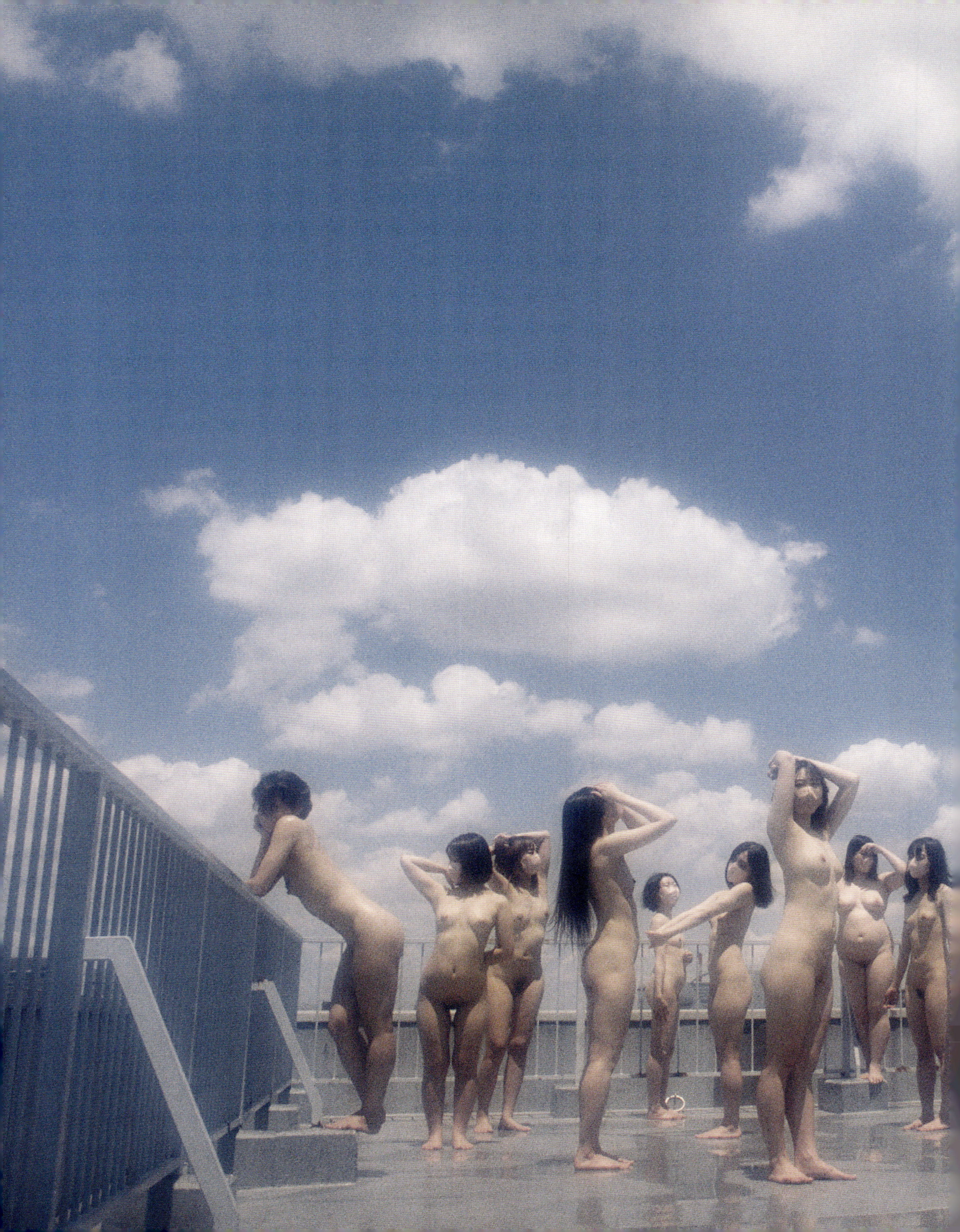

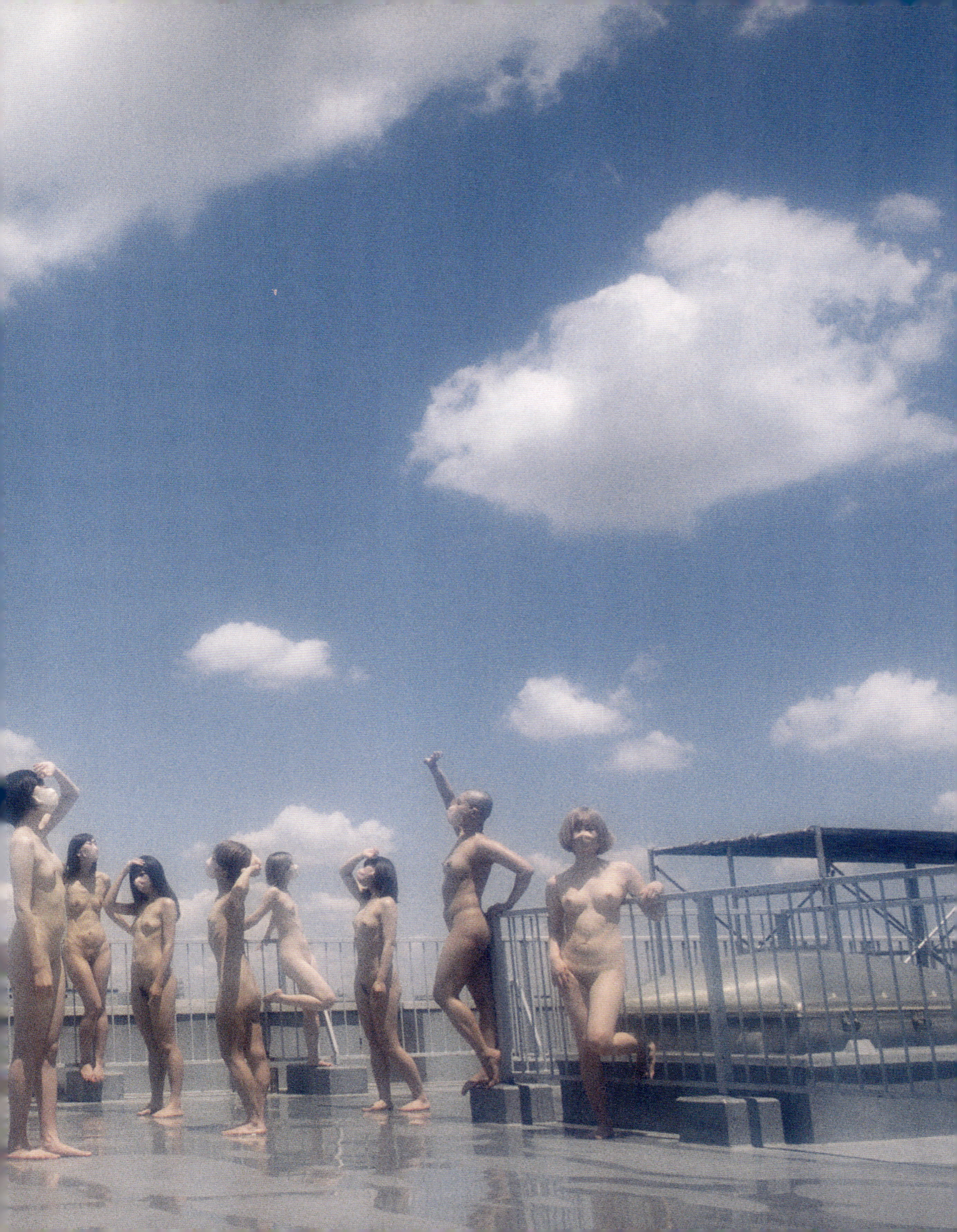

MALCOLM SINCLAIR LOBBAN

ÁLFKONA

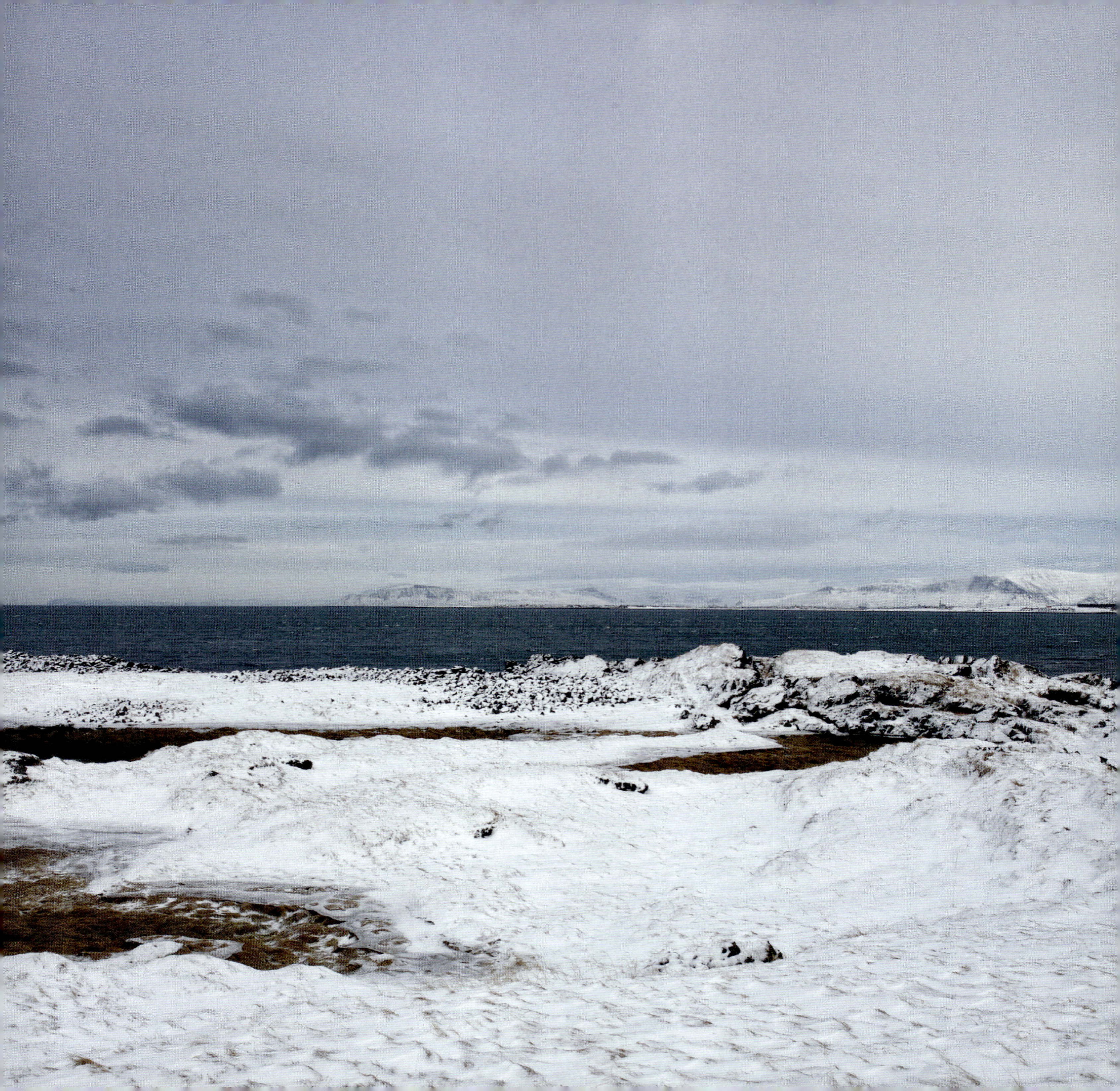

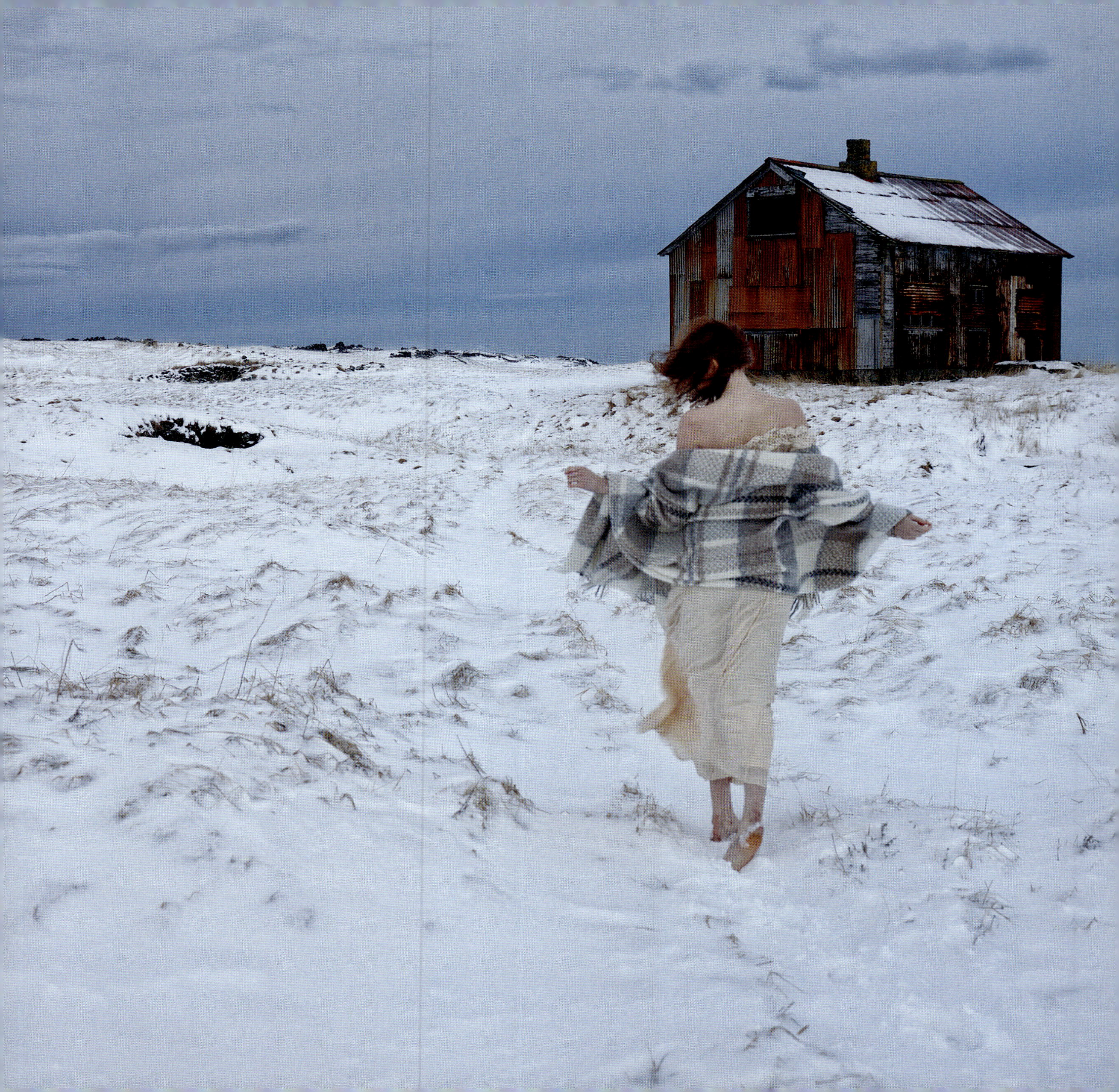

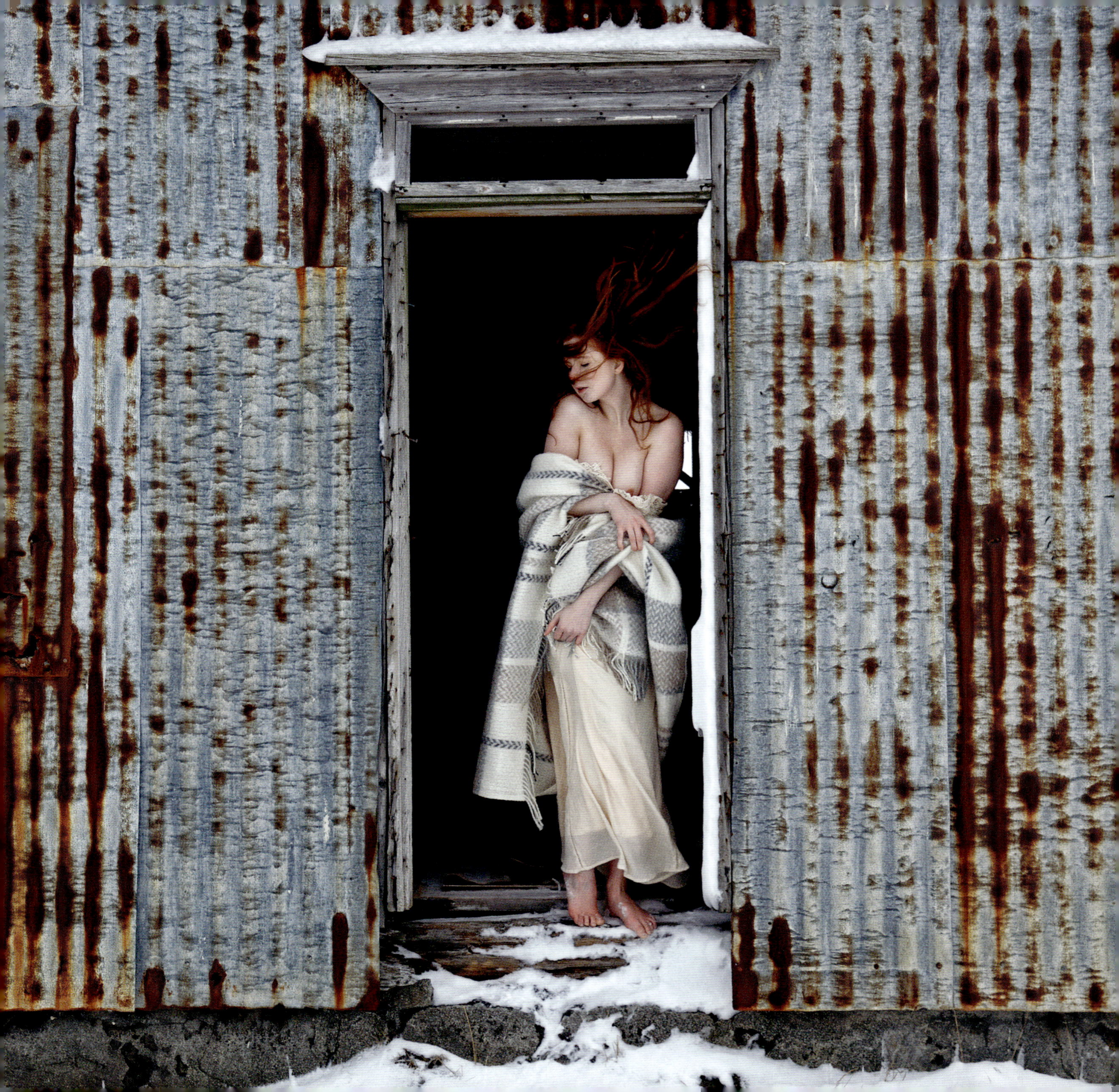

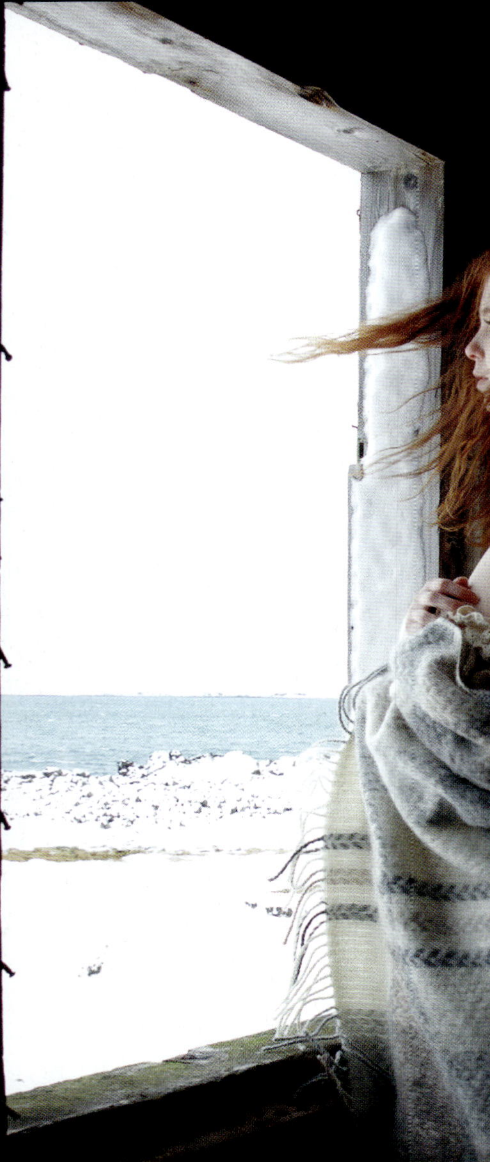

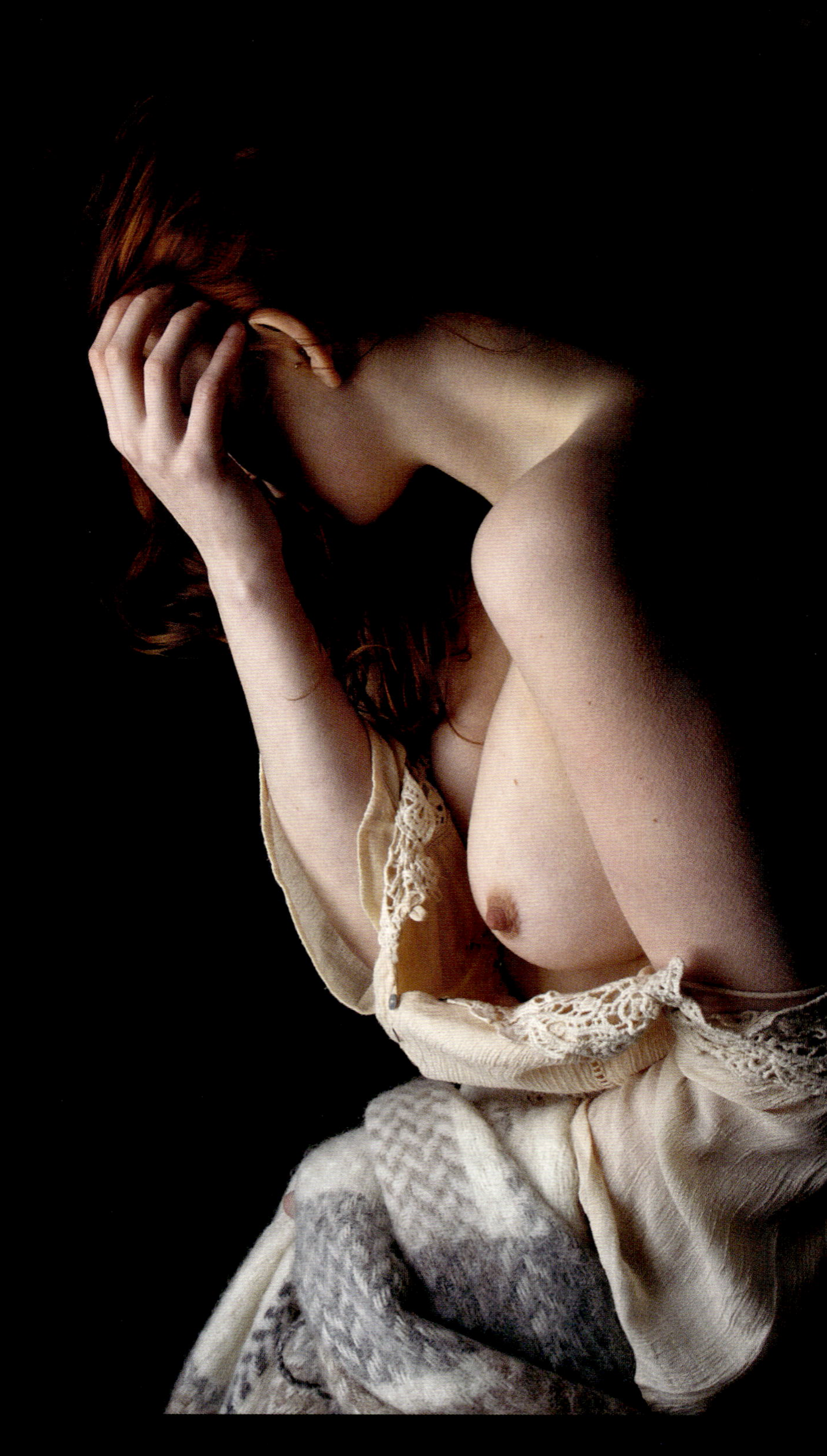

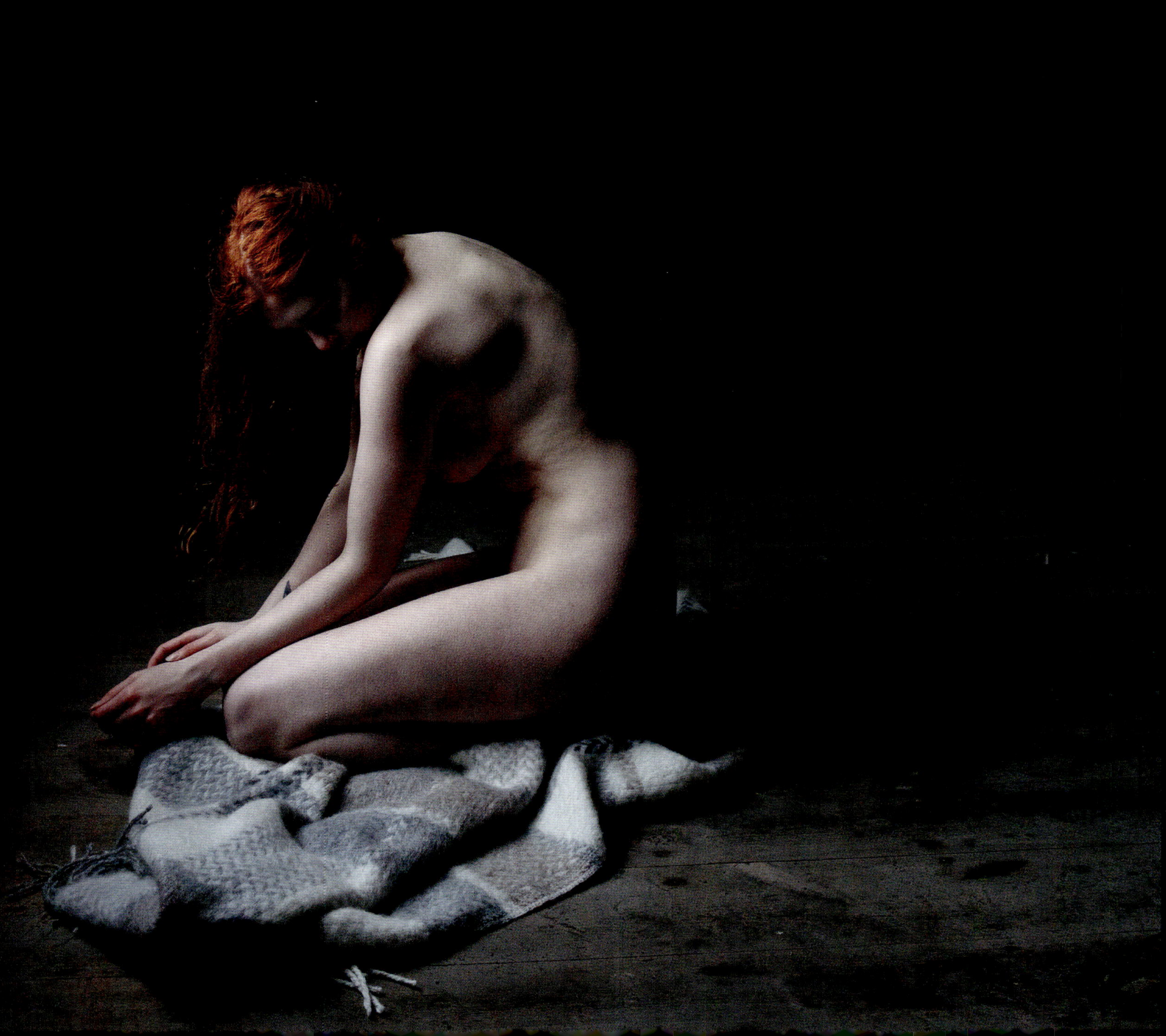

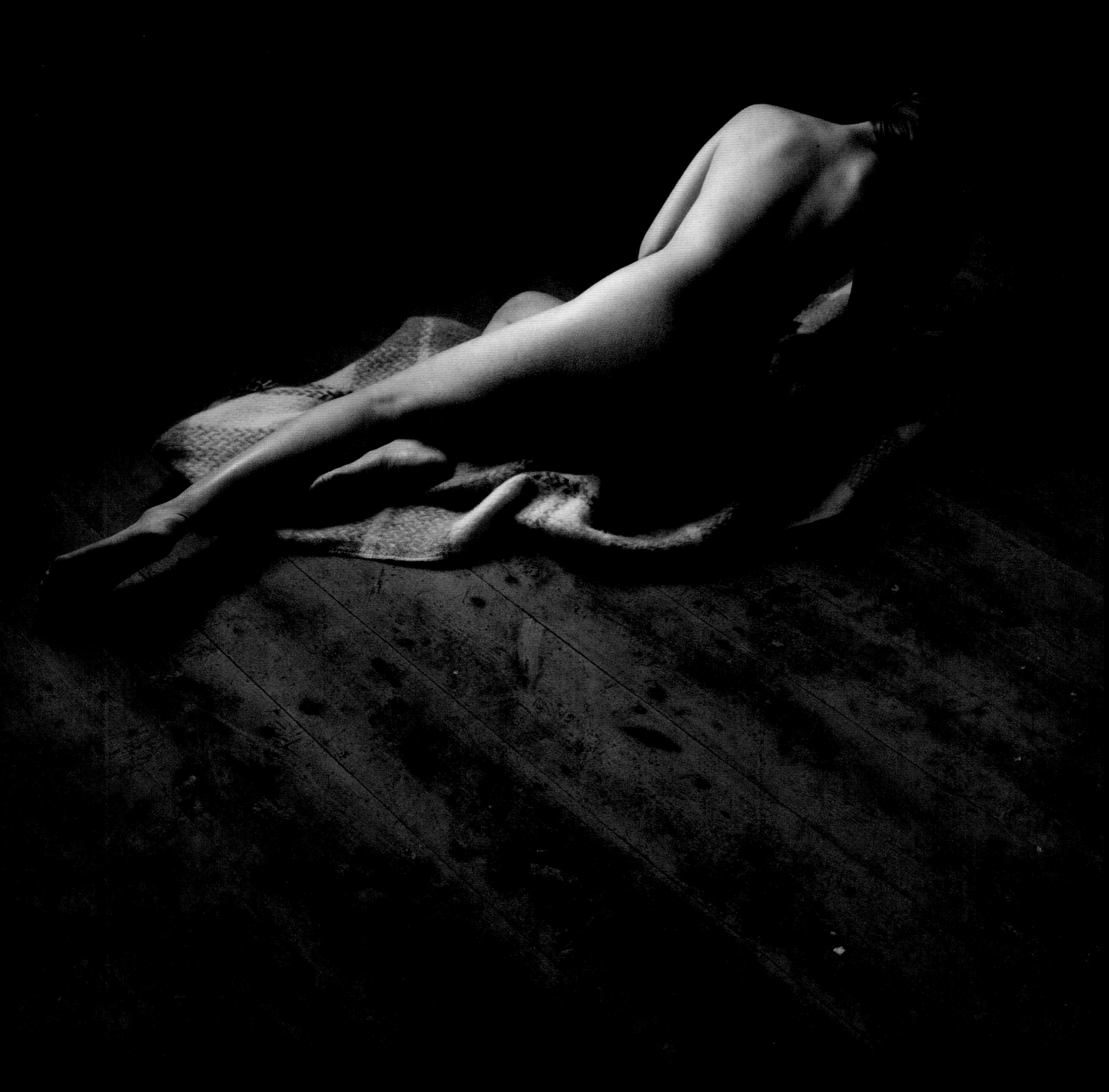

V. THANATOS

EXPLORING DEATH, MORTALITY, AND THE FATE OF THE HUMAN RACE. THESE STORIES EXPLORE THE LIMITS OF HUMAN LIFE. THEY SURVEY THE INEVITABILITY OF DEATH AND THE TENSION BETWEEN MORTALS AND THE DIVINE.

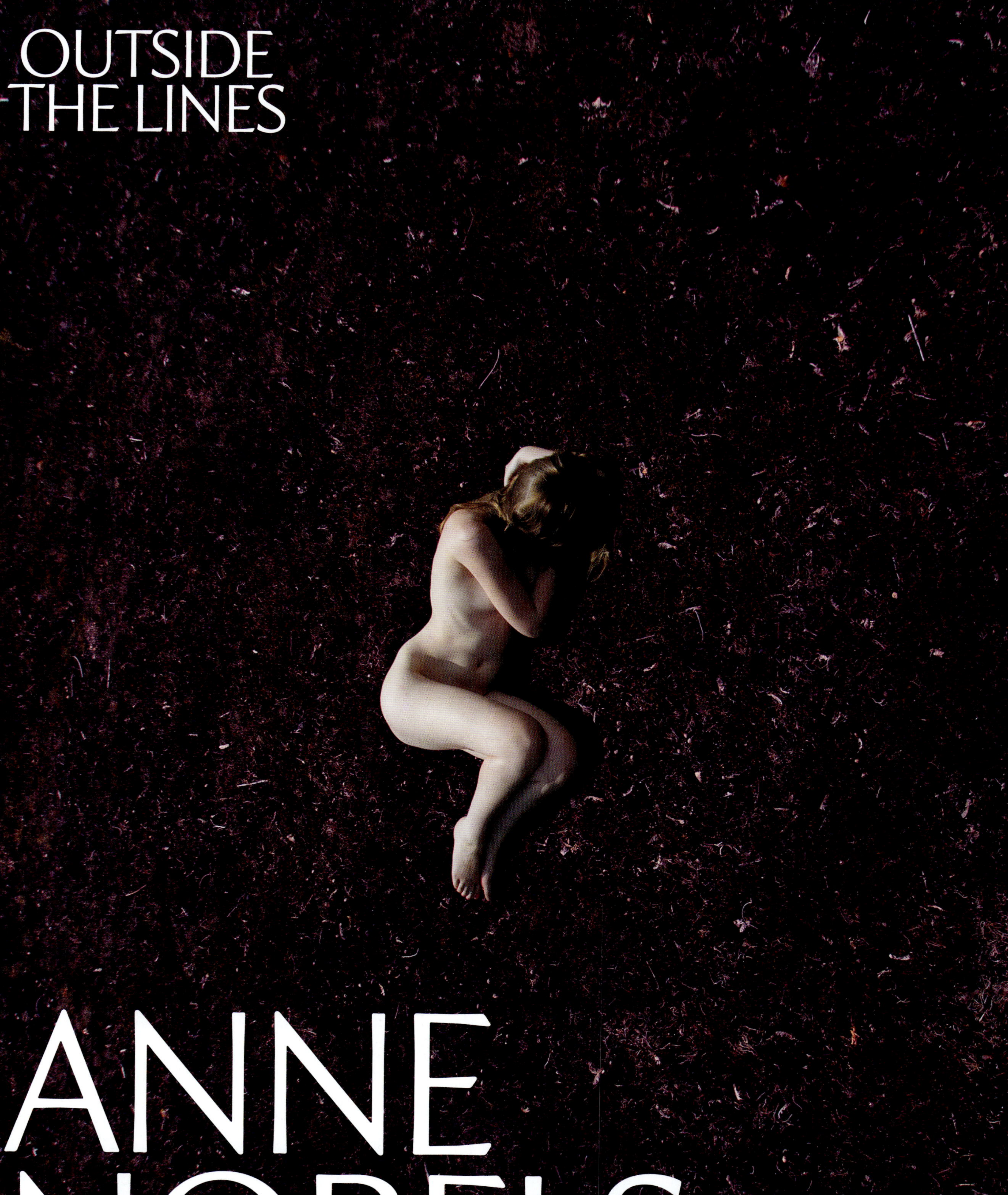

OUTSIDE THE LINES

ANNE NOBELS

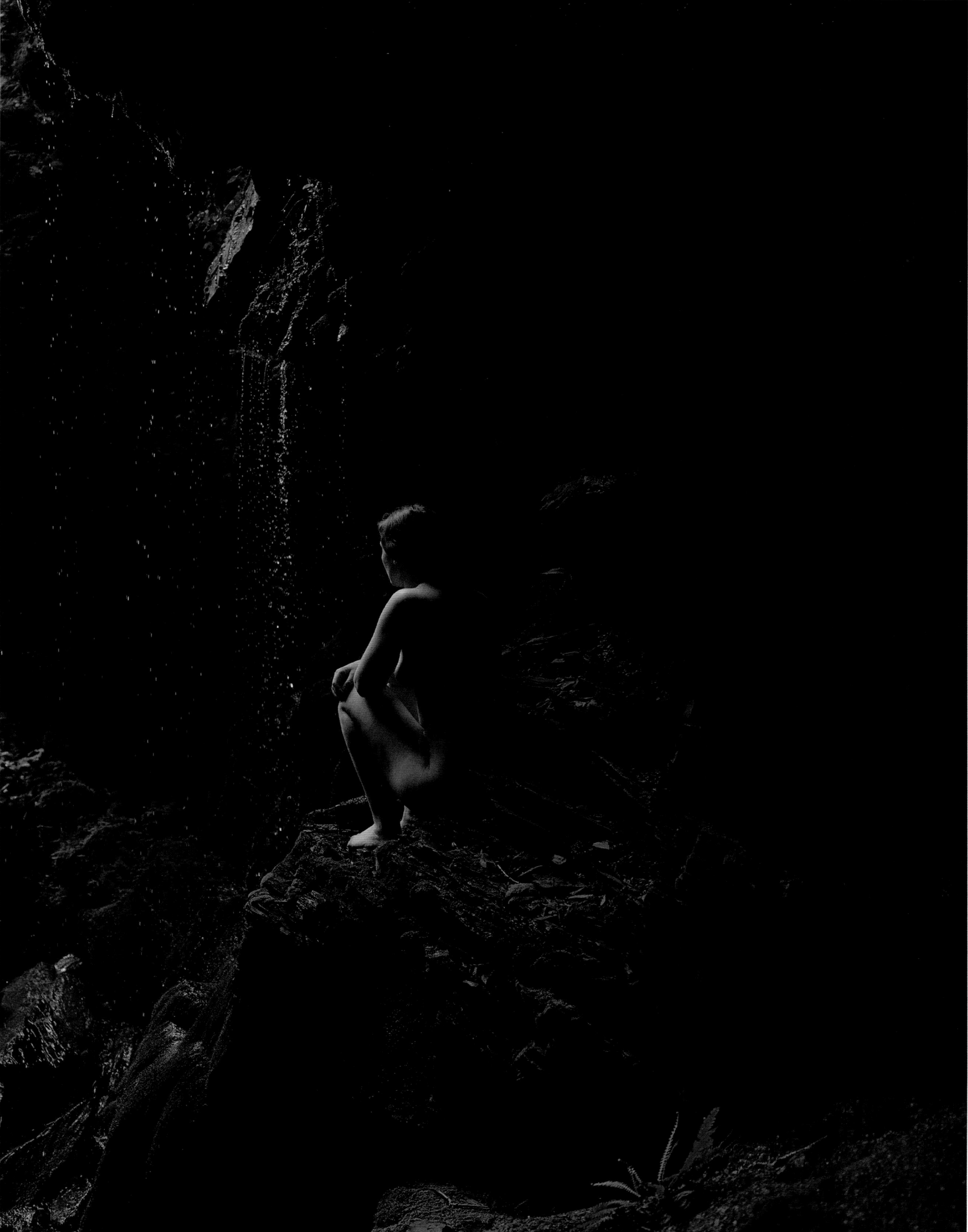

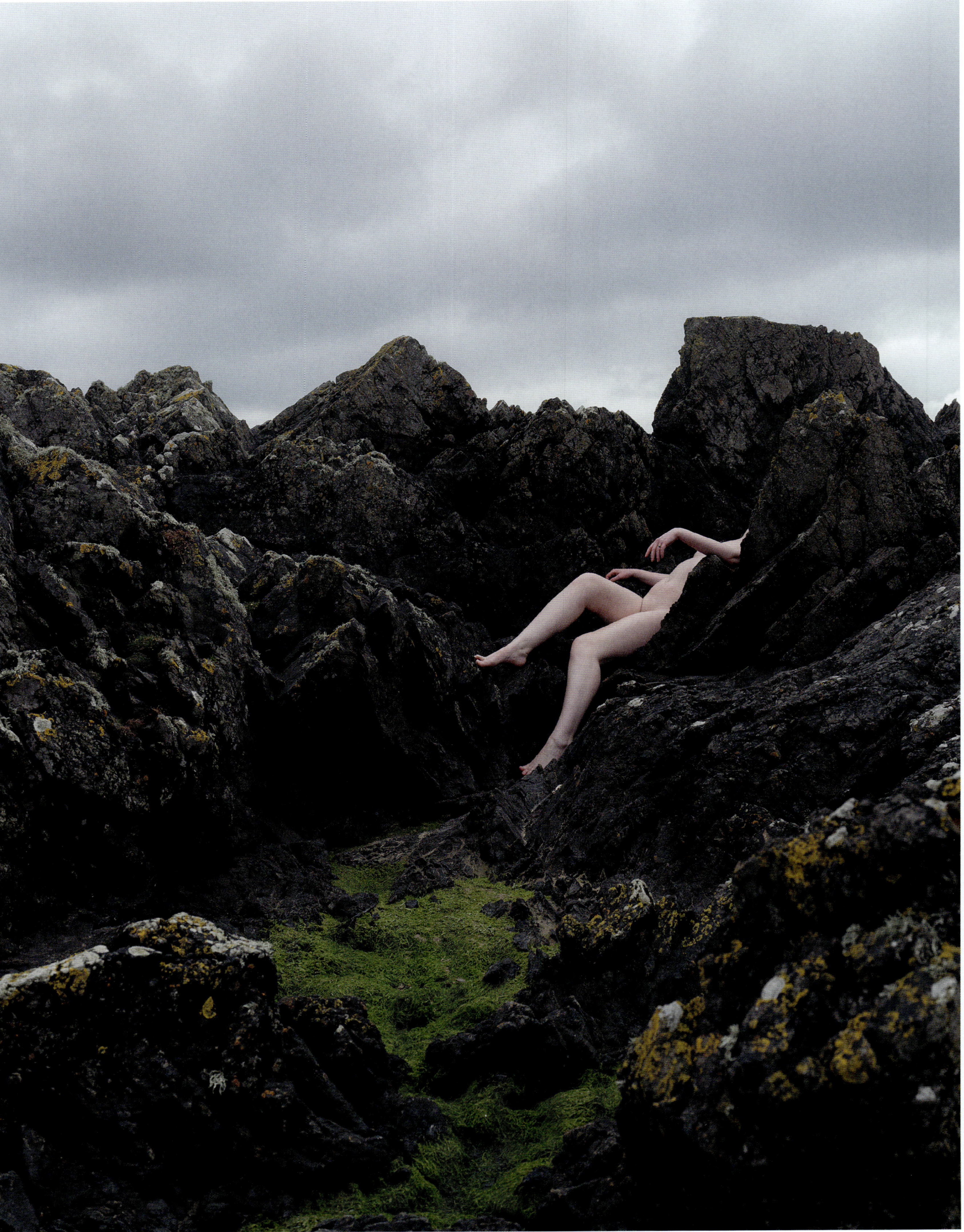

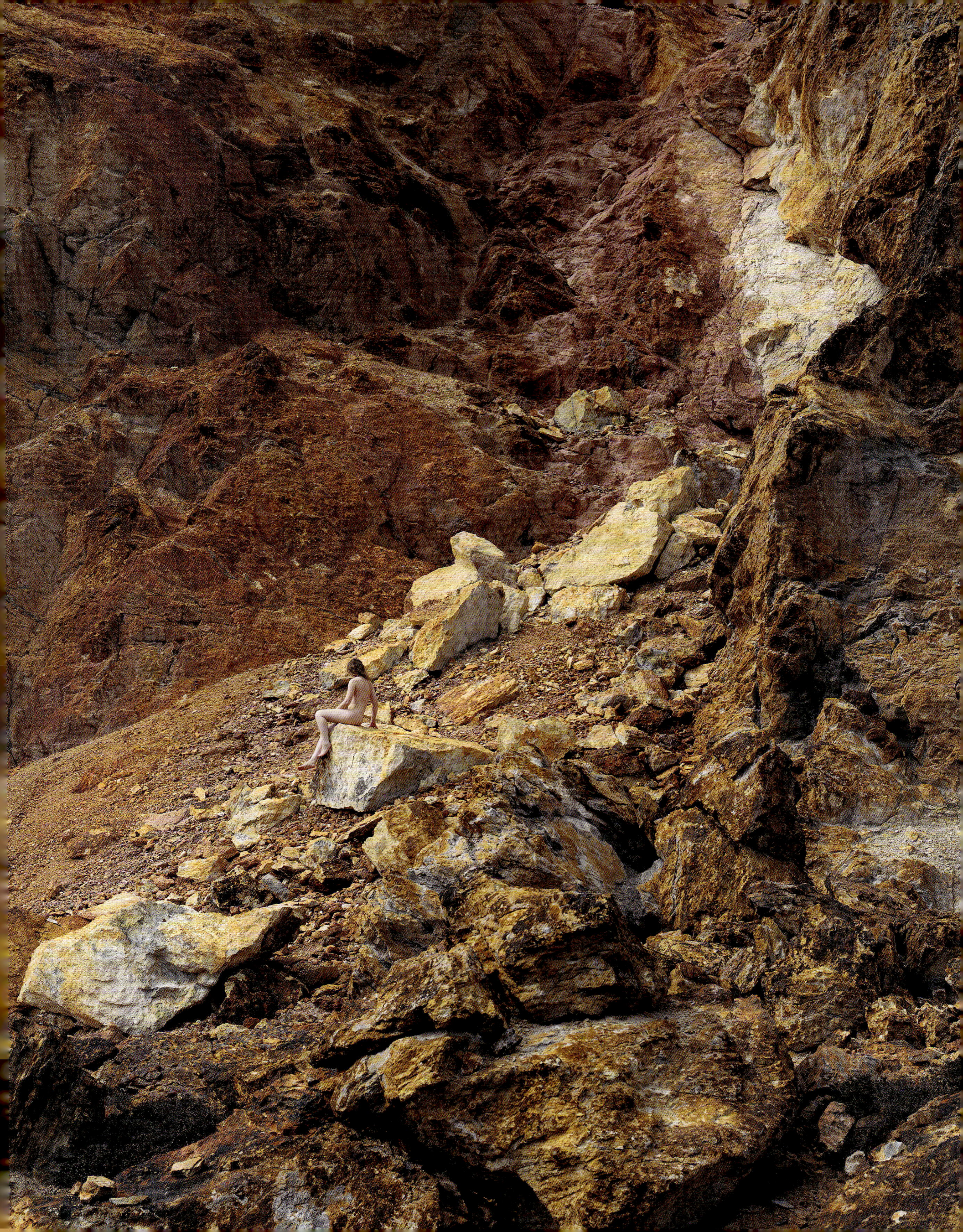

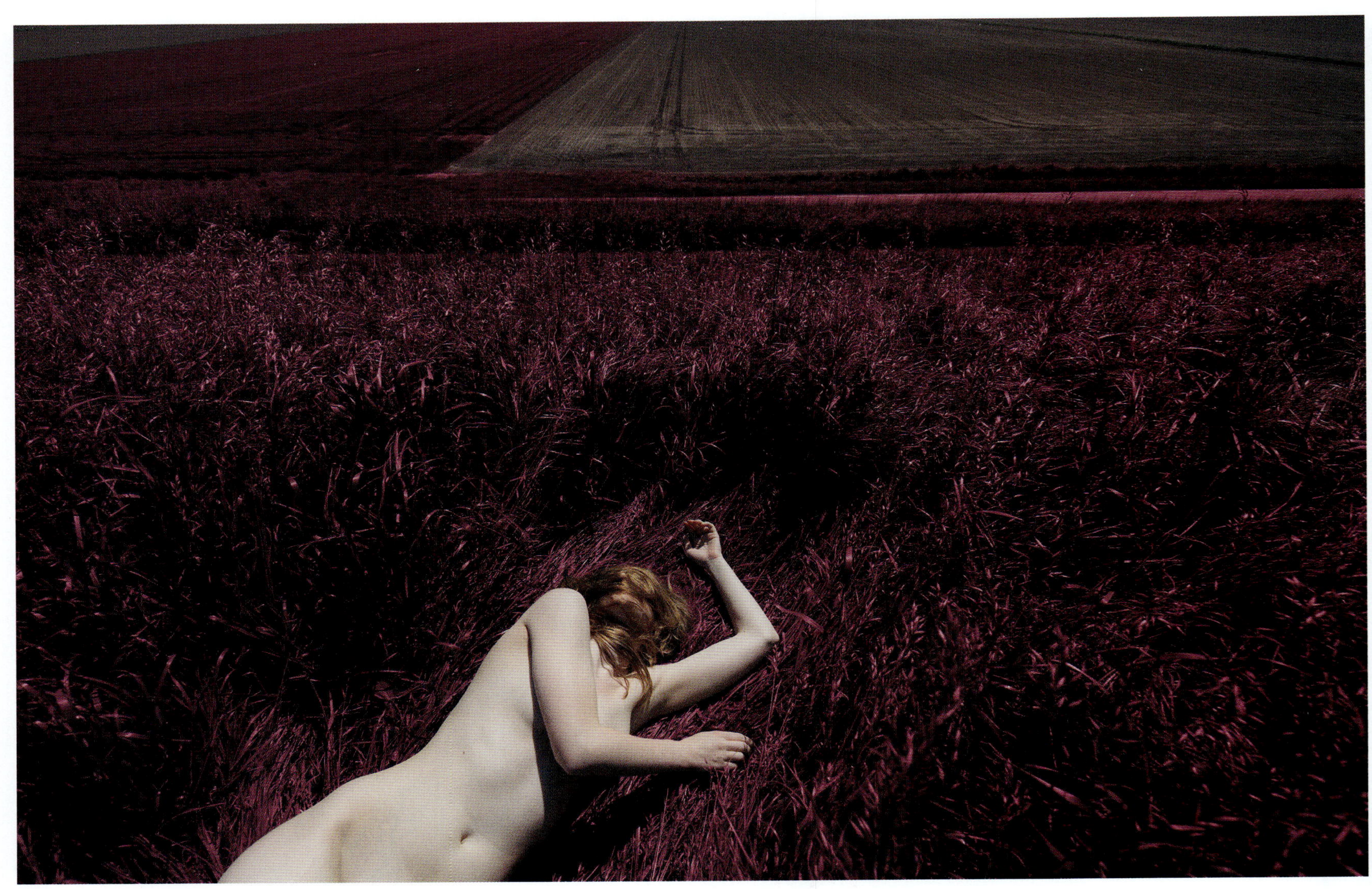

170

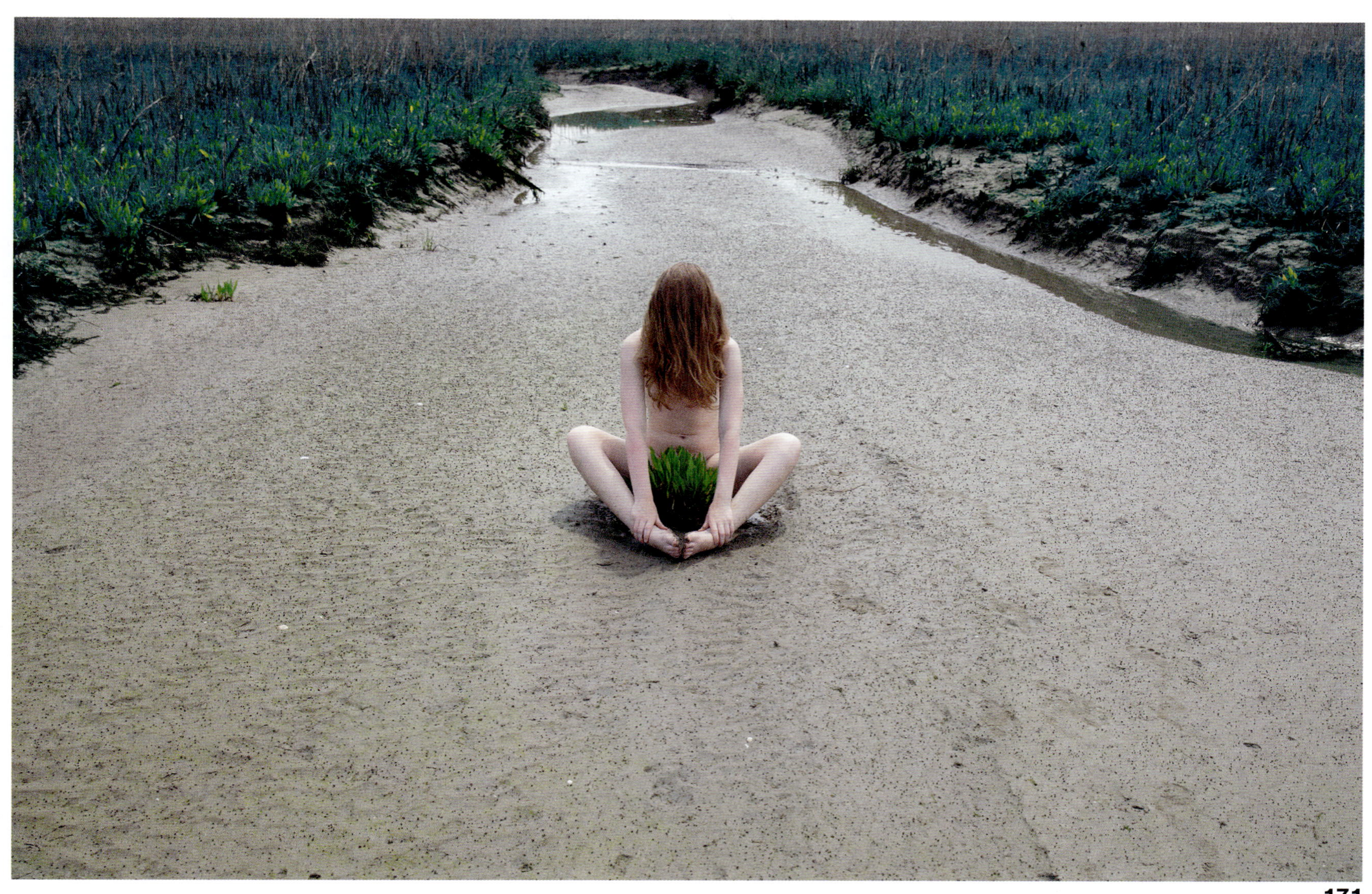

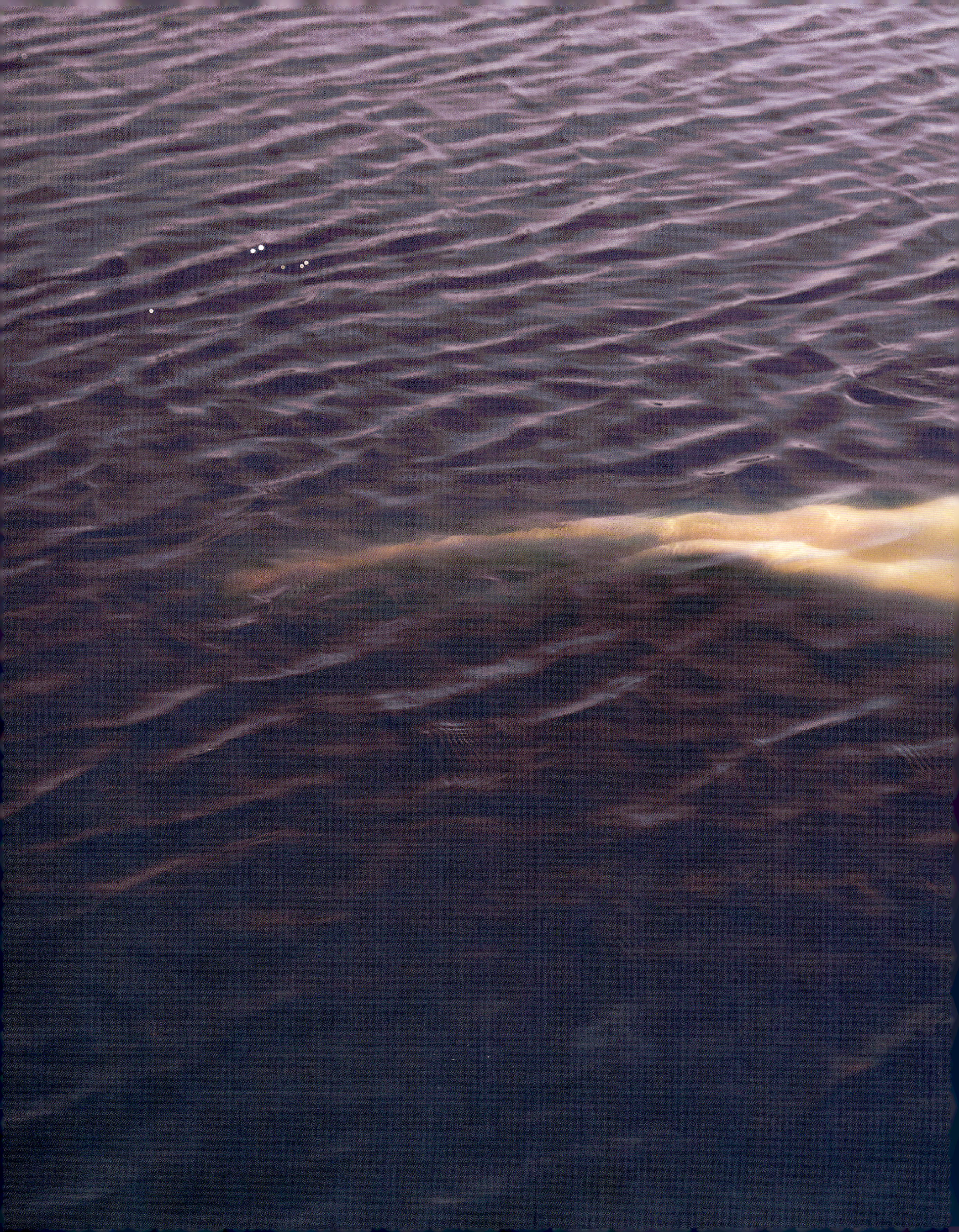

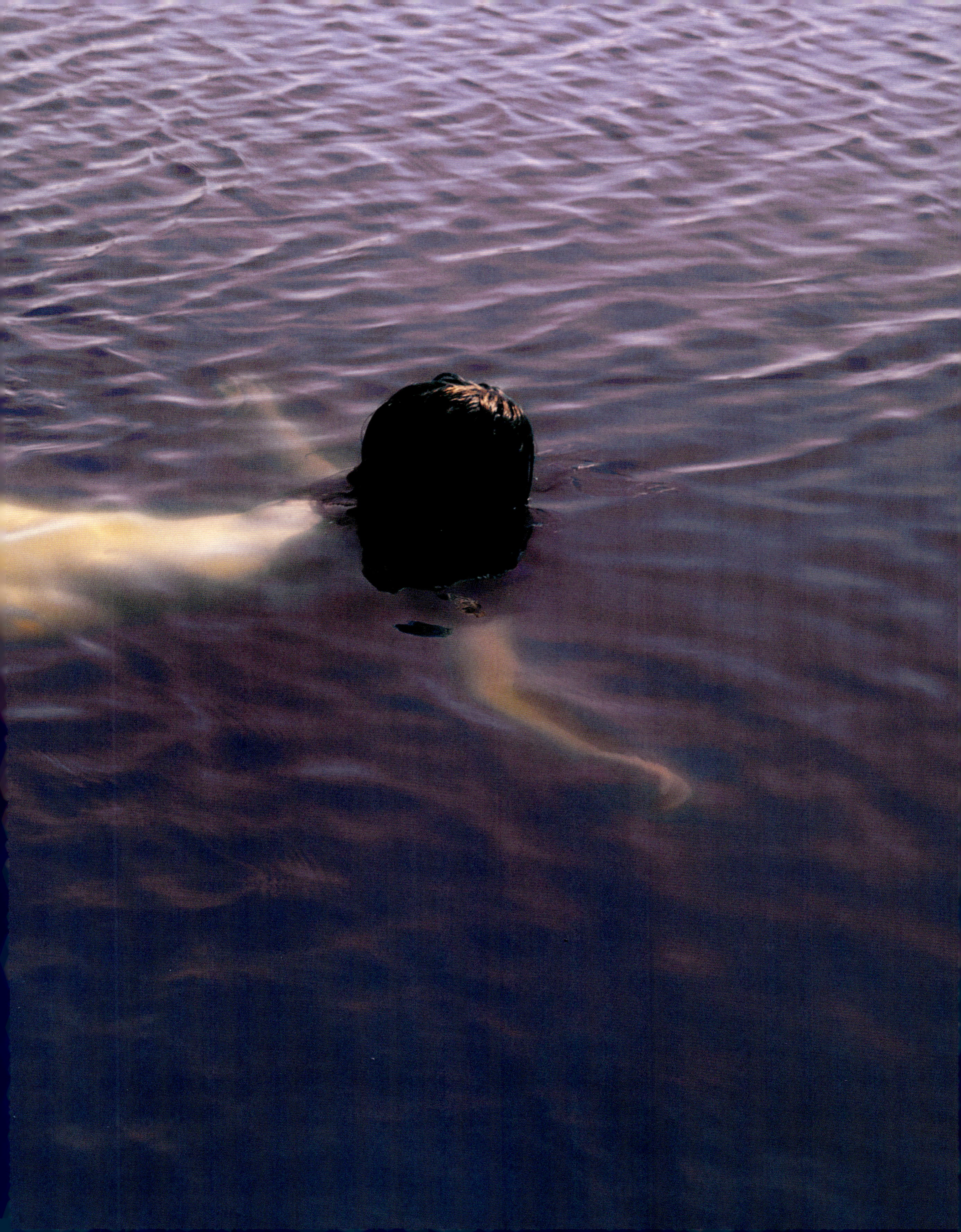

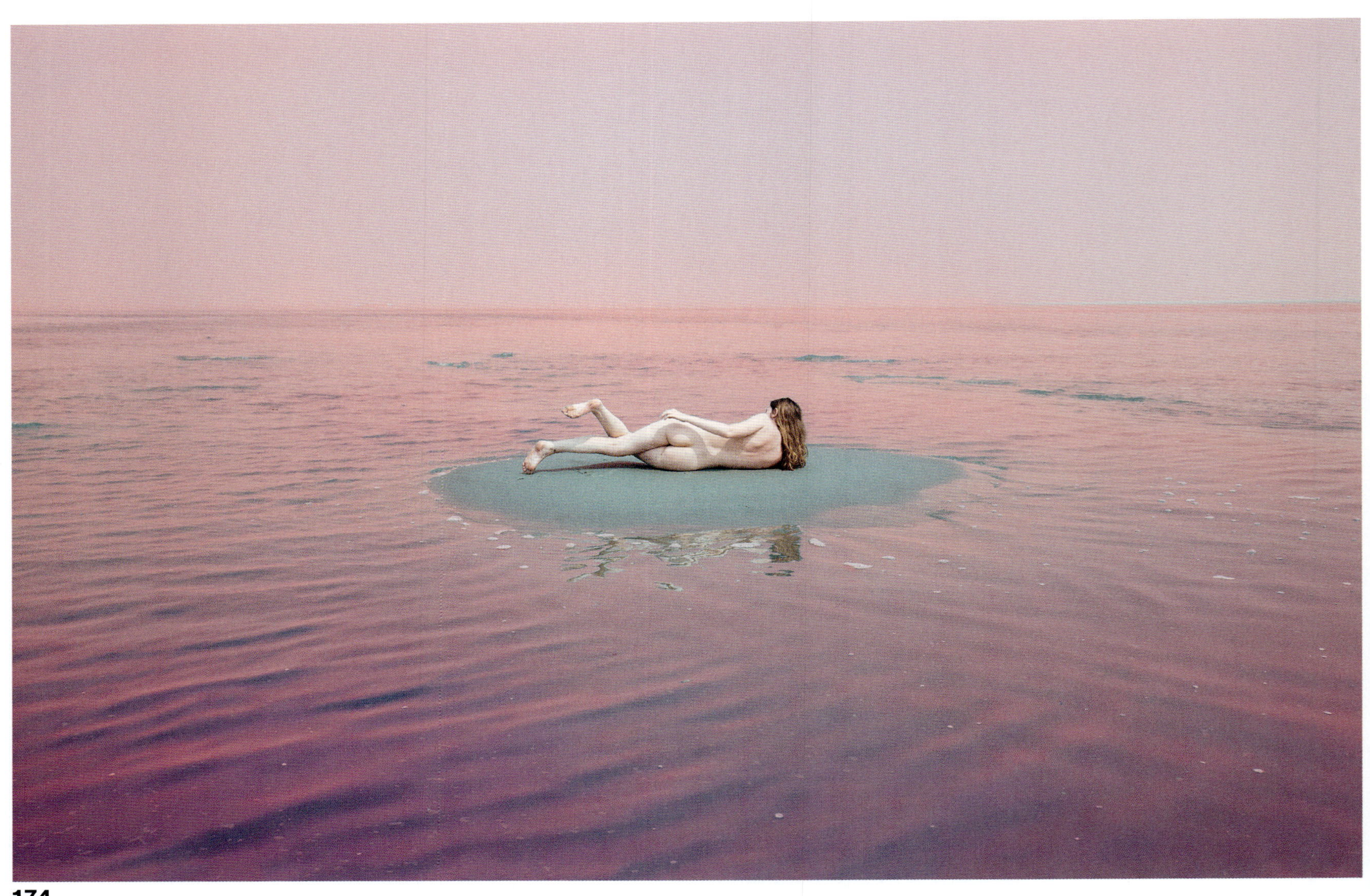

174

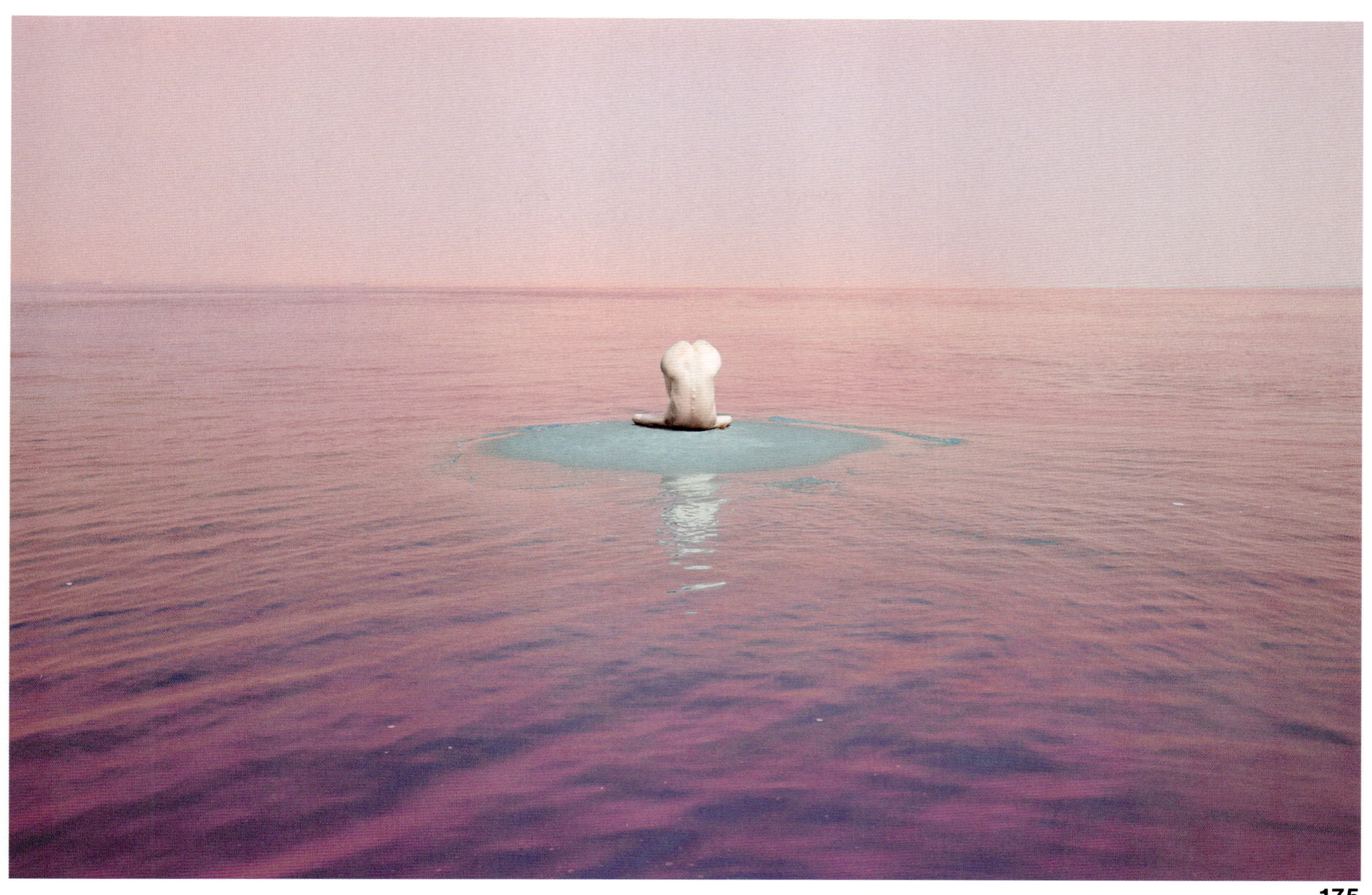

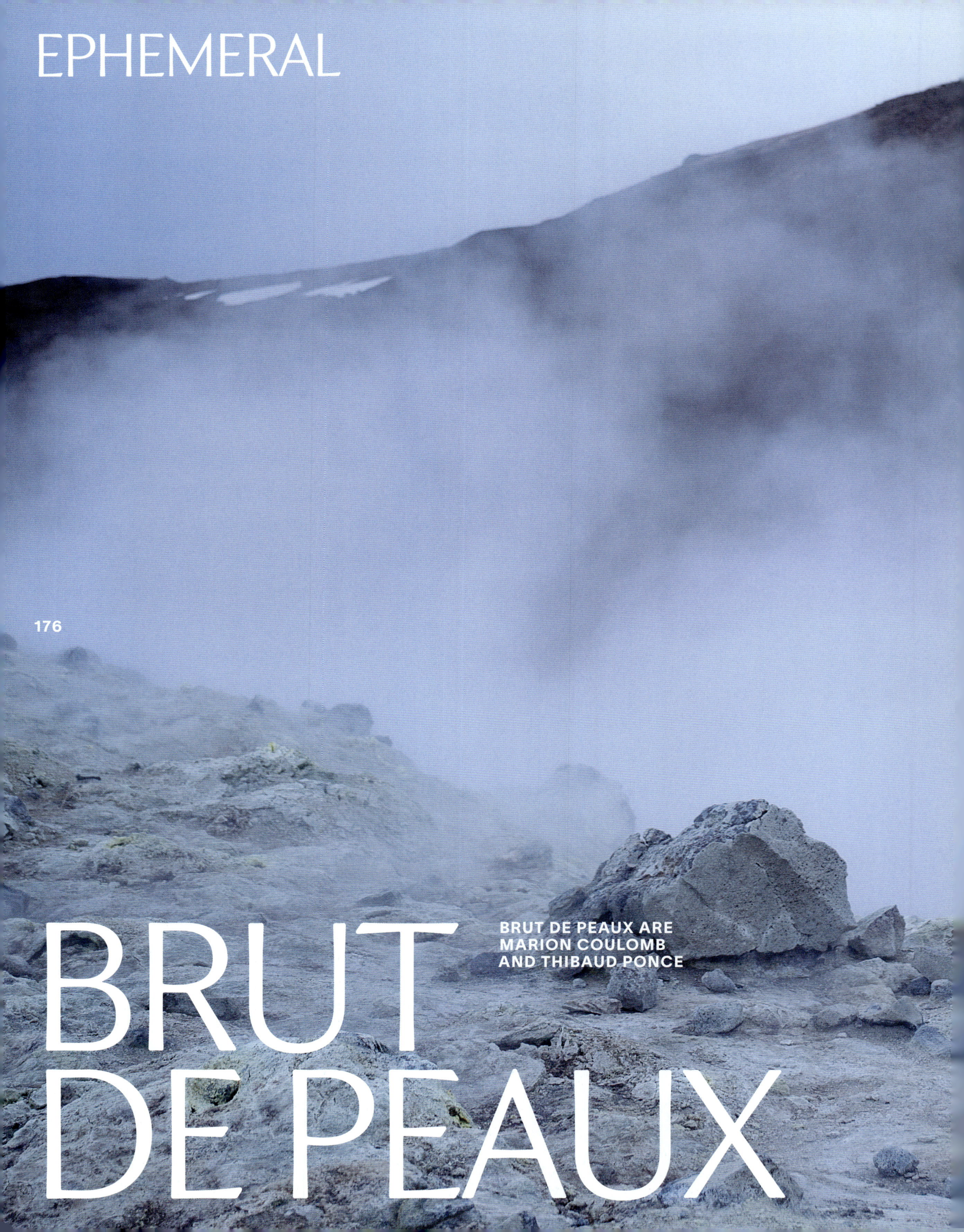

176

BRUT DE PEAUX

BRUT DE PEAUX ARE
MARION COULOMB
AND THIBAUD PONCE

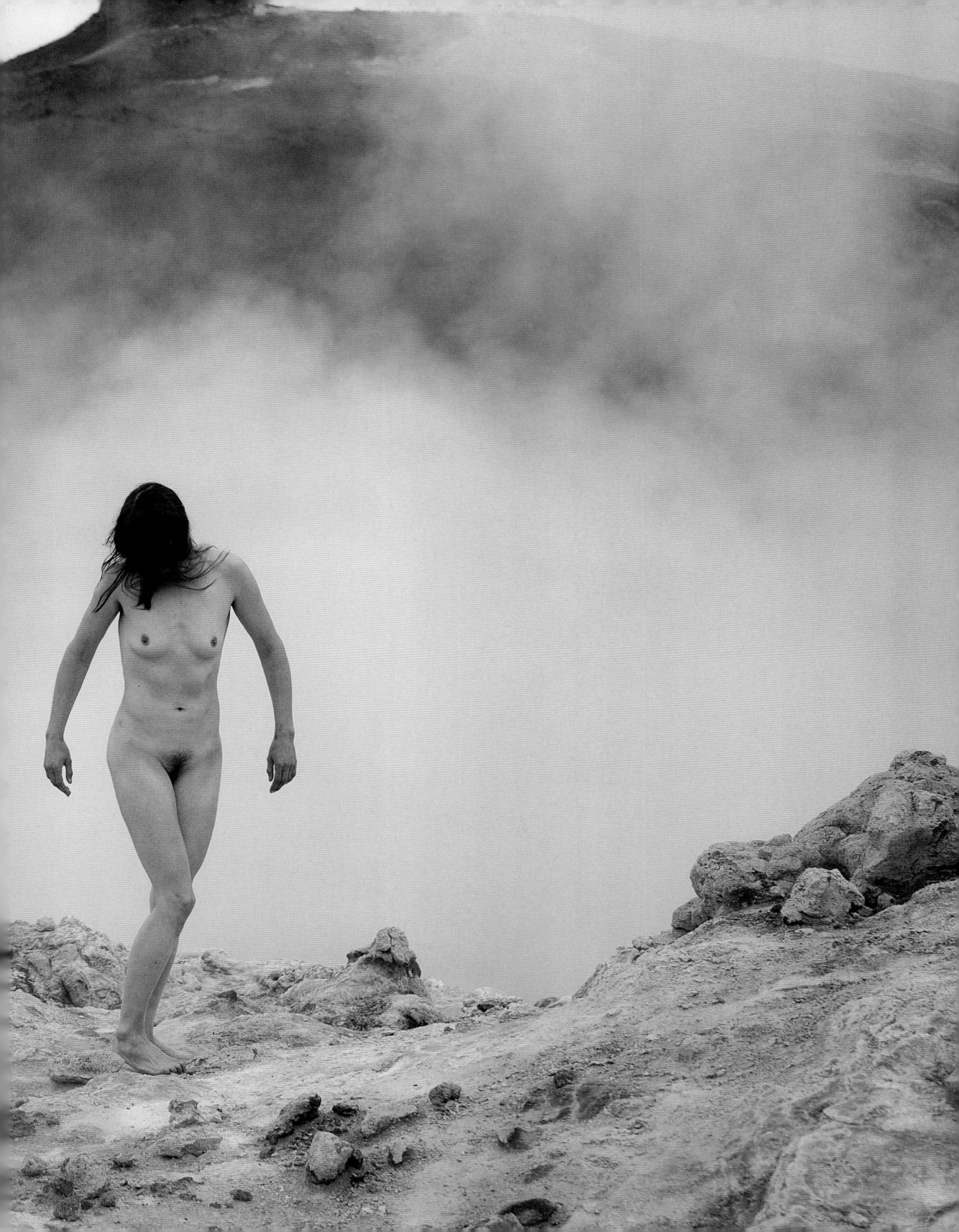

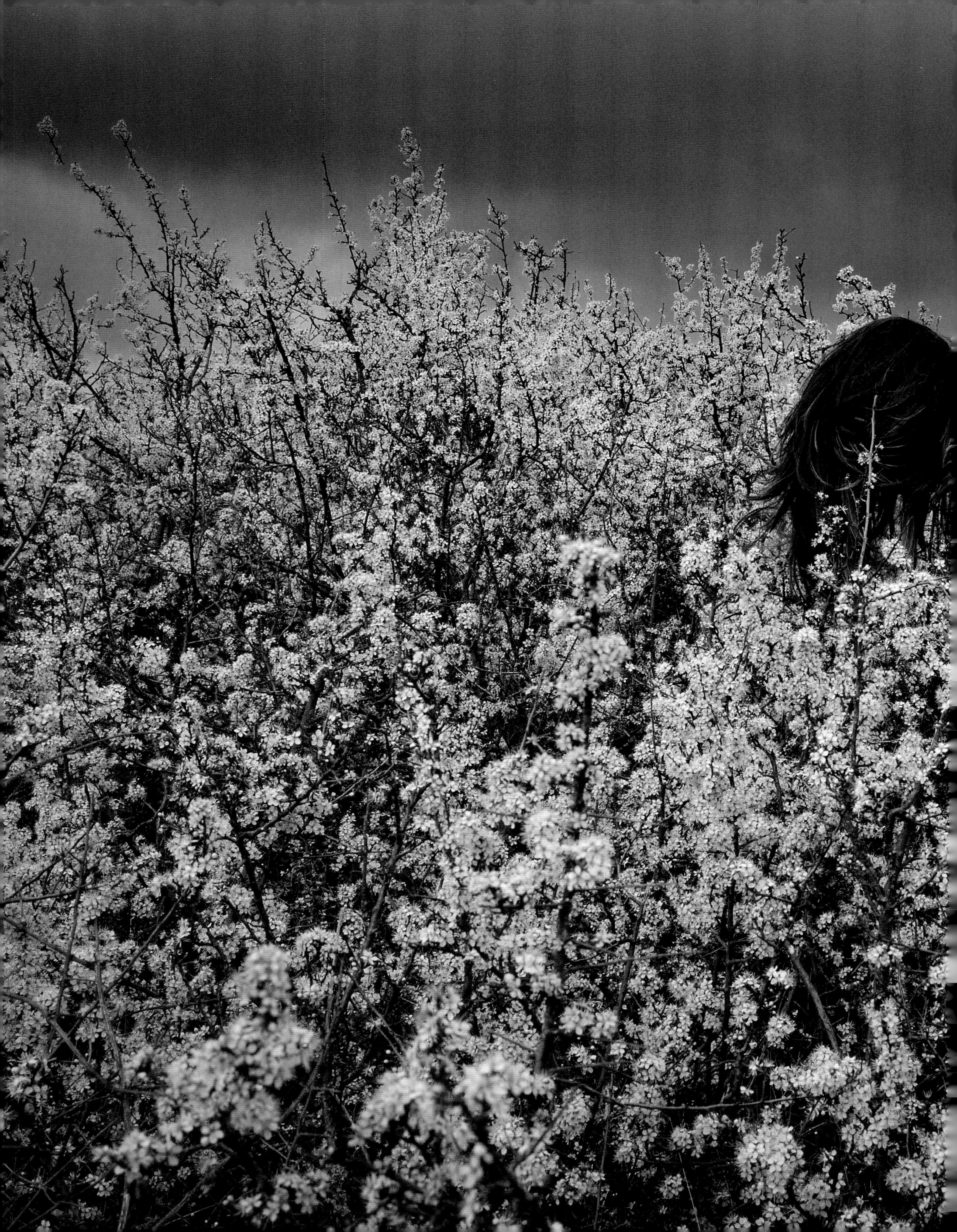

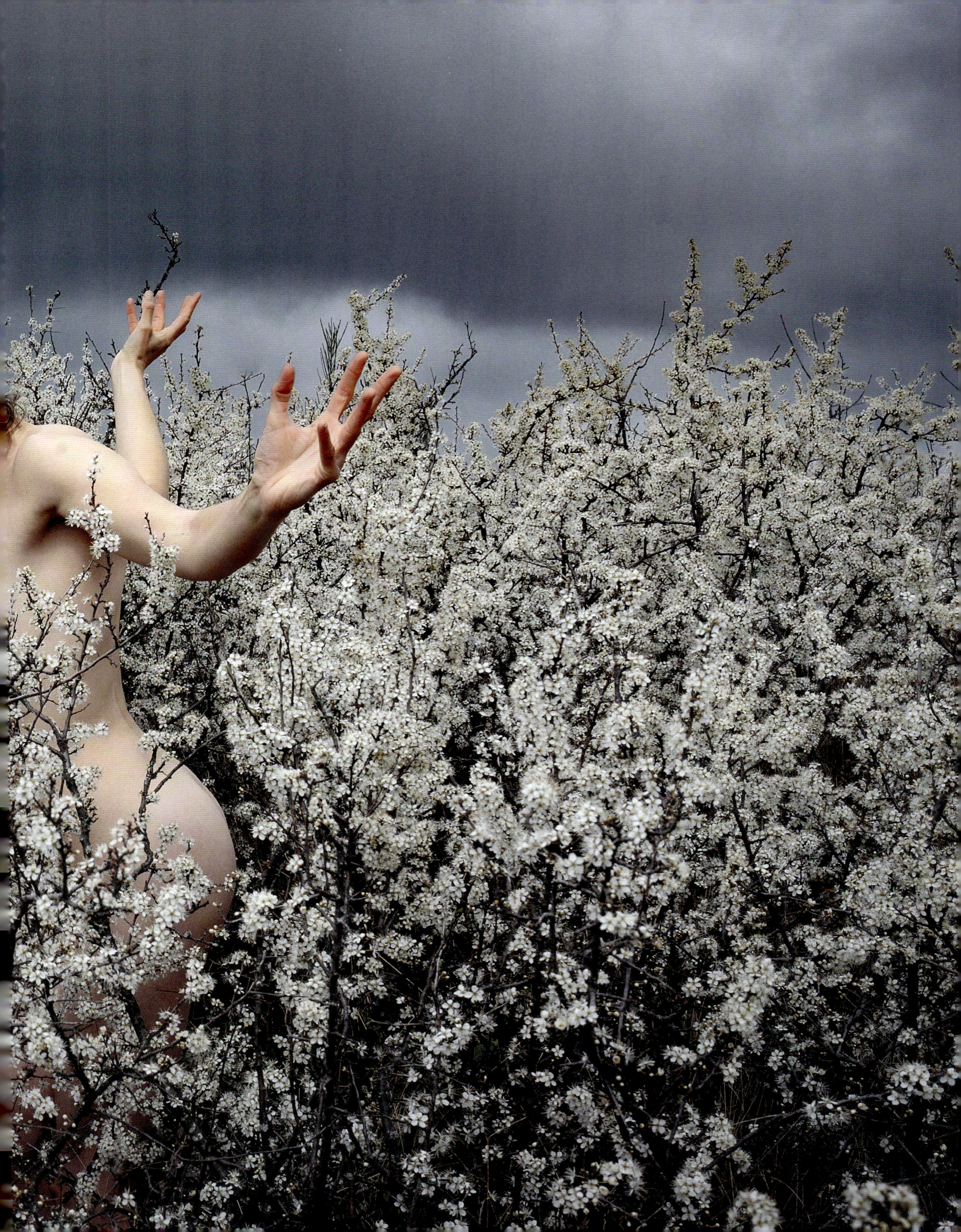

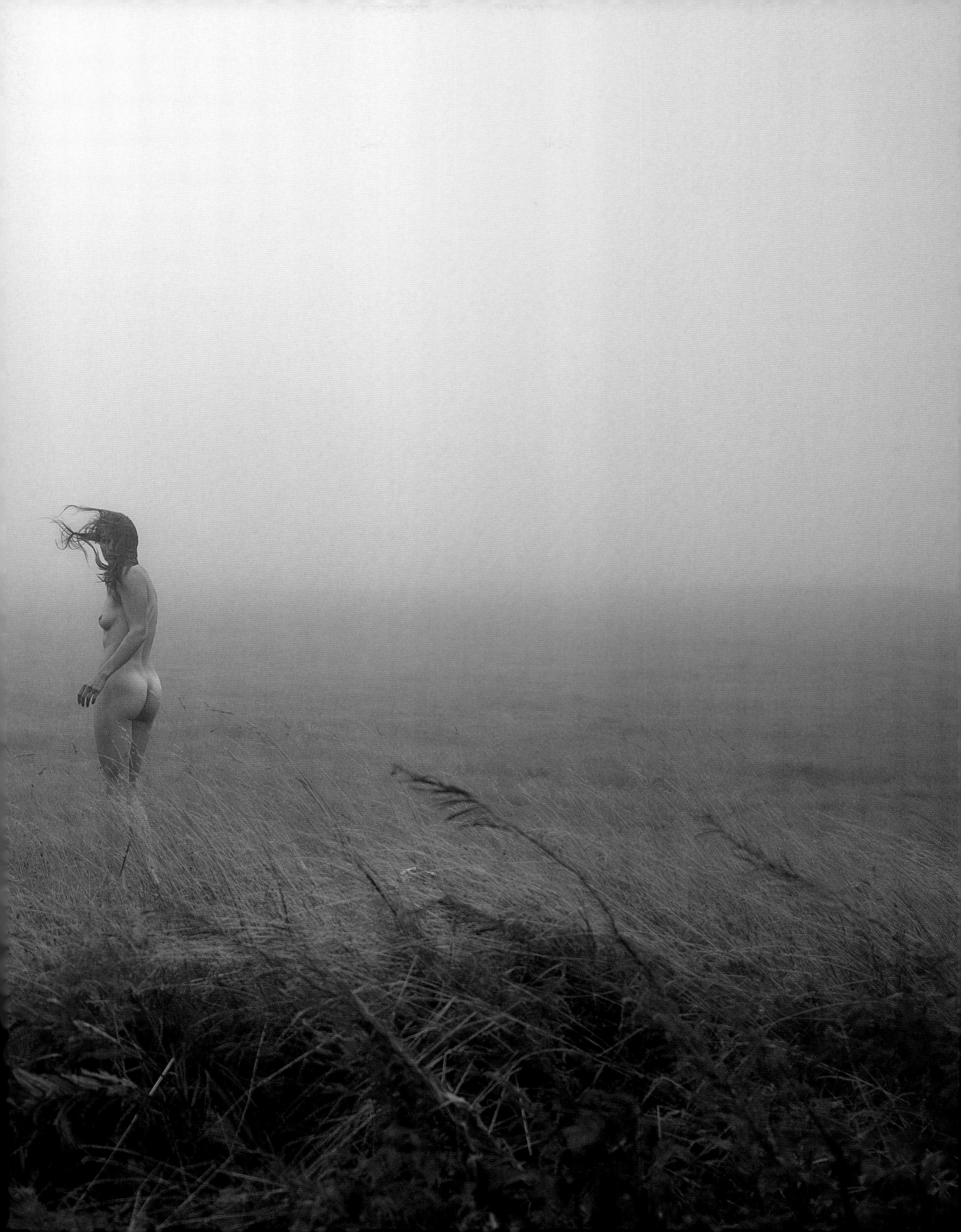

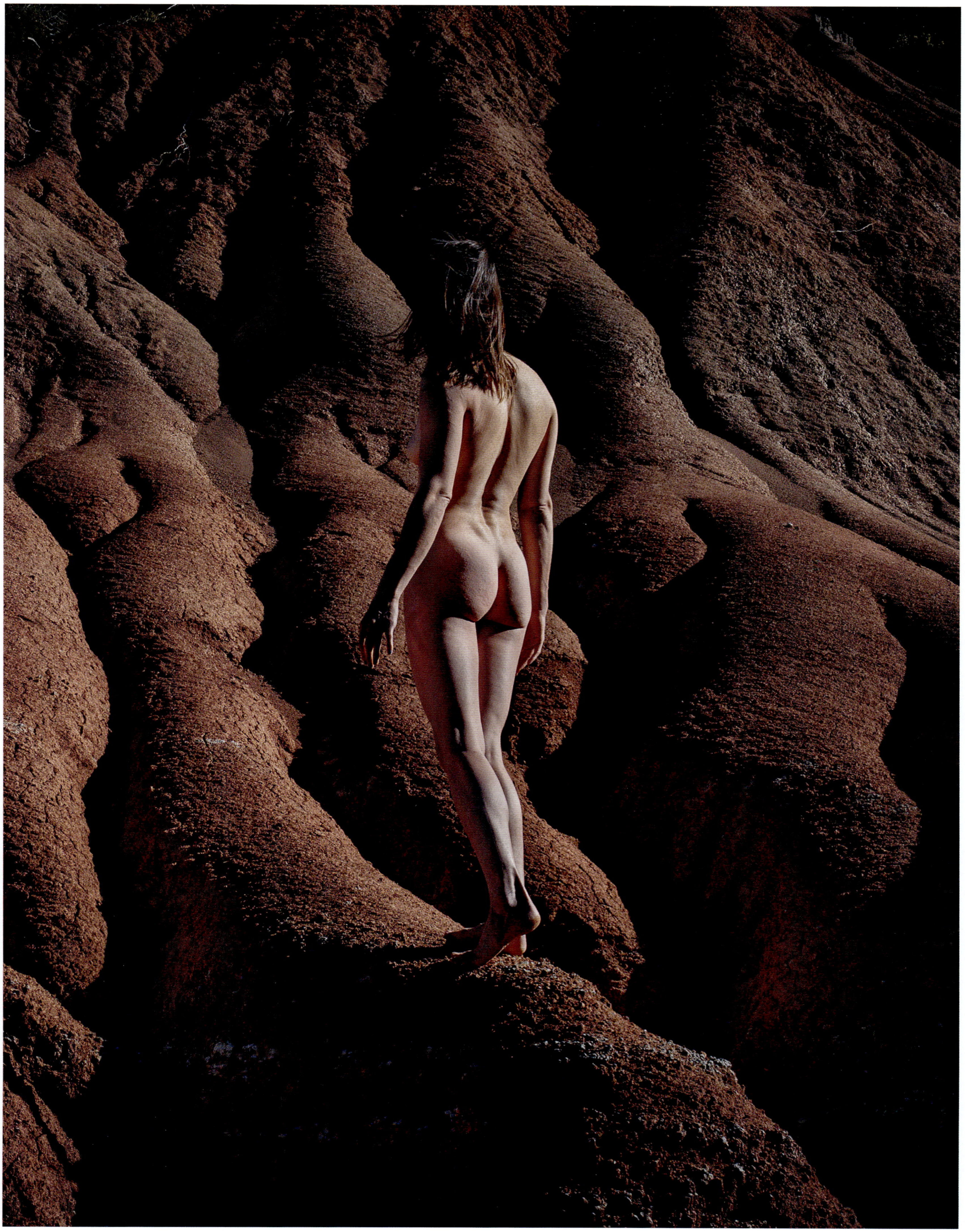

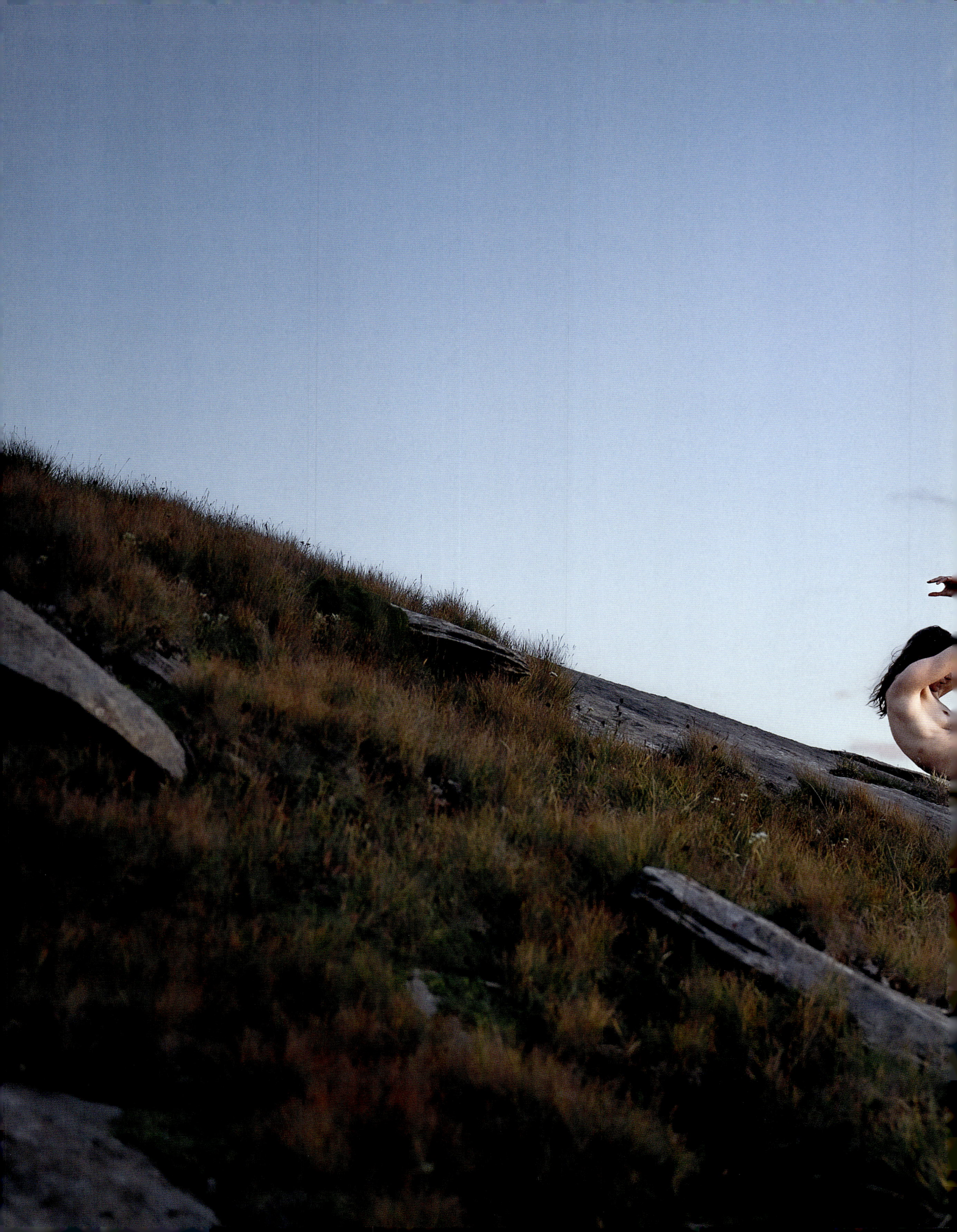

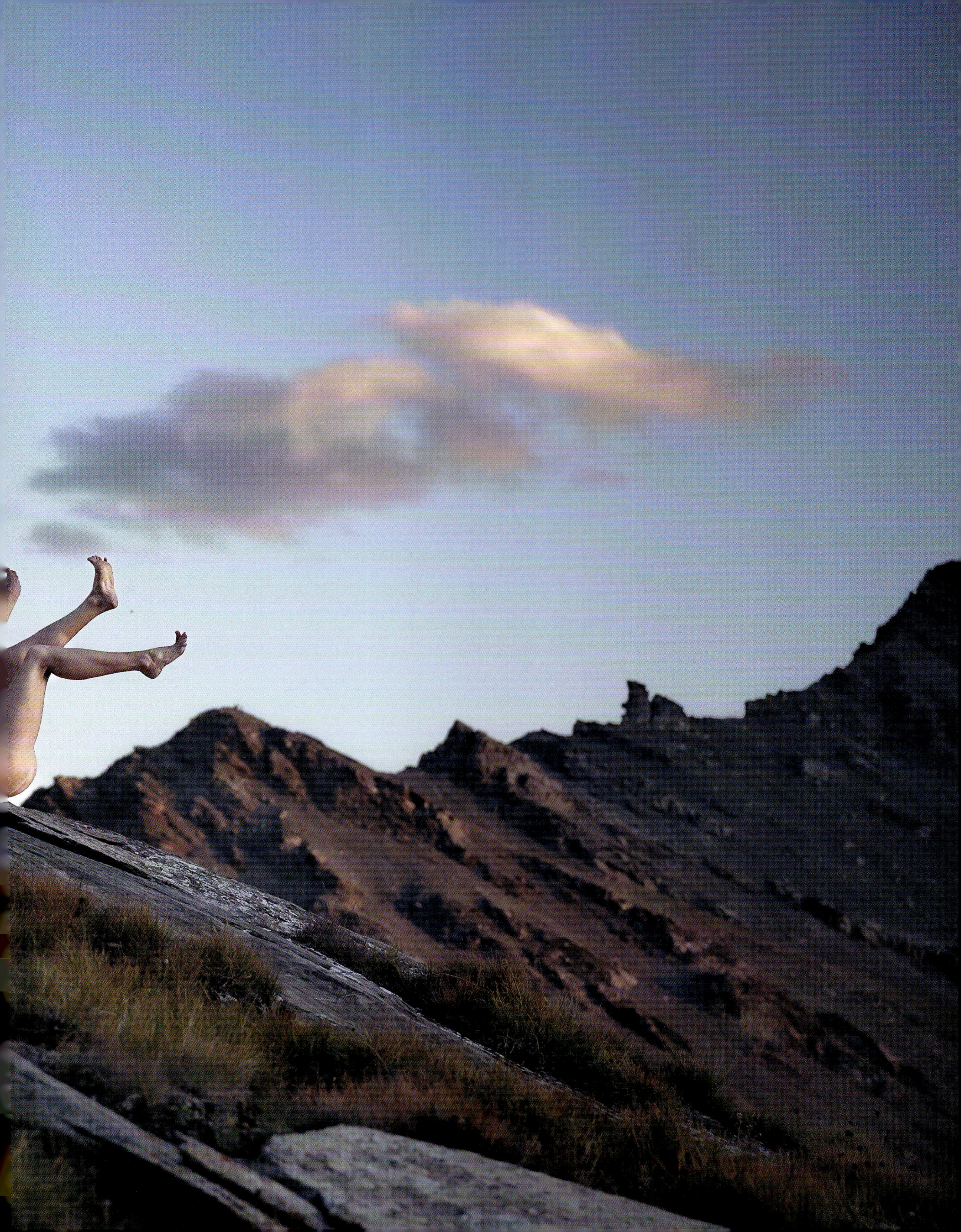

NASTYA SPACEY

AMPHITRITE

MODEL:
DARIA GAITUKIEVA

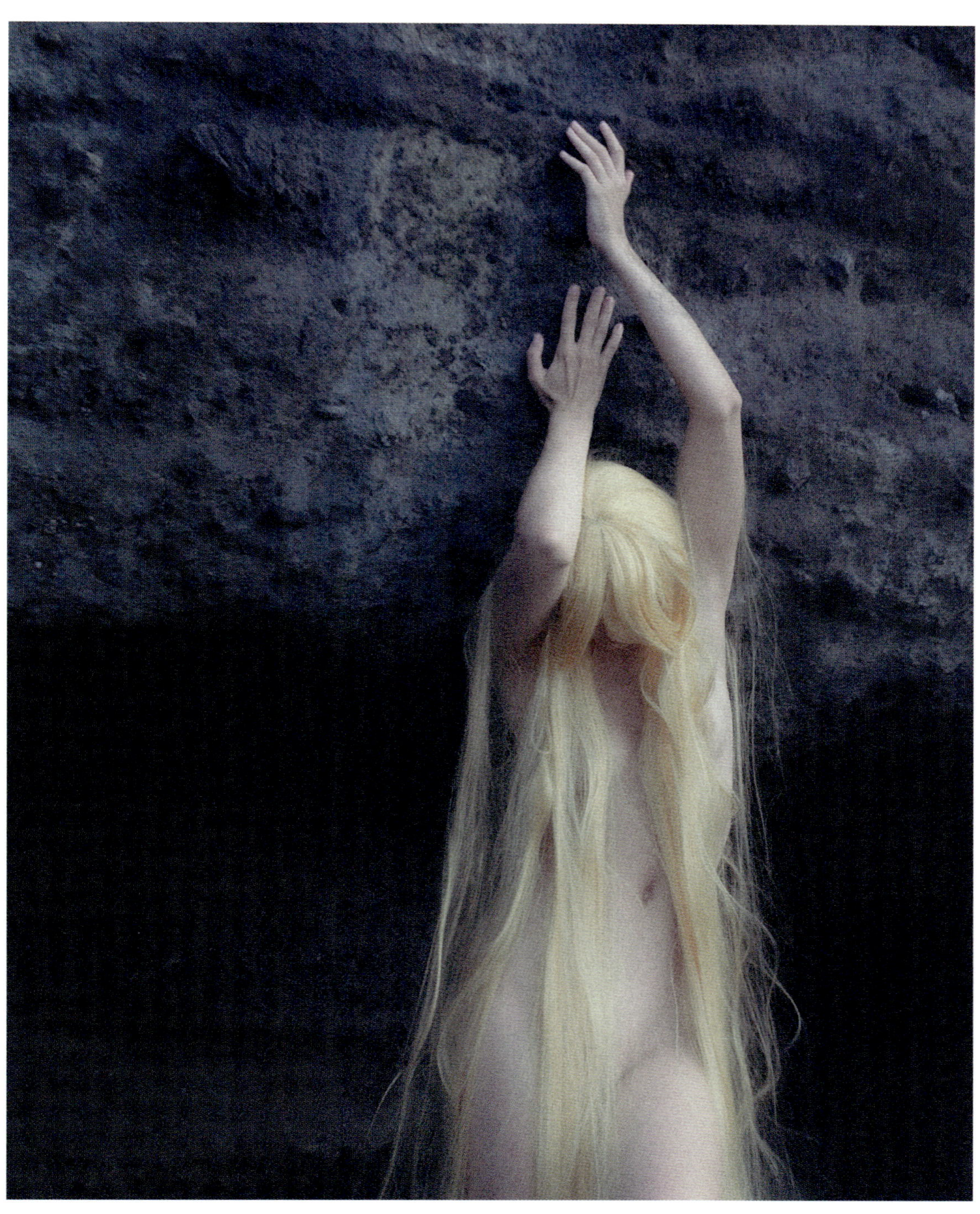

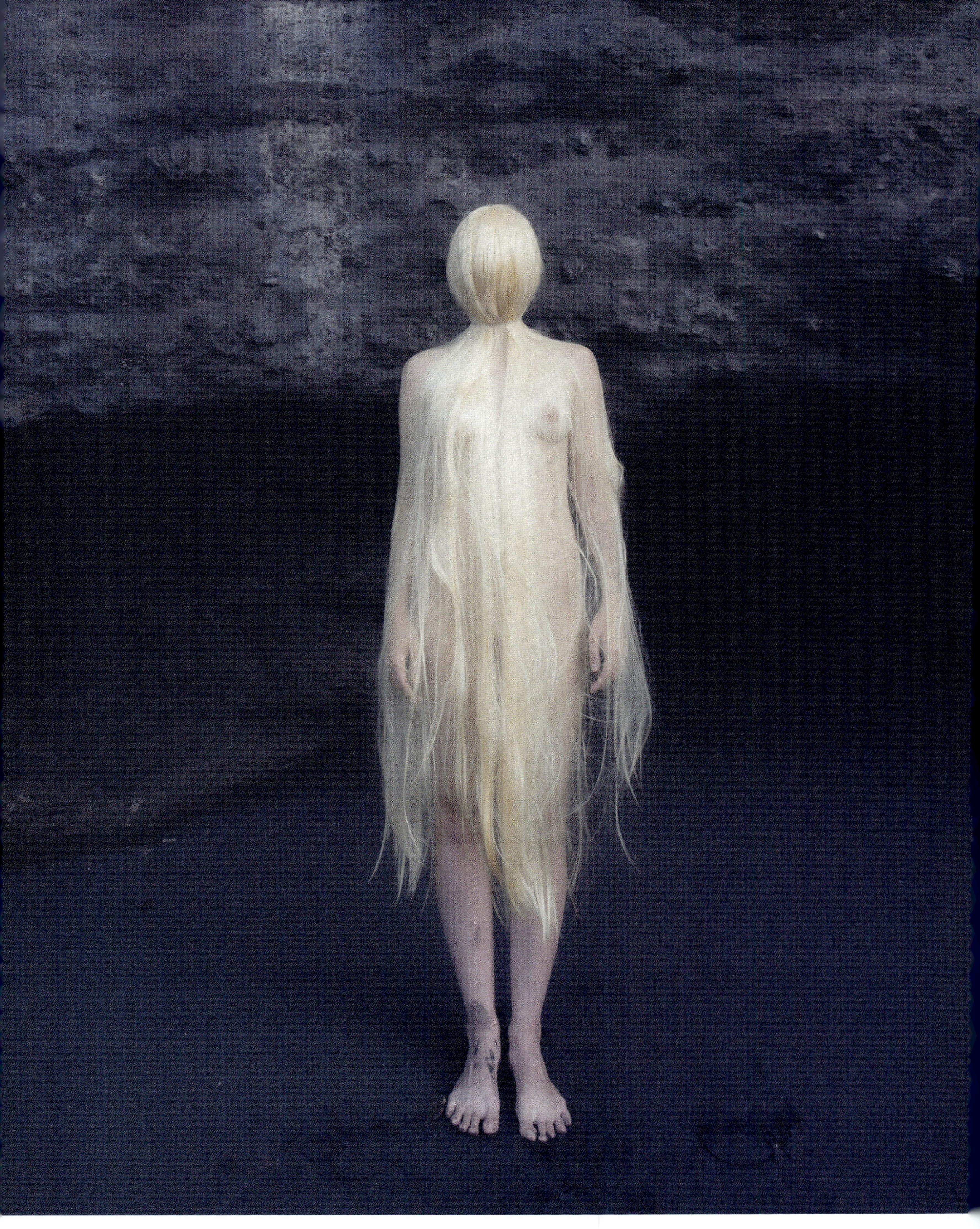

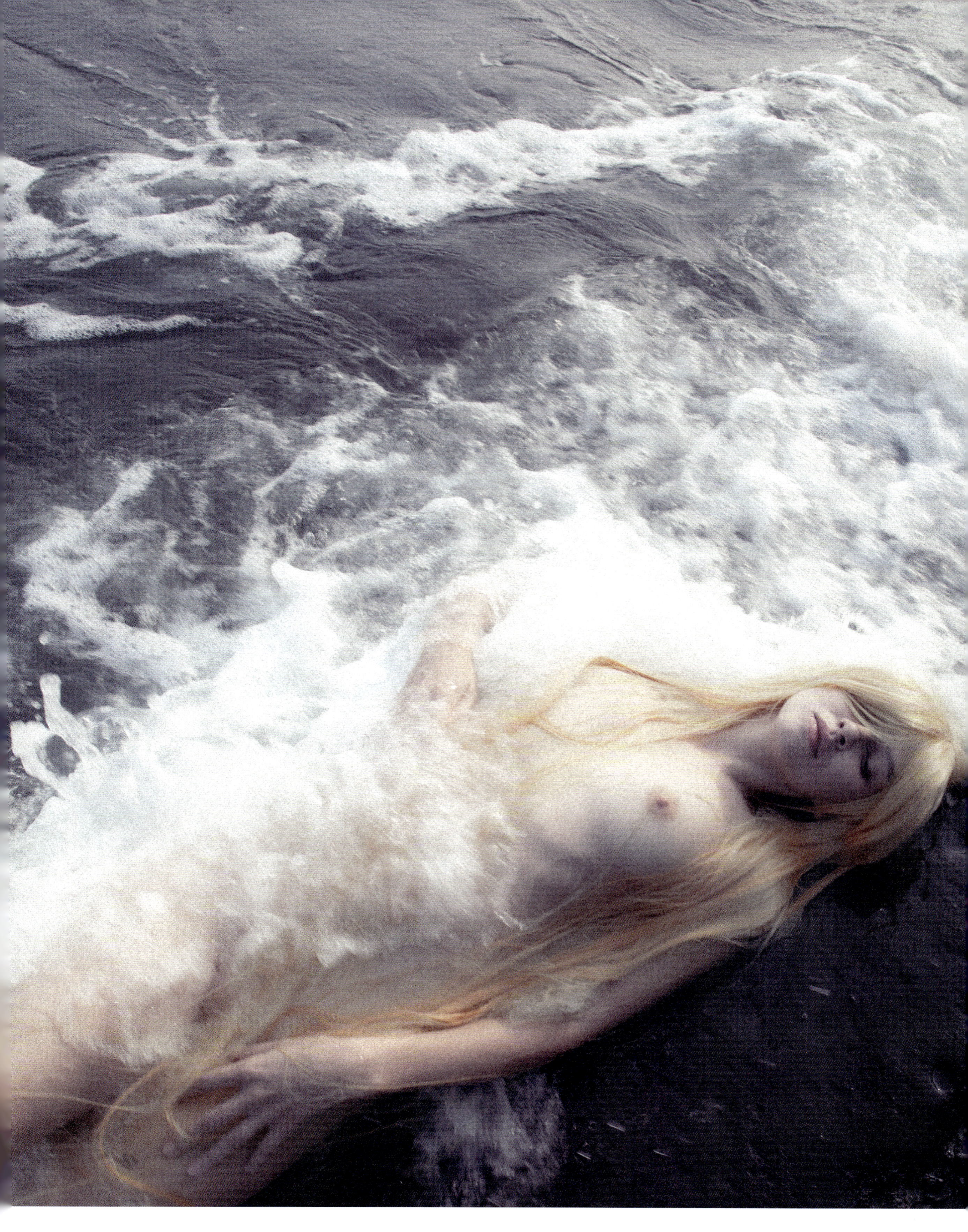

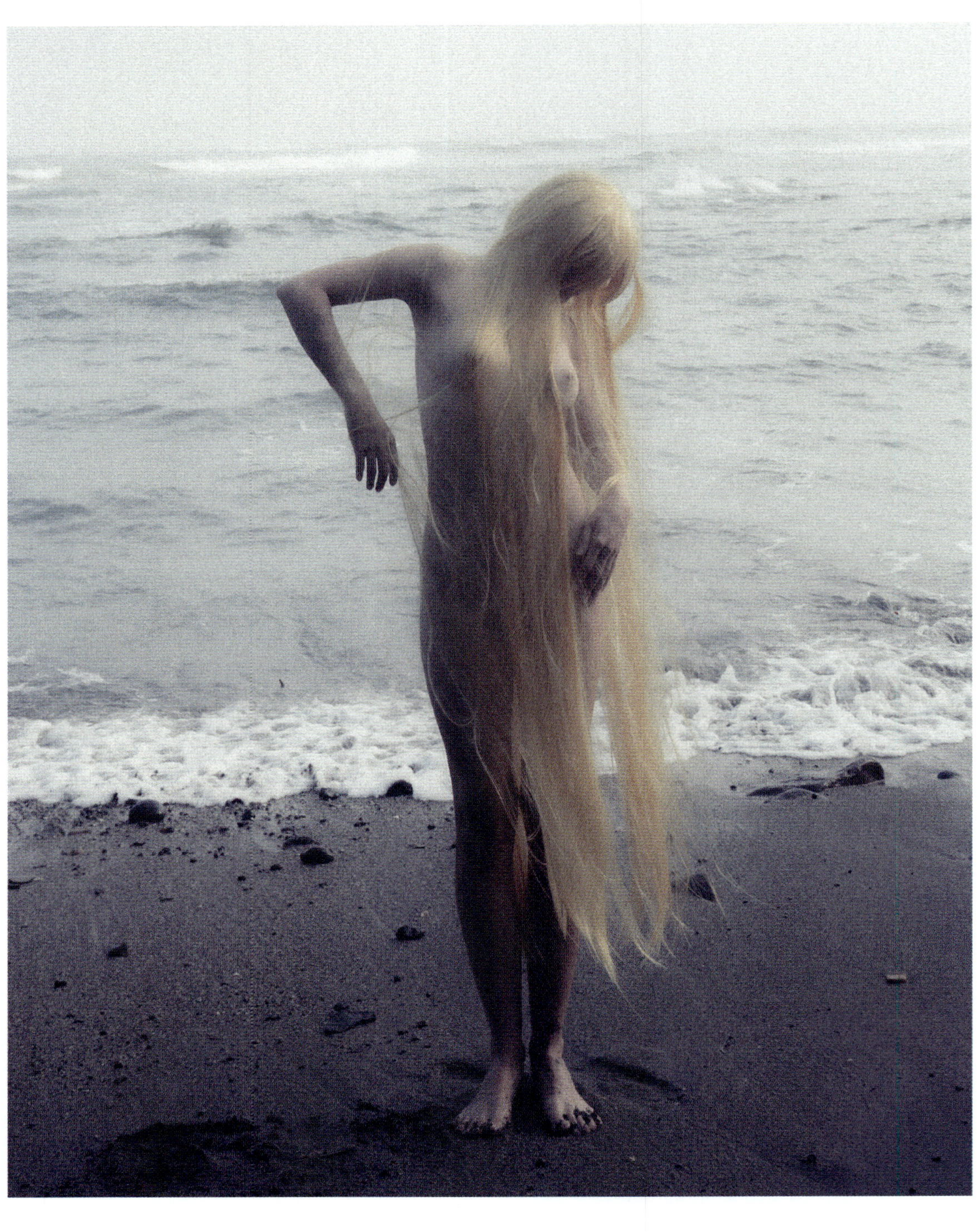

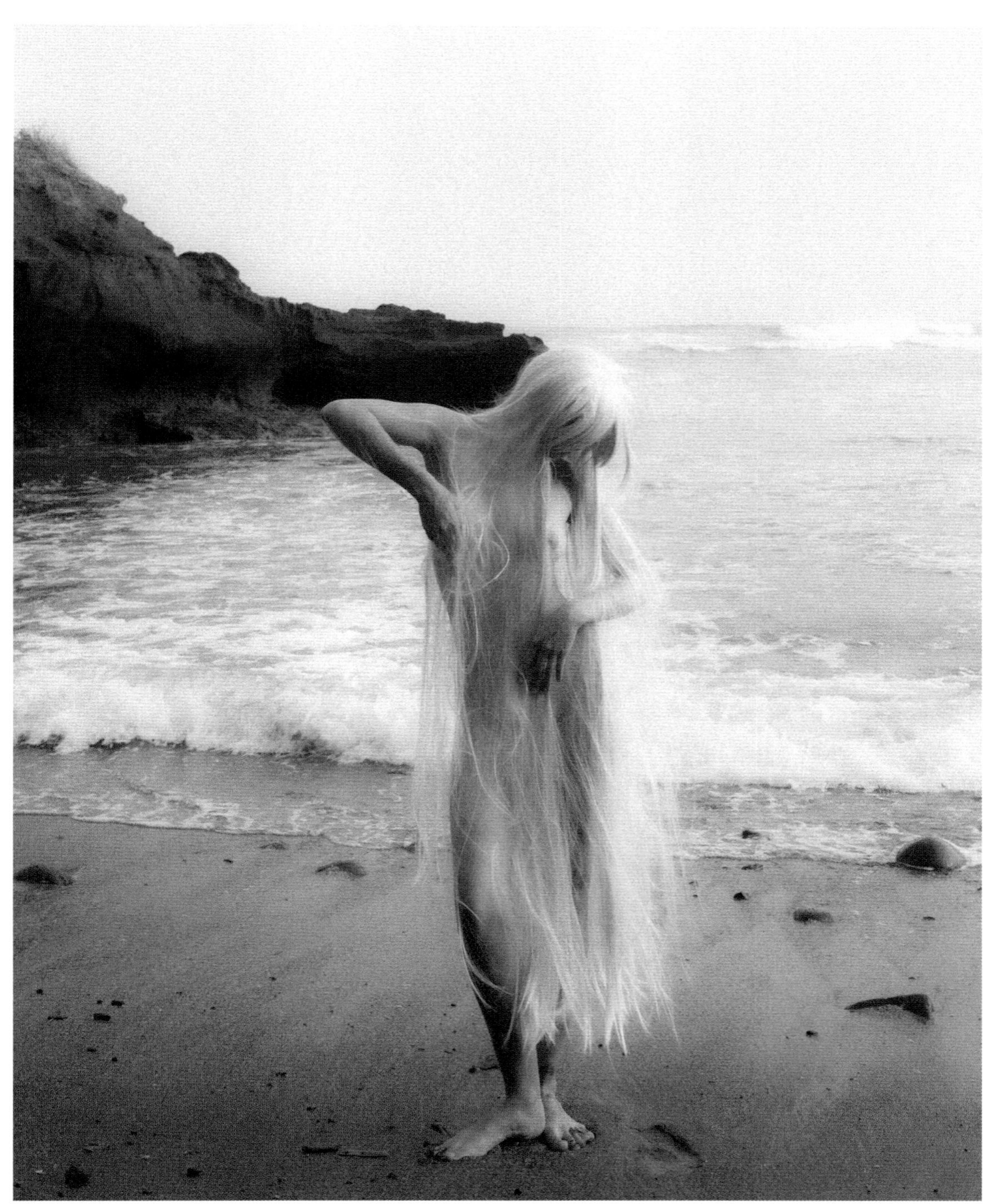

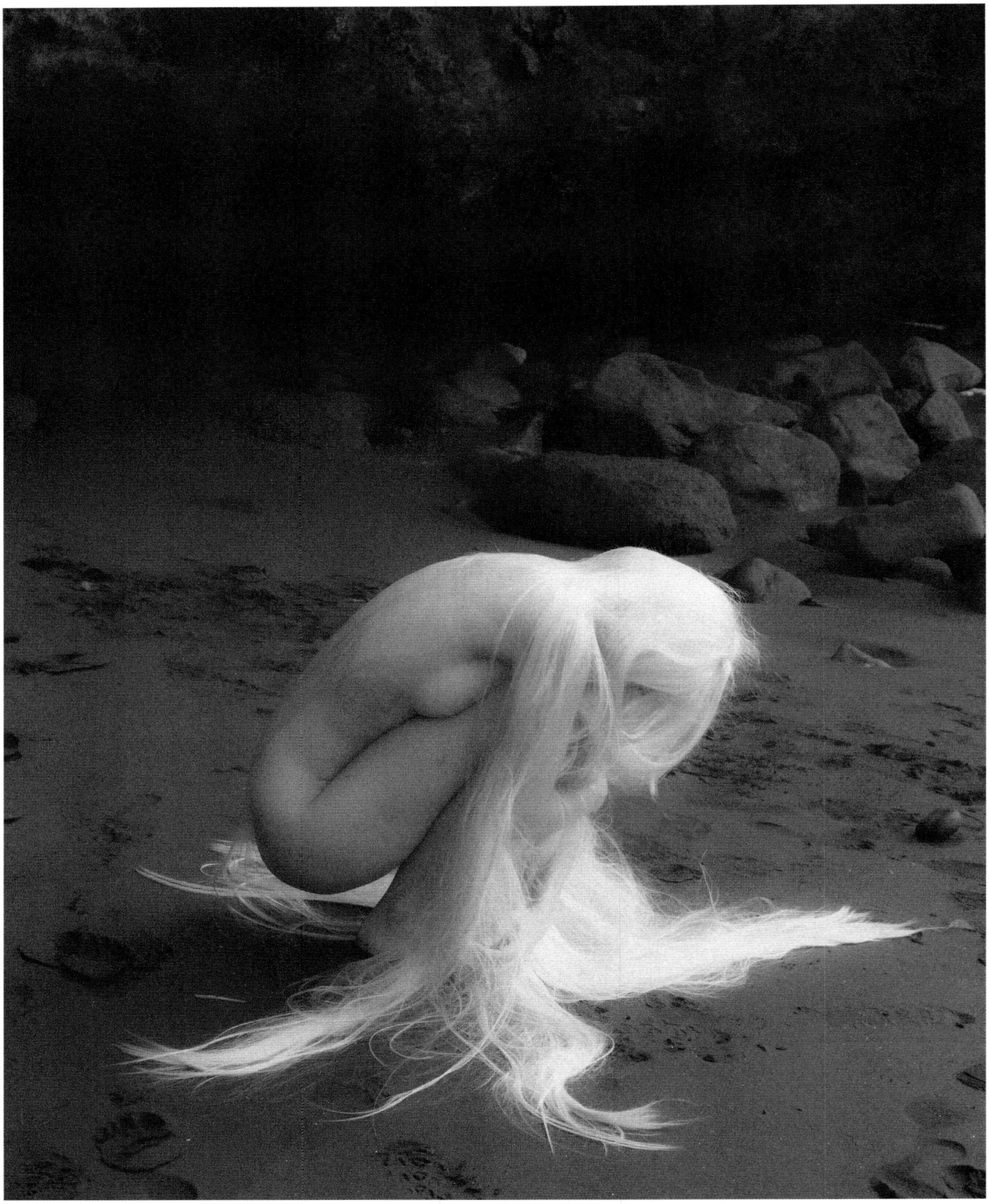

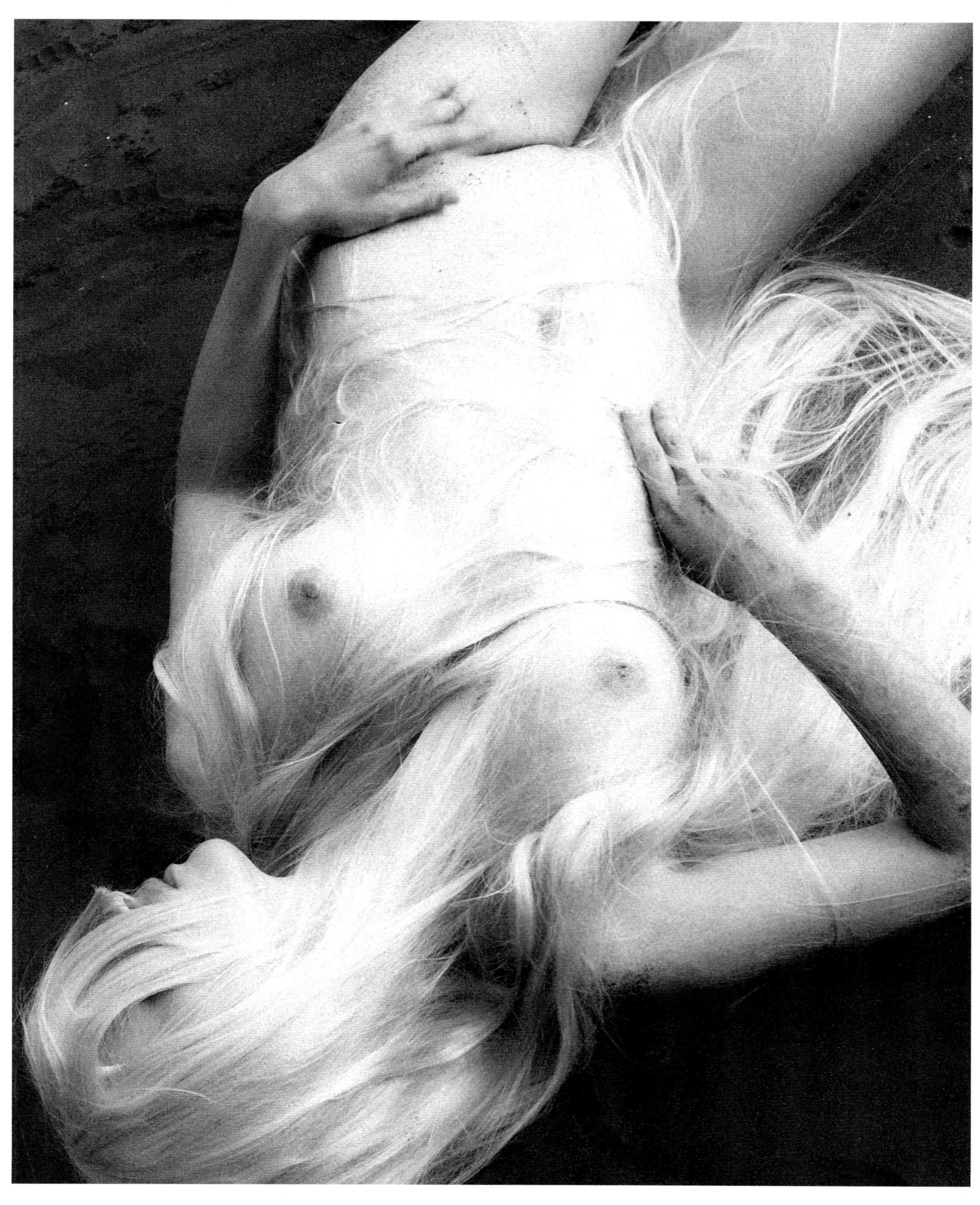

LISA LIND

A BABY, A BEAST

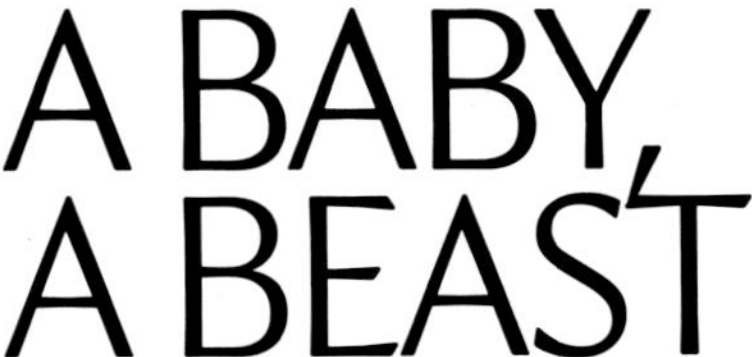

ARTWORK BY:
MARI KOPPANEN

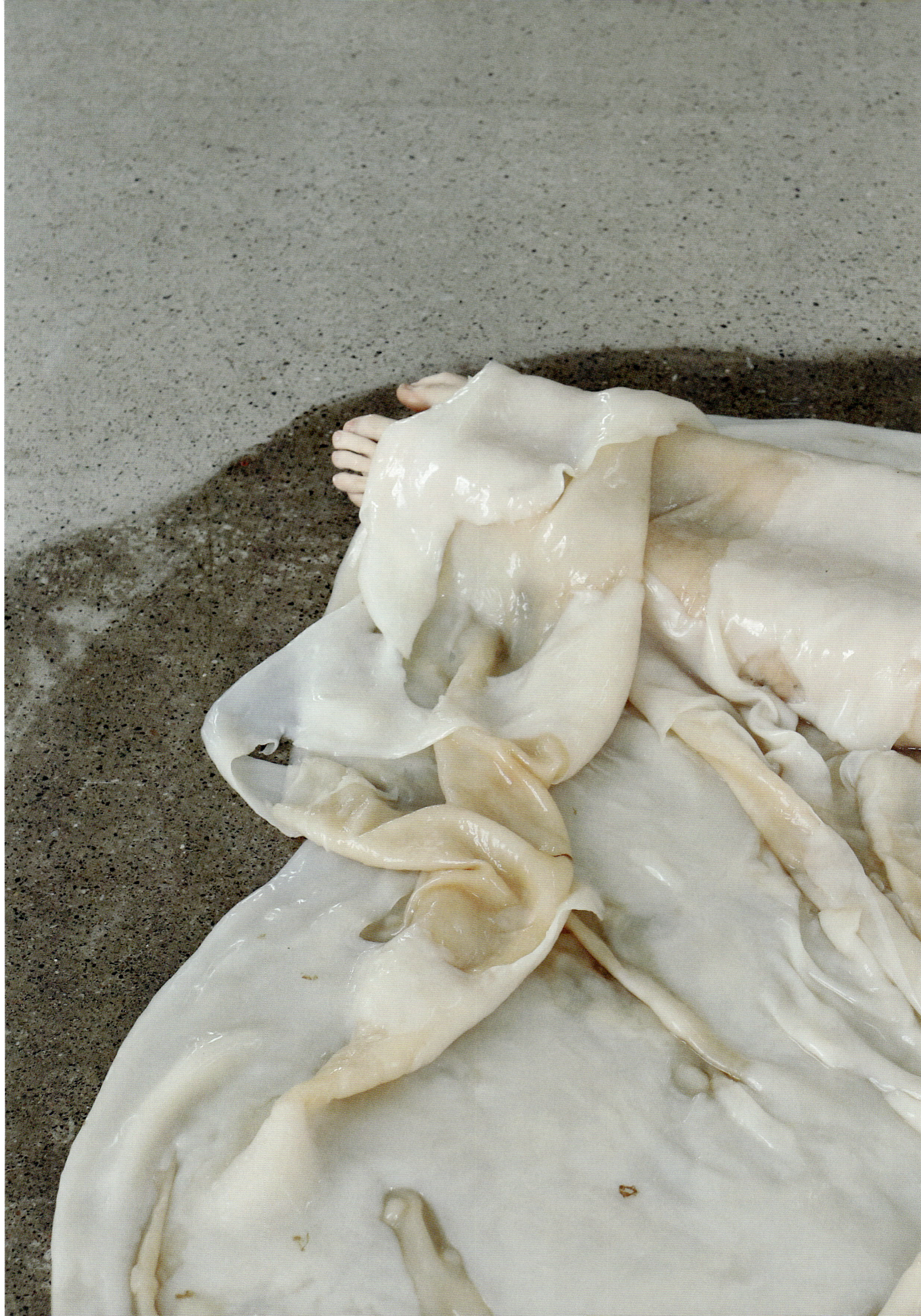

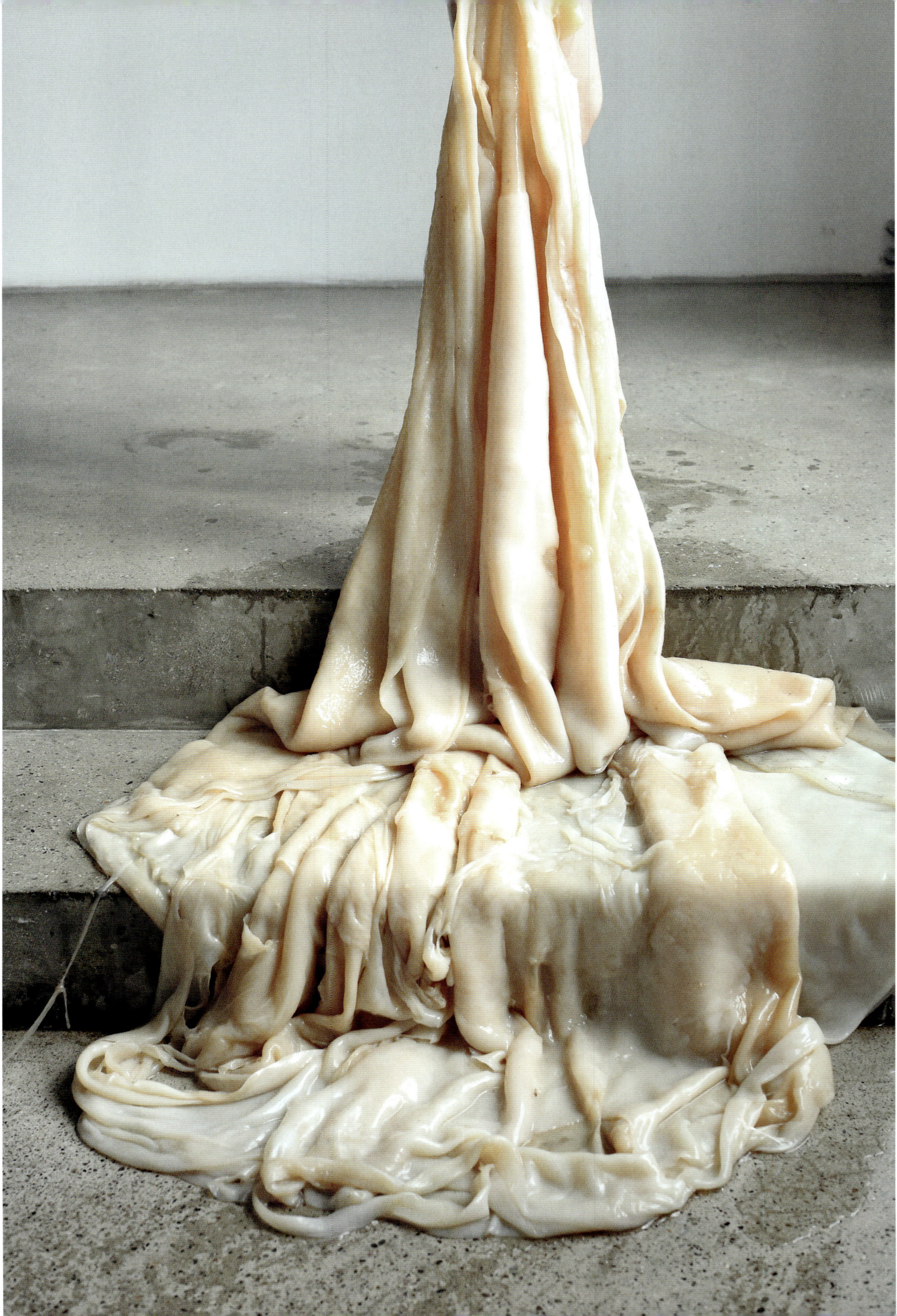

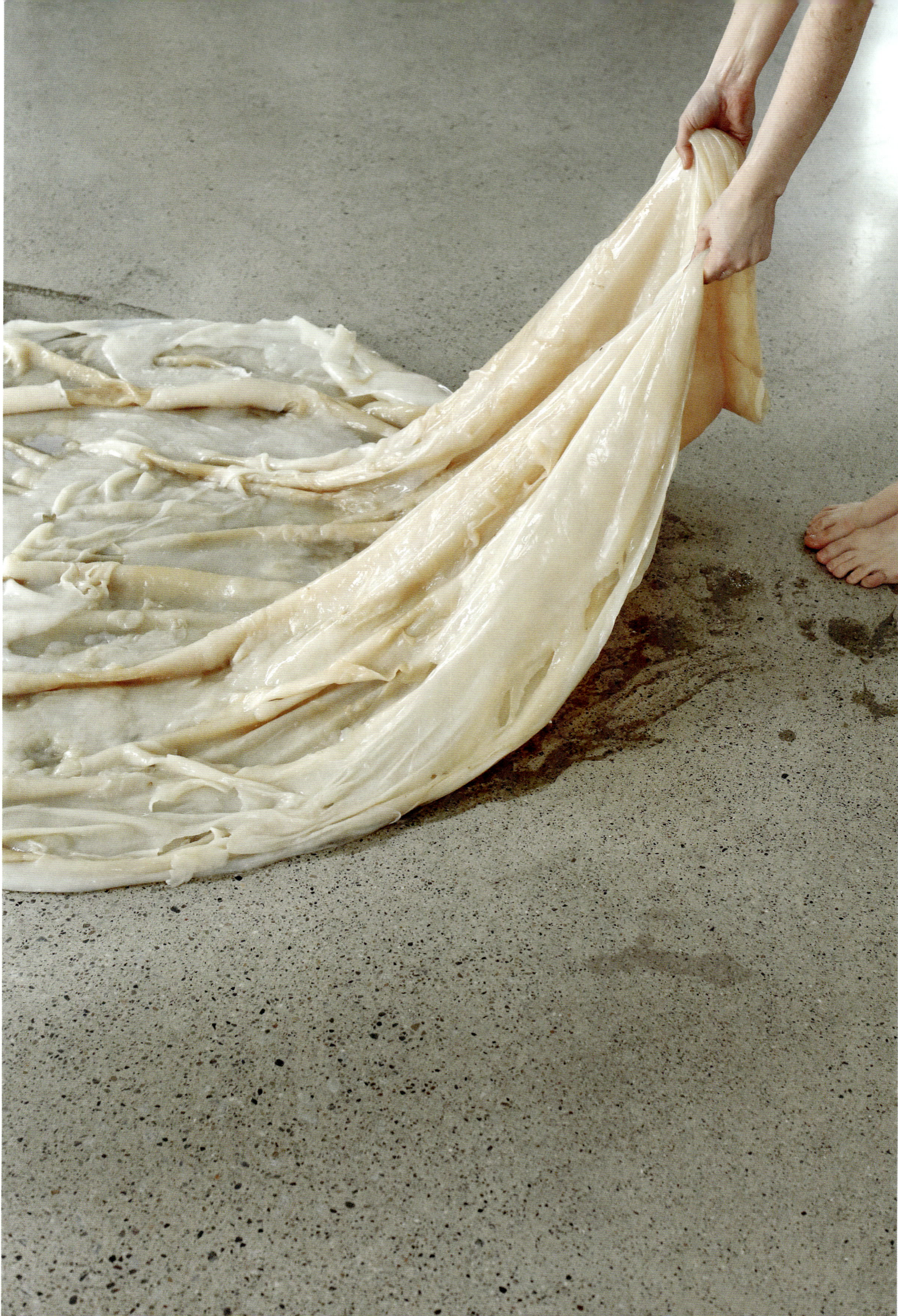

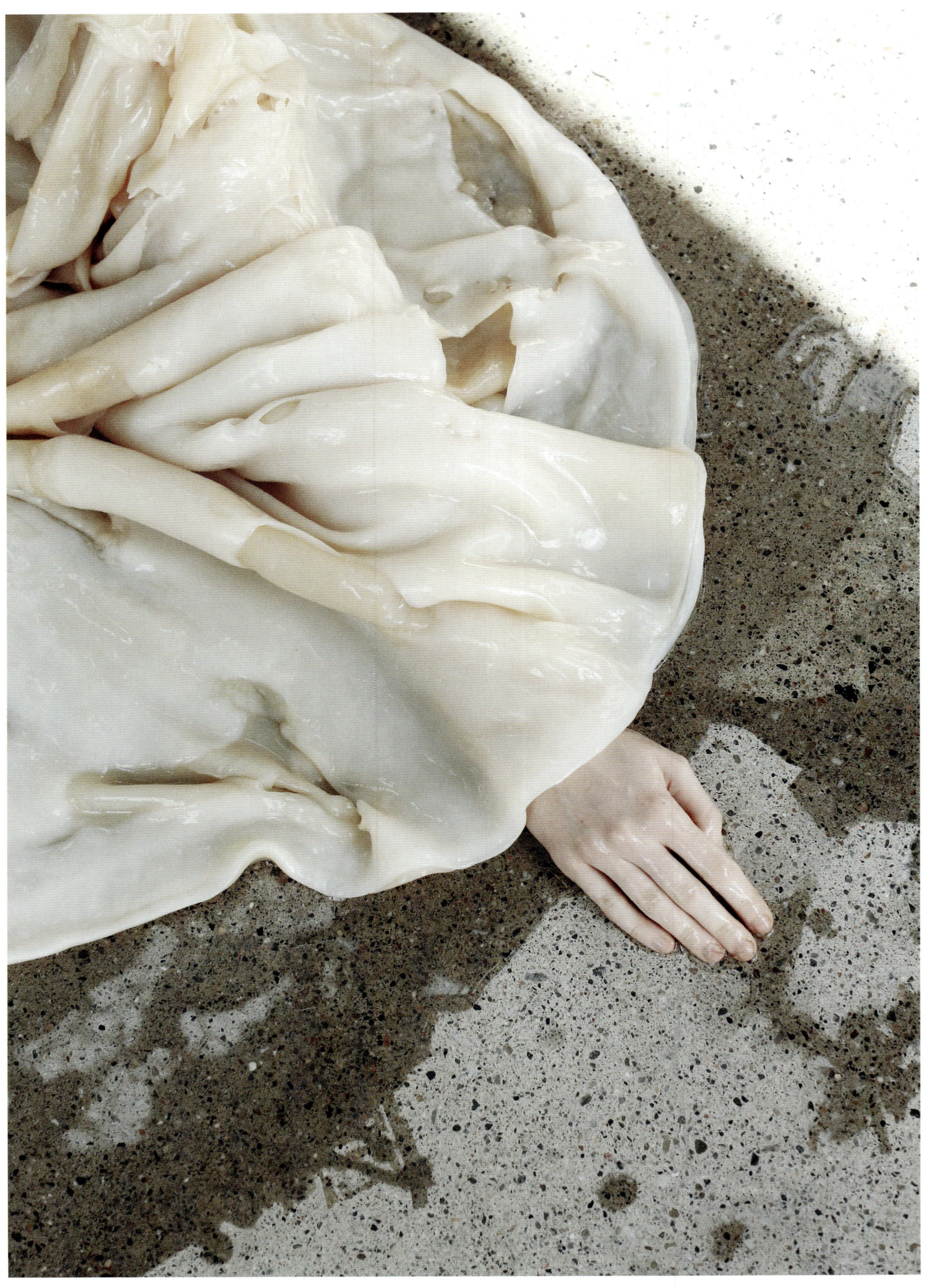

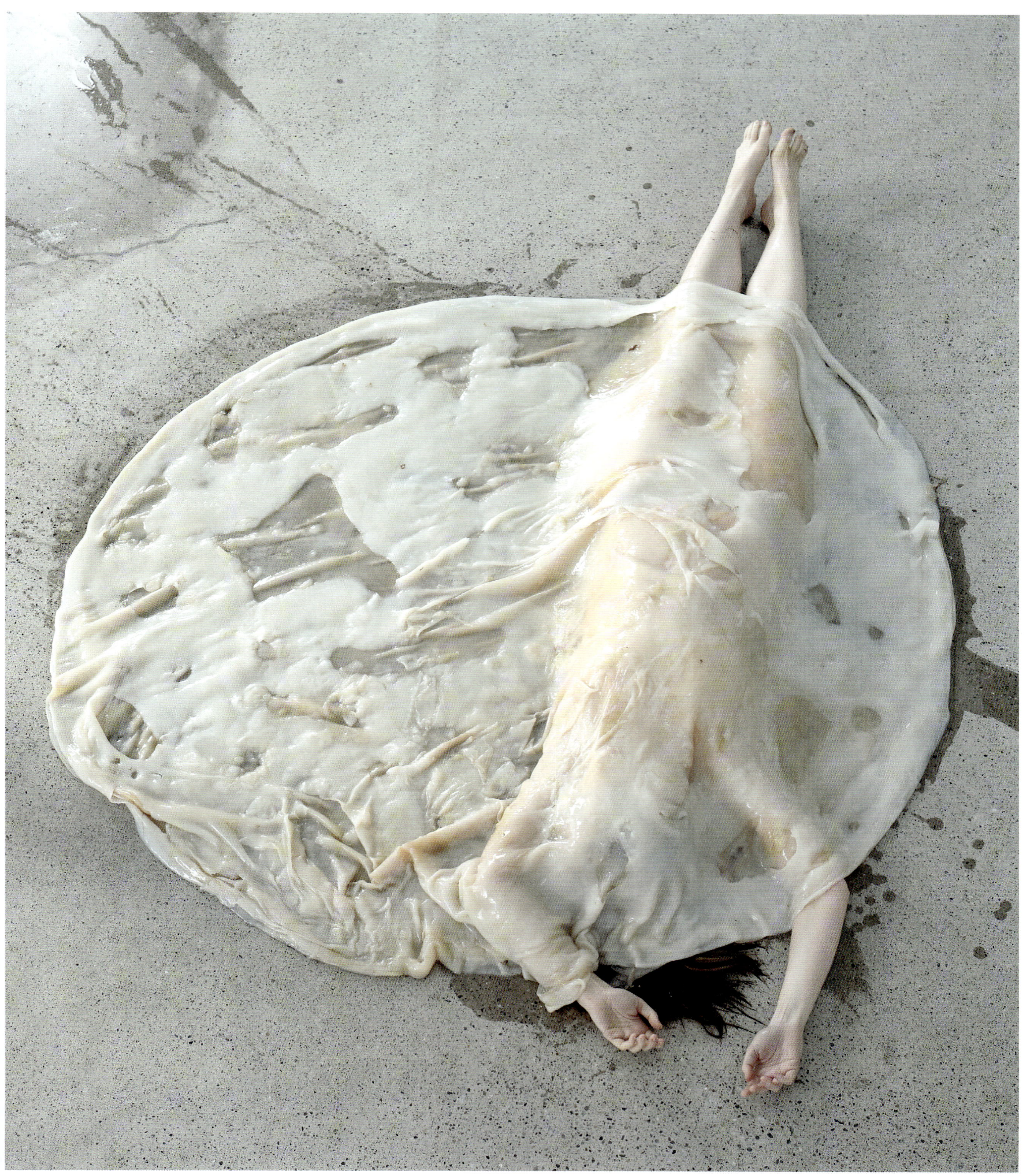

SMPH

SMPH ARE
STEFAN MILEV AND
PHIL HOFFMANN

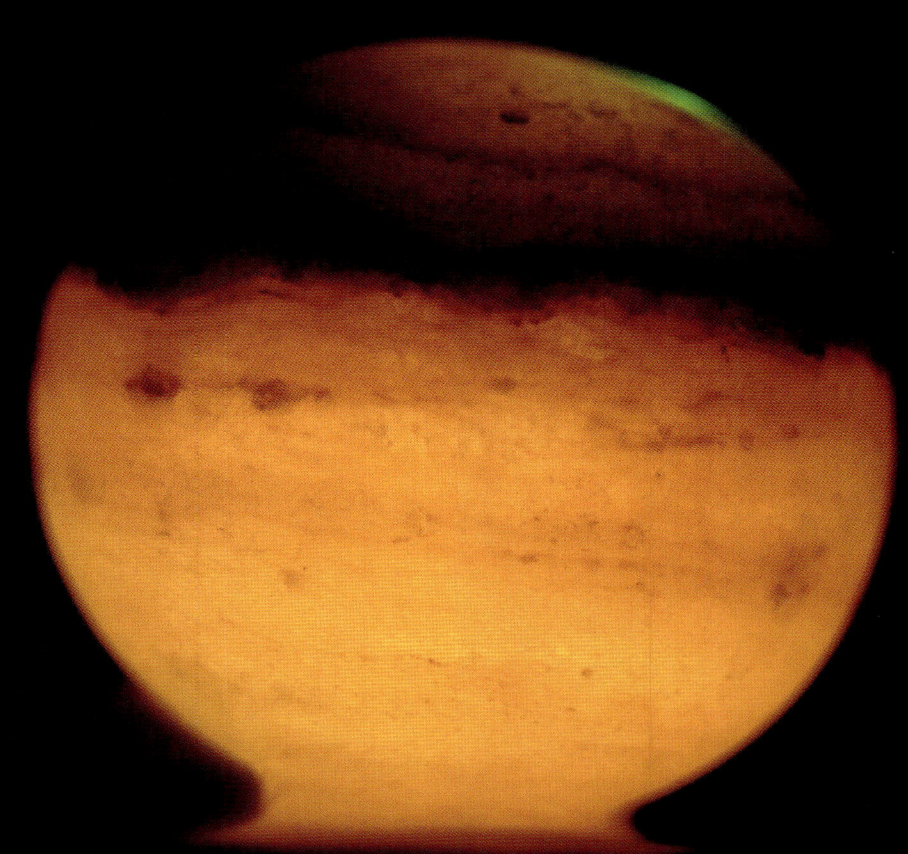

SILENCE

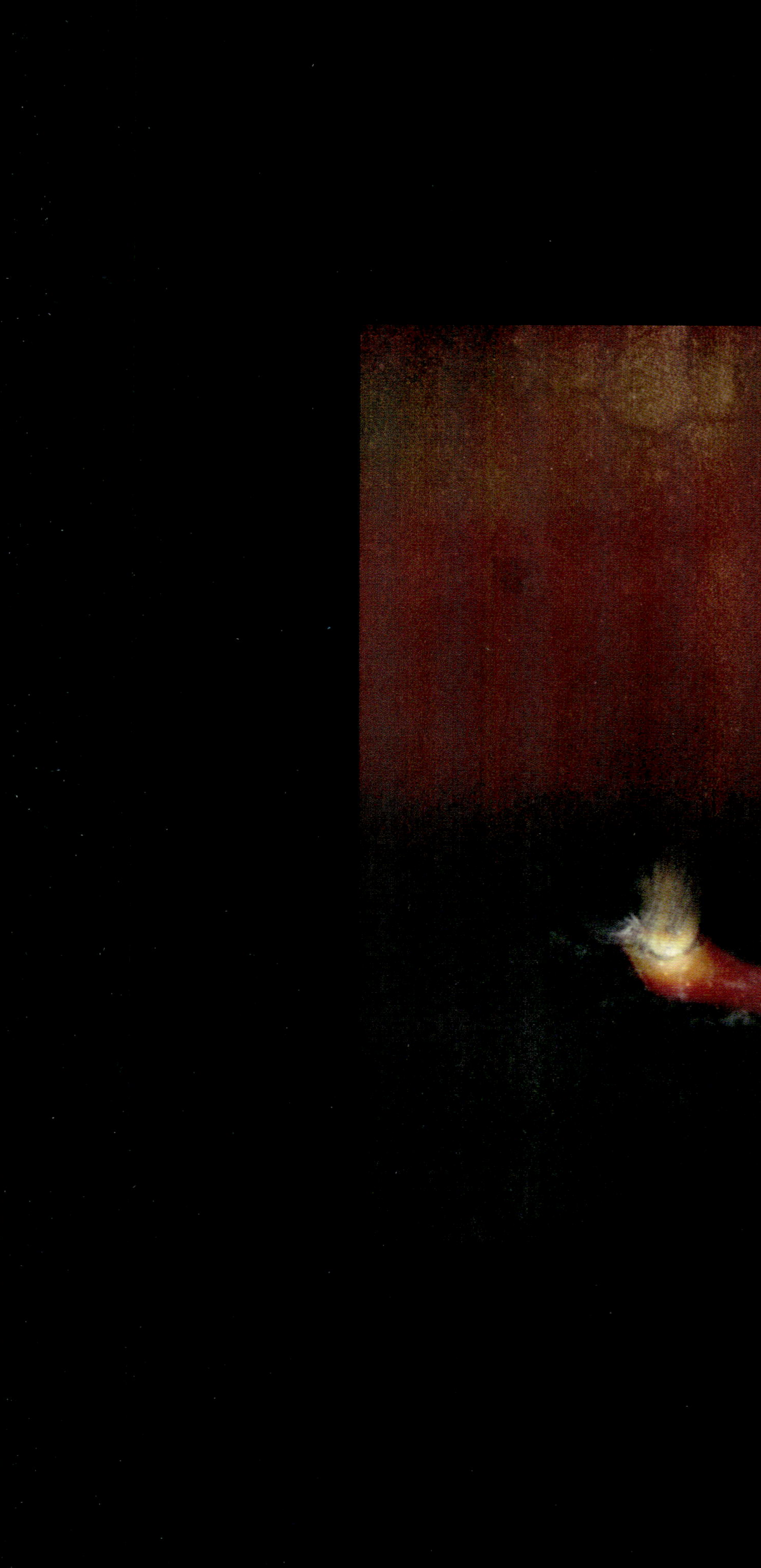

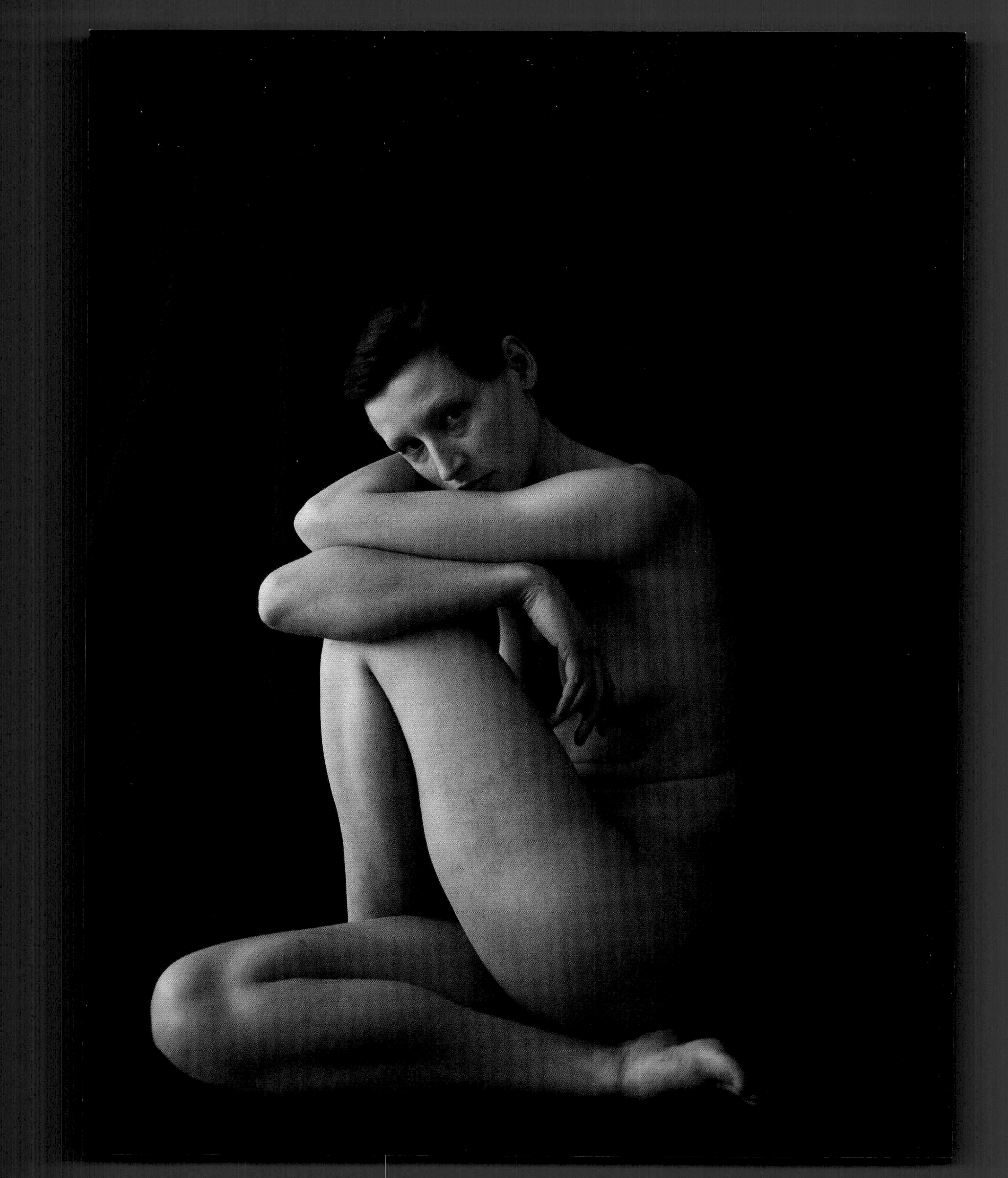

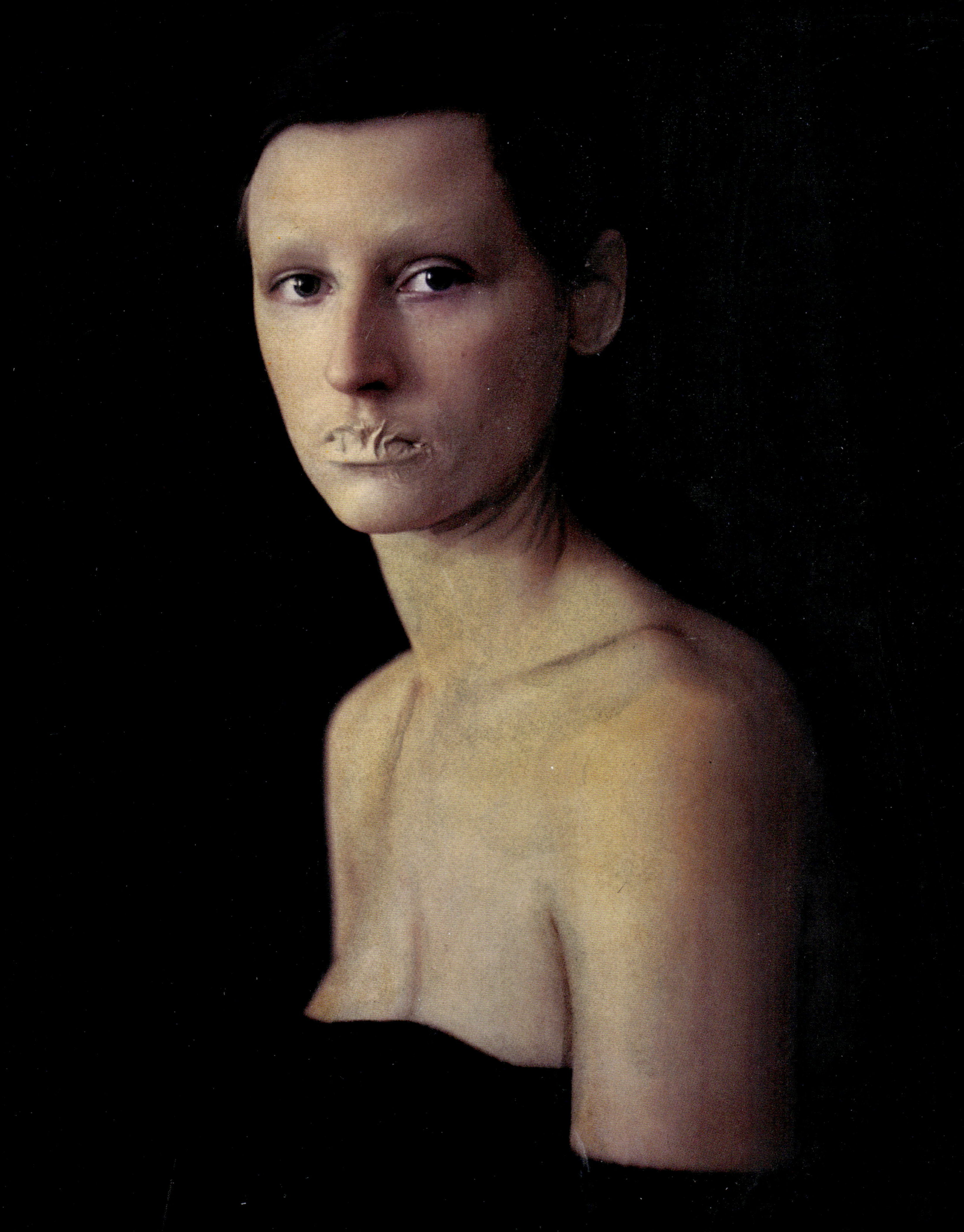

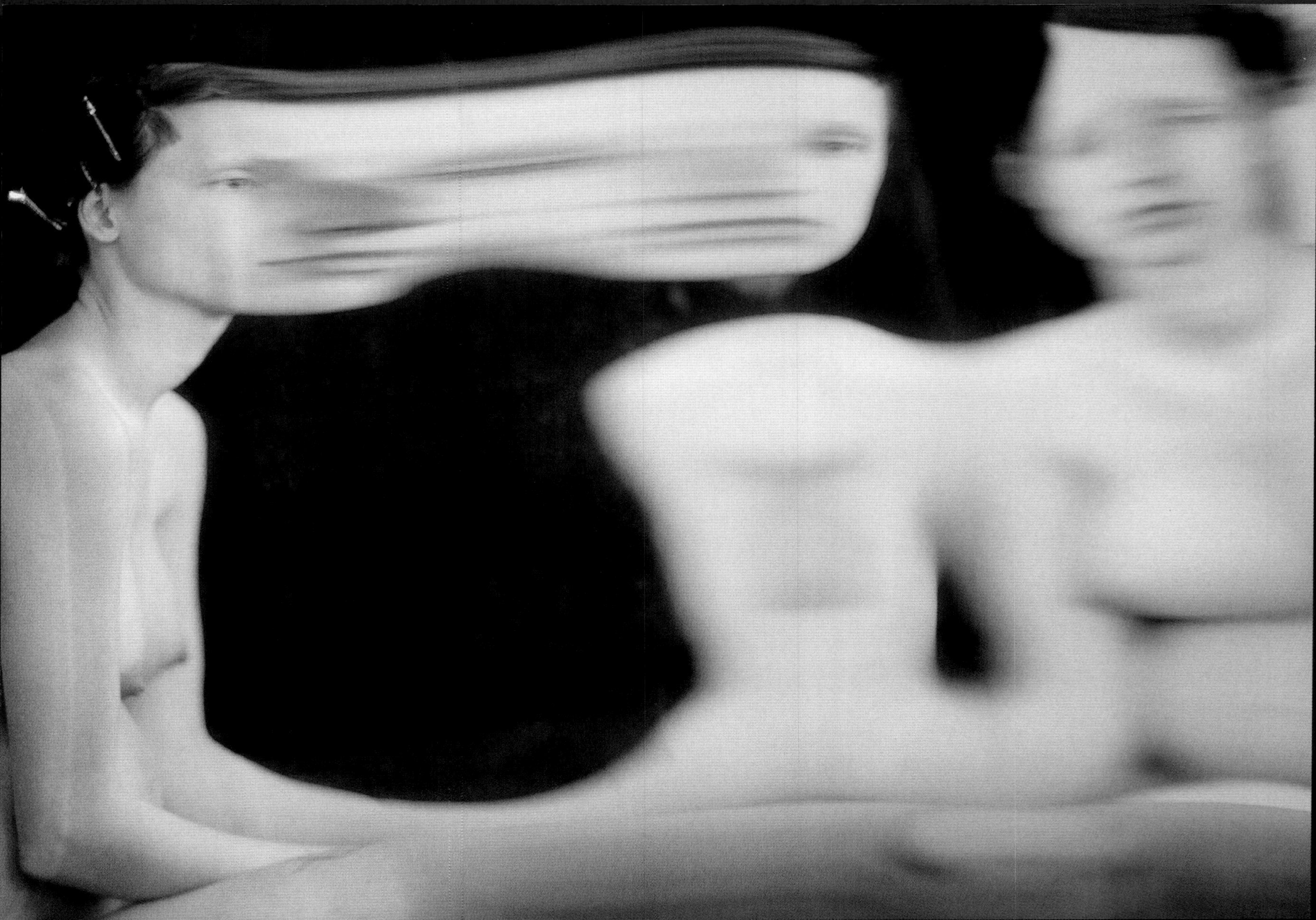

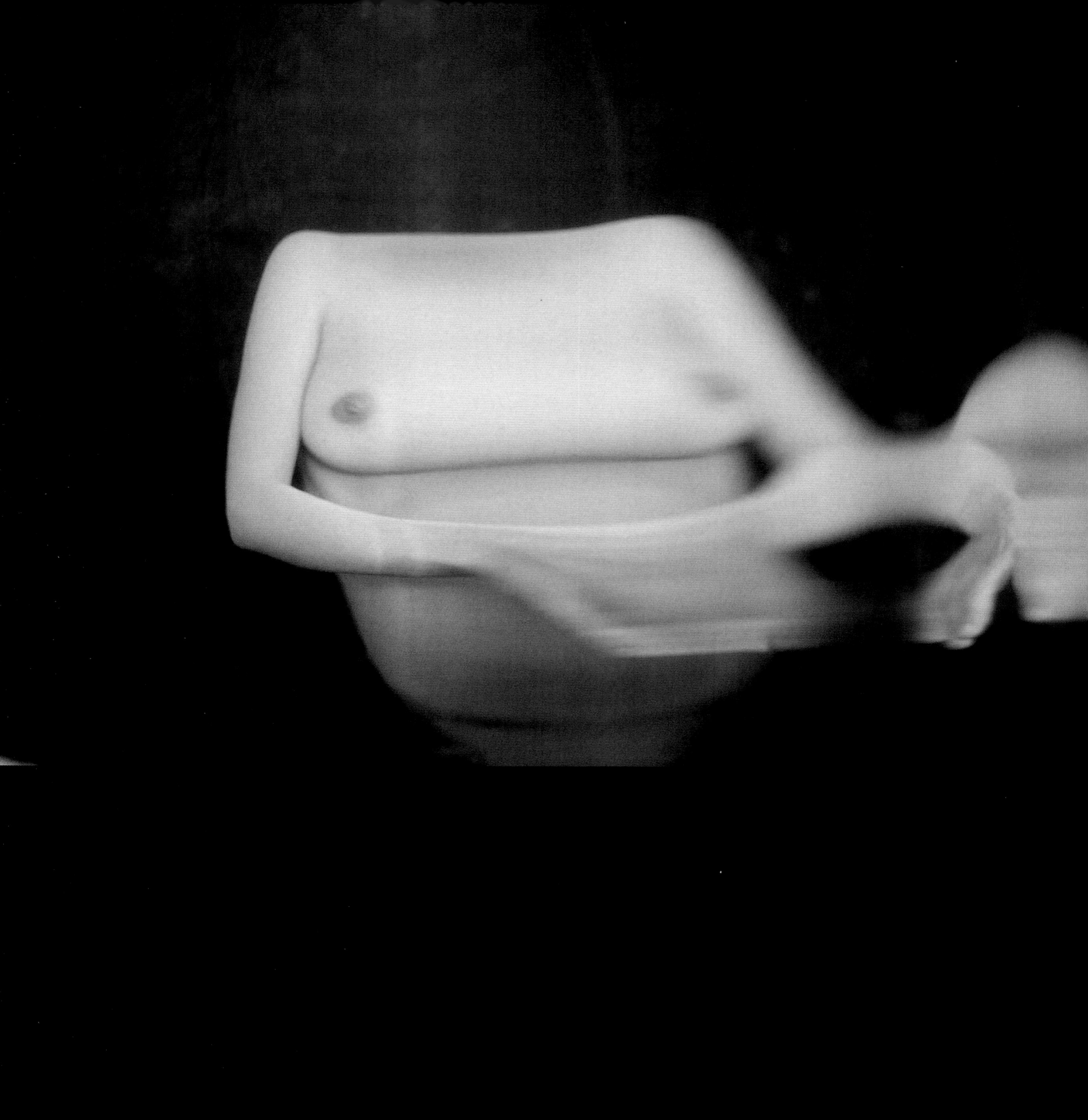

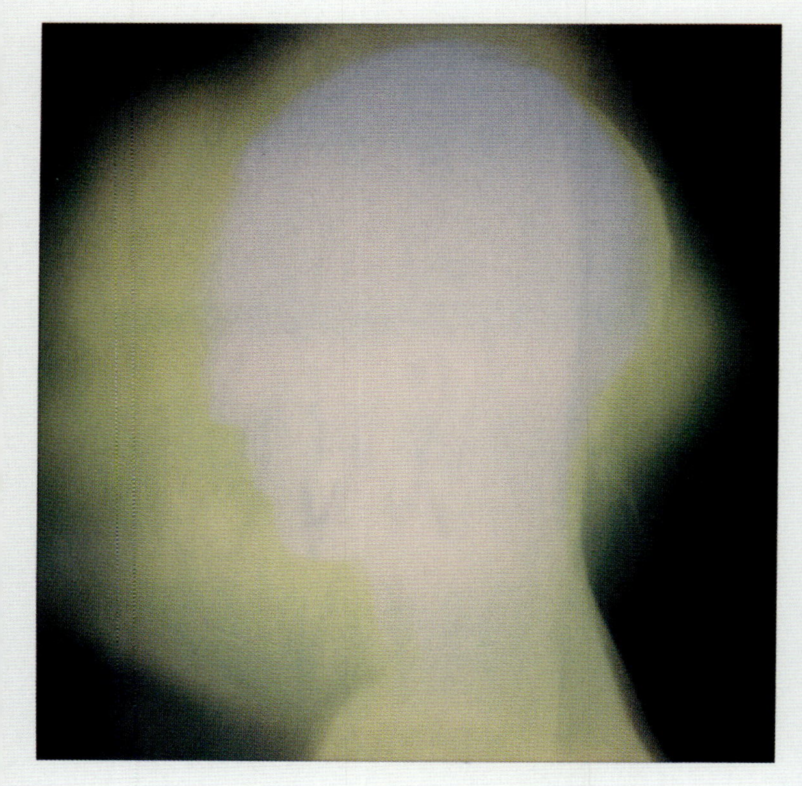

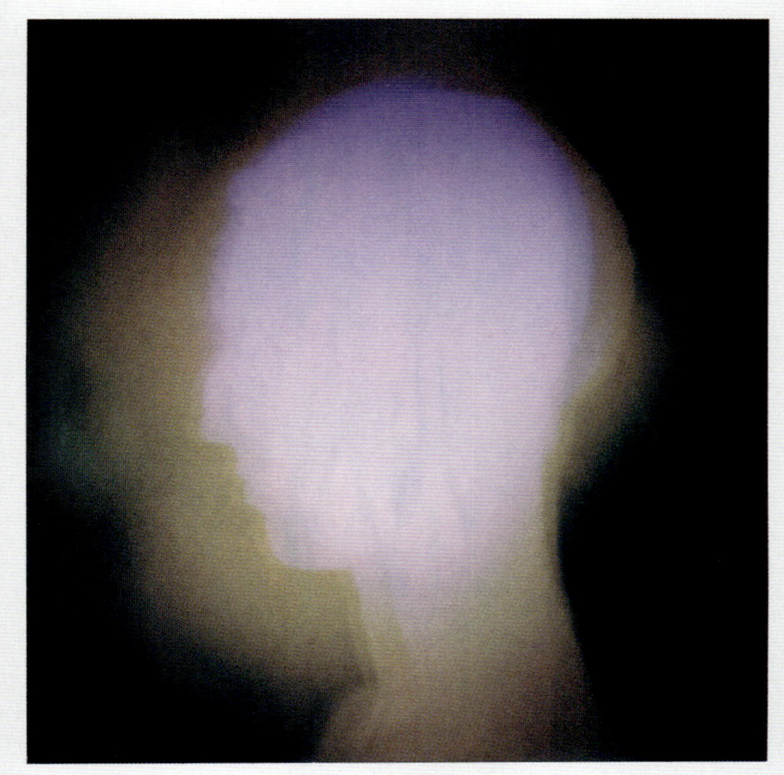

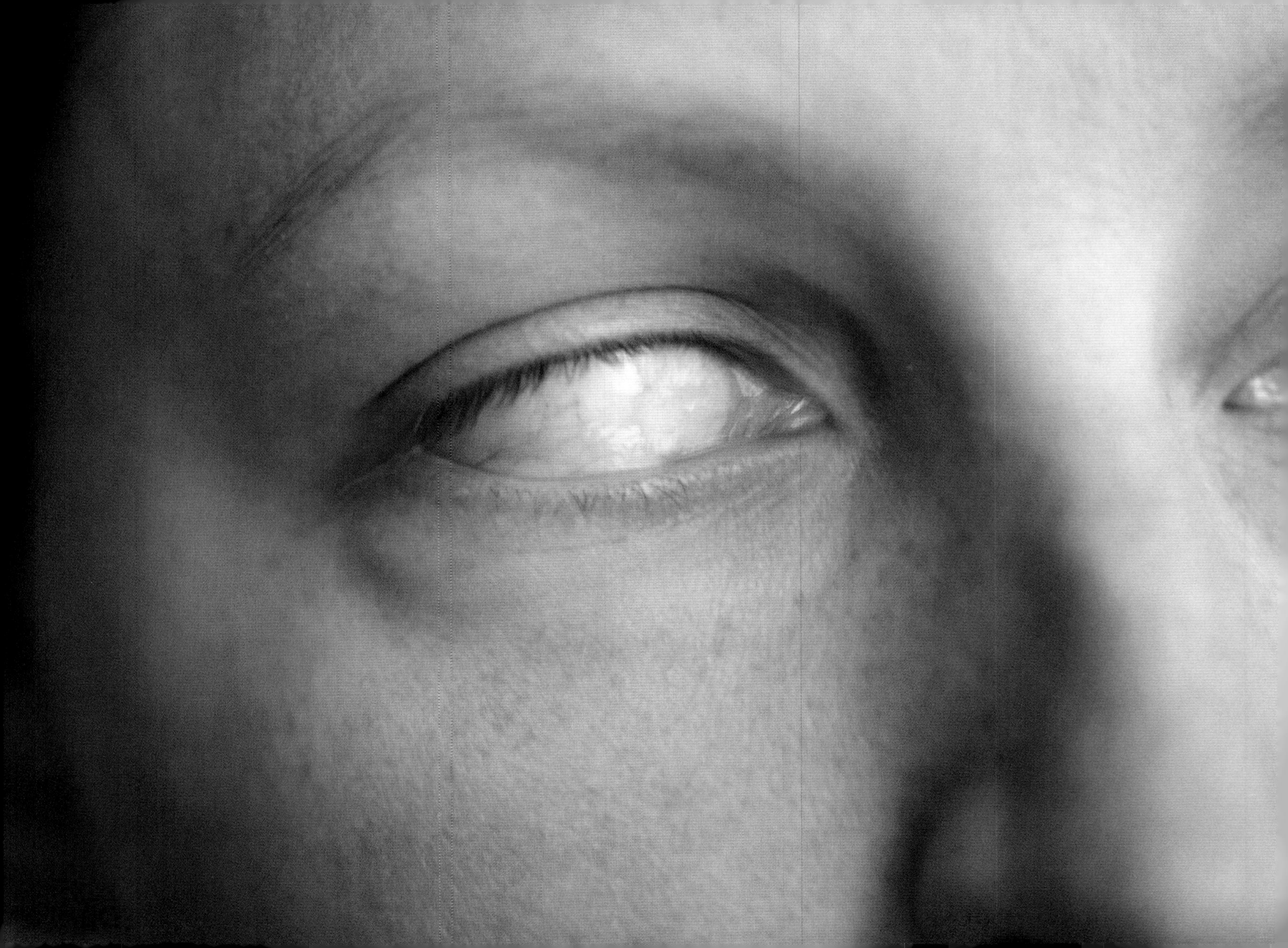

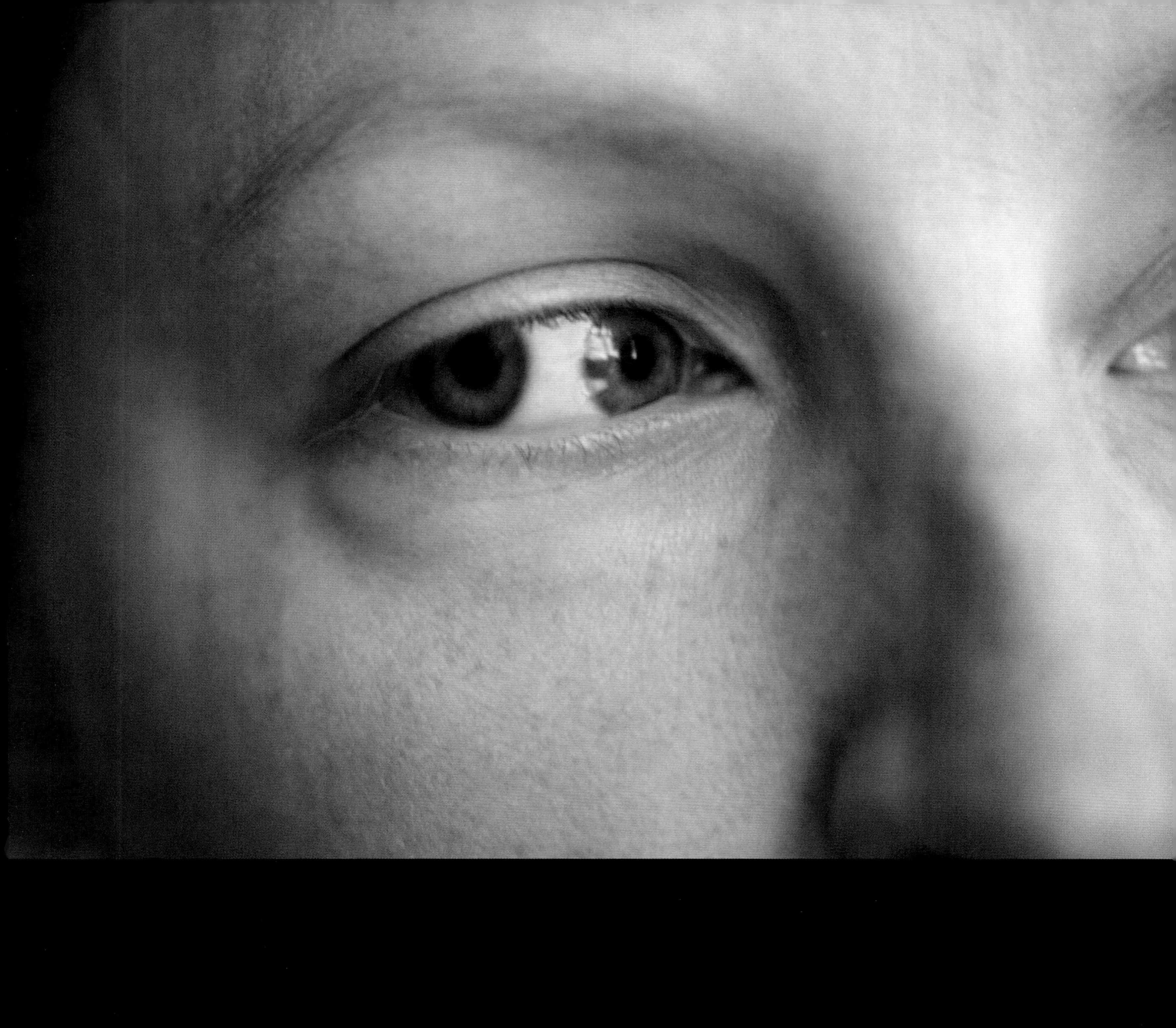

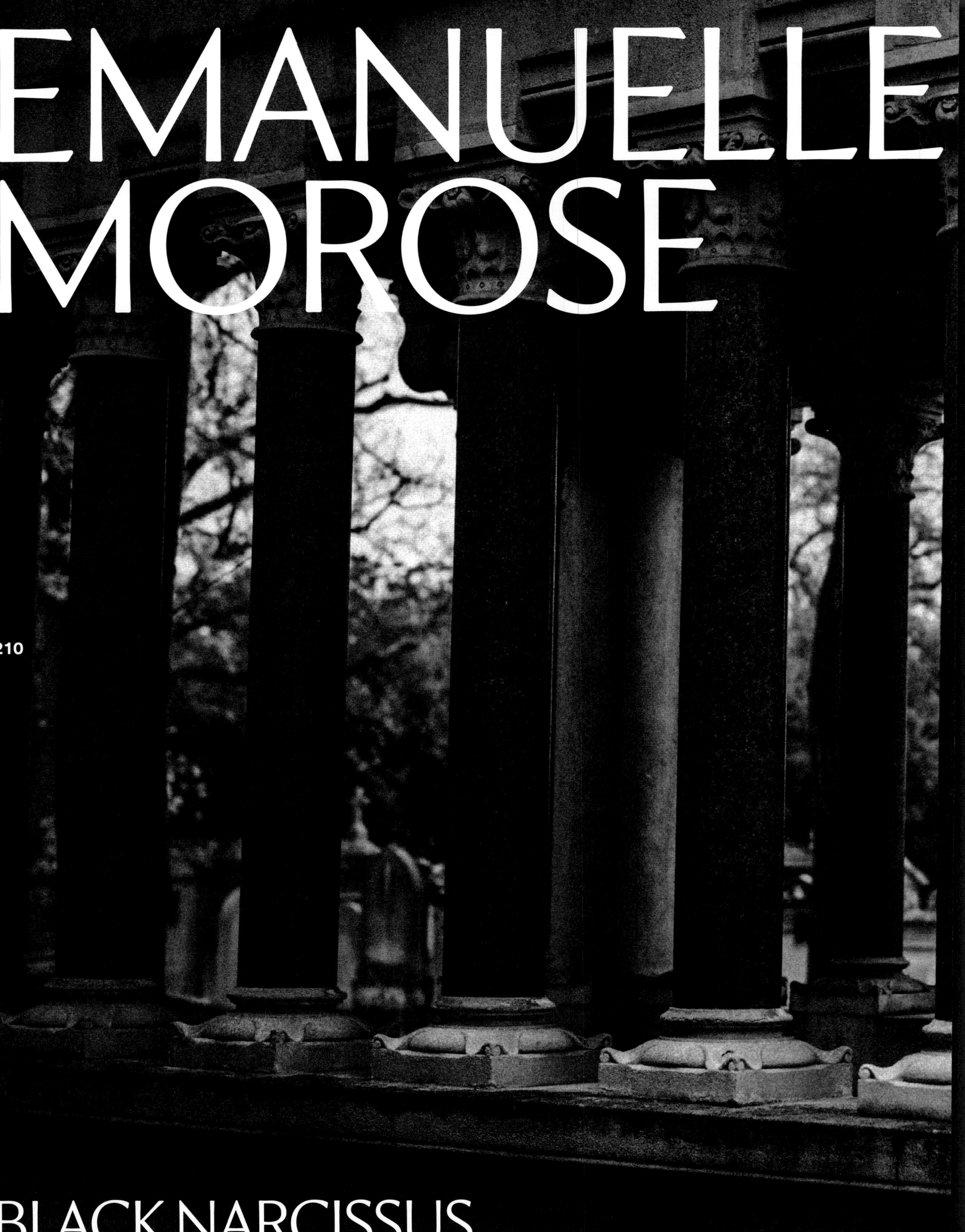

EMANUELLE
MOROSE
210
BLACK NARCISSUS

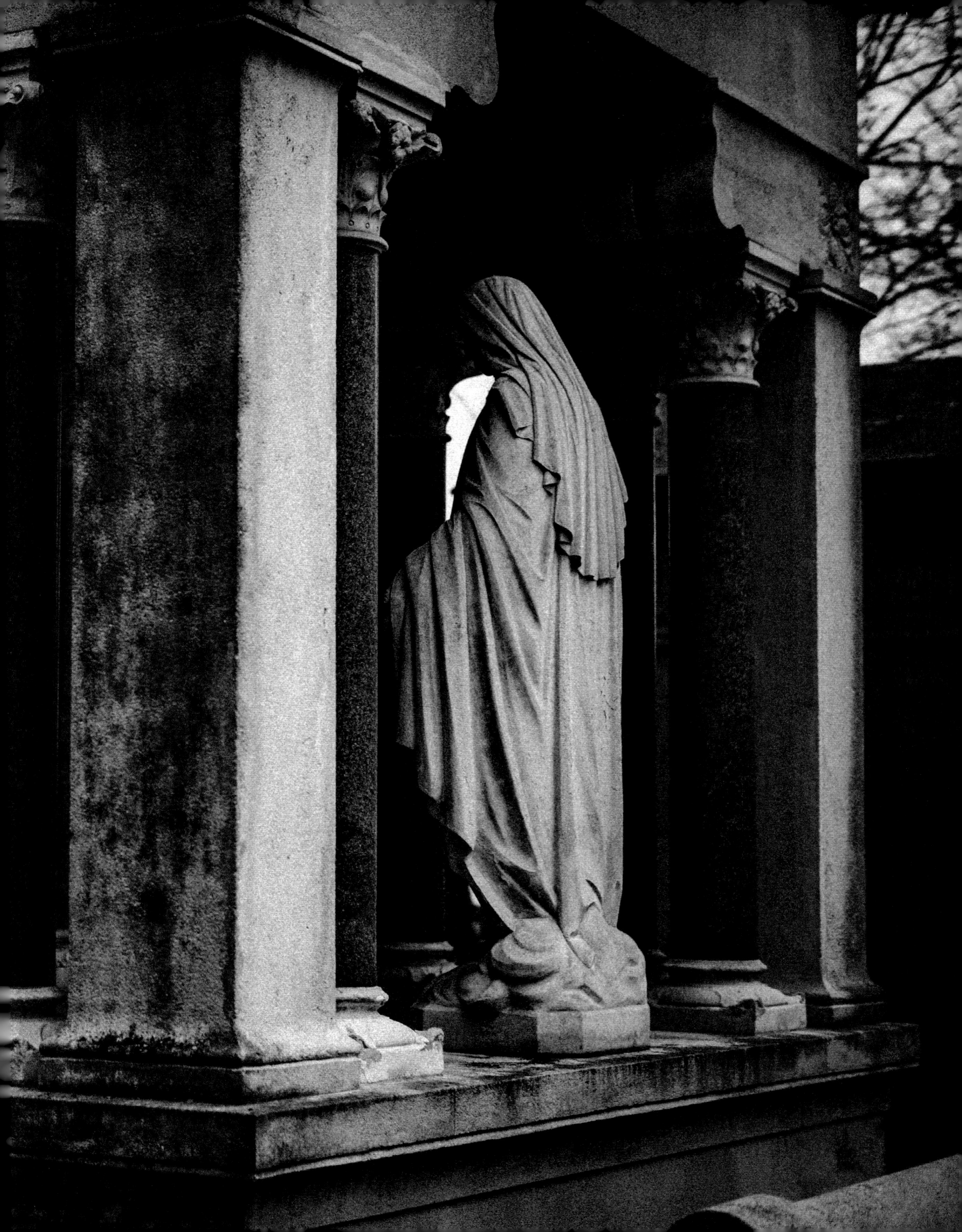

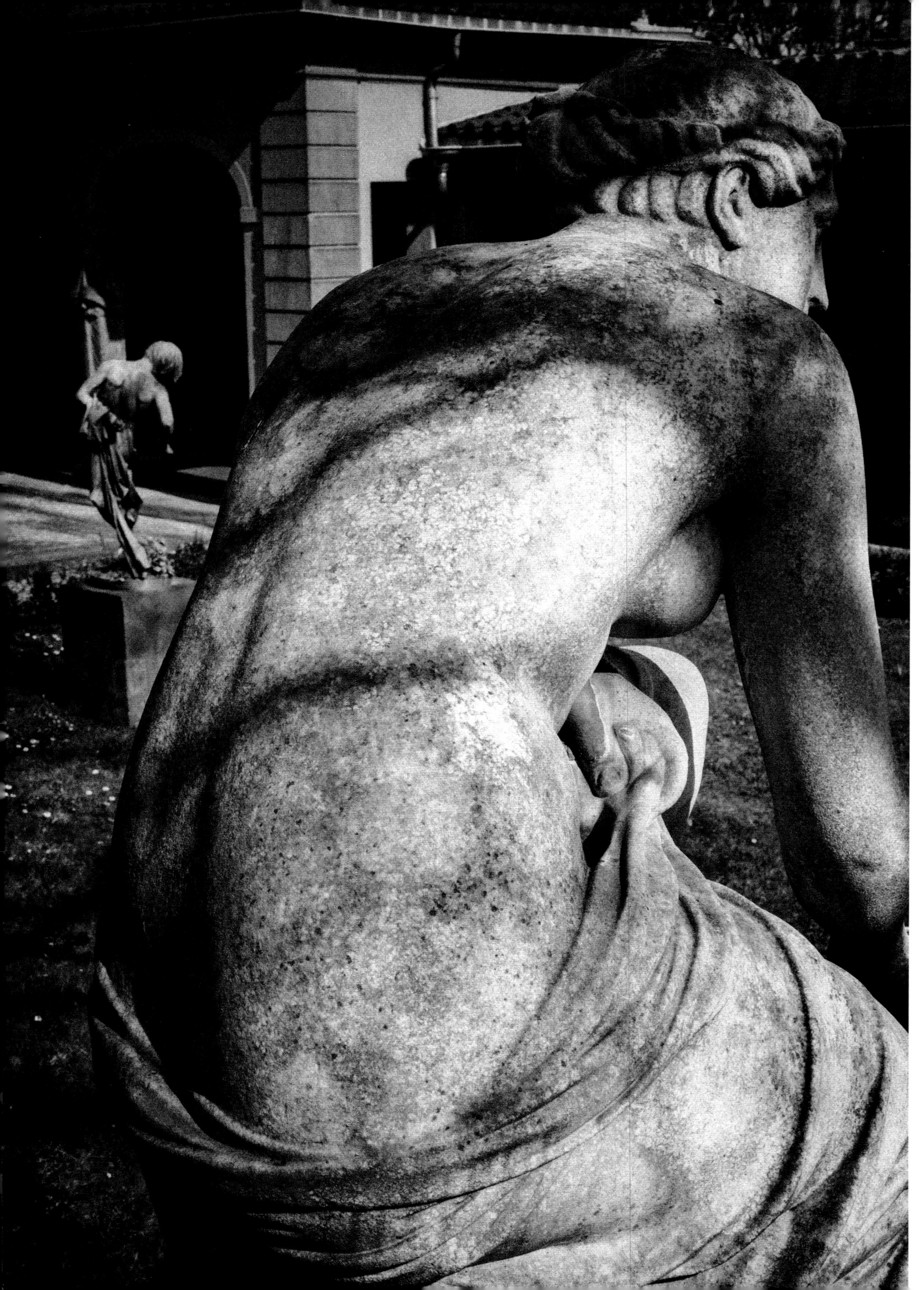

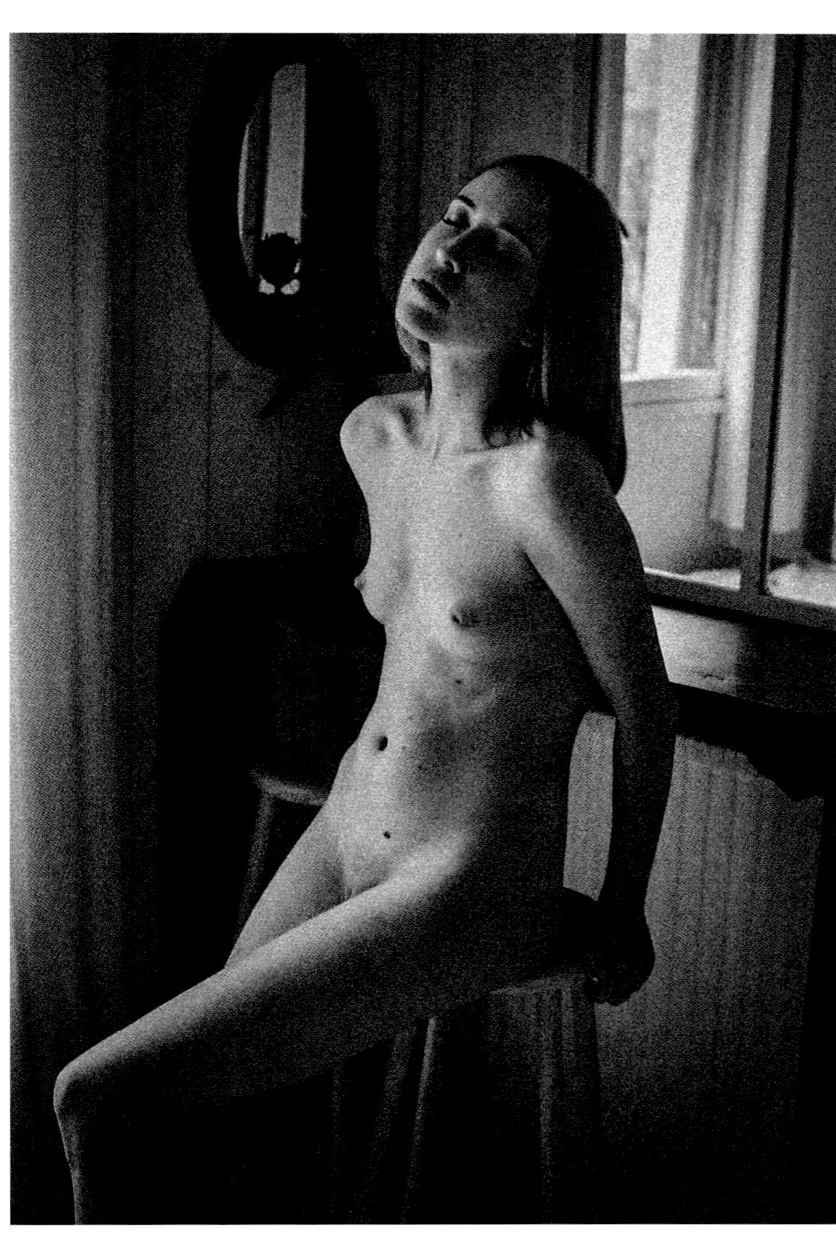

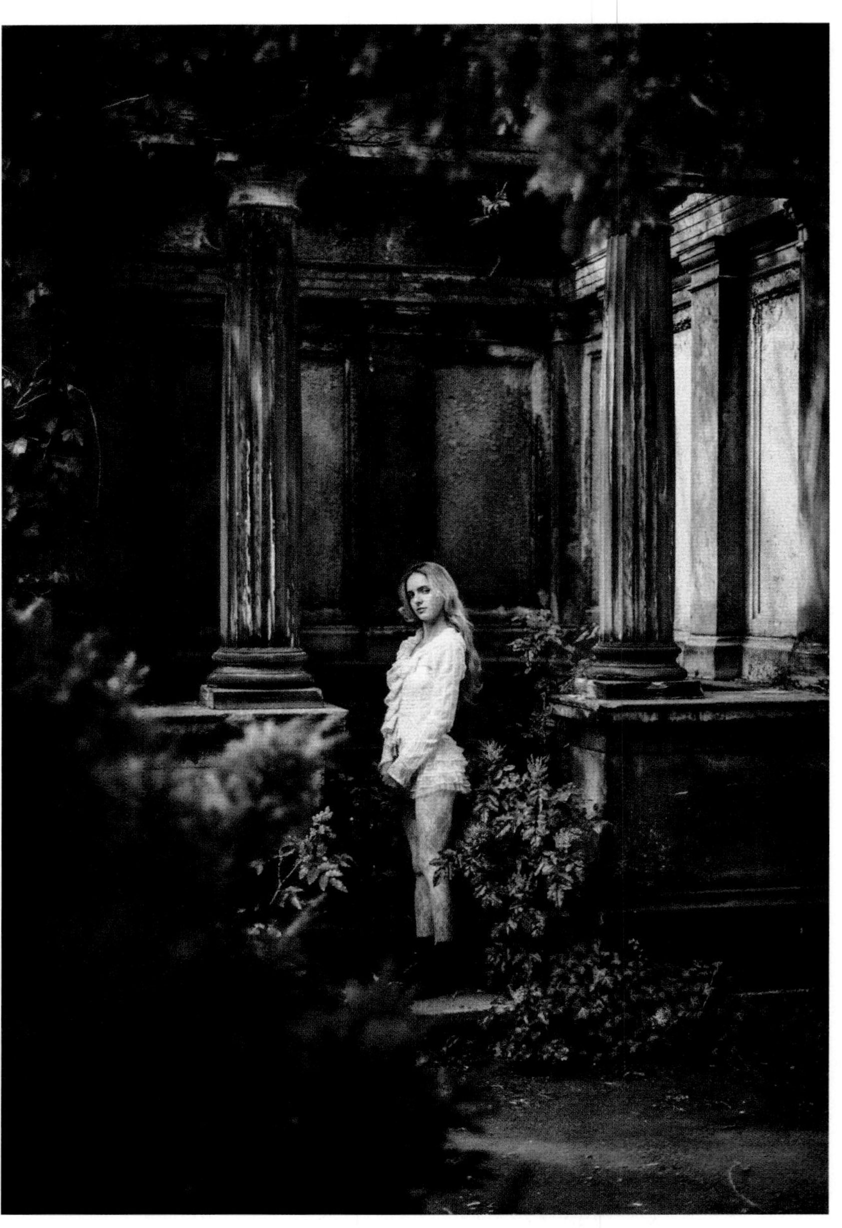

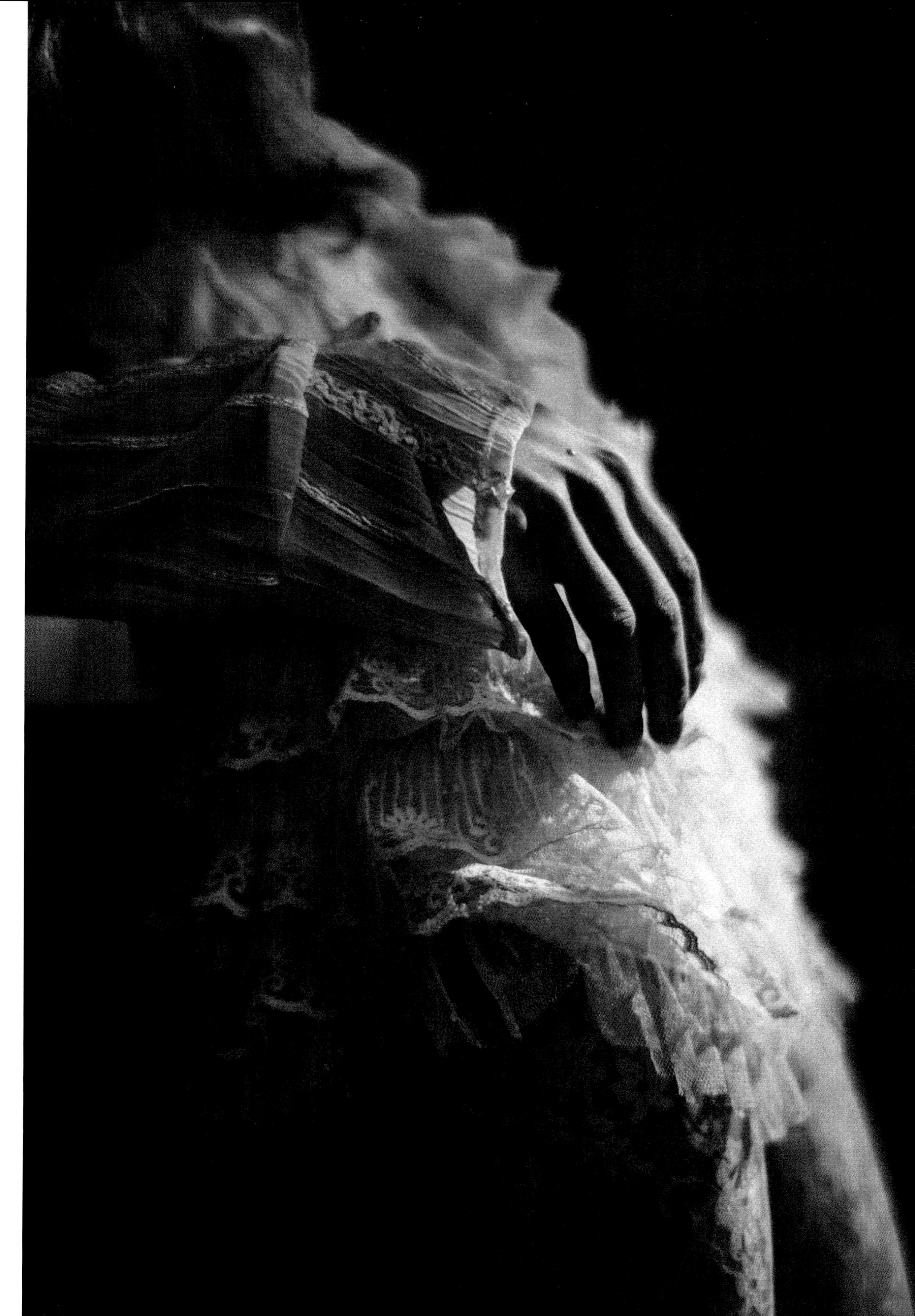

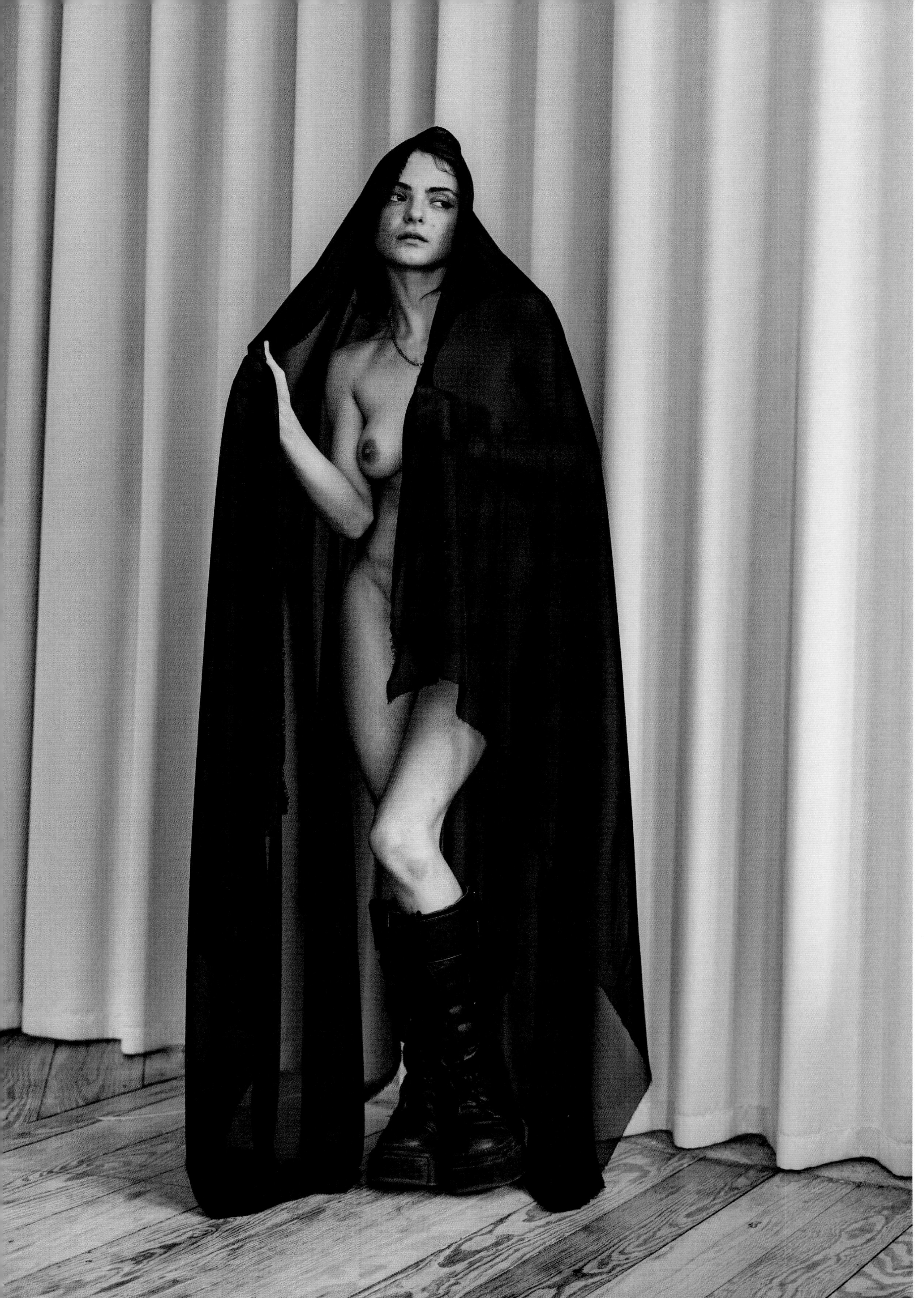

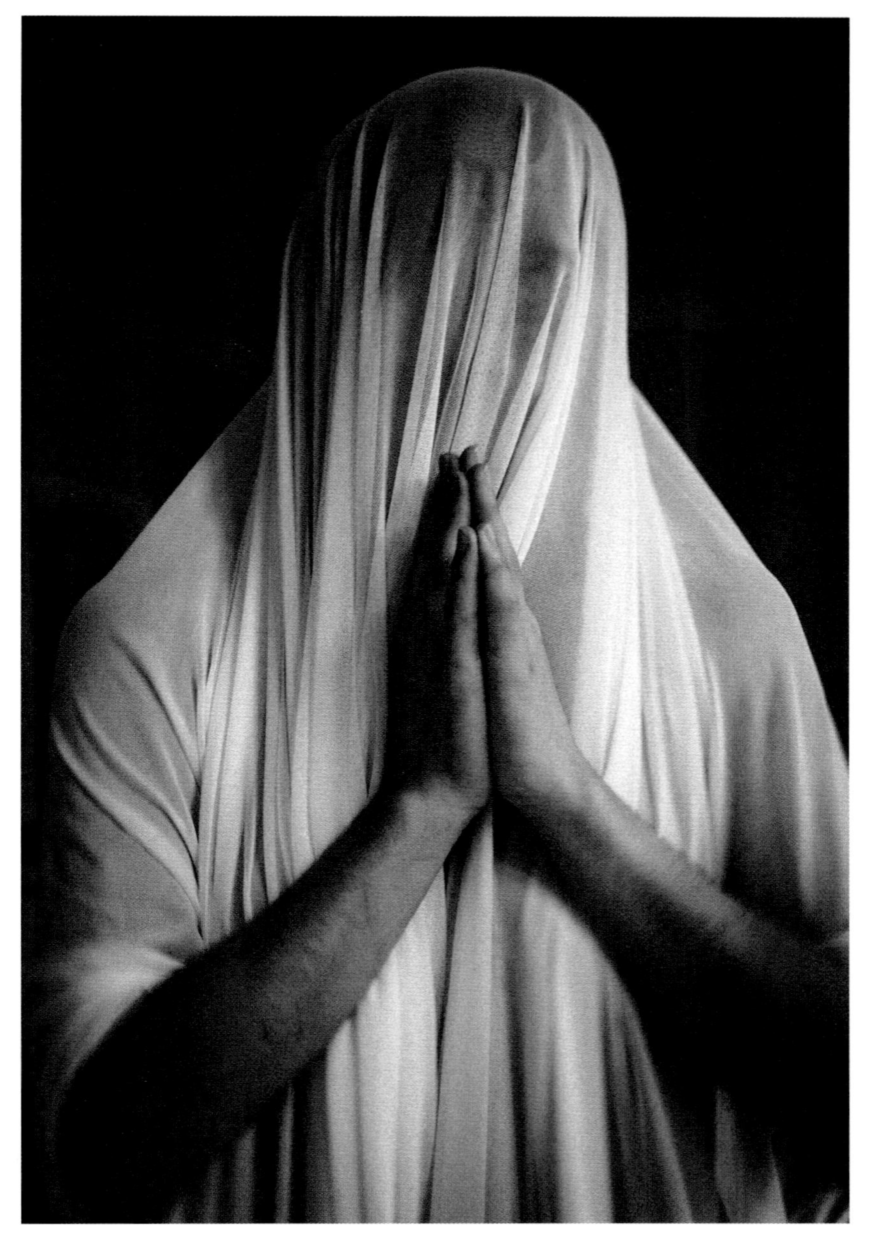

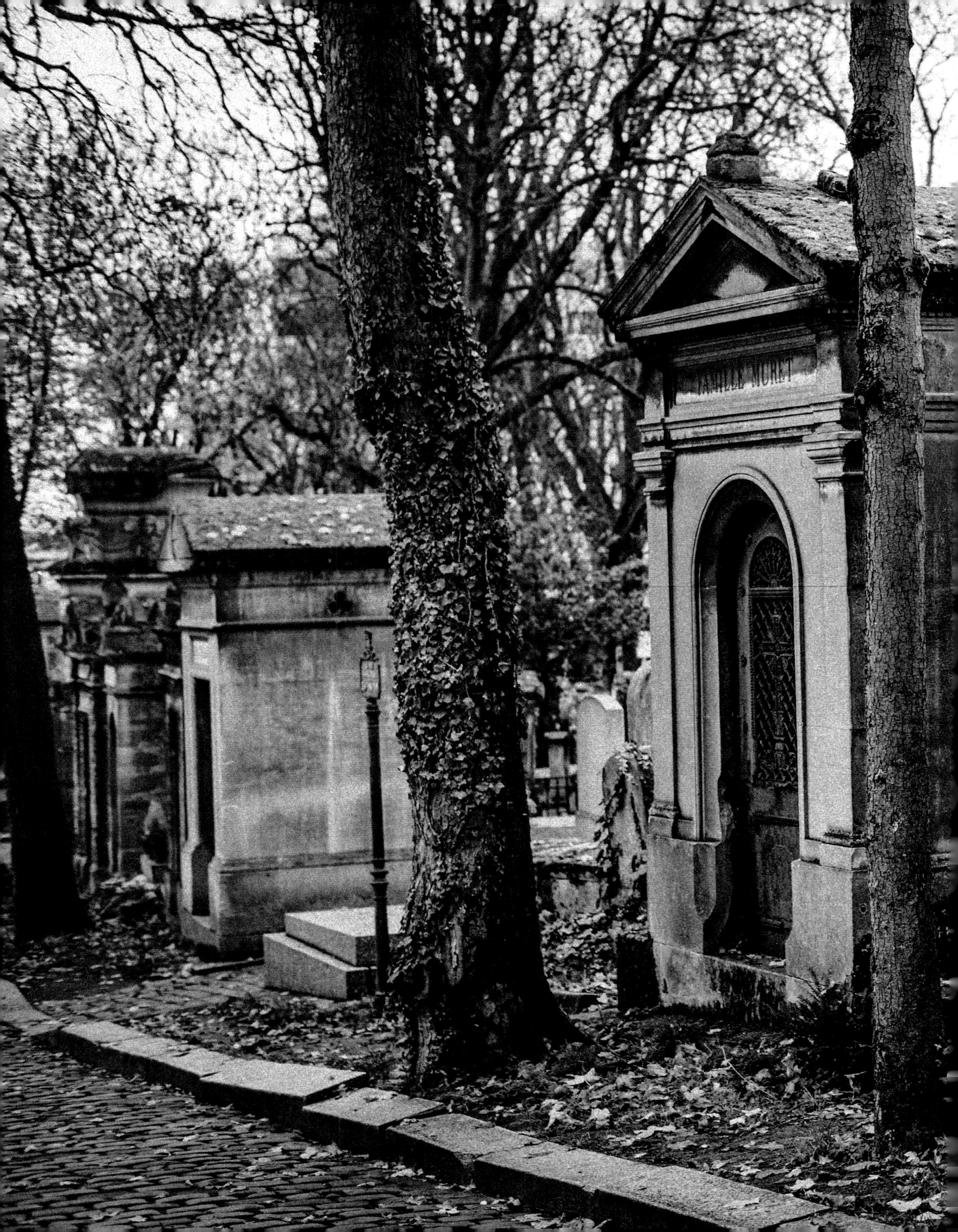

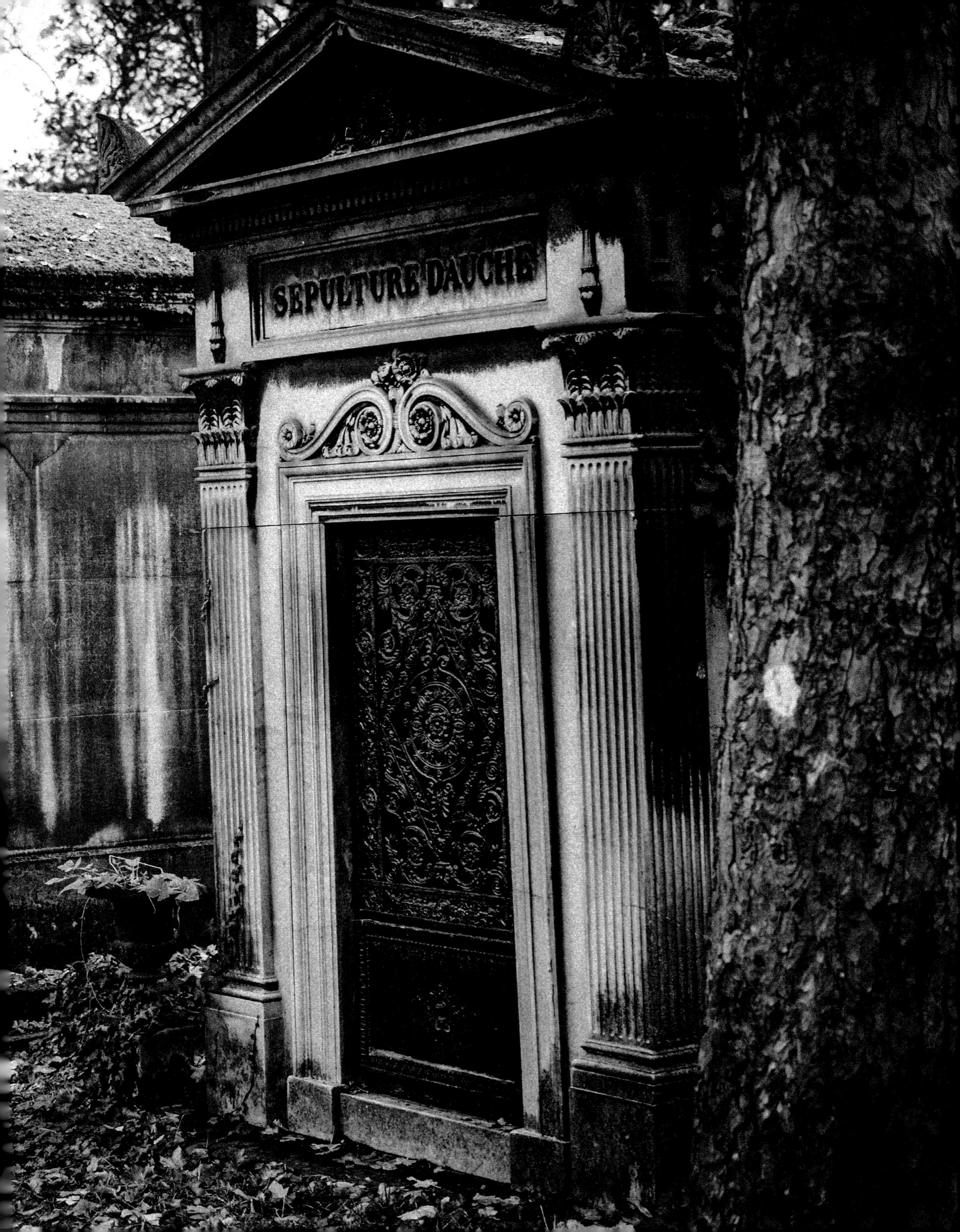

SEPULTURE DAUCHE

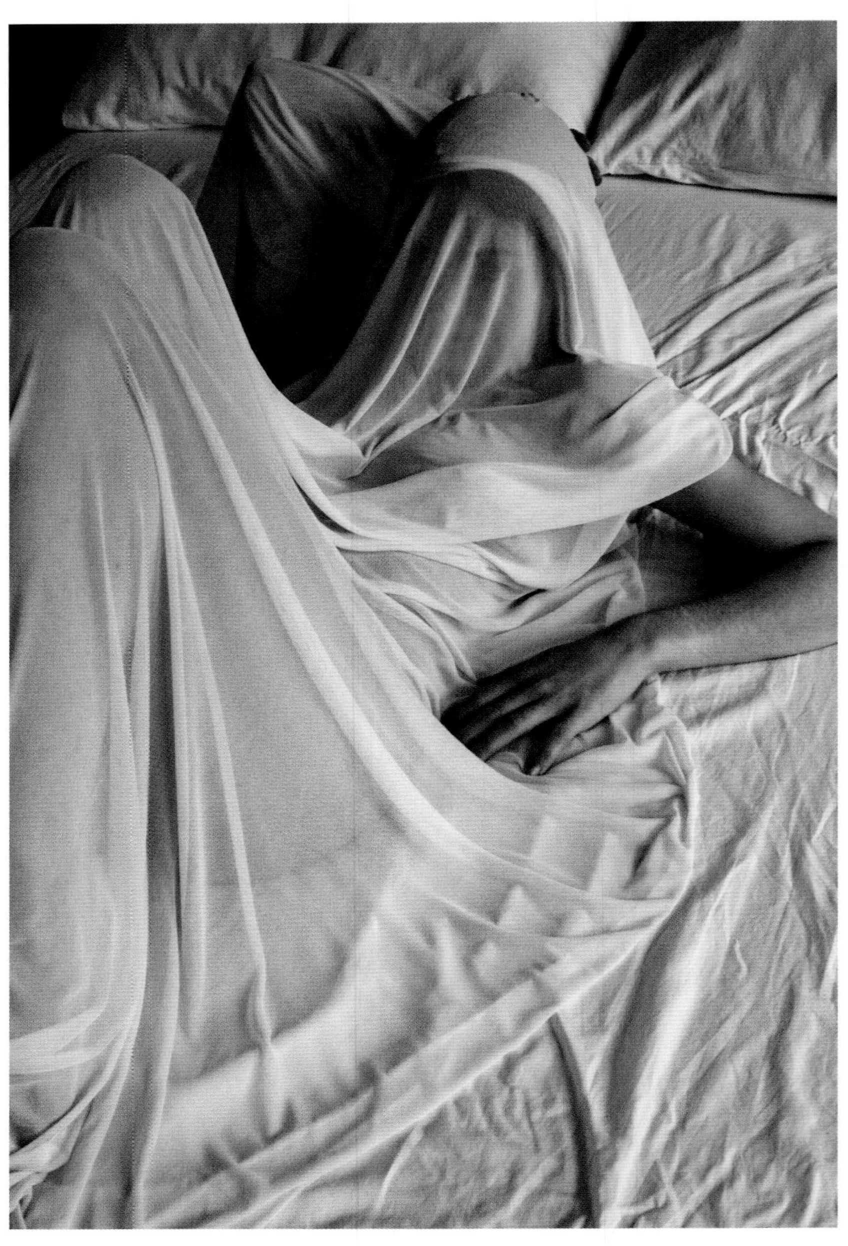

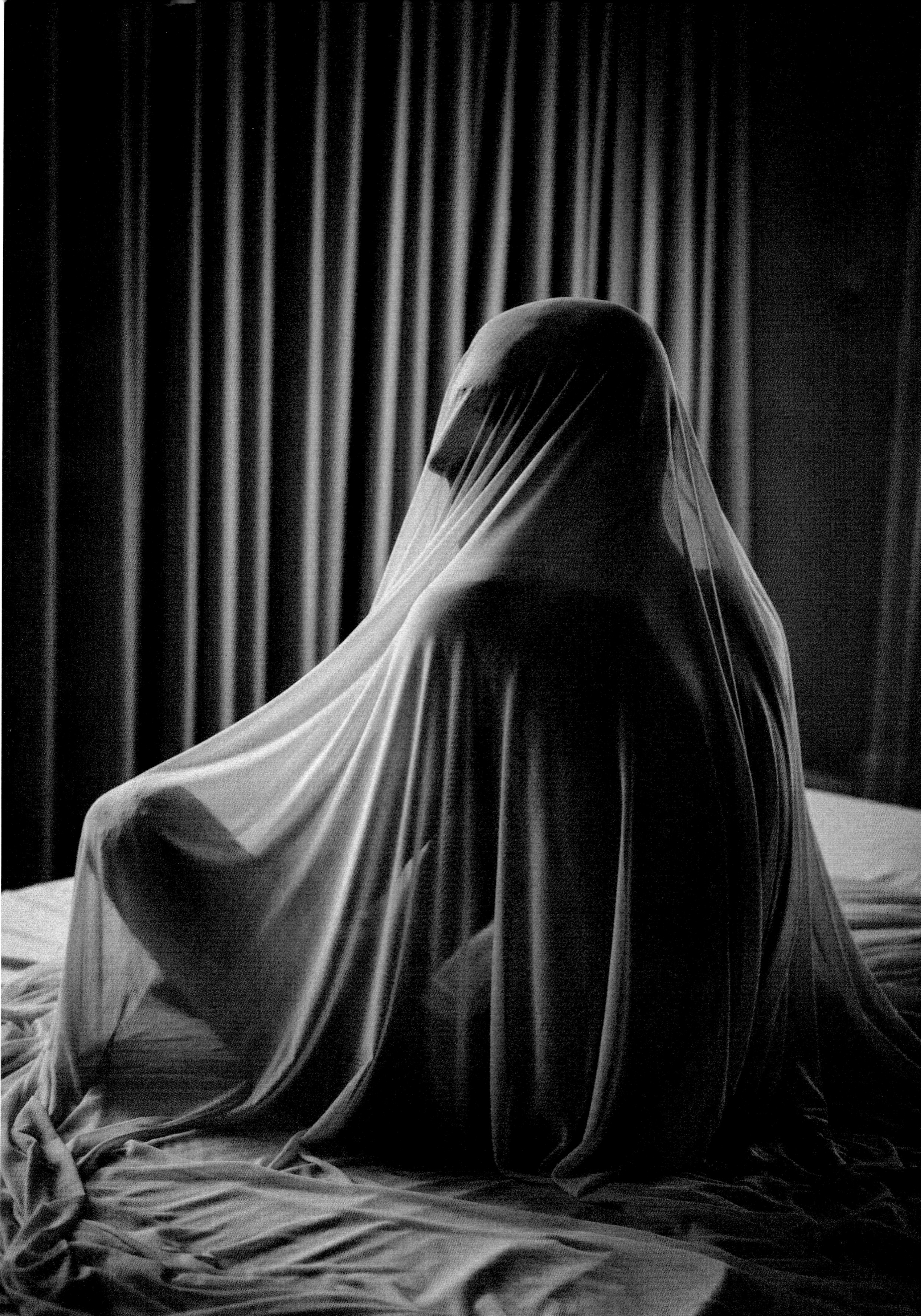

COLOPHON

MERCI BEAUCOUP.

I WOULD LIKE TO EXPRESS MY GRATITUDE FOR YOUR TRUST IN FUNDING THIS BOOK THROUGH KICKSTARTER. THANK YOU TO ALL BACKERS AND SUPPORTERS — WITHOUT YOUR PASSION FOR ART BOOKS AND PHOTOGRAPHY, THIS PROJECT WOULD NEVER HAVE BECOME A REALITY!

SPECIAL THANKS ALSO GO TO MY PARENTS, ROSE AND MICHI, FOR THEIR ENDLESS SUPPORT AND LOVE.

YOURS, MATTHIAS

THE OPÉRA
VOLUME XIII
MYTHOS

EDITOR
MATTHIAS STRAUB

ART DIRECTION
STUDIO TILLACK KNÖLL,
DESIGN PRACTICE
STUDIOTILLACKKNOELL.COM

PROOFREADING
HANNE MÄCHLER
HANNEMAECHLER.DE

PRODUCTION
JENS BARTNECK,
KERBER VERLAG

PROJECT MANAGEMENT
VERENA SIMON,
KERBER VERLAG

TYPEFACES
TWK ISSEY &
TWK LAUSANNE
WELTKERN.COM

COVER
NASTYA SPACEY

PUBLISHED BY
KERBER VERLAG GMBH & CO. KG
RUDI-DUTSCHKE-STRASSE 26
D-10969 BERLIN
+49 30 25928-280
+49 30 25928-272 (F)
INFO@KERBERVERLAG.COM
WWW.KERBERVERLAG.COM

KERBER PUBLICATIONS
ARE DISTRIBUTED WORLDWIDE

ACC ART BOOKS LTD
RIVERSIDE HOUSE,
DOCK LANE,
MELTON WOODBRIDGE,
SUFFOLK,
IP12 1PE, UK
+44 1394 38 99 50
+44 1394 38 99 99 (F)

ARTBOOK | D.A.P.
75 BROAD STREET,
SUITE 630
NEW YORK, NY 10004, USA
+1 (212) 627 19 99
+1 (212) 627 94 84 (F)
WWW.ARTBOOK.COM
ORDERS@DAPINC.COM

AVA VERLAGSAUSLIEFERUNG AG
CENTRALWEG 16
8910 AFFOLTERN AM ALBIS, CH
+41 44 762 42 50
+41 44 762 42 10 (F)
AVAINFO@AVA.CH

ZEITFRACHT MEDIEN GMBH
DISTRIBUTION GERMANY
+49 711 7860 2254
SERVICE.ZEITFRACHT.DE

THE DEUTSCHE NATIONAL-
BIBLIOTHEK LISTS THIS
PUBLICATION IN THE DEUTSCHE
NATIONALBIBLIOGRAFIE,
DNB.DE

ISBN 978-3-7356-1089-8
WWW.KERBERVERLAG.COM
WWW.THE-OPERA-MAGAZINE.COM
PRINTED IN EUROPE